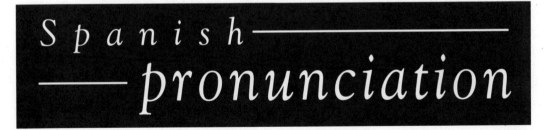

Spanish pronunciation

theory and practice

THIRD EDITION

Spanish

pronunciation

theory and practice

THIRD EDITION

John B. Dalbor

Holt, Rinehart and Winston
Harcourt Brace College Publishers

Fort Worth   Philadelphia   San Diego   New York   Orlando   Austin   San Antonio
Toronto   Montreal   London   Sydney   Tokyo

VP/Publisher	Rolando Hernández-Arriessecq
Developmental Editor	Irwin Stern
Project Editor	Tashia Stone
Production Manager	Debra A. Jenkin
Art Director	Bill Brammer
Cover Image	Yves Courbet

ISBN: 0-03-018077-5
Library of Congress Catalog Card Number: 96-77795

Address for Editorial Correspondence:
Harcourt Brace College Publishers
301 Commerce Street, Suite 3700
Fort Worth, TX 76102

Address for Orders:
Harcourt Brace & Company
6277 Sea Harbor Drive
Orlando, FL 32887-6777
1-800-782-4479 (outside Florida)
1-800-433-0001 (inside Florida)

Printed in the United States of America

6 7 8 9 0 1 2 3 4 5   039   9 8 7 6 5 4 3 2 1

Contents

Appendix

Maps

Diagrams

Charts

Preface to the Instructor

Spanish Pronunciation: Theory and Practice, Third Edition, continues to be several books in one: an introduction to phonetics and phonology in general—with their various tools and techniques; an analysis of the sound system of American Spanish, including a look at the sound features of its principal dialects; a rigorous contrastive analysis of this system and that of North American English; and, most important of all, a manual of theory and practice for English speakers learning Spanish.

This book was first written specifically for my own undergraduate Spanish phonetics course at Penn State University. The second edition presented many changes on the basis of about a dozen years' personal experience in using the first version. This third edition has even more extensive and substantive changes, based in part on the experience of my colleagues and myself, but also on more recent changes in the philosophy and practices of foreign-language pedagogy in general. It is hoped, of course, that these changes will improve the book greatly, but also that the material and features retained will continue to be of value to the student.

This edition, like its two predecessors, is intended for college-level students who have studied Spanish at least three years—including in high school—and who need not only a solid grounding in Spanish phonetics and phonology, but also a systematic and workable program for aiding them to learn to speak Spanish with as authentic an accent as is within their capabilities.

The most radical change in this edition and the most immediately obvious one to users of the book is a new order of presentation of the material. The majority of my colleagues have recommended that

I present suprasegmentals first, then vowels, and finally consonants—the exact opposite of the order of the first two editions. In fact, many of them have informed me that this is the way they taught the course anyway with this book. Intonation is probably the area of the target sound system most resistent to mastery by the language student and thus the one that requires the most practice. By studying suprasegmentals before segmentals, students can practice these features of stress, intonation, and rhythm for a much longer period of time. In addition, the new order can better handle the crucial role of stress in vowel combinations since it now precedes them.

This change in order, however, is not without a few drawbacks. Previously going from the standard place-and-manner analysis of sound production to the presentation of phonological rules for consonants and their articulation seemed smooth, logical, and natural. Since this particular transition can no longer be made in this way, I felt it necessary to divide the area of sound production into two sections: *phonation* first, followed by the suprasegmentals, and then *articulation,* followed by vowels first, then consonants. Thus the material on sound production previously found in Chapter 4 of the second edition has been divided into "Producing Speech Sounds: Phonation" (now Chapter 4 and followed by suprasegmentals, rhythm, and paralanguage) and "Producing Speech Sounds: Articulation" (now Chapter 11 and followed by vowels and consonants). This has caused some inevitable repetition of basic points as well as the presentation of the complicated rule for unstressed /I/ as one of the first ones in the book instead of the relatively simple /p/ rule, as the first two editions had it. However, in my opinion, the benefits from this change far outweigh its slight disadvantage. And, as some of my colleagues have suggested, the new order provides students with more time to absorb and practice the more resistant material.

Other changes regarding the content of several of the chapters have also been made. The strong vowels /a e o/ are now grouped in Chapter 15. The consonants /b d g/ are now together in Chapter 22, and /y/ and /w/ in Chapter 23. The consonants /ĉ f x (h)/ are together in Chapter 25. Consonant combinations and consonant + vowel combinations have been combined in Chapter 29. The pedagogy chapter, formerly the penultimate one of the book, is now at the end (Chapter 32) and follows ''Orthography,'' Chapter 31. Though many of the chapter titles have changed, the material covered remains the same.

Another fundamental change—even more important in my opinion—is the nature of the exercise material, now listed under the friendlier rubric of ''Practice'' rather than the now harsh-sounding term, ''drill.'' Reliance on minimal pairs as a teaching device has been reduced, and greater emphasis is placed on more communicative activities. Some exercises are open-ended in the sense that they have no correct answer that the student can check in the Answer Key (Appendix C). Although most of the regular chapters start the practices with an exercise or two in auditory discrimination, they all include more production activities, such as reading aloud, carrying on short conversations, answering questions, and generating original contributions on suggested topics. It is hoped that these activities will help the student use the sounds accurately in the context of speaking normal Spanish rather than just in individual words and phrases, as was too often the case with the audio-lingually oriented materials of years past. Many introductory and most review chapters now also include discussion questions, each with a few suggested answers given in the Answer Key.

Another new feature is the addition of a glossary of linguistic terms (Appendix A), with Spanish equivalents and a brief definition, often with ex-

amples for each. I intend for this new section to serve the instructor and student not only as a source of Spanish terminology for specialized terms, but also as a quick reference section as well as a study guide for the student. The terms are listed twice: first in English with the Spanish equivalent and a brief definition, then in Spanish.

Although the structuralist concept of the phoneme and allophones is still dominant in the book and phonemically transcribed examples abound in the text, phonemic transcription practice by the student has been discontinued. Doing both phonemic and phonetic transcriptions occasionally confused students unnecessarily, particularly when checking their answers in the Answer Key. Also, since Spanish orthography is already so much more phonemic than that of English and other commonly studied European languages, phonemic transcription, I felt, had limited value in comparison with phonetic transcription. As a colleague in French linguistics once told me, only half in jest, ''You people in Spanish phonetics are luckier than we are—you have all those allophones!''

The phonological rules have been revised slightly. When they present a choice of allophones, in free variation in a given environment, the first choice in braces before the diagonal line for phonetic environment is almost always representative of careful, slower speech and the second one of more rapid, casual speech. For example, the /i/ of **mi,** in **mi amigo,** has two realizations: either the first listed, the full vowel [i], as in [mi-a-mí-g̶o], or the second one listed, the semi-vowel [i̯], as in [mi̯a-mí-g̶o]. This practice is followed as closely as possible throughout the book. Also in all practices where speech style would make an important difference in the student's transcription, the style to be used is indicated either in the instructions or after the practice sentence itself.

In addition, since intonation now comes before vowels and consonants, all practices for the latter sounds include several sentences for which the suprasegmentals of stress, pitch, and juncture are to be shown in the transcription as well. Formerly, because of the order of presentation, these intonational features were transcribed in examples and exercise answers only at the very end of the book.

The analysis of some Spanish segmental sounds has been modified somewhat. In the direction of simplification, the open [ẹ] has been eliminated for two reasons. If this variant is deemed important enough to be analyzed and practiced in transcriptions, then the next logical step would be to do what treatments like those of Navarro and Cressey (see the Bibliography, Appendix E) do, namely extend the concept of vowel openness to [ị], [ụ], and [ọ] as well. But this would represent an unnecessary complication in a book such as this. My feeling now is that this feature (occurring mainly in closed syllables anyway) is largely as redundant for English speakers as it is for Spanish speakers. Many important vowel problems confront the English-speaking student of Spanish; [e] vs. [ẹ] is really not one of them. Also changes in the analysis of English vowels, described below, have made this subtle difference even more dispensable.

The sound [ĉ] is now analyzed as alveolo-palatal, as are its homorganic resonants [l̃] and [ñ], as in **colcha** and **ancho,** respectively. However, in the interest of simplicity, these sounds, when presented phonemically, are considered just palatal and are shown as such in the phoneme charts.

The palatalized [sʲ] before front vowels, as in the Argentinian pronunciation of **nación,** has been added as a dialectal variation.

The symbol for palatal *l* has been changed to [l̃], simply to make it analogous to palatal [ñ]. The fricatives [p̸ b̸ d̸ g̸] are now written with a slash rather than a hyphen since it was considered easier to see in printed form and is also widely used in other Spanish phonetic studies.

The analysis of English vowels has been revised. The vowels of *sin, pen, soot,* and *but* are presented now as [I], [ɛ], [U], and [ʌ], respectively. The so-called long vowels of English are still analyzed as diphthongs, as in *seen* [sIyn], *pain* [pʲɛyn], *suit* [sUwt-], and *boat* [bowt-]. Thus the close vowels [i], [e], and [u] occur only in Spanish, not English, producing the following distinctions: English *mill* [mIɫ] and *meal* [mIyɫ] and Spanish **mil** [mil];

English *soot* [sUt-] and *suit* [sUwt-] and Spanish **sus** [sus]; English *less* [lɛs] and *lace* [lɛys] and Spanish **les** [les]; English *coal* [kʲowɫ] and *call* [kʲɔɫ] (in eastern dialects of the U.S.) and Spanish **col** [kol]. Schwa [ə] is used only for unstressed syllables; [ʌ] is the stressed central vowel, as in *above* [əbʌv].

The final chapter on language learning now attempts to classify the English speaker's errors in Spanish according to their importance: Class A "critical," Class B "serious but not critical," and Class C "important but not serious." Obviously the aim of all serious students of Spanish should be to acquire an absolutely authentic native Spanish accent, but realistically we know this is very difficult for many and perhaps even impossible for some. All errors are not equal and should be ranked somehow. Yet the ranking of errors is admittedly subjective and just not as straightforward and clearcut as the recent oral proficiency testing criteria in the profession imply. It is difficult to isolate and focus on errors that "virtually never interfere with understanding and rarely disturb the native speaker." There is precious little research on how learner's errors affect native speakers—at least in Spanish—so I have tried to base this section on my own experiences (which I presume have been fairly typical) in learning Spanish and teaching it to English speakers.

Most instructors rightly emphasize phonemic contrasts first over allophonic subtleties in their instruction on the grounds that, through the correct use of the target phonemes, communication can properly take place. This is probably true, yet, if one had to choose (and one does not, of course) between having an English-speaking student miss an occasional /r/-/r̄/ contrast, pronouncing, for example, **quería** with the latter phoneme and **enterrado** with the former, and the use of the notorious English "dark *l*" [ɫ] in syllable-final position in Spanish, I would definitely be more tolerant of the former phonemic error than the latter allophonic one. This is admittedly based on how "foreign" I think this sounds to the average native speaker of Spanish. Others may disagree.

Thus the classification and hierarchy of errors is meant to serve more as a guide to the student than as a definitive analysis and is simply based on what I feel to be the errors that most readily cause communication to break down. A breakdown in communication happens not only when a phonemic distinction is missed, but just as often because the mispronunciation causes the native-speaking listener to attend less to *what* the learner is saying and more to *how* he or she is saying it. This distraction, of course, is the bane of every speaker of every language in the world in face-to-face linguistic communication. Thus, although both of the above errors are critical, the first one—even though allophonic—is absolutely essential, in my opinion, to achieving a good Spanish accent, and the second one—even though phonemic—is serious but not critical to doing so.

The third edition presents much more material in the form of charts and tables, and all of them, including all diagrams except regular facial diagrams, have been titled and numbered consecutively throughout the book for easier reference.

The Answer Key (Appendix C) has also been changed slightly. Alternate possibilities in the phonetic transcription answers continue to appear in the line immediately above the principal line of transcription, but such alternatives appear only for sounds that have formally been taken up. Thus [ŷ] is not given as an alternate to [y] until after /y/ (in Chapter 23) has been actively presented. Although, obviously, such alternates are always possible, I felt that it was confusing to the student to be given additional correct choices in the Answer Key until he or she understood the nature of these choices.

Appendix D consists of four new dialogs, intended to provide the student with pronunciation practice as well as practice in phonetic transcription if the instructor wishes. They are recorded, of course, and can be used in a variety of ways—both in and out of class. For example, the dialogs can be read in class by pairs of students; the instructor can have the students make phonetic transcriptions of portions of them—either from the written text or by listening to the cassette in class; the instructor can use portions of them for testing purposes, as well.

Also in this third edition, the Bibliography (Appendix E) has been greatly reduced. Now with the widespread appearance and use of computerized bibliographies and data bases, finding references in Spanish phonetics and phonology is easier in one sense than it was 20 or 30 years ago, but perhaps more difficult in another because of the overwhelming wealth of materials now available. Thus the new bibliography is highly selective and includes not only a few very recent studies in Spanish linguistics but retains a few hoary classics, such as Tomás Navarro's pivotal and pioneering work in Spanish phonetics, whose influence and importance continue in the field even though the study was originally done some eighty years ago.

The Appendix section on the phonological rules has been eliminated from this edition since all the rules—with examples—are found in the appropriate place in the corresponding chapters.

The cassette tape program contains all oral practices in the textbook that could appropriately be recorded (not the open-ended dialogs or question-answer practices, for example), plus the four dialogs in Appendix D.

Certain problematic and somewhat controversial areas, however, remain unchanged in this third edition. Another suggestion by some of my colleagues has been to write the new edition in Spanish. This has not been followed, however, for one principal reason. Spanish phonetics in particular and phonetics and phonology in general as disciplines continue to be unfamiliar and rather imposing—at first, at least—to the average user of this book. Much of this material is undeniably but necessarily technical and somewhat "mathematical" in its appearance. In addition, unfortunately, the average user of this book—based on my personal experiences and abundant reports from colleagues—is not always comfortable in reading expository technical prose in Spanish and consequently must spend a great deal more time in doing so than if the information is presented in English.

Most of my colleagues and I have always taught this course in Spanish and found a book written in English to be an aid, not a hindrance. Students are able to prepare the material in advance faster and more confidently and review it after class more thoroughly. And, as already mentioned, even though most of the critical terms are cognates in both languages, a glossary with Spanish equivalents (Appendix A) has been added. This particular issue in Spanish language textbooks—from elementary programs all the way to advanced texts in language, literature, and linguistics—is still a moot one, as witnessed by the large number of successful Spanish language texts at all levels still written in English.

Presenting the dialect situation in American Spanish is a particularly thorny matter. The dialect zones established for Spanish America and the language areas shown for Spain in the second edition have been retained, although it must be borne in mind that our maps, as all dialect maps, can be misleading if interpreted too literally. Maps of this sort still remain a necessary evil in linguistic geography, and a dialectal study can be damned for their omission and damned by their inclusion. For example, no study of American Spanish can be complete without reference to the ever increasing number of Spanish speakers in the continental United States, particularly in the metropolitan areas, yet it is virtually impossible to represent this situation adequately with maps.

The concept of General American Spanish is still thought to be valid, although now it is admittedly almost as much a social concept as a regional one. As I have said, the efforts to establish Spanish American dialect regions with accompanying maps is fraught with difficulties. The results are inevitably inaccurate, somewhat misleading, and out of date, and the author is often accused of oversimplification. Yet some attempt to provide visual information of this sort for the student must be made, despite the pitfalls. And this had been done once more.

The third edition of *Spanish Pronunciation* is still replete with repetition and review. My experience is that it is always good pedagogy to tell students what you are going to tell them, then tell them, and then tell them what you have told them. What may seem repetitive to the instructor, in my opinion, is usually welcomed—secretly, if not openly—by the student, as long as the repetition is modified in some way to make it interesting and palatable. Thus I have continued to follow the practice of introducing a concept, studying it in detail, and then reviewing it. Chapter 5 introduces suprasegmentals, Chapter 14 vowels, and Chapter 20 consonants, and Chapters 10, 19, and 30 review them, respectively, with the expected analysis and practice in between. In my opinion, an attempt to cover this material just once, with little or no advance preparation and little or no followup, inevitably leads to superficiality. Most good instructors, regardless of the text they use, undoubtedly provide such redundancy and reinforcement in their teaching and their use of supplementary materials, and I feel that it is appropriate and convenient for all to have the textbook do this, too.

The phonetic analysis is still largely traditional place-and-manner, despite the admitted shortcomings of this approach. I feel that an approach based purely on a distinctive feature analysis, a generative analysis, or some analysis based on an offshoot of these two, while probably superior from a purely theoretical point of view, is doomed to failure when it comes to teaching Spanish pronunciation to undergraduates. Thus, as illustrated in Chapter 26 (on nasals), the phonemic analysis is still ''modified structuralist,'' with a few departures, such as phonemic overlap, and occasional ventures into item-and-process as opposed to item-and-arrangement, which characterizes most of the phonological analysis in the book.

Acknowledgments

I would like to acknowledge with gratitude the contribution of the many students and colleagues who have made valuable criticisms, comments, and suggestions, many of which I have followed in this third edition. However, I take full responsibility for the inevitable errors and omissions that show up in a work such as this. I would also like to thank the following reviewers of the manuscript:

David Barnwell, University of the Virgin Islands

María Cecilia Colombi, University of California, Davis

William R. Glass, The Pennsylvania State University

William H. Klemme, Indiana University at Fort Wayne

Francisco Ocampo, University of Minnesota

My particular thanks go to Irwin Stern, of Colombia University, for his valuable suggestions in the planning, writing, and production of this book and his review and editing of the manuscript; to Diana Mejía, native of Colombia and currently of the Pennsylvania State University, for serving as my Spanish language informant and for writing the dialogs found in Appendix D; and to Steven-Michael Patterson for his careful and painstaking copyediting of what was necessarily an extremely difficult manuscript to work with.

JBD
State College, PA

1

Introduction

A longstanding and widespread belief among English speakers is that Spanish is the easiest of all foreign languages for them to learn. This seems unquestionable when it is compared with such languages as German, Russian, Latin, Japanese, Chinese, Arabic, and perhaps even a commonly studied language like French.

The average English-speaking North American—from the U.S. or Canada—believes this for several reasons. Spanish not only has many grammatical similarities with English but a large number of easily recognized COGNATES, such as **animal**, **televisión**, **música**, and so forth. In addition, our language is now filled with borrowed Spanish terms: **taco**, **sombrero**, **fajitas**, **rodeo**, to name a few.

But probably the main reason for the reputation Spanish enjoys as an ''easy'' language is the fact that it is supposedly so easy to pronounce—especially when compared with French or German or Russian. However, what people who think or say this really mean, without realizing it, is that Spanish is much easier to spell than most other languages, including English, of course. Spanish uses the familiar Roman alphabet, unlike the so-called exotic and ''hard'' languages like Russian, Chinese, or Japanese. For example, the Russian word for the first-person singular pronoun *I* is pronounced [yá], exactly the same as the Spanish word **ya** meaning *already*. But the Russian word is spelled Я, so, even though the sounds involved are identical and certainly not hard for English speakers, the written characters of Russian's Cyrillic alphabet make the language just seem intrinsically more difficult than Spanish. Russian actually is more difficult for North Americans than Spanish, but this writing difference is only a superficial and temporary obstacle, having little to do with the real stumbling blocks in the path of the English-speaking student of Russian.

Even with a more familiar language like French, which, like English and Spanish, uses the Roman alphabet, the problem is similar. One set of sounds—[dɔ-né], for example—can be spelled **donner**, **donnez**, **donné**, **donnés**, **donnée**, or **données**, depending on grammatical function and meaning. This French ''legacy'' is also reflected in the spelling of such English words as *beauty* or *buffet,* carried down or borrowed from French. But in Spanish—unlike both English and French—different spellings most often represent different sounds, and, conversely, different sounds are always also spelled with different letters.

People commonly refer to Spanish as a "phonetic" language—just an imprecise way of saying that in Spanish ORTHOGRAPHY (the spelling system) there is a close and consistent correspondence between the written symbols and the sounds they stand for. This is not so in other languages commonly studied by North Americans. Worst of all, of course, is our own English, whose spelling is so idiosyncratic and variable that few native speakers ever learn it completely. How long can the best educated English speaker go in serious writing endeavors without consulting a dictionary just for spelling, let alone meaning? In fact, the author, as he wrote these very lines, hesitated over whether the word *correspondence* has an *e* or an *a* at the beginning of its last syllable and checked his dictionary just to be sure. Educated Spanish speakers need very little such help in spelling their own language. Spelling bees have little point in Hispanic countries because learning to spell properly is just not the great accomplishment for these children that it is for English-speaking children. And it is also quite likely that you, as an English-speaking student of Spanish, now beyond basic courses, will learn to spell Spanish better than English.

But despite this fact, even the best students make occasional or even frequent and noticeable errors in their pronunciation of Spanish, since its sounds are inherently as difficult for an English speaker as those of French or Russian or German. In fact, a close comparison of the sound systems of English and Spanish reveals that very few sounds in one language are exactly the same as the other's, and even the few that are the same or similar are found in different patterns of occurrence, making them just as difficult as though they were different. For example, the Spanish consonant [p], as in **pino**, has no puff of air (ASPIRATION) with it in any position of any word. English has exactly the same unaspirated or "unpuffed" [p] sound, but only after an *s* at the beginning of a word, as in *spin*. But the [pʰ] in the word *pin* has a puff of air with it (notice the special symbol after *p* indicating this), causing the English-speaking student of Spanish to use it mistakenly in Spanish words, producing **pino**, for example, as [pʰí-no]. It sounds just as strange or wrong in Spanish to say it this way as it does to pronounce English *pin* with the unaspirated [p]. Try to do it this way, if you can, to hear the effect.

To repeat, not only are the sounds of Spanish different from the seemingly "same" ones in English, but they are distributed or patterned differently, complicating the learning task and impeding mastery of the sound system by learners of each language. Spanish is not at all unusual in this regard; this is the norm. Yet this fact is too often overlooked because of the relatively simple and consistent orthography of Spanish.

Mastery of the sound system of Spanish, as you suspect, can come hard for the average English-speaking student. Naturally some students have an excellent ear and are just naturals when it comes to doing it. Unfortunately, the majority are not and, if they hope to master Spanish pronunciation and get to sound like a native (at least as far as pronunciation is concerned), they must proceed carefully and painstakingly, through analysis, trial and error, correction, and constant practice. Without a systematic approach to the problem, even living in a Hispanic country for a period of time or spending time with Spanish-speaking friends might not be enough for adolescent and college-age speakers.

If you are considering a career in teaching Spanish and are fortunate enough to have already mastered a pretty good Spanish accent—even without the ''sweat and tears'' alluded to above—you will have the task of trying to get your own students to achieve an equally satisfactory pronunciation. Unless you are equipped to help them attack the problem soundly and systematically, you can only hope that they will have the same talent and good fortune to learn just through imitation. With all this in mind, this book has several purposes.

1. To teach you as English-speaking students the correct pronunciation of Spanish—through analysis, imitation, and practice.
2. To point out and analyze the important contrasts and useful similarities between the sounds of North American English and Spanish.
3. To introduce you to the field of linguistics, mainly in two areas of sound analysis, which are referred to as PHONOLOGY and PHONETICS.
4. To teach you some of the methods, techniques, and tools of phonetics, such as ARTICULATORY DESCRIPTION, FACIAL DIAGRAM, and PHONETIC TRANSCRIPTION.
5. To acquaint you with the most important pronunciation differences between the varieties of Spanish, both in America and, to a lesser extent, Spain.

With regard to this last point, the sound differences between American Spanish and standard peninsular Spanish (CASTILIAN) have been greatly exaggerated and are really fewer in number and in importance than those between North American English and British English, to say nothing of the English of Australia or India, for example.

American Spanish has several main varieties or DIALECTS (''dialect groups'' might be a better term), and most of them are included in this book. There is a broad and somewhat amorphous group of Spanish dialects lumped together and termed GENERAL AMERICAN SPANISH. This is analogous to the concept of General American English, which is heard all over the United States and Canada and has become the norm for radio and television announcers, even in places where it is not the normal speech, such as coastal New England or the Southern United States. General American Spanish is also the norm on Spanish American radio and television and is also used in daily life by educated speakers, particularly in Mexico, Central America, and the Andean countries of South America (Colombia, Ecuador, Peru, and Bolivia). This matter of language varieties or dialects is a complicated and touchy issue for many speakers of both languages, but it is really more a social than a linguistic one. Just as with North American English, all dialects of Spanish—both American and peninsular—are mutually comprehensible. No speaker of any one of them has any great difficulty in communicating with speakers of another—at least as far as pronunciation is concerned. (Obviously, vocabulary is another matter.) The Peruvian farmer (if he has learned Spanish), although probably a Quechua Indian, can enjoy a movie about Spaniards made in Madrid, just as you can follow a Masterpiece Theater program or understand Paul McCartney in a TV interview without major difficulties. (There will be much more on this in Chapter 3, ''Language and Dialects.'')

Finally, a word on the best way to use this book. Read the presentation at the beginning of each chapter, referring as directed to parts of other chapters and the Appendix. Of particular value to you will be Appendix A, a glossary containing definitions of the key linguistic, specialized, and technical terms used in the book, along with their Spanish equivalents. The inclusion of such terms in the glossary is indicated by the use of all CAPITAL LETTERS for the first appearance or two in the text. The glossary consists of two parts—one listing and defining the terms in English along with Spanish equivalents, and the other an alphabetical listing of the Spanish terms with English equivalents. There are other useful summaries and charts in Appendix B, practice dialogs in Appendix D, and a brief selective bibliography in Appendix E containing the works cited in footnotes and other important ones as well. There is also an end vocabulary, which you can check for the meaning of unfamiliar Spanish words that occur in examples and practices throughout the book.

The practice material at the end of each chapter is meant to be done regularly by you and prepared for class as directed by your instructor. You should also prepare the written transcription practices, the answers to all of which are found in Appendix C, Answer Key. Cassettes of material for listening and speaking practice accompany this book, and your instructor will indicate how you should use this material as well.

2

Language and Linguistics

Acquisition of Language

LANGUAGE is undoubtedly the most important—and perhaps at the same time, most mysterious—accomplishment of human beings. Every normal human on the face of the earth learns to talk and uses language quite effectively for a variety of communicative purposes. Yet few people understand much about this marvelous skill they possess and utilize every day. Physiologically and psychologically normal children in every linguistic community are adept at speaking their own language by the age of five or six, and many even well before that. Yet relatively little is known about the exact process the child's brain and nervous system go through to acquire this skill.

Even though animals have intelligence as well as a vocal mechanism—in some cases closely resembling that of humans—none of them have language or speech in the sense that we have it. Linguists believe that this is due to two principal factors: the human brain and the unique configuration of the fully developed human VOCAL TRACT, that is, the shape of the mouth and throat and the position of the TONGUE and LARYNX or "voice box."

Current theory holds that the capacity to learn and use language is genetically transmitted—like the shape of one's eyes or nose or the desire and ability to walk at a certain age—and that the human brain is pre-programmed, in a sense, to construct "rules" or strategies for interpreting and producing speech. We know that this brain capacity doesn't even depend wholly on hearing since the deaf, with special training, can learn to use language, although not in exactly the same way that hearing people do. At any rate, no physiologically and psychologically normal child on the face of the earth fails to learn the language or languages he or she is exposed to as a baby. In fact, language ability is not necessarily dependent on intelligence, since the mentally retarded often learn to use language quite well and sometimes at an even earlier age than other children.

Vocalization

The fully developed human vocal tract has a shape unique among all animals, a shape that permits a variety of open sounds, VOWELS, for example. Other primates, such as apes and gorillas, seem to have a similar vocal tract at first glance, but it is different enough to preclude the pronunciation of basic vowel contrasts such as /a/, /i/, and /u/, the minimum three vowels of all human language. (Most languages have more, of course.) The vocal tract of human infants is likewise incapable of making these sounds at first, but in a relatively short period of time—within a couple years at most—develops so that it can make them quite easily and consistently. The vocal tract of other animals never changes in a significant way, and thus these animals can never produce the vowel sounds of a normal two-year-old human. And, without vowels, speech is impossible.

As the human baby begins to vocalize, these sounds cause a reaction on the part of the individuals in its environment. They, in turn, respond vocally, and the baby is encouraged to keep babbling and even try to imitate the sounds it hears; in other words, the baby begins to figure out the system or "crack the linguistic code," so to speak, and begin to use it, too.

A baby at first probably produces practically every sound capable of coming from its vocal mechanism, but after a time begins to discard the ones it never hears, that is, those that are absent from the language of the surrounding individuals. Gradually the baby learns how to produce the sounds it hears in some fairly consistent fashion, and it becomes aware of certain meaningful contrasts between them. It begins to see how these sounds are related to the objects in its environment, and it begins to understand how their production in a particular way can have very practical results as well as provide psychological satisfaction. But, above all, the baby never stops practicing with its caregivers. After a couple of years the baby has control of many, if not most, of the truly fundamental patterns of sound, form, and arrangement in its language(s), and by adolescence he or she has complete mastery of all of them. The human child speaks the language fluently and sometimes even perfectly, even though there are literally hundreds (perhaps thousands) of words that he or she does not know and never will in a lifetime.

culture (with a *c*) and Culture (with a *C*)

All this time the child, along with the language, has been learning the CULTURE, too. It should be pointed out at the outset that the term "culture" is used here in the anthropological sense rather than the aesthetic one. Sometimes referred to as "culture with a small *c*," it means the totality of the patterns of human behavior which often differ markedly from one ethnic and linguistic group to another. This "culture" consists of the ways that humans have developed to solve the problems of existence—providing food and shelter, dealing with the surroundings, coping with the realities of life and death, and, above all, interacting with one another. Both elements—the language and culture in this sense—are so closely related and intertwined that it is sometimes difficult to tell which one has a greater influence on the other.

When they hear the term "culture," many people think first of aesthetic accomplishments, such as art, literature, and music, which we refer to as "Culture with a capital *C*."

This type of "culture," however, is produced by relatively few members of any LINGUISTIC COMMUNITY and not even always appreciated by all its members. But everyone without exception, every day of his or her life, is using and participating in his or her culture with a small *c*. It is interesting to note how much time and effort is spent on teaching each of these different concepts of culture in the average foreign-language program. Until recently the anthropological approach to culture (with a small *c*)—at least in the United States— was not always presented as systematically in language courses as would have been de- sired. Traditionally, many language programs spent a sizeable amount of time on the other concept of Culture (with a capital *C*), particularly, of course, literature. And this is still true in some places. The reasons for the emphasis on Culture are historical and have little to do with linguistics or even language itself. The results, however, have always had an effect on the students.

The Role of Language in culture (with a *c*)

Although one can learn a foreign language without also learning its culture, it is virtually impossible for anyone to understand, let alone learn, a foreign culture (with a small *c*) without first knowing its language. When this fact is ignored or paid lip service by officials in charge of planning and administering programs in education, government, social work, or law enforcement—programs that involve other language groups—the pro- grams are destined to be less than successful. On the other hand, the relative success of some groups, like the religious missionaries and the business professionals who devote a great deal of time and effort to learning the language of the culture they wish to understand and function in and whose members they seek to influence, is proof that knowing the language is an indispensable factor to learning the culture.

But "knowing the language" means different things to different people. For some it is primarily being able to translate it into one's own native language and/or being able to read, understand, and appreciate its literature and other written manifestations. Some in the past even denied or downgraded the importance of the spoken as opposed to the written language. This attitude went hand-in-hand with and probably even stemmed from the commonly held notion that language is primarily writing rather than sound. When the two conflict—as they inevitably do—many felt (and still do) that sound should cede to writing. "Just pronounce it the way it's written!" is the impatient admonishment. Rarely do we hear, "Why don't we write it the way we really pronounce it?" (although this is exactly what children and foreign-language students sometimes do at first).

Sounds and Letters

The confusion between sounds and letters is widespread among educated speakers and hard to dispel. If one asks the average educated North American how to make the plural of nouns in English, the answer is frequently something like this: "Add *-s* if the word ends in a vowel or certain consonants, as in *table-tables* or *chair-chairs*; add *-es* in some cases like *dish-dishes*; and change a *-y* at the end to *-ie-,* and add *-s* as in *berry-berries.''* This individual may very well be surprised and perhaps even feel that his leg is being pulled if he is told that the real rule is ''to add the sound /s/ after a final /p t k f θ/, /ɨz/ after a final /s z š ž č ǰ/, and /z/ everywhere else, as in *cat-cats, horse-horses,* and *dog-dogs.''*

The first individual may object to the last part about /z/, citing something like *pen-pens* to prove that his rule is the right one, namely that regular plural nouns in English basically end in *-s.* Actually, both rules are right in a sense, but they each pertain to different aspects of the language—the letters of the written language, covered in the first one, and the sounds of the spoken language (the *real* language for many), covered in the second one. The first rule tells a native English speaker how to *spell* his own language, which he already knows how to speak; the second one tells a foreigner how to *pronounce* the new language, which he does not yet know how to speak.

Writing Language

Unfortunately, the more formally educated a person is, the more deep-seated these misconceptions about the nature of language and the role of writing. Such individuals can hardly help thinking of language as the set of symbols that merely *represent* language. Yet writing cannot possibly be synonymous with language. The majority of the inhabitants of the earth can neither read nor write (for a variety of reasons), yet they all speak languages as complicated, sophisticated, beautiful, and logical as English or Spanish. Some think of an ILLITERATE as a person who does not even know his own language, but this is far from the truth. Illiterates cannot read or write their own language—many because they never learned to do it and many simply because they speak a language that has no written form.

''Written form'' in this case refers principally to an ALPHABET or a system in which each graphic symbol (or sometimes two graphic symbols) purports to represent one sound. Some languages, like ancient Egyptian or classical Mayan, an Indian language of Mexico and Central America, used HIEROGLYPHICS or PICTOGRAPHS—pictures or icons—to represent objects, people, or concepts. Other languages, like Chinese, have a system of IDEOGRAPHS, which represent semantic concepts, like words or morphemes (units of words). A few languages, like Japanese, have SYLLABIC WRITING, in which the symbols, as the name implies, represent spoken syllables rather than single sounds, units of meaning, words, or entire concepts. But the majority of the world's languages with writing systems use ALPHABETIC or PHONEMIC WRITING, as do English, Spanish, French, German, Russian, etc., that is, the languages most commonly studied by North Americans.

Prescriptive versus Descriptive Approaches to Language

Most people, particularly educated speakers, take what is called a PRESCRIPTIVE APPROACH to language. For them the written form is primary; there is really only one correct way of putting words together, and most words have one basic meaning, which is the "true" one regardless of how current speakers use or "misuse" them. This approach has been notably unsuccessful in teaching students about their own native language, let alone a foreign language. Think of the rules you may have learned in school, but that you know now (and probably even knew or suspected then) were not observed by anybody in ordinary conversation, regardless of their educational level or social status. All native speakers of English use prepositions to end their sentences ("What did you talk about?" instead of the stilted "About what did you talk?"), say "It's me!" (instead of the formal "It's I!") when answering the question "Who is it?" asked by someone who is expected to know who it is (like your roommate), and complain that "The weather was awful" (when you know it did not inspire awe but ruined your picnic), and so forth.

Linguists and many language teachers, however, take what is called a DESCRIPTIVE APPROACH to language. For them the spoken form is primary: spelling for many languages like English or French is inconsistent, illogical, and varies inexplicably; the meaning of words changes over time to become what native speakers (through some sort of an unwritten and unplanned consensus) decide it should be; and the language just keeps on evolving, not degenerating or becoming corrupted. If this were not the case, Spanish speakers would still be speaking Latin, the language from which Spanish evolved, and North Americans would still be speaking Anglo-Saxon—that is, Old English, the form of our language spoken a thousand years ago and now studied only in some English language and literature courses.

The issue is not an important one for linguists, who are much more interested in studying the language as it actually is (or was) spoken by native speakers. Language or language arts teachers, who are supposedly teaching native speakers their own language—the one these students have already been speaking fluently for years—tend to be more conservative and are too often concerned with maintaining standards in the language. Some even feel that it is their mission to preserve the purity of the language and save it from corruption or, worse yet, extinction.

Foreign-language teachers have an easier time of it in the sense that they can dodge this issue since they feel justified in correcting you, as English-speaking students of Spanish, and requiring you to try to use the language the way Spanish speakers do. Yet even many teachers of Spanish are reluctant to go too far and teach things that are supposedly incorrect but now commonly said all over the Spanish-speaking world by educated speakers—things like **Hubieron tres muertos en el accidente** "There were three deaths in the accident" (instead of the theoretically correct **Hubo tres muertos en el accidente**), or **Le conté el incidente a mis padres** "I told my parents about the incident" (instead of the theoretically correct **Les conté el incidente a mis padres**) or even **¿Adónde fuistes?** "Where did you go?" (instead of the theoretically correct **¿Adónde fuiste?**). Admittedly these three examples have varying degrees of acceptability throughout the Spanish-speaking world, but none ever appear in textbooks for foreign learners as viable alternatives to the so-called correct or standard forms.

General American Spanish

The situation with Spanish sounds is fortunately not so thorny or controversial. Few would argue with the concept that you English-speaking students should be taught to speak Spanish using the sounds that educated native Spanish speakers do, since you are already educated speakers of your own language, too. The problem arises when it comes to choosing which variety of Spanish to teach. The answer we have chosen for this book is the so-called General American Spanish (introduced in Chapter 1 and taken up in detail in Chapter 3, ''Language and Dialects''). This is akin to teaching foreign students the English of Seattle or Detroit or Los Angeles or Toronto rather than the English of Tuscaloosa or Boston or Little Rock or the Bronx—all equally correct varieties of English. North Americans from all over, including these last named areas, seem to be satisfied to hear so-called General American English rather than New England, New York, or Southern English from the mouths of national radio and television announcers. Our decision to use General American Spanish as the standard in this book is similarly motivated and no more controversial.

Studying the Sounds of Language

Linguistics has many interesting subdivisions. One of the most basic is the study of the sound system, which can be divided roughly into two parts. One is PHONOLOGY (formerly PHONEMICS), the study of the function and patterning of speech sounds, and the other is PHONETICS, the study of the quality of individual sounds, exactly how they are produced by the human vocal mechanism, how they are transmitted as sound waves, and how they are interpreted by the listener. The majority of our work will be in this second area, in a branch of phonetics known as ARTICULATORY PHONETICS, and is designed to help you achieve a good Spanish accent. There will be times when phonological theory will be brought in to help you understand why certain Spanish sounds are used where they are and also particularly why you find some of them so difficult to pronounce and what you can do about it. To a lesser extent we will also learn why Spanish speakers have problems with English sounds, although this is peripheral to the main thrust of the book. We can predict the problems you have with Spanish sounds, explain why you may make certain errors, and isolate these problems for analysis and practice so you can conquer them and achieve ultimate mastery of the Spanish sound system. Our assumption is that, as a serious student of Spanish, your goal is to ''have a native accent in Spanish.'' Most everything in this book is designed to help you reach it.

Review and Discussion

Following are some questions to help you review and remember the material of Chapter 2. Suggested answers are found in Appendix C.

1. In the news media there are often items and features about the ''language'' of such animals as dolphins, chimpanzees, and parrots. Do you think their systems of communication are really language? Why or why not?

2. How can any baby manage to learn the language it is exposed to from birth in such a relatively short time when some of these languages seem so hard for us to learn as adults? Is it mainly ''nature'' or ''nurture''?

3. What does language have to do with human culture (that is, culture with a small *c*)?

4. Have you ever studied Hispanic Culture (with a capital *C*)? Where? How?

5. What actually constitutes a language—letters or sounds? Defend your position.

6. What is the difference between letters and pictographs?

7. Give an example of a statement about English that represents the prescriptive approach to language, then one about the descriptive approach. Now do the same for Spanish if you can.

3

Language and Dialects

Geographical Varieties of Language

We all know that a Bostonian does not speak like a Mississippian and that someone from Denver or Baltimore thinks that both of them have a very definite accent. The average individual's ear (apparently among speakers of all languages) is remarkably attuned to dialectal differences in speech—regardless of how little linguistic knowledge he or she may have. These differences and this ability to perceive them provide a great source of humor, fun, arguments, and, unfortunately, even prejudice. However, even though most speakers of a given language can immediately pick out a speaker from a different geographical region solely on the basis of his or her speech, few really understand the nature of these regional pronunciation features. Their knowledge of the production of speech sounds does not come anywhere near to matching their ability to perceive the corresponding auditory differences. They might even be able to imitate the dialect, but they rarely can explain exactly what they are doing and how they are doing it.

Not only is the average person perceptive of regional dialect differences, he or she often has subjective, impressionistic, and even erroneous opinions about not only these dialects but their speakers. Fact and fancy are mingled in such a way that widespread popular misconceptions abound in our thinking. Although there is no such thing as one typical New York accent or one typical Southern accent, hearing what we identify as such an accent may quickly conjure up stereotypical images with social, ethnic, racial, and educational implications that are no longer true or important and perhaps never were. For example, a recent survey taken for an automobile manufacturer revealed that the Americans polled thought that a Boston accent sounded the most ''intelligent,'' a New York accent the most ''untrustworthy,'' and a Southern accent the ''sexiest.''[1] These unfounded feelings have long been exploited in movies and on television, and the use of regional dialects has probably created as much controversy and perhaps ill will as it has provided humor and entertainment.

---

[1]As reported in the *Centre Daily Times* (State College, PA), Mar. 23, 1995, p. 2A.

Spanish speakers naturally have similar notions about speakers from other dialect regions of the Hispanic world. But it is interesting to note that speakers of one language do not always hold these opinions about speakers of another language that they have learned. The Spanish speaker new to the U.S. is at first not aware of the images associated with the different dialects of American English. Likewise, the English speaker—even though he or she may also speak Spanish as a formally learned language—does not always share the same linguistic impressions about speakers from Madrid or Havana or Buenos Aires that a Mexican, for example, might have.

Dialect or Language?

Dialect or language variation is one of the areas of linguistics of greatest interest and fascination to the non-professional or layman, but it is, at the same time, a concept extremely difficult to define and explain with precision. Sometimes it is even impossible for language professionals to decide whether a given speech mode is really another language or just a different dialect of the same language. Several factors are used to determine this. The main one is mutual intelligibility or comprehensibility. If speakers of two different speech "modes" can understand each other, even though with some difficulty at first and after some practice (assuming, of course, that neither has formally studied whatever it is that the other speaker is speaking), these modes are usually considered to be different dialects of the same language. An individual from Minneapolis or Winnipeg may have some difficulty in communicating easily at first with an individual from Johannesburg, South Africa, or New Delhi, India, but this difficulty won't last long or really impede communication in any serious way because they are all speaking dialects of the same language, English. The same is true when an individual from Las Palmas on the CANARY ISLANDS confronts someone from Arequipa, Peru, since they are both speaking varieties of Spanish.

Fortunately, for us this issue is clear-cut and relatively simple in both Spanish and English. But it is a major problem in other languages, such as Italian, German, or Chinese. Sometimes the solution is conventional, convenient, even political, and not based solely on linguistic reality. We speak of the various dialects of Italian (Neapolitan, Piedmontese, Tuscan, Calabrese, Sicilian, Venetian, and so on), yet some of these modes are really mutually incomprehensible (Neapolitan and Venetian, for example). But rarely do we speak of the different "languages" of Italy. On the other hand, this is exactly what most linguists say about Mandarin and Cantonese, which are likewise mutually incomprehensible; thus, linguists refer to them as languages. Most people really mean Mandarin when they say "Chinese" since it is the official language of China and the one with the most speakers.

Another case, closer to home for us, is that of Spanish and CATALAN, two of the main languages of the Iberian peninsula. Both are spoken by many of the same speakers in northeastern and eastern Spain and the BALEARIC ISLANDS in the Mediterranean off the eastern coast of Spain. These people are politically, ethnically, and culturally united with the rest of Spain, yet Spanish and Catalan are unquestionably two different languages. Many North Americans who knew Spanish were surprised to find that they could not read the signs shown or understand many of the words spoken by Spaniards during the televising of the 1992 Olympics in Barcelona. This is because these words were not Spanish but Catalan, the official language in this part of Spain, Catalonia, although the vast majority of its citizens are bilingual. These two languages started centuries ago as dialects of Latin but have diverged to the point where they now have such significant grammatical and phonological differences that they are now separate. In this case political, ethnic, and cultural unity has not been as significant as linguistic reality.

It is a historical accident or at least a series of historical events that has made Castilian and not Catalan the official language of all of Spain, and, therefore, the official language of the countries of Spanish America as well. Castilian was the language of the people who led the reconquest of Spain from the MOORS in the Middle Ages and became the dominant force on the Iberian peninsula. It has been said facetiously that ''a language is just a dialect that had a strong army and navy at one time in the past.''

But almost all languages in turn have different geographical varieties or dialects of their own. A speaker from Boston and a speaker from Minneapolis both write the word *here* the same way, and it means exactly the same thing to both. Yet the first speaker says /hÍh/ *heah* without any final *r* consonant, and the second speaker says /hÍr/, with his tongue curled back for a very prominent and definite final *r*. Each understands the other's pronunciation of the word despite never saying it that way. Both the uniform meaning and the written form of thousands of words just like *here*, combined with the crucial fact of mutual intelligibility, lead us to the obvious fact that the New England and Midwestern speech modes are two dialects of the same language, English. But, in contrast, the Spanish word **buzón** and the Catalan word **bustia** mean exactly the same thing, and the speaker of each language can even easily pronounce the word in the other language correctly when he or she sees it written. Yet neither speaker—unless he or she already knows the other language—realizes that the unknown word means exactly the same thing—*mailbox*. In this case, mutual incomprehensibility (plus other differences, of course) shows clearly that Spanish and Catalan are two distinct languages.

Mutual comprehensibility, of course, depends on more than sound and meaning. The grammatical structures of different dialects of the same language differ only slightly, but those of different languages, even though related—like Spanish and French—usually differ radically. It is difficult to think of significant grammatical differences between the various dialects of English or between the various dialects of Spanish. But the grammatical differences between *any* dialect of English and *any* dialect of Spanish are so numerous and difficult that, as you should well know by now, it may take years of study to master them.

When all is said and done, the definitive solution (if there is one) to the problem of language versus dialect is perhaps more one of quantity than quality. Catalan, peninsular or Castilian Spanish, and Argentinian Spanish all originally came from Latin, but Catalan is considered a separate language. The latter two are just different varieties of the same language; the differences between Catalan and Castilian Spanish or Catalan and Argentinian Spanish, for example, are far greater than those between Castilian and Argentinian Spanish. In some languages like German or Italian, the determination of language versus dialect is quite arbitrary and open to question, but in the cases of the two languages we are concerned with here, Spanish and English, linguists agree quite readily on whether a given speech mode is a different language or just a different dialect of the same language.

Social and Educational Varieties of Language

In addition, dialectal differences can be analyzed not only on a geographical or regional basis but also along social and educational parameters. There are noticeable and important differences in the speech of people of different socio-economic backgrounds, different ages, and different educational levels. This is a complicated question, and these speech variations are changing and diminishing relatively rapidly in the developed countries because of increased travel, more higher education, a transient population, upward social mobility of more people, and particularly the influence of the mass media—television, films, and popular music. English in the United States and Canada is moving toward greater uniformity, especially with the younger generations. The same thing is true of Spanish, particularly in highly industrialized countries like Spain and Argentina, although this dialect leveling is not proceeding as fast in American Spanish because of the difference between the role of social, economic, and educational factors in the Hispanic world and in the U.S. and Canada.

There is also a difference in the way the two parameters of regional and social factors intersect in English and Spanish. In English, although there is more leveling among younger speakers, more mature speakers still show marked regional variation in their speech with socio-economic factors being largely irrelevant. For example, a lawyer from Boston, with regard to pronunciation, sounds more like a dockworker from Boston than he does a lawyer from Los Angeles or New Orleans. Bill Clinton, from Arkansas, and Ted Kennedy, from Massachusetts, even with the similarity of their educational backgrounds and their professions, clearly have different accents—both regional from the point of view of General American. One accent is Southern Midlands and the other, New England. And, more importantly, as is typical with older speakers, neither has shown any interest in changing his speech for any reason—political or otherwise.

But in Spanish the situation is somewhat different. Regional differences with more highly educated people, who are normally also in a higher socio-economic class, are not as prominent. Thus, a doctor from Mexico City, for example—in his pronunciation at least—sounds somewhat more like a doctor from Bogotá or Buenos Aires than he does like a laborer from the outskirts of his own city or a peasant from a nearby village. The reasons for this are complex and based on the social and educational differences in Hispanic and North American culture and society.

In addition, certain regional or geographical varieties or dialects in every linguistic community have greater prestige, or, better said, greater acceptability. ''Acceptability'' means that the dialect in question does not particularly attract attention or is certainly not annoying to the majority of individuals who do not speak it. They are able to attend more to what the speaker is saying rather than to the way in which he or she is saying it. The prestige or standard dialect for both Spanish and English—that is, the one with the greatest acceptability—is the one currently dominant on national television and radio in both linguistic communities. (We are referring, of course, mainly to announcers and newspeople rather than to dramatic and musical performers.)

Varieties of North American English

An oversimplified but convenient division for the United States shows four general regional speech areas (although each, of course, can be subdivided): Eastern, Midlands, Southern, and Midwestern or General. "Eastern" is coastal New England and the immediate New York city area (including nearby New Jersey but not eastern Long Island, for example). "Midlands" starts in southern Pennsylvania, Ohio, Indiana, and Illinois (what might be termed the northern sector of the Ohio River valley) and proceeds southward through the Appalachians, down through the Ohio valley and the Mississippi valley, starting around St. Louis and extending considerably to the west of the Mississippi, veering above Louisiana westward into Texas. "Southern" starts around Washington, DC, and moves south fairly close to the Atlantic coast and then westward south of the Appalachians through what is known as the "Deep South" until it melds with Midlands in eastern Texas. Florida does not fit neatly into this area because of the influx of speakers from other areas of the eastern United States, plus, of course, the Hispanics since the early sixties. "General American" is basically everything else, including the Mid-Atlantic area (excluding the regions already mentioned), the Great Lakes area, the Midwest, the Great Plains, the Rocky Mountains, the extreme Southwest, and the Far West (from the Pacific coast to the Rockies and from the Mexican border actually all the way to Alaska). The speech of most English-speaking Canadians, at least west of Quebec, is very similar, and in most cases almost identical, to the speech of the neighboring areas of the U.S.

Unquestionably, General, or Midwestern English, with all its subdivisions and varieties, is the default dialect in the United States, the one with the greatest acceptability throughout the country and the one spoken by the greatest number of people in North America. The truth of this is shown by the curious fact that an individual born and raised in Manhattan will not get a job as a television announcer or perhaps even an on-camera news person on a national network, whose headquarters, of course, are in Manhattan unless he or she speaks more like someone from Detroit or Los Angeles than with the so-called typical New York accent. An individual born and raised in Georgia will not get an announcer's job on an Atlanta radio or television station with a wide reception area unless he uses General American rather than Southern speech. Yet an individual with an Eastern accent (Franklin Roosevelt, from near New York City) and an individual with a Southern accent (Jimmy Carter, from southwest Georgia) both got to be president of the United States. Despite this, individuals with regional accents will most certainly never get to be anchor persons on nightly network news broadcasts. The most popular television person-alties have been speakers of General American (Johnny Carson, Oprah Winfrey, and David Letterman, for example), although there are exceptions (like Jay Leno and Regis Philbin, both speakers of Eastern).

The Language Situation on the Iberian Peninsula

The Hispanic world is also divided into various dialect areas, but the situation here is even more diverse. Education is still not as widespread as it is in the United States and Canada, yet it is much more uniform because of the educational systems in Hispanic countries. In Spain and Spanish America there are greater regional dialectal differences among the middle and lower socio-economic classes than among educated speakers be-cause of this uniformity of education and closer agreement on linguistic standards which dictate how an educated speaker should speak his or her own language.

There are four languages on the Iberian peninsula: SPANISH (CASTILIAN), CATALAN, GALICIAN-PORTUGUESE, and BASQUE (see Map 1 on p. 18). The first three are Romance languages and the fourth, **vasco** or **vascuence**, is unrelated to any other language spoken in the world today. Some linguists believe it to be a descendant of the language spoken on the Iberian peninsula when the Greeks, Phoenicians, and Romans arrived before the Common Era. Basque is now spoken in a small area in northern Spain. Catalan (**catalán**) and its dialects are spoken by virtually everyone in northeastern Spain and in the Balearic Islands and is an officially recognized language. Galician (**gallego**), spoken in northwestern Spain, can be lumped with Portuguese to form a larger language unit known as Galician-Portuguese (**gallego-portugués**). Portuguese, of course, is the national language of Por-tugal, but Galician, now in essence a dialect of Portuguese, is a regional language of Spain heard more in rural than urban areas and lacking the prestige and status that Catalan, for example, enjoys in the other corner of Spain. Spanish (**español**), that is, Castilian (**cas-tellano**), is the official national language of Spain and is spoken all over the country, including the Canary Islands (not shown on the map). Spanish is spoken by virtually all the inhabitants of the other language areas (except the very young who have not yet gone to school and some of the very old who perhaps never went). These individuals are true bilinguals since they speak the national language in addition to their native regional lan-guage, in most cases equally well.

Naturally there are also dialects within **castellano** itself. The main one, the official national standard dialect, has no particular name other than **castellano**. It is spoken all over Spain (whether natively or not), is used in schools, is heard on radio and television and in the movies, and is used for business and social intercourse throughout the nation. One of its principal regional dialects is ANDALUSIAN (**andaluz**), spoken in southern Spain and in the Canary Islands. Most of the relatively few sound differences that characterize it are also heard in American Spanish. The reasons for this are mainly historical and are presented later in this chapter.

Map 1   Languages of the Iberian Peninsula

GALLEGO-PORTUGUÉS

CATALÁN

ESPAÑOL (CASTELLANO)
(with the dialect **andaluz**)

VASCUENCE

There are very few important sound differences between standard **castellano** and **andaluz** or between **castellano** and American Spanish (all of which will be taken up in subsequent chapters). The principal one is the distinction or contrast in **castellano** between /s/ (as in ca**s**a *house*) and /θ/ (''th'') (as in ca**z**a *hunt*), the former always being spelled with **s** (po**s**o *sediment*, **s**e**s**o *brain*, **s**ierra *mountain range*) and the latter with **z** (po**z**o *well*) and **c** + **e** (**c**e**s**o *I stop*) or **c** + **i** (**c**ierra *s/he closes*). From now on in this book the term **castellano** will be used only to refer to the national standard language of Spain, spoken natively by people from central and northern Spain and characterized mainly (but not solely) by DISTINCTION or **distinción**, the contrast between /s/ and /θ/, as illustrated above.

Most Spaniards in the areas where **vasco** (**vascuence**), **gallego**, and **catalán** are spoken are, as we said, bilingual. Some speak their native language mainly at home and in other informal situations, but others, such as the **catalanes** in northeastern Spain, speak it virtually all the time until, of course, they encounter those who speak only **español**. During the autocratic regime of the dictator Francisco Franco (1936–1975), these three languages became symbols of political separatism and defiance of the central government, which thus attempted to suppress them in all forms. But these languages have recently experienced a vigorous revival and perhaps even glorification under the subsequent democratic regime of the constitutional monarch, Juan Carlos, who, himself, has delivered speeches in **catalán**, for example. Some Spaniards, however, are still not in total agreement with a policy that permits and fosters other recognized languages, as evidenced by their displeasure at the fact, for example, that King Juan Carlos opened the 1992 Olympic Games in Barcelona by speaking Catalan first, then Spanish. **Vasco** has also become an important symbol and tool for the Basque separatists. Regardless of all this linguistic disagreement and even conflict, the visitor to Spain today can depend on being able to use Spanish with virtually everyone of school age or older anywhere in the country.

Judeo-Spanish

One other dialect of Spanish, JUDEO-SPANISH (**judeo-español** or **ladino**), should be mentioned before passing to America. In 1492, along with the Moors (those of North African descent), most Jews were expelled from Spain and fled to Portugal, North Africa, and the eastern Mediterranean, particularly Greece and Turkey. These Sephardic Jews (so-named from *sepharad,* the Hebrew word for Spain) lived close together, usually in segregated districts, and maintained along with their religion and social customs the language they had brought from Spain. Although many foreign words have since entered this dialect of medieval Spanish, it is considered to be phonologically quite similar to what it was in the days of Columbus. This is particularly interesting and valuable to linguists because it gives them a good idea of how all Spanish was pronounced at that time. Such a situation is a very fortuitous and practically unique one for scholars. This dialect of Spanish is different from modern Spanish for several reasons, the principal one being that it did not participate in the sound changes of the sixteenth and seventeenth centuries. For example, it does not have the sound **jota** [x] as in **jardín** or **hijo** since this sound developed years after the Spanish or Sephardic Jews were forced to leave their homeland. In the twentieth century many of them emigrated to other countries, and early in this century there were significant groups in the large Eastern cities of the United States, although these groups have grown much smaller over the years since the younger members are abandoning the use of Spanish. But there are now vital Sephardic communities throughout Europe and in Israel, where newspapers, magazines, and other writings in **ladino** (often written with Hebrew rather than Roman characters) are regularly published.

The Indian Languages of Spanish America

Unlike the situation in the U.S. and Canada where the number of speakers of native Indian languages is small and even diminishing, there are still many areas of Latin America where Indian languages are the main means of communication. In Mexico and Central and South America there are millions of speakers of the principal indigenous languages, many of whom are bilingual with Spanish, but many of whom do not know Spanish very well or at all.

In Mexico among the Uto-Aztecan languages still spoken, Náhuatl is the most important with nearly a million speakers. This was the language of the Aztecs of central Mexico. In Meso-America, which includes southern Mexico, the Yucatan peninsula, and nearby areas of Central America, Mayan and Mayan-related languages are spoken by several million. Quechua, the language of the Indian peoples ruled by the Incas when the Spaniards first reached Peru, is spoken by over seven million in Ecuador, Peru, and Bolivia. Over a million Bolivians and Peruvians speak Aymará, and Guaraní is spoken and preferred for daily use by Paraguayans, most of whom are bilingual with Spanish. The governments of these countries have at various times made concerted efforts to teach all their citizens Spanish with varying degrees of success. The influence of these indigenous languages on Spanish vocabulary is noticeable at first but really minor in the overall picture. It consists mainly of specialized words having to do with animals, plants, food, implements, and other things that were unknown by the Spaniards when they arrived in the New World—words such as **barbacoa** (*barbecue*), **batata** (*sweet potato*), **canoa**, **cóndor**, **coyote**, **chocolate**, **gaucho**, **hamaca** (*hammock*), **huracán**, **jaguar**, **llama**, **poncho**, **tamal**, **tomate**. Many of these words, of course, are quite familiar to North Americans since they have been taken into English in almost the original Indian form. The influence of the grammar of the Indian languages on Spanish, though, is virtually nil.

Varieties of American Spanish

American Spanish today is much closer in pronunciation to **andaluz** than to standard **castellano**, and there are two principal theories to explain this. One holds that the majority of the Spanish **conquistadores** and settlers were from southern Spain or had lived there for a period of time and naturally carried their speech to America. Also a very high percentage of the women, deemed more influential than men in child language acquisition, were from southern Spain. And even many of the men and women not from this area of the country spent considerable time—sometimes a year or more—in southern cities such as Seville awaiting passage to the New World.

The explanation, however, is not quite so simple. Although a majority of these immigrants to America were from southern Spain or had spent time there, a sizeable number were not. In addition, although most features of the **andaluz** dialect are found in American Spanish today, some are not. Another theory holds that both the Spanish of southern Spain and that of America underwent certain similar sound changes at about the same time in history and consequently are quite close today. Thus the Spanish of America evolved in the same direction as the Spanish of southern Spain, but independently, according to this theory.

In addition, American Spanish, as might be expected, now shows many regional variations of its own. Some linguists feel that these differences can be attributed to the influence of the SUBSTRATUM INDIGENOUS American languages that the Spanish settlers came in contact with. In other words, the native Americans, who had to learn Spanish in most areas of Spanish America, put the peculiar stamp of their Indian languages on their Spanish, thus making American Spanish what it is today.

Other linguists feel that it is not logical that the language of the conquered peoples should have such a strong influence on the language of the conquerors, and there must be another explanation for the regional varieties of American Spanish. These differences are mainly due to the migration and settlement patterns of the sixteenth and seventeenth centuries. They feel that all American Spanish can really be divided into two broad groupings, sometimes referred to as highland Spanish and lowland Spanish, or inland Spanish and coastal Spanish, or administrative and government Spanish and trade and maritime Spanish. These distinctions refer, respectively, to the Spanish spoken in the mountainous inland regions (the Andean region of South America and the valley of Mexico), both regions that were the sites of two of the most important administrative and cultural centers of the colonial period—Bogotá and Mexico City. These were regions relatively removed from the waves of immigration coming in from Spain, as opposed to the low-lying, coastal regions (the Caribbean islands and Gulf Coast areas of Mexico, Central and South America, the Pacific coast of South America, and the River Plate area on the lower Atlantic coast of South America). These were regions of maritime trade and commerce, where all the new immigrants from Spain first arrived and mixed with each other. Many, of course, settled here permanently. This first type of region (highland/inland), coincidentally perhaps, also encompasses the two most influential Indian languages, Náhuatl and Quechua, lending some credence to the first substratum theory.

For purposes of study and analysis, in this book we will present American Spanish in five main areas, each of which has also been subdivided by specialists, just as linguists for American English can find several regions in each of the broad areas we have already indicated for the United States. Such divisions are somewhat arbitrary and difficult to delimit with great precision, yet they are defensible. For example, everyone who has lived in the two cities knows that New Yorkers do not speak exactly like Bostonians, yet these two dialects are undeniably much closer to each other than either is to the variety of English spoken in Nashville, Tennessee. Thus New Yorkers and Bostonians are both considered to be speakers of ''Eastern.'' The same arbitrariness is true of Spanish. Cubans and Puerto Ricans can easily be shown to speak somewhat different forms of Spanish, yet the typical speaker from each of these islands sounds much more like his counterpart than either do to a speaker from La Paz, Bolivia, for example. Thus, they are both considered to be speakers of ''Caribbean Spanish.''

Map 2   Dialect Areas of American Spanish

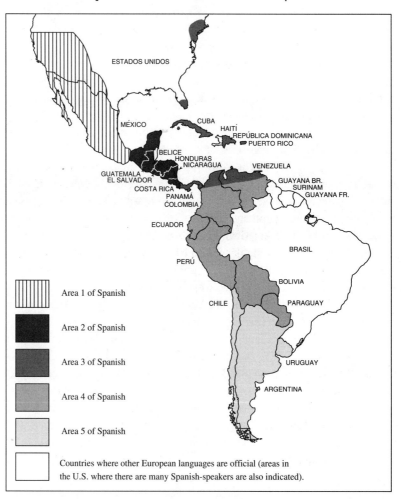

The following are the geographical divisions of American Spanish (see Map 2, above).

1. *Mexico* (most parts) and *Southwestern United States*, including California.
2. *Central America:* southern Mexico and the Yucatan peninsula, Guatemala, Honduras, El Salvador, Nicaragua, and Costa Rica.
3. *Caribbean:* Panama, Cuba, Puerto Rico, Dominican Republic, the northern coast of Colombia and Venezuela, the northeastern United States containing Puerto Rican populations, Florida and the Gulf Coast areas of the United States having Cuban populations.

4. *Highland and Inland South America:* interior of Venezuela; most of Colombia, Ecuador, and Peru; Bolivia and Paraguay.
5. *Southern South America:* Argentina, Uruguay, and Chile. (This area is also called the Southern Cone.)

General American Spanish

This is necessarily an oversimplification, and exceptions can easily be found, but this rough division will be satisfactory for our purposes. The variety of Spanish that will serve as the basis for the examples transcribed phonetically and heard on the tapes can be called General American Spanish. Many of the same criteria used above in the discussion of General American English have been used to establish this division. American Spanish is quite uniform in its grammar, that is, its MORPHOLOGY (form of words) and SYNTAX (order of words). The regional dialectal distinctions are in vocabulary—interesting, but not the province of our study in this book—and in pronunciation, the main theme of this book. General American Spanish is spoken by *educated* speakers all over Spanish America and is heard as the principal form on radio and television. It enjoys, if not necessarily the greatest prestige, certainly the greatest acceptability. We have already defined this concept as the quality of a dialect which calls the least attention to itself, thus permitting listeners to concentrate more on the message than the method of delivering it—the aim of verbal communication in any language.

However, General American Spanish characterizes not only the Spanish of educated speakers in most parts of Spanish America, but also the Spanish of the majority of urban speakers, whether educated or not, in areas 1, 2, and 4. A TV news announcer in any Spanish American city is more likely to have the features that characterize the accent of an educated speaker from Mexico City, San José (Costa Rica), or Bogotá than one from Havana, Santiago (Chile), or Buenos Aires, provided, of course, that the latter speaker is using his or her normal pronunciation. These pronunciation features will be examined in detail in subsequent chapters.

It is also interesting to note that Spanish speakers who record language instruction tapes prepared by publishers for purchase and use by North American students of Spanish virtually always use General American Spanish (whether it is their normal dialect or not). This is almost exactly like the situation already described for General American English. Since most of you are learning Spanish as a foreign or second language, it is most practical for you to start with the dialect enjoying the greatest acceptability throughout the Spanish-speaking world. Later, if you visit and live in another dialect area of the Hispanic world, you can decide if you want to try to modify your Spanish accordingly. This is advisable and rarely difficult to do; in fact, for young students it is usually difficult to avoid.

In the last analysis, the matter of regional dialects should not represent a problem for the student of Spanish. It should be asserted once more that any educated speaker of Spanish can be easily understood by any other educated Spanish speaker anywhere in the world. Your problems in learning to speak with a good Spanish accent will always stem much more from the interference of your native language than to any Spanish dialectal variations that you may encounter along the way.

Review and Discussion

Remember that suggested answers are found in Appendix C.

1. Does everyone have an "accent," that is, speak a dialect of his or her language?
2. What are some features that enable one to decide whether a given speech mode is just a different dialect from another one or really another language?
3. Explain the truth underlying the quip, "A language is just a dialect that had a strong army and navy."
4. Is the matter of dialect solely a question of where a given speaker grew up? Explain.
5. What general dialect of English or Spanish (if you are a native speaker of Spanish or a bilingual) do you speak?
6. What languages are spoken on the Iberian peninsula?
7. Why do some citizens of Israel speak Spanish natively today?
8. What is one explanation for the fact that most Latin Americans speak a form of Spanish today that is closer to the Spanish spoken in Seville (southern Spain) than in Bilbao (northern Spain), for example?
9. Is Spanish the only important language spoken in Spanish America?
10. If you had to delineate some broad geographical dialect divisions for American Spanish, what are a couple of strategies for trying to do this?
11. Is your own dialect of English or Spanish (if you are a native speaker of Spanish or a bilingual) the same as most others in your home town or city? If not, how do you explain it?

4

Producing Speech Sounds: Phonation

The Human Vocal Mechanism

The parts of the human body used for producing speech sounds are also there for other purposes, such as eating, breathing, or lifting. Man, alone among animals, has developed the use of these organs and structures for systematic communication.

We find that the components of the human vocal mechanism are precisely the parts of the body that humans use to breathe, to ingest food and drink, and to tense the abdominal muscles in exertion, such as lifting (pretend to lift something very heavy and notice what happens to your vocal cords).

Starting from the bottom and proceeding upward (following the path of sound production), we have the DIAPHRAGM,[1] which pushes upward squeezing the lungs and forcing the air out, up through the BRONCHIAL TUBES and the TRACHEA or windpipe (see no. 1 on Diagram 1 on p. 26). When the airstream gets to the LARYNX (no. 2 on Diagram 1) or voice box it passes between bands of elastic tissue—the VOCAL BANDS (also referred to as the vocal cords, no. 3). The movement of air causes these bands to vibrate. They can be tightened or relaxed, creating a small triangular opening between them, called the GLOTTIS (not shown). If the bands are tightened, the passing air makes them vibrate faster, and the resulting sound waves have a higher frequency, which, in turn, causes a higher musical pitch (see Diagram 2 on p. 27). This pitch can be lowered by relaxing the vocal bands, thus slowing the rate of vibration and lowering the frequency, that is, the number of sound wave CYCLES PER SECOND (CPS) or HERTZ (HZ). The size and thickness of these vocal bands differs with age and sex, thus creating a deeper or higher voice, depending on whether the speaker is a man, a woman, or a child (of either sex). An infection or inflammation such as laryngitis can temporarily change the size and shape of these bands, making one's voice hoarse, husky, squeaky, or even inaudible. The vocal bands of males

---

[1]Most of the technical and specialized terms in this and other chapters can be found in Appendix A, Glossary. Included are brief definitions and the Spanish equivalents.

Diagram 1 Organs of Speech

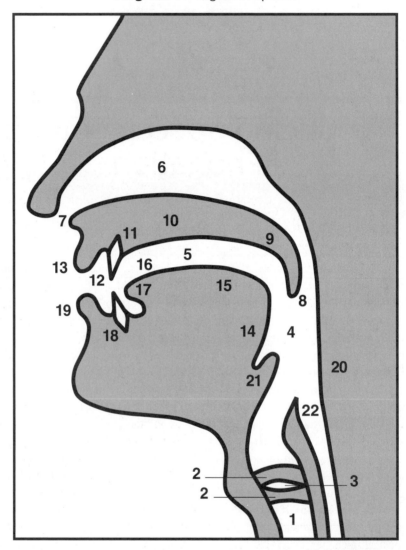

1 trachea	9 velum	16 blade or front of the tongue
2 larynx	10 palate	17 tip of the tongue
3 vocal bands	11 alveolar ridge	18 lower front teeth
4 pharynx	12 upper front teeth	19 lower lip
5 oral cavity	13 upper lip	20 wall of the pharynx
6 nasal cavity	14 root of the tongue	21 epiglottis
7 nostrils	15 dorsum or back of the tongue	22 esophagus
8 uvula		

Diagram 2   Sound Wave Frequency

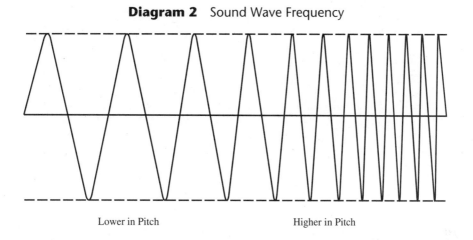

Lower in Pitch   Higher in Pitch

thicken rapidly at puberty, creating the so-called "change of voice" in teen-age boys and the deeper voice of men when the change is complete. The vocal bands in later life become weaker and lose their elasticity, creating the typical weak or shaky voice of the very elderly.

Singers have greater control than the average person over the extent and precision with which these bands can be tightened or relaxed and thus can achieve greater accuracy in the resulting musical notes. The rest of us cannot do it as well and, thus, often sing off key or "out of tune." This is because pitch in music is absolute; a note must have an exact frequency or number of sound wave cycles per second (cps) or Hz. But pitch in language is relative; the rises and falls of the human voice resulting from the greater or lower frequencies are compared to each other, not to a mathematical absolute.

The vocal bands vibrate for all vowel and many consonant sounds. This tone resulting from vocal band vibration is called PHONATION or VOICING. The glottis is open; the bands are kept apart and do not vibrate for consonants like [t] or [s], which are thus called VOICELESS or UNVOICED. You can easily hear the difference by placing your hands tightly over your ears and pronouncing first the voiceless consonant [s] in a prolonged manner— *s-s-s-s-s-s*—and then the voiced consonant [z] in the same way—*z-z-z-z-z-z*. You should not only be able to hear the voicing, but also feel the vibrations of your vocal bands resonating in your head, nose, and throat.

The force with which the air is expelled from the lungs through the larynx controls the VOLUME or loudness of the sound by increasing or decreasing the AMPLITUDE or size of the sound waves (see Diagram 3 on p. 28).

The airstream, now modified by the vibrating vocal bands, reaches the PHARYNX (no. 4 on Diagram 1), a cavity formed by the root of the tongue and the wall of the throat. From there the air can be exhaled through one of the two RESONANCE CHAMBERS, the ORAL CAVITY (5) or the NASAL CAVITY (6). If the VELUM (9) is lowered (as it is in Diagram 1), the air passes through the nasal cavity or passage and comes out through the NOSTRILS

Diagram 3   Sound Wave Amplitude

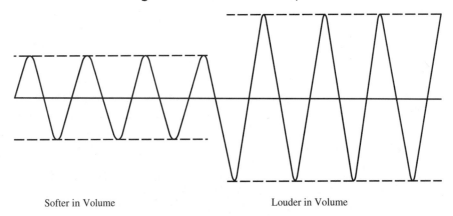

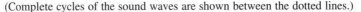

Softer in Volume   Louder in Volume

(Complete cycles of the sound waves are shown between the dotted lines.)

(7). In this case the resulting sound is a NASAL like [m] or [n]. The size and shape of this passage are not subject to voluntary control although the passage, of course, can be deliberately blocked off by pinching or closing the nostrils. A head cold or sinus infection can cause the lining of this passage to swell and can reduce the size of the passage or even close it off, thus modifying certain sounds. When this happens, the nasal sounds cannot be made properly—[m] sounds like [b] (*Barry* instead of *marry*), [n] sounds like [d] (*dough* instead of *no*), and [ŋ] sounds like [g] (*rig* instead of *ring*). This is actually the reverse of the popular notion that you sound like you are talking through your nose when you have a bad cold. In reality, you *cannot* talk through your nose, and, consequently, the nasals, no longer being very nasal, just don't sound right.

Most sounds, however, are produced by expelling the air through the oral cavity or mouth, and, thus, are known as ORAL SOUNDS. The LOWER or MOVABLE ARTICULATORS— the LOWER LIP (19), LOWER FRONT TEETH (18), and TONGUE (14–17)—move to make contact or come very close to the UPPER or FIXED ARTICULATORS—the UPPER LIP (13), the UPPER FRONT TEETH (12), the ALVEOLAR RIDGE (11) or gum ridge behind the upper front teeth, the hard PALATE (10), the VELUM or soft palate (9), the UVULA (8), and sometimes even the PHARYNX wall (20). The sound-producing area of the tongue can be divided into four main parts—the TIP (17), the BLADE or front (16), the DORSUM or top (15), and the ROOT or extreme rear (14), which is used in making sounds in Arabic, for example, but not in Spanish or English. The role these parts of the vocal tract play in the production or articulation of sounds is taken up in greater detail in Chapter 11.

In the front of the pharynx, below the root of the tongue, is the EPIGLOTTIS (21), which, although not functional in speech, is extremely important in the ingestion of food and liquid and can actually be a matter of life and death. As you swallow, it closes off the air passage to the larynx so that the food and liquid will go down the ESOPHAGUS (22) rather than to the larynx and trachea (windpipe). Occasionally, however, the epiglottis does not close fast enough, the food goes down "the wrong way," and coughing, choking, and perhaps even strangulation can result. The Heimlich Maneuver (familiar to CPR and restaurant personnel) is designed to force the air violently up through the vocal tract from the lungs, thus dislodging the foreign material stuck in the glottis (opening between the vocal bands) or even down in the trachea.

In the production of sound, the exhaled air is modified or controlled in several important ways.

1. VOLUME—the force with which the diaphragm and lungs expel the air, thus increasing the amplitude of the sound waves and making the sound louder, or decreasing their amplitude and making the sound softer.
2. VOICING or the lack of voicing—whether or not the vocal bands are tense enough to vibrate, thus causing phonation or the production of sound waves.
3. PITCH—how high or low a tone the sound has, depending on how tense or loose the vocal bands are, thus increasing or decreasing the frequency of the sound waves.
4. RESONANCE—whether the resulting sound waves resonate (reverberate, "bounce around") in just the oral cavity or both the oral and nasal cavities.
5. PLACE OF ARTICULATION—which articulators approach or contact each other: that is, which achieve what is known as MAXIMUM CLOSURE, the final position of the articulators—whether close to or far from each other—to produce the sound.
6. MANNER OF ARTICULATION—the way in which these articulators contact each other during maximum closure and how they modify the airstream.

Speech sounds can be divided into two basic categories: CONSONANTS, if the airstream is stopped or impeded in any way, and VOWELS, if it is not. There is a third intermediate category, known as GLIDES (or SEMI-CONSONANTS or SEMI-VOWELS), that is, sounds that seem to fit in neither category but form their own. In this book, however, some of these sounds will be considered to be basically consonants and the rest, basically vowels. The articulation of vowel and consonant sounds will be taken up in detail in Chapter 11.

Review and Discussion

1. Which of the following body parts do you think are essential or at least significant in the production of normal speech sounds? Why or why not?
   molars, nasal cavity, diaphragm, sinuses, glottis, epiglottis
2. Why do you abruptly close your vocal bands tightly when you exert yourself, such as when lifting something heavy, for example?
3. Why do adult males normally have deeper voices than adult females?
4. How is phonation or voicing created?
5. Why is it so important in language?
6. Name the three resonating chambers in the vocal tract.

7. Why is the popular notion that you sound ''nasal'' when you have a head cold really a misconception?
8. Describe from a physiological and an acoustic point of view what happens when you make a sound louder, that is, give it more volume.
9. Do the same for sounds that are higher in pitch.
10. What is the fundamental difference between vowels and consonants?

5

The Melody of Spanish (Suprasegmentals)

Vowels and consonants are known as SEGMENTAL sounds, small segments in the stream of speech. Some of them can be modified in several important ways by other sound features, known as SUPRASEGMENTALS, or features overlaid on the individual sound segments. These modifications are also referred to as INTONATIONAL or PROSODIC features, and they create the melody of the language.

These suprasegmental sound modifications are so important in human communication that the listener often heeds them much more than the individual sound segments. In fact, you can literally contradict the meaning of the words you utter just by your intonation. When you answer the question, "What do you think of it?" with the words, "It's just great!", if your voice starts quite high in musical pitch on the first part of *great* and drops slightly lower within the word, you really mean what the words arranged in this sequence seem to mean, namely that you highly approve of whatever it is. But if your voice starts very low on the first part of *great* and drops even slightly lower within the word, you are being sarcastic, or sound disappointed for some reason, or at any rate seem to mean just about the opposite of what these words indicate at their face value.

Or if you say about your friend's favorite movie and TV star, "He's a good actor!" with a high tone on *ac-* and drop to a low tone on *-tor,* you are praising him. But if you start on a low tone with *ac-* and raise the pitch quite high on *-tor,* you are not only denying this fact but even belittling your friend's judgement on the matter and criticizing him or her as well as the actor in question.

The common expression, "It's not what you say but how you say it" is soundly based on a linguistic reality—the complicated and subtle (for a foreign learner of a language) but essential suprasegmental system of the target language. Spanish, too, works this way although it has slightly fewer intonational contrasts than English.

Stress

The first suprasegmental feature is STRESS, which is the relative loudness, volume, or INTENSITY (controlled by the amplitude of the sound waves) of a given syllable in a word or in the stream of speech. Stress is CONTRASTIVE (that is, PHONEMIC) in English and enables you to distinguish between *implant* (verb) versus *implant* (noun) or *a moving van* (any such vehicle moving along the street) versus *a moving van* (a special truck for transporting household goods). It is equally significant in Spanish, enabling Spanish speakers to distinguish between **célebre** *famous* and **celebré** *I celebrated,* or turn a logical answer **Porque vive todavía** ''Because he's still alive'' into a bizarre question, **¿Por qué vive todavía?** ''Why is he still alive?''

Pitch

The second suprasegmental feature is PITCH, which is the musical tone (produced by the frequency of the sound waves) of a given syllable. In music, as we indicated in the previous chapter, pitch is absolute. The sound waves of the note A above middle C, for example, must have a frequency of exactly 440 cps or Hz and not 438 or 445, if it is to be exactly A, ''concert pitch'' (used for tuning musical instruments properly). But in language, pitch is relative and is manipulated within ranges rather than on an exact scale of proportionally separate notes. Relative pitch is what enables you to distinguish between ''What?'' with a sharp rise at the end and ''What?'' with a slow drop at the end, both answers to the statement, ''I have something to tell you.'' The first means ''I didn't hear you; please repeat,'' but the second means ''What do you want to tell me?'' In Spanish, **Está lloviendo** with a drop in pitch on the final **-do** explains why you come in wet or why you can't play tennis, but **¿Está lloviendo?** with a sharp rise in pitch on the final syllable is a question about the weather meant to be answered by your INTERLOCUTOR.

Juncture

The third suprasegmental feature is subtler and even somewhat problematic in the analysis of Spanish pronunciation. These are the so-called TERMINAL or EXTERNAL JUNCTURES, which describe what the voice does at pauses in the discourse where there is necessarily a slight change in pitch, volume, and tempo as your vocal bands stop vibrating or phonating momentarily. You can lower the pitch of your voice and trail away gradually into silence to indicate finality, or completion of the utterance. Or you can raise the pitch and cut off the volume abruptly to indicate doubt or simply a question. You can also sustain the pitch on a level note, prolonging the last syllable and lowering the volume slightly to indicate hesitation or incompletion. ''He won't do it'' in the first case (indicated by ↓) conveys resignation and acceptance of his refusal. But said in the second way (indicated by ↑) you convey disbelief or perhaps anger. And, if said in the third way (indicated by →), "He won't do it, but . . . ," you imply that the matter is far from over or perhaps you have another solution.

Normally these terminal junctures simply follow and continue the rises and falls in pitch or tone, but in Chapter 7 we will see instances where the pitch and the junctures do not match. For example, the voice can drop on the last syllable only to rise slightly and sharply at the very end, actually with the last few vibrations of the vocal bands.

Rhythm

The last suprasegmental feature is RHYTHM, which depends mainly on the relative length of stressed and unstressed syllables. For this reason, rhythm is very difficult to analyze in a comprehensive system of DISCRETE units, as we can do with vowels and consonants. Nor does it regulate meaning in the precise way that stress, pitch, and the individual segmental sounds do because syllable or vowel length is not contrastive in Spanish. But, nonetheless, the role of rhythm is just as critical to the acquisition of an authentic "native" Spanish accent as these other sound features are.

The linguistic role in language of these suprasegmentals, their auditory aspect, their physical properties, and their physiological origin are shown in the following chart.

Chart 1   Suprasegmentals

Linguistic Role of the Sound (SUPRASEGMENTALS)	Auditory Perception of the Sound	Physical Properties of the Sound	Physiological Source of the Sound
STRESS	loudness (volume, intensity) of sound	amplitude of sound waves (DECIBELS)	muscular effort in expelling air from lungs
PITCH	"musical tone" of sound	frequency of sound waves (cps or Hz)	tension of vocal bands
RHYTHM	syllable (or vowel) length	duration of sound waves (centiseconds)	timing of the muscular effort to stop and start outward air flow

Foreign-language teachers in the United States have generally neglected the area of suprasegmentals, probably because textbooks have, too. This is true not only because in the past, scientific studies on stress, pitch, juncture, and syllable length were relatively few in number and highly technical, but also because most teachers and textbook authors were really not convinced of the importance of these features in the beginning stages of language instruction. The few teachers that fully appreciated the problem lacked adequate instructional materials. Even today language textbooks typically devote much less space to suprasegmentals than to segmentals, and many teachers (depending on their experience in linguistics) omit the sections of their textbooks devoted to the explanation and practice of intonational features. Today linguistic studies of these features are more numerous, and teachers have become more aware of their importance in the total picture of language learning. Despite this improved situation, suprasegmentals are still more difficult for linguists to analyze, for instructors to teach, and for students to learn than vowels and consonants.

Thus, the element of Spanish most difficult for you to master remains proper intonation. This is ironic because you acquired the INTONATION of your native language so early, so quickly, so easily, and so thoroughly. And now it lies so firmly embedded at the base of your linguistic system that it stubbornly resists your efforts to learn the intonation of the target language. But even though your Spanish grammar may be perfect, your vocabulary extensive, and your individual sounds accurate, you will retain a noticeable foreign accent until you master the suprasegmental system of Spanish. But it can be done, so **¡Manos a la obra!**

6

Stress in Spanish

The Role of Stress in Language

The force with which the air is expelled from the lungs through the larynx controls the amplitude of the resulting sound waves and thus the volume or loudness of the sound. This loudness is perceived mainly in the vowels but also in certain voiced consonants that can be hummed or "sung," such as the nasals [m n ñ] or the lateral [l]. Stress in both Spanish and English is FUNCTIONAL (contrastive, phonemic) since it affects meaning. In both languages, in all multisyllabic words, certain vowels are pronounced louder than the others, thus determining the meaning of the word: **célebre** (*famous*) versus **celebré** (*I celebrated*) or *implant* (noun) versus *implant* (verb).

Stress has other functions, too: it may characterize an individual's unique way of speaking, it may show emphasis, or it may show mood, attitude, and emotion. For example, in Spanish **Dígamelo** is the normal way to say *Tell me*, but **Dígamelo** is emphatic and shows impatience or irritation. In English you can say, "Well, I'm not going," to exclude yourself from the group of those who are going, or you may say, "Well, I'm not going," to indicate your firm intention to remain. Or in French one may say **C'est impossible**, the normal way of indicating the impossibility of something, or **C'est impossible!**, an emphatic way of stating the impossibility of the matter.

But for our purposes here the most important role of stress is the first one mentioned above: lexical. This means that in both Spanish and English shifting the stress from one syllable to another changes or even destroys the meaning. If you say in Spanish **Así habló**, you mean, "That's the way he talked," but if you say **Así hablo**, you are saying, "That's the way I talk." Or if you say **Esto es muy bueno**, you have simply distorted the word **bueno** so that it sounds strange and abnormal. In English if you say *survey*, you are using a noun, but if you say *survey*, you are using a verb.

Occasionally, of course, the stress in words is different from dialect to dialect. If you are from Argentina, you say **boina** (*beret*), but if you are from Colombia you may call the item a **boína**. If you are from Detroit, you say, *Detroit,* but if you are from Pittsburgh, you may very well say *Detroit.* Both ways in both of these examples are correct, but each way sounds unusual to the other speaker who does not place the stress that way.

Fortunately for you, the stress system of Spanish is simpler than that of English since it has only two degrees of stress. A strong or heavy or primary stress is marked with ´ over the vowel, and a weak stress can be marked with ˘ over the vowel in the examples where it is necessary to mark the vowel in some way, though weak stress is left unmarked in a regular phonetic transcription. Thus **casa** can be transcribed [ká-să] in an example just to make it clear that the last syllable, unlike the first one, is unstressed or weak-stressed. However, normally **casa** is transcribed [ká-sa] in a regular phonetic transcription, leaving only the strong or stressed syllables marked.

Stress in English

English has four degrees of stress. The vowel of the PRIMARY or HEAVY-STRESSED syllable is marked with ´; SECONDARY STRESS with ˆ; TERTIARY STRESS with `; and WEAK STRESS with ˘. Unstressed or weak-stressed syllables in English normally contain either a HIGH CENTRAL VOWEL called ''barred-i'', transcribed [ɨ], or a MID CENTRAL VOWEL called ''schwa,'' transcribed [ə]. Thus the stresses in the phrase *Kentucky Derby* are shown as [kʰɨnt'ʌkÌ̀ydɔ́rbÌ̀y]. This same phrase with the stress over the second vowel of *Kentucky*— [kʰɨnt'ʌkÌ̀ydɔ́rbÌ̀y]—would imply that there is another ''derby,'' in addition to the famous one.

Some more words and phrases to illustrate the English stress system (with all the stresses marked) are ăppéar, ăn ápplĕ, táblĕ, básebàll, thís bâll (not *that one*), hîgh tíme, twô yéars (not *months*), twó yêars (not *three*), and so on. Many subtle contrasts and interesting historical developments are revealed in these English stress patterns. For example, there is a town in Pennsylvania, *Steelton,* pronounced [stɨ́yltŏn], schwa [ə] being the most frequent vowel in unstressed syllables in English. The name came from the phrase *steel* town, that is, one where steel is produced, pronounced [stɨ́ylt'àwn]. Of course, there is no such phrase in English as *steel town*, pronounced [stɨ̂ylt'áwn], which would mean ''a town made out of steel.'' Yet we can stress *town* in a sentence like ''Steelton is a small town [smâlt'áwn]'' (a town that is small). Many foreign learners of English, particularly speakers of French, which has no phonemic stress whatsoever, simply cannot at first understand such phrases as ''Every white house is not the White House,'' or ''A crow may be a black bird, but it is not a blackbird,'' or ''Greenhouses are almost never green houses.'' There are hundreds of such contrasts in English, based solely on the interplay of these various degrees of stress.

Stress in Spanish

The stress system in Spanish is simpler than that of English because there are only two degrees of stress: strong, marked ´, and weak, which is rarely marked in a Spanish transcription for reasons of simplicity. Some linguists analyze the Spanish stress system as having three degrees. What they call ''secondary'' stress occurs mainly in the first part of adverbs like **naturalmente** or in some compound words like **bienvenida** or **veintidós**.

They even claim that native speakers can distinguish between the word **abrelatas** *can opener* and the phrase **Abre latas** "He/She opens cans" *solely* on the basis of the stresses and not the context. This claim is doubtful, and the few cases where some speakers might sometimes react as though they heard a difference are simply not enough to warrant complicating our analysis with another degree of stress. In English the four degrees of stress are easy to demonstrate; in Spanish it is extremely difficult to verify a third degree of stress.

Another important difference between the stress systems of the two languages is the fact that in English either the mid central vowel *schwa* [ə] or the high central vowel *barred 'i'* [ɨ] occurs in virtually every weak-stressed syllable. Spanish lacks both of these vowels; the vowels in the weak- or unstressed syllables in Spanish are of virtually the same length and quality as their stressed counterparts (with some exceptions, as we will note later, with certain speakers in Mexico and in the Andes region of South America). Thus the first /a/ of **casa** is like the second one in all respects, except, of course, for its loudness or stress.

All Spanish words *in isolation* have at least one primary or heavy stress. **Para**, pronounced alone as [pá-ra], may be the verb *he/she stops* or the preposition *in order to* or *for*. But in the stream of speech certain parts of speech "lose" their main stresses. Thus in Spanish there can be a contrast between ¡**Para el carro!** "Stop the car!" and **para el carro** *for the car*. This difference can be shown in phonetic transcription: [pá-ra-el-ká-r̄o] versus [pa-ra-el-ká-r̄o]. Or **El perro, ¿qué tiene?** [ké-ti̯é-ne], for example, means "What's wrong with the dog?", but **el perro que tiene** [ke-ti̯é-ne] **pulgas. . .** is the beginning of an incomplete sentence, "The dog that has fleas . . ."

In English certain short words are normally unstressed or weak-stressed in the stream of speech and undergo extreme shortening and even sound loss: *her* becomes just *'er*, as in "Tell her"; *him* becomes just *'im*, as in "Trust him"; *my* might even become *'muh'*, as in "My man." But for emphasis or contrast we can easily put a heavy stress on these forms (thus, changing the vowel from [ə] or [ɨ] to other ones), as in "Tell *her*, not *me*!" or "Trust *him*! Why should I do that after what he's done?" or "This is *my* problem, and I'll handle it myself."

Spanish speakers can create contrasts like this, too, but rarely through the stress system, as we do in English. The favored way in Spanish is to change the word order of the sentence by putting words susceptible to heavy stress near the end. Thus many short Spanish words, such as **la** *her* or **lo** *him or* **mi** *my*, which do not occur with stress in the stream of speech, must be replaced or accompanied by such phrases and words as **a ella** *her,* or **a él** *him*, or **mío** *my* (to convey emphasis). Looking around a room for a familiar face, a Spanish speaker says, **Ah, la conozco a ella** "Oh, I know *her*." Or, in answer to the question "Who did you see running away from the scene?", the response for *him,* while pointing to the suspect, is **a él**. Often, as we have said, the new form requires a recasting of the sentence (from the point of view of English, of course): **Este carro es mío** "This is *my* car." (In some dialects this could be said as in English **Este es mi carro**, but in most **mío** would be used after the noun instead of **mi** before it.)

This problem is actually a double one for you as an English speaker. First, you must learn which words do not normally carry strong stress in Spanish in the stream of speech, and, secondly, you must learn the lexical and grammatical methods for conveying the emphasis and contrast you are trying to express. This second consideration, although crucial in learning the language, is not the main concern in this book, although we do want you to realize that since certain Spanish words are not said with heavy stresses, you must find an alternate way of expressing yourself, utilizing words that can be stressed.

Free Forms versus Bound Forms

In Spanish some words are considered to be UNBOUND or FREE FORMS, that is, words that can also be uttered in isolation. The words **mujer** or **venga** or **guapo** or **aquí** can be uttered in isolation as answers to questions or simply expressions of meaning. They happen to be, respectively, a noun, a verb, an adjective, and an adverb, and these words, as you probably know, are the main "parts of speech" or form classes in both Spanish and English. Such free or unbound forms usually take heavy stresses in the stream of speech because of their grammatical status, which, in a somewhat circular fashion, is indicated by their ability to be said in isolation.

But most other short grammatical classes—sometimes referred to as FUNCTION WORDS—are normally never uttered in isolation because they are BOUND FORMS, and thus never take heavy stresses in the stream of speech. Such words as articles (**el, la, las, un**), short possessives (**mi, tu, sus**), short prepositions (**con, sin, de, a, para**), object pronouns (**la, lo, me, te, nos**), subordinating conjunctions (**que, cuando**), and others to be examined later always occur in natural speech in the "company of," or in close proximity to a word in one of the four main classes already indicated: noun, verb, adjective, or adverb. Naturally we have to make a few trivial exceptions. A Spanish speaker would never say **le** in isolation, that is, without an accompanying verb (as in **Le gusta**), except to answer a question like, —¿**Cuál pronombre se usa con gustar, le o lo?** —**Le**.

Such usage occasionally puzzles English speakers, who, of course, are used to hearing many of these short forms in isolation with heavy stresses. In English, as we offer coffee to someone and point to the cream, we can ask "With or without?" But in Spanish the words **con** and **sin**, since they are short prepositions, are "bound" to one of the main parts of speech, are rarely said in isolation, and thus do not take what would be a heavy stress in these situations. The Spanish speaker thus asks, ¿**Con leche o sin leche?** with heavy stresses only on the noun **leche**. Batman shouts to Robin, "*After* him!", but in the Spanish dubbed version the words come out, ¡**Tras él!** because **tras** is a short preposition and can neither be said in isolation nor with a heavy stress. The humorous English misinterpretation might be that Batman is really saying "After *him*!" rather than "After *her*!", but no such thing is implied in Spanish.

Although there are exceptions to this phenomenon of free versus bound forms and stressed versus unstressed forms, a handy rule-of-thumb is that free forms are always stressed in the stream of speech in Spanish whereas bound forms almost never are. If the speaker wants to emphasize one of the unstressed, bound forms, she/he must choose a related word and recast the sentence. In English normally all we do is say the emphasized word louder regardless of what type of form it is and where it occurs in the sentence.

Following are the types of words in Spanish normally considered free and therefore susceptible to taking heavy stress anywhere in the stream of speech. In the accompanying examples, the stressed words are *italicized* with the stressed syllables underlined. Remember that written accents, although obviously related to voice stress, are another matter. Some stressed syllables have written accents just because of the rules of Spanish orthography (spelling), but the vast majority of stressed syllables have no written accents. This will be taken up in detail in Chapter 31.

Chart 2   Stressed Forms in Spanish

NOUNS	La *señora* pidió una *ensalada*.
NOMINALIZED FORMS (any other part of speech that functions as or replaces a noun)	*Lo* de ayer es increíble. El *otro* me gusta más. Por fin compró el *azul*.
VERBS	La señora *pidió* una ensalada. No lo *tenemos* todavía.
ADJECTIVES	Por fin compró el carro *azul*.
ADVERBS	*Ayer* no más me mandó un mensaje electrónico. *Aquí* a la residencia.
DISJUNCTIVE PRONOUNS (those used without verbs)	*Yo* no lo vi. ¿Todo esto para *mí*?
NUMERALS (both cardinal and ordinal)	Tiene *dos* impresoras. No, por *primera* vez.
NEGATIVES	*No* viene *nadie*.
POSSESSIVES (post-posed and pronouns)	Es un amigo *mío*. El *suyo* costó mucho más.

(*Continued*)

(*Continued*)

DEMONSTRATIVES	*Este* aparato tiene capacidad de fax.
INTERROGATIVES	*¿Cuándo* regresa?
EXCLAMATIVES	*¡Qué* bien!
DETERMINERS (sometimes called "limiting adjectives")	Tengo mi *propia* computadora ahora. Sí, *cualquier* día está bien. Estoy ocupado *todos* los días de esta semana. *Algunos* estudiantes de la clase son hispanos.

Chart 3   Unstressed Forms in Spanish

(Remember that these italicized example words have no underlined syllables because they are not stressed in the stream of speech.)

SIMPLE (one-word) PREPOSITIONS	Gracias, lo prefiero *con* leche. Esto es *para* el carro. ¡*Tras* él!
CONJUNCTIVE PRONOUNS (those used only with verbs)	No *lo* conozco. *Me* da lo mismo. Creo que *se* va en este momento.
ARTICLES (indefinite and definite)	*Un* pájaro en *la* mano vale cien volando.
CONJUNCTIONS (both coordinating and subordinating)	Así con papel *y* lápiz. *Cuando* venga, se lo diré. *Para que* lo sepas, hombre.

(*Continued*)

(*Continued*)

POSSESSIVES (pre-posed)	*Mi* **amigo me los mandó.** *Su* **carro costó mucho más que el mío.**
RELATIVE PRONOUNS	**La mujer** *que* **nos dirigió la palabra es una arquitecta muy conocida.** **¡Sálvese** *quien* **pueda!**

There are a few forms that fit in either or both categories, that is, they may or may not be stressed in the stream of speech, depending on various factors, such as dialect, emphasis, or attitude. Thus the italicized words may not necessarily be stressed in all cases.

Chart 4   Variably Stressed Forms in Spanish

QUALIFIERS (both intensifiers and diminishers of adjectives)	**Creo que es** _más_ (or *más*) **listo que el diablo.** **Es el** _menos_ (or *menos*) **conocido de todos.**
Unos (meaning *some* in the sense of *a few*)	_Unos_ (or *unos*) **estudiantes acudieron a ayudarle.**
Haber (one-syllable forms)	**Lo** _ha_ (or *ha*) **dicho sólo para meter su cuchara.**
Es	**Epifanio** _es_ (or *es*) **de Sevilla, ¿no lo sabías?**
First element of a COMPOUND	_veintidós_ (or *veintidós*) _bienvenida_ (or *bienvenida*) _sacacorchos_ (or *sacacorchos*) _guardaespaldas_ (or *guardaespaldas*)

Sentence Stress

In addition to word or lexical stress, there is another type of stress known as SENTENCE STRESS. In virtually every utterance one of the several primary word stresses is louder than the others. Usually this sentence stress (marked here with two accent marks ˝) coincides with either the first or the last stressed syllable of the breath group or utterance, where, as we shall see in the next chapter, the pitch also changes: **¿Por qué** [ké̃] **dices esas cosas?**, where the emphasis is on *Why*, or **¿Por qué dices esas cosas** [kó̃-sas]**?**, where the emphasis is on *things*. In the first case, **qué** is even louder than the **di-** [dí-] of **dices**, the **e-** [é-] of **esas**, and the **co-** [kó-] of **cosas**, which also have primary stresses because of their grammatical status (see Chart 2 on p. 39). In the second case, **co-** is louder than **qué**, **di-**, and **e-**, still with primary stresses, because of the shift in emphasis. The heavy sentence stress of the first sentence indicates that you are seeking the reason for which the other person has said these things; the heavy sentence stress of the second sentence indicates you wonder why it is *these* things and not others that have been said.

Occasionally this feature of sentence stress ˝ is used to emphasize a short word that normally is unstressed in the stream of speech (see Chart 3 on p. 40). Although there are no particular rules for this phenomenon, a common form to receive sentence stress is often the last object pronoun attached to a command form, as in **¡Pues, hombre, dígamelo!** [di-ǵa-me-ló̃] or **Sí, señor, siéntese** [sien̦-te-sé̃]. Also, as we have seen, some speakers use both normal lexical stresses and sentence stresses on the short pre-posed possessives, particularly in emotional speech: **¡No quiero tu** [tú̃] **dinero!**

Frequently the extra loudness of sentence stress obscures the other primary stresses and makes their presence hard to detect for the foreign learner. However, if the other primary stresses are changed, the meaning of these words is also changed in Spanish. For example, in the sentence **¡No hablo así a nadie** [ná̃-đie]! "I don't talk that way to anyone!", although **nadie** has a heavy sentence stress, the syllables **no**, **ha-**, and **-sí** still have their normal primary stresses. If the **ha-** of **hablo** did not have its proper primary stress, its meaning would be obscured, and the verb could even be interpreted as **habló**, changing the sentence to "She didn't talk that way to anyone!"—not at all what you meant.

Since sentence stress is so dependent upon emotion and emphasis (and even the speaking style of some individuals), its occurrence and position in the sentence are difficult, if not impossible, to predict theoretically. Thus, we will mark it only in the transcriptions where you are told specifically that one of the words has extra emphasis and leave it unmarked in all other transcriptions.

Stress Phrases

In Spanish a group of unstressed syllables clustered around one primary stressed syllable is called a STRESS PHRASE or STRESS GROUP. These phrases have less importance in Spanish phonetics and phonology than larger syntactic groups like clauses and sentences since there are no pauses between them. An utterance like **Los hombres que conocimos en la fiesta son futbolistas** has four stress phrases but is only one sentence or one breath group: **Los hombres // que conocimos // en la fiesta // son futbolistas.** As you can see, most stress phrases—unless they are very long words—are relatively short in Spanish since there are so many word classes that have primary stress (see Chart 2). These primary stressed syllables are normally not accompanied by a great many unstressed syllables, although very long words are an exception to this: **agriculturización** or **constitucionalidad.**

English is noticeably different in this respect. It is normal to have many syllables—with weak, tertiary, and secondary stresses—clustered around one primary stress, as in the example *Kentucky Derby* [kʰɪntʼʌkɪ̀ydə́rbɪ̀y]. This is also true of breath groups, that is, the stream of speech between two pauses. The groups may be phrases, clauses, or even sentences, as long as they are said without a pause anywhere, which would create a new breath group: ''my first Kentucky Derby'' (seven syllables with the single primary stressed syllable underlined); ''when I saw my first Kentucky Derby'' (ten syllables); ''It rained all day at my first Kentucky Derby'' (twelve syllables). Thus, as you see, English can have fairly long stress groups, whereas in Spanish they are rarely longer than three or four syllables (the primary stressed syllables are also underlined): **Fui** (one syllable) **a ver** (two syllables) **la Vuelta** (three syllables) **a Colombia** (four syllables). Exceptions are very long words, such as those in the previous paragraph. Such long Spanish words, however, have only one heavy stress. You, as an English speaker, must guard against raising the degree of stress in these unstressed syllables, as you do in English. In English the word *responsibility* comes out [rɪ̀yspânsɪ̀bɪ́lɪ̀tɪ̆y], with one primary stress, one secondary stress, one tertiary stress, and three weak stresses. But in Spanish the word **responsabilidad** comes out [r̄es-pon-sa-βi-li-ɖáɖ] with one primary stress and five weak stresses.

The difference in the length and nature of these stress groups creates quite different rhythms in the two languages (to be examined in greater detail in Chapter 8). Spanish has a smoother, more even-flowing rhythm—''legato'' in musical terms—because of this alternation of weak and strong stresses in the breath group (and other reasons, too), whereas English has a choppier, less even-flowing rhythm because of the interplay of all four degrees of stress in one breath group. You can see this in the transcription of *Kentucky Derby* above, and you can hear it by saying the English sentence, ''It rained all day at my first Kentucky Derby'' normally and then listening to a native speaker of Spanish say **Fui a ver la Vuelta a Colombia** or **Los hombres que conocimos en la fiesta son futbolistas**.

Word Stress Categories

Spanish words can be classified according to the position of their lexical stress.

Chart 5 Classification of Spanish Words by Stress

LAST-SYLLABLE STRESSED (**aguda**)	**hablar, feroz, animal, habló, nación, estás**
PENULT (next-to-last syllable) STRESSED (**llana**)	**hablo, hablan, hablas, césped, fácil, lápiz**

(*Continued*)

(*Continued*)

ANTEPENULT (third-from-last syllable) STRESSED (**esdrújula**)	<u>lá</u>pices, <u>rá</u>pido, <u>dí</u>game
PREANTEPENULT (fourth-from-last syllable) STRESSED (**sobresdrújula**)	<u>dí</u>gamelo, dic<u>ié</u>ndonosla

There are really no single Spanish words in the last category, "preantepenult" or **sobresdrújula**, since all such forms are verbs with object pronouns attached.

Notice that in the first category only words ending in a vowel letter, **n,** or **s** have written accents; in the second category only words ending in consonants *other* than **n** or **s** have written accents; and in the third and fourth categories *all* words have written accents. The rules for the use of written accents in Spanish are obviously dependent on the spelling as well as on the position of the lexical stresses, and these rules will be examined briefly in the last section of this chapter and in greater detail in Chapter 31, "The Orthography of Spanish."

A handful of nouns in Spanish shift their lexical stress when pluralized: **ca<u>rác</u>ter** is a **llana** word, but in the plural form the stress shifts forward one syllable, to **ca<u>rac</u>teres**, still a **llana** word. **<u>Ré</u>gimen** is an **esdrújula** word, but in the plural form the stress shifts forward one syllable to **re<u>gí</u>menes** and is thus still an **esdrújula** word. In this case, however, if the stress did not shift we would have an impossibility in Spanish—a **sobresdrújula** *noun*: ***<u>ré</u>gimenes**.[1] Shifting the stress like this is very unusual in Spanish. However, many Spanish words, although the stress does not shift, are in different stress *categories* when pluralized: **ciu<u>dad</u>** (**aguda**) - **ciu<u>da</u>des** (**llana**); **<u>jo</u>ven** (**llana**) - **<u>jó</u>venes** (**esdrújula**). This fact is more important for the correct placement of the written accent than it is for achieving the right pronunciation.

A few Spanish nouns with two adjoining vowels have two variant pronunciations based on stress shift: a formal one with the stress on the first vowel and an informal one with the stress on the second vowel. In this latter case sometimes the first vowel turns into a semi-vowel: **océano**, either [o-sé-a-no] (formal) or [o-se-á-no] or even [o-si̯á-no] (informal); **período**, either [pe-rí-o-đo] (formal) or [pe-ri̯ó-đo] (informal). However, even speakers who use the informal stress-shifted pronunciation retain the accent in writing.

---

[1]An asterisk * before an item in linguistics means two things. In historical or diachronic linguistics it means that the marked form probably existed due to what we know about the laws, processes, and history of the language, but no evidence of it has ever been found in written form. But in descriptive synchronic linguistics an asterisk means that the form is non-existent because it is incorrect and ungrammatical, that is, it would never be said normally by a native speaker. That is how we use it in this book.

Double-Stressed Words

Adverbs ending in **-mente** have two strong stresses, reflecting the words' true nature as compounds, made up of the adjective + **-mente: igualmente** [i-ǥuál-mén̦-te], **rápidamente** [r̄á-pi-ɗa-mén̦-te]. (The written accent on **rápidamente** is really because of **rápida-**, an **esdrújula** word, all of which have written accents in Spanish.) Some compounds likewise have two heavy stresses: **veintidós** [béi̦n-ti-ɗós], **camposanto** [kám-po-sá̦n-to], **sacapuntas** [sá-ka-pú̦n-tas]. Some speakers, however, pronounce these compounds (except for **-mente** adverbs) with just one heavy stress: [bei̦n-ti-ɗós], [kam-po-sá̦n-to], [sa-ka-pú̦n-tas].

Stress and Cognates

The last important aspect of Spanish stress is the fact that so many words have different stress patterns from their English cognates, thus misleading you as to their correct pronunciation. Such words as **acróbata** *acrobat*, **comunica** *communicate*, **demócrata** *democrat*. **preocupo** *preoccupy*, **teléfono** *telephone* are often mispronounced by English speakers because of the conflicting stress patterns. This is usually not a major problem, however, once it is brought into your awareness.

Stress and Orthography

The lexical primary stresses in Spanish are always indicated either directly or indirectly by the spelling. If a word has a written accent, obviously that syllable carries the voice stress: **país, continúa, pasó, andén, inglés, césped, fácil, nácar.** But you can also tell where to place the lexical voice stress in any Spanish word indirectly, that is, just by its spelling, even though there is no written accent. All words without written accents that end in any consonant letter *other than* **n** or **s** are **agudas**, or stressed on the last syllable: **unidad, anorak, animal, escribir, reloj, maguey, alcatraz.** All words without written accents that end in vowel letters, **n**, or **s** are **llanas**, stressed on the next-to-last syllable: **casa, rico, clase, cursi, tribu.** All **esdrújula** words (voice stress on the third-to-last syllable) and **sobresdrújula** forms (voice stress on the fourth-to-last syllable) carry a written accent: **capítulo, énfasis, dígame, dígamelo, dándonoslas.**

A written accent found on an **í** or a **ú** next to another vowel within a word indicates that the /i/ or /u/ is *stressed* and is thus not a SEMI-VOWEL forming part of a diphthong: **mío, leíste, grúa, baúl.** If the /i/ or /u/ next to a vowel is *not* stressed—and in properly spelled forms you can always tell by the lack of a written accent—it is the semi-vowel [i̯] or [u̯] and forms part of a DIPHTHONG: **paisano, siete, causa, suave.** It is easy to be misled by the presence of an /i/ or /u/ nearby. In the word **siete**, for example, remember that the /e/ is really the stressed part of the syllable, not the /i/. But in a word like **ríe**, the /i/ *is* stressed and thus bears a written accent.

There are two exceptions to this rule of a written accent on a stressed /í/ or a stressed /ú/ next to another vowel. In words where the letter **u** comes between a **q** or a **g** and an **i**, the **u** represents no sound at all and thus the /i/ does not need a written accent: **quito**, **seguir**. There are a great many words like this in Spanish. Also in words where a stressed /í/ follows a /u/ or vice versa, there is no written accent : **ruido**, **viuda**. There are just a handful of Spanish words like this.

The written accent in all its functions will be covered in detail in Chapter 31.

Practice

A.

Pronounce the following words and give the stress category in each case, as in the examples below.

está   aguda (because the last syllable is stressed)
figura   llana (because the next-to-last syllable is stressed)
número   esdrújula (because the third-to-last syllable is stressed)
muéstraselos   sobresdrújula (because the fourth-to-last syllable is stressed)

1. animo	13. leones
2. lóbrego	14. irá
3. devuélvamelo	15. oportuno
4. caminar	16. manifestaciones
5. oportunidad	17. diciéndotela
6. avergüenzo	18. juvenil
7. golondrina	19. telefoneo
8. impónganselos	20. partidario
9. análisis	21. dándoselo
10. desperdicio	22. depósito
11. glotón	23. honradez
12. inverosímil	24. insignificancia

B.

*Your instructor will say one word or phrase from either column **a** or column **b**, going in numerical order. Repeat it, indicate which column it is in, and give the meaning if you know it. Then say the corresponding word or phrase from the other column, and also give the meaning if you know it. For example,* INSTRUCTOR: **la calle.** YOU: **la calle**—*column **a**—the street.* **La callé**. *I made her be quiet.*

a	b
1. la calle	la callé
2. baño	bañó

3.	la corte	la corté
4.	lástima	lastima
5.	la ópera	la opera
6.	tarde	tardé
7.	viaje	viajé
8.	la vera	la verá
9.	la sábana	la sabana
10.	refresco	refrescó
11.	celebro	celebró
12.	célebre	celebre
13.	celebre	celebré
14.	¿yo, filósofo?	¿yo filosofo?
15.	seria	sería
16.	tenia	tenía
17.	bajo	bajó
18.	domino	dominó
19.	deposito	depósito
20.	depósito	depositó
21.	papa	papá
22.	abra	habrá
23.	peso	pesó
24.	preocupo	preocupó

C.

Pronounce the following words (or repeat them after your instructor if you need help). Be careful to use only one primary stress and make all the remaining weak-(un-) stressed syllables equal in length and value although, of course, not as loud as the stressed syllable.

1. norteamericano	13. permutabilidad
2. matemático	14. generalizar
3. carnicero	15. generalización
4. cántaro	16. estacionar
5. aseguro	17. estacionamiento
6. aseguró	18. impermeable
7. exámenes	19. impermeabilidad
8. decímetro	20. abandonamiento
9. refrigerador	21. alfabetización
10. laboratorio	22. homogeneidad
11. institucional	23. agriculturización
12. institucionalidad	24. impresionabilidad

D.

*Pronounce the following words and phrases (or repeat them after your instructor).
In each case there are two primary stresses.*

1. igualmente
2. lícitamente
3. naturalmente
4. generalmente
5. cumpleaños
6. anglosajón
7. cubrecama
8. salvavidas
9. enhorabuena
10. regularmente
11. casa cuna
12. informalmente
13. literalmente
14. pararrayos
15. guardabrisa
16. hazmerreír

E.

*Say the English word or phrase first (or your instructor will say it); then pronounce
the corresponding Spanish cognate, which, of course, will have a different stress
pattern.*

1. *permanent*   permanente
2. *acrobat*   acróbata
3. *opportunity*   oportunidad
4. *antidote*   antídoto
5. *preoccupy*   preocupo
6. *solicitous*   solicito
7. *democrat*   demócrata
8. *democracy*   democracia
9. *anecdote*   anécdota
10. *versatile*   versátil
11. *character*   carácter
12. *characters*   caracteres
13. *cartilage*   cartílago
14. *regimens*   regímenes
15. *deposit*   depósito
16. *deposited*   depositó
17. *communicate*   comunica
18. *felicitous*   felicito
19. *I deposit*   deposito
20. *I imagine*   me imagino

F.

Read the following phrases and sentences aloud, being careful to place primary stresses only on the free forms that take them and leave all other words unstressed. If your instructor wishes, you can give the meaning of the Spanish utterance.

1. No vivo aquí.
2. No vino nadie.
3. No vino ninguno.
4. No tiene ninguna.
5. Es mi amigo.
6. Es un amigo mío.
7. ¿Tiene dos impresoras?
8. No, tiene sólo una impresora.
9. Lo de ayer es increíble.
10. No lo ve en ninguna parte.
11. Elizardo y su esposa vienen a visitarnos la semana que viene.
12. ¿Lo tomas sin azúcar o con azúcar?
13. El habla es propia de los humanos.
14. Él habla pero no dice nada.
15. Si esto vale mucho, nadie lo sabe.
16. Sí, esto vale mucho, y todos lo saben.
17. Es para mi amigo.
18. Es para mí, amigo.
19. No se espera más.
20. No sé, espera un poco más.
21. Se lo digo siempre cuando viene.
22. Se lo diré. ¿Cuándo viene?
23. —El perro, ¿qué tiene? —No sé.
24. El perro que tiene pulgas se rasca.
25. Venden trigo, maíz, vegetales, así como carne de vaca y otros productos.
26. Así como carne de vaca—cortándola en trocitos.
27. ¡Cuanto tengo es tuyo!
28. ¡Cuánto te quiero!
29. ¿Que vale mucho? No sé.
30. ¿Qué vale tanto? No se sabe.

G.

Rephrase the Spanish sentence so that the word indicated in parentheses (or the concept represented by the word) now receives an emphatic heavy sentence stress.

Normally such words go at or near the end of the sentence in Spanish. There may be more than one possible answer. For example,

Es mi libro. (mi)   →   ¡El libro es <u>mío</u>! ¡Ese libro es <u>mío</u>!

1. Es su amigo. (su)
2. Me gusta la lucha libre. (me)
3. Nadie lo ha visto. (nadie)
4. O es un loco o es un genio la persona que siempre se habla. (se)
5. ¿La conoces? (la)
6. No es tu vídeo; no lo puedes tomar. (tu)
7. ¿También le gusta la lucha libre? (le)
8. Creo que la Mafia se llama entre los ''miembros'' ''Nuestra cosa''. (nuestra)
9. Tampoco lo comprendo. (lo)
10. ¿Por qué siempre critica lo que escribo? (yo)

H.

Using conventional orthography (regular spelling), indicate the primary stresses by underlining the proper vowel. Written accents have deliberately been left off all words. Then check your work in Appendix C.

1. Se comunica con los ingleses por medio del telefono.
2. Si, es lo que llaman ustedes un caracter, pero tenemos muchos caracteres como el por aqui.
3. Imaginese que ya se va la señora Martinez.
4. El chico cuyo padre era el candidato democrata el año pasado es alumno mio.
5. —¿Tienes suficiente papel? —Si, esta caja me basta.
6. Figurese, me conto la anecdota en la que no pudieron encontrar el antidoto a tiempo.
7. —Solicito ayuda de unos alumnos que sean muy, muy diligentes, con mucha responsabilidad. —¿Los has encontrado? —Todavia no y francamente no me lo explico.
8. —Celebre usted la llegada de un hombre tan celebre. —Ya lo celebre.

7

Intonation in Spanish

The second important suprasegmental feature of the Spanish sound system is INTO-NATION. As we have seen, your interlocutor often pays more attention to the way you say things than to what you seem to be saying with the actual words. At least, if your tone and emphasis contradict the words and grammatical constructions, the former elements usually override the latter. The intonation of the language is one of the first things an infant learns, long before individual sounds, lexical items, and syntactic constructions. Perhaps this is the reason that learning the intonation of a foreign language is so difficult for the adult; the native intonation is so deeply and firmly embedded that it resists the acquisition of a new intonation.

Pitch

Pitch, the main component of intonation, is the musical tone of the voice, or the effect produced by the frequency of the sound waves created by the vibration of the vocal bands in the larynx. Singers have such great control over their vocal bands that they can produce a desired frequency exactly, such as 440 vibrations or cycles per second (cps) or hertz (Hz) for the note A above Middle C, known as "concert pitch." Pitch in ordinary language use, however, is relative rather than absolute as it is in music. Although women and children typically have higher voices than adult males, all speakers, regardless of their age and sex, manipulate their vocal bands in pretty much the same way to create such important distinctions as question versus statement, command versus request, ordinary utterance versus emphatic utterance, and so on. Although the exact tones or frequencies vary with age, sex, and individual speaker, the word "What?", said with a sharp rising tone by any native speaker of English means "I didn't hear you. Repeat it." And "What?", said with a gradual dropping tone by the same speaker means, "What do you want?" or "What is it that I'm supposed to do?" or "What do you have to tell me?"; in other words, this "What?" ↓ is a request for more information, often in response to a question that has been perfectly understood, unlike the first "What?" ↑, which is an admission of not having heard the other speaker's utterance.

Intonation, that is, this interplay of rising, sustained, and falling vocal tones, not only conveys lexical and grammatical meaning, but, just as importantly for human communication, also expresses the speaker's intentions, attitudes, emotions, personality, and psychological state. We all know people whom we refer to as "business-like, no-nonsense" types, or whining and complaining types, or hesitant and meek types, or assertive and aggressive types, and so on. Intonation plays a key role in our evaluation of such personality types, along with the accompanying facial gestures, body language, actions, and words, of course.

This means that, if you carry over all your English intonational patterns into Spanish, you run the risk of not only being misunderstood occasionally but, perhaps worse, creating a false impression of yourself—at least in the initial stages of your relationship with Spanish speakers. Thus, although individual segmental sounds, such as vowels and consonants, may be mastered to perfection, failure to pronounce them with the proper intonation will spoil what might otherwise be a pretty good Spanish accent. Thus we present suprasegmentals before segmentals in this book—not only because of their intrinsic importance, but also their relative difficulty for you as an adult learner of Spanish.

Tone Languages and Intonation Languages

Intonation is a system of contrasting pitch levels, manipulated almost exclusively on the sentence level: to distinguish between questions and statements, to produce contrast and emphasis, and to provide new as opposed to known information. Languages that utilize intonation solely for these purposes include most European languages and thus most of those commonly studied by North Americans. But some languages (mainly in Asia and Africa), like Chinese, Vietnamese, Thai, and Hottentot manipulate pitch on the lexical or word level, and are thus called TONE LANGUAGES. This means that the same sequence of segmental phonemes (vowels and consonants) has a different *lexical* meaning according to the way the pitch changes from syllable to syllable or even within the same syllable. For example, in Vietnamese the sound sequence /ma/ means six different things, depending on the level and direction of the tones. The syllable /ma/ means *mother* if said with a high tone that rises even higher at the end, *cheek* with a high tone that rises slightly at the end, *ghost* with a high tone that is sustained on the same level, *tomb* with a mid tone that rises quite high at the end, *young rice plant* with a low tone that rises slightly at the end, and *but* with a low tone that falls slightly at the end.[1]

Languages like Spanish and English, however, use pitch to control grammatical rather than lexical meaning on the phrase, clause, and sentence level and, for this reason, are called INTONATION LANGUAGES. For example, both languages generally use a final pitch drop to indicate that an utterance is a declarative statement: **Vive en ese apartamento** ↓, "She lives in that apartment" ↓, and a final pitch rise to indicate a question: **¿Vive en ese apartamento?** ↑, "She lives in that apartment?" ↑. Our previous illustration of

[1]This information was conveyed to me in a personal communication from a native speaker of Vietnamese, Kim Martínez.

"What?," said with either a rise ↑ or a fall ↓, despite the fact that it is only one word, is not a counter-example since the first "What?", although just one word, is really short for "What did you say?", and the second "What?" is really short for "What do you want?" or "What am I supposed to do?" Thus both Spanish and English employ pitch in basically the same way, unlike tone languages like Chinese or Vietnamese.

Pitch Levels in English

In English there are four contrastive pitch levels: LOW /1/, MID /2/, HIGH /3/, and EXTRA-HIGH or emphatic /4/, but in Spanish there are only three: low /1/, mid /2/, and high or emphatic /3/. Speakers of both languages can lower their voices below pitch level /1/, and English speakers can raise them above level /4/ and Spanish speakers above level /3/, but these extremes are what we call EXTRA-LINGUISTIC or PARALINGUISTIC. This means that such extreme rises and falls in the voice are beyond the linguistic system, unlike virtually all the sounds—both segmental and suprasegmental—that we will deal with in the two languages. This paralinguistic aspect of the sound system is taken up in Chapter 9.

The pitch levels, although numbered for convenience, are relative and vary in actual tone from speaker to speaker. All pitch levels of a child, for example, are ordinarily higher than those of an adult, and those of a woman are higher than those of a man in both languages. Yet each speaker of Spanish and English, at least in the same dialect, manipulates the pitch of his or her voice on the same relative levels to achieve the same meaning: statement, question, command, emphatic statement, and so on.

In English this can be demonstrated by the following four minidialogs. The relevant stressed syllables are indicated by underlining. The numbers that correspond to the lines for the four pitch levels are indicated on the right.

1. **Speaker A:** "Where does he live?"

   Speaker B: "He lives in Ben<u>sa</u>lem."   3 / 2 / 1

   [*Bensalem* is the needed new information, thus pitch level 3.]

2. **Speaker A:** "Does he live or work in Bensalem?"

   Speaker B: "He <u>lives</u> in Bensalem."   3 / 2 / 1

   [*Lives* is the needed new information, thus pitch level 3.]

3. **Speaker A:** "Who lives in Bensalem?"

   Speaker B: "<u>He</u> lives in Bensalem."   3 / 2 / 1

   [*He* is the needed new information, thus pitch level 3.]

4. **Speaker A:**   "No, I think he lives in Willow Grove."

        4
        3

    Speaker B: "No, he lives in Bensalem."   2
        1

[*Bensalem* is strongly emphasized; thus pitch level 4.]

Notice that if you, as Speaker B, give the response in dialog 4 for Speaker A's question in dialog 1, with *Bensalem* on the emphatic pitch level 4 instead of the normal 3, you sound annoyed or overbearing. Why be so emphatic about the name of the town in dialog 1 when Speaker A has still done nothing to dispute your information? But pitch level 4 in dialog 4 is appropriate because you are now trying to convince Speaker A of something he apparently did not believe when you answered the question for the first time in dialog 1.

Pitch Levels in Spanish

Here, as in all future examples of both English and Spanish, intonation will be marked as follows. The line for level /1/ is a line below the letters (or later phonetic symbols), the line for level /2/ is immediately below the letters or symbols, the line for level /3/ is right above the letters or symbols, and the line for level /4/ is a line above that. Following are illustrative examples for Spanish.

5. **Speaker A:**   —¿Dónde vive?

    Speaker B: —Vive en Santo Domingo.   2
      1

6. **Speaker A:**   —¿Vive o trabaja en Santo Domingo?

      3

    Speaker B: —Vive en Santo Domingo.   2
      1

7. **Speaker A:**   —¿Quién vive en Santo Domingo?

      3

    Speaker B: —Juan vive en Santo Domingo.   2
      1

8. **Speaker A:**   —No, creo que vive en San Pedro de Macorís

      3

    Speaker B: —No, vive en Santo Domingo.   2
      1

You will notice immediately several differences between the pitch levels of English and those of Spanish. Perhaps the main one to focus on now is the fact that, since Spanish has only three contrastive pitch levels, /3/ serves as the emphatic level, the role that /4/ fulfills in English. This means, of course, that the so-called ''normal'' pitch level for the final words of these examples in English (level 3) sounds emphatic in Spanish, and the so-called ''normal'' pitch level (level 1) in the Spanish words make the speaker sound somewhat disinterested in English, although neither impression is accurate. For example,

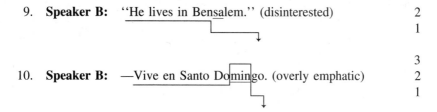

Junctures

Another phonological suprasegmental feature—along with stress and pitch—is JUNC-TURE, that is, what the voice does immediately before a pause in the discourse, usually a slight change in pitch, volume, and tempo. When the speaker of either Spanish or English comes to the end of a breath group, that is, makes a pause, however slight, she/he can terminate it in one of three ways: by lowering the pitch of the voice slightly and trailing away into silence / ↓ /, by raising the pitch slightly and cutting off the volume rather sharply / ↑ /, or by sustaining the pitch, prolonging the last syllable of the phrase, and diminishing the volume slightly /→/. These ways of ending a breath group are called TERMINAL JUNC-TURES and are contrastive in the two languages. They represent a change in pitch, but one which is not quite to the next level, and a change in both volume (amplitude of the sound waves produced by phonation or voicing) and tempo (length of the phonation or voicing). Normally they follow the direction of the voice from one pitch level to the next, but it is also possible to lower the pitch of the voice one level and then raise it slightly before the pause and, vice versa, to raise the pitch of the voice one level and then lower it slightly before the pause.

The normal meaning of the three junctures is basically the same in both languages: / ↓ / indicates finality or completion; / ↑ / indicates either questioning or continuation; and /→/ indicates uncertainty, incompletion, or hesitation.

English Statements and Questions

Actually the number of different intonation patterns is large in both languages and depends on dialect, emotion, personality of the speaker, and so forth. Yet a few basic patterns in each language emerge as significant and fairly uniform from dialect to dialect and speaker to speaker. These are the ones presented in this book, both to enable you to sound more like a native speaker of Spanish as far as intonation goes and also to keep you from conveying the wrong message about your utterance or yourself by incorrectly carrying over an English pattern into Spanish. So there are several correct intonation patterns you can use in Spanish to express basically the same thing, but there are some *incorrect* ones—almost always stemming from your native English (or perhaps another language that you learned as a child)—that you should *not* use in Spanish.

It should be emphasized that these intonation patterns are used mainly in General American English. Other dialects of English, both in and outside of North America, may use other patterns; in fact, intonation is one of the best instant markers of dialect. Here are a few examples in English, so you can see how the pitch levels and terminal junctures are marked, along with the function of each pattern.

ORDINARY STATEMENT: /2 3 1 ↓/

	3
11. I'd like to order some pizza.	2
	1

This is the answer to a question about what you are going to order for your meal. Remember that the first syllable of *pizza*, on level /3/, is not particularly emphatic, just normal in English.

EMPHATIC STATEMENT: /2 4 1 ↓/

	4
	3
12. No, no, I want pizza.	2
	1

But now for some reason the word *pizza* has been emphasized—indicated by pitch level /4/. This is no longer a simple response to a question about what you are going to order, but indicates a small disagreement about the food to be ordered or perhaps a repetition to the listener, who did not at first hear the name of the food you wanted.

ORDINARY INFORMATION QUESTION: /2 3 1 ↓/

	3
13. What do you want to drink?	2
	1

Although all questions usually seek information, we term questions that begin with *wh-* or interrogative words and seek new information (in place of the interrogative word) information questions to distinguish them from other types. The intonation is basically the same as that of statements because the few *wh-* words in English automatically signal a question to the listener, who then is supposed to supply the corresponding new information requested in the interrogative word at the beginning of the question. Just as with statements, there is an emphatic form, which puts the new information on pitch level /4/ for basically the same reasons already mentioned: you are repeating the question or emphasizing a certain element of it.

EMPHATIC INFORMATION QUESTION: /2 4 1 ↓ /

14. What do you want to drink?

```
                                    4
                                    3
                                    2
                                    1
```

English speakers know that if they use the intonation of question 14 instead of that of question 13, their motives or mood will be questioned. Question 14 indicates that something special has happened in the discourse, and the ordinary intonation of question 13 is not sufficient to convey our intended meaning.

YES-OR-NO QUESTION: /2 2 3 ↑ /

15. Do you want to eat here?

```
                                    3
                                    2
```

Yes-or-no questions are distinguished from information questions, by the fact that they already include all the basic information. All you want your interlocutor to do is confirm it or deny it, unlike your desire in information questions, which is to request the interlocutor to supply information new and presumably unknown to you. If the response to question 15 is yes, you know where your friend wants to eat because he has confirmed the information you have given him, but if the answer is no, you still theoretically do not know where he wants to eat. It is possible, of course, to ask question 15 with falling intonation, as in question 16.

ALTERNATE YES-OR-NO QUESTION: /2 3 1 ↓ /

16. Do you want to eat here?

```
                                    3
                                    2
                                    1
```

The question said with this intonation pattern has a variety of implications, which are far beyond the extent of our analysis here, but we do know that the utterance is a question, despite the falling intonation, because of the syntax: "Do you ... ?" As we will see, Spanish is quite different with regard to questions of this nature.

CHOICE QUESTION: /2 2 3 ↑ 2 3 1 ↓ /

17. Do you want to eat here, or take this home?   3
                                                                    2 .
                                                                    1

Choice questions, as the name implies, supply the listener with two (or more) possible answers and request selection of one of the possibilities. The first part has basically the same intonation of a yes-or-no question; the second part the same intonation of a statement. Notice that if you repeat the intonation of the first part in the second part, you are implying a third possibility that you have not yet mentioned.

OPEN-ENDED CHOICE QUESTION: /2 2 3 ↑ 2 2 3 ↑ /

18. Do you want to eat here, or take this home . . . ?   3
                                                                    2
                                                                    1

This is still a choice question, although now truncated or cut off; you have just not supplied the third choice.

The last English pattern to be mentioned is the so-called VOCATIVE, that is, the mention of your interlocutor's name or title. Since vocatives are usually quite short in nature—just a couple of syllables—we mark only two pitch levels and the juncture.

VOCATIVE, following an INFORMATION QUESTION: /2 3 1 → 1 1 ↑ /

19. How're you doing, Kim?   3
                                                                    2
                                                                    1

Notice that now the terminal juncture following the question has a level, sustained juncture → instead of the expected fall ↓ . In virtually all of the intonation patterns above, the level → can replace the falling ↓ to indicate lack of finality, that is, that something more is coming—in this case, your interlocutor's name, the vocative. But the important thing with the vocative in General American English is the rise, usually from a low pitch level. This seems to indicate friendliness, interest, and amiability. A level → might indicate that something more will shortly follow. The falling ↓ has a strange sound of finality, gruffness, or resignation, a feeling that the speaker probably does not want to convey. This intonation seems particularly true when the vocative follows a statement or question. If the name *Kim* is said alone for any reason, a rise ↑ probably indicates that you are not sure it is really Kim or that you are surprised to see her. A fall ↓ on the name *Kim* alone has other meanings, but probably not the rather negative ones that this intonation would imply if *Kim* immediately followed a previous utterance.

These distinct intonation patterns are admittedly difficult to explain, analyze, and demonstrate out of context, but they are such a vital and universal part of human language that any native speaker who switches them or misuses them does so at his or her own peril. We all know that the wrong intonation pattern at the wrong time can cause a distinct (although perhaps temporary) change in the relationship that exists between two interlocutors. Even the least educated and most naive speakers can manipulate intonation masterfully in their own native language just like a talented violinist manipulates the strings of the instrument. Needless to say, it is much more difficult to do this in a foreign language. If your intonation in Spanish is often wrong, you will find that your interlocutor begins thinking more about you, your background as a Spanish student, where you have spoken Spanish before, and so on, rather than on what you really want him or her to think about: namely, the message you are attempting to convey. And we all want people to concentrate on *what* we are saying, not *how* we are saying it.

Spanish Statements and Questions

The following examples for Spanish are marked in the same way, although only three pitch levels are indicated for reasons explained above. The first number within slash bars refers to the level up to but not including the last stressed syllable of the breath group; the second number represents the pitch level of the last stressed syllable itself, and the last of the three numbers within slash bars refers to the syllables following the last stressed syllable of the group. If the group ends on a stressed syllable, the pitch, of course, must change *within* that level and is thus indicated by the last *two* numbers. For example, in the emphatic statement **Vive en Santo Domingo**, the stressed syllable **-min-** is on pitch level 3 (because it has the last stress of the group), and the **-go** falls to level 1. You can indicate this by bringing the pitch line down between these last two syllables.

/2 3 1↓/

			3
20.	Vive en Santo Domingo.		2
			1

But in the emphatic statement **Vive en San Pedro de Macorís**, the last stressed syllable of the group is *also* the last syllable of the group, so the pitch level must start on level 3 and drop to level 1 within the syllable **-rís**.

/2 3 1↓/

			3
21.	Vive en San Pedro de Macorís.		2
			1

Actually in Spanish the voice pitch starts on level 1 in the first unstressed syllable or the first few unstressed syllables and rises to level 2 on the *first* stressed syllable of the group. This seems quite natural for English speakers to do and has little significance in the overall intonation patterns of either language. What the voice does at the *end* of the group is most significant—either on the *last* stressed syllable before a pause, the last syllable whether stressed or not, or both of these syllables. Thus for the sake of convenience, we mark all Spanish and English intonation patterns as beginning on pitch level 2, with a couple exceptions as noted below.

In a few of the following examples, alternate patterns are given. This means that the difference between them is slight and subtle; you will hear both, and, thus, you may use both in Spanish to convey the indicated meaning.

ORDINARY STATEMENT: /2 1 1 ↓ /

22. Vive en Santo Domingo.	2
	1

ALTERNATE STATEMENT: /2 2 1 ↓ /

23. Vive en Santo Domingo.	2
	1

EMPHATIC STATEMENT: /2 3 1 ↓ /

	3
24. Vive en Santo Domingo.	2
	1

ORDINARY INFORMATION QUESTION: /2 1 1 ↓ /

25. ¿Dónde vive Eduardo?	2
	1

ALTERNATE INFORMATION QUESTION: /2 2 1 ↓ /

26. ¿Dónde vive Eduardo?	2
	1

EMPHATIC INFORMATION QUESTION: /2 3 1 ↓ /

	3
27. No, hombre, ¿dónde vive Eduardo?	2
	1

ORDINARY YES-OR-NO QUESTION: /2 2 2 ↑ /

28.   ¿Quieres tomar <u>al</u>go?↑   2

Notice there that although **al-** is the last stressed syllable of the group, the pitch rises on the very last syllable of the group **-go**, even though it is not stressed.

There is an alternate yes-or-no question, which is often is used more by woman than men, but is acceptable when used by either sex in any dialect.

ALTERNATE YES-OR-NO QUESTION: /2 2 3 ↑ /

                                                                3

29.   ¿No quieres tomar un <u>refres</u>co?   2

Just as in example 28 the pitch rises on the very last syllable **-co**, even though the final stress falls on **-fres-**.

There is a third yes-or-no question, which is sometimes used in any dialect to request confirmation of something already expected by the speaker or sometimes to indicate surprise or slight disagreement. It is also used by speakers in the Caribbean area for any yes-or-no question, that is, in place of example 28.

CONFIRMATION YES-OR-NO QUESTION: /2 3 1 →/

                                                                 3

30.   ¿No quieres tomar un <u>re</u>fresco?   2

                                                                 1

This intonation pattern is a good illustration of how terminal junctures, although they usually continue the pitch direction, do not necessarily have to do so. In emphatic statement 24, the pitch of the voice drops to level 1 on the last syllable of the utterance and drops just a bit farther (shown by ↓), indicating finality. But in the confirmation yes-or-no question 30, although the pitch drops to level 1 on the last syllable, there is a slight leveling off of the voice shown by →, indicating not finality now, but rather some interest in continuing the dialog.

CHOICE QUESTION: /2 2 2 ↑ 2 1 1 ↓/

31.   ¿Quieres comer una <u>pizza</u>↑ o algo más <u>fuerte</u>?   2
                                                                 1

Slight variations exist here, too: the first part of the question can end with 3 ↑ (as in question 29) instead of 2 ↑ , and the second part of the question can end with 2 1 ↓ (as in statement 23). (These variations are not listed as separate examples.)

In virtually all of the intonation patterns illustrated above, the level juncture → replaces the final falling juncture ↓ to show that more information immediately follows the question or a statement. Thus, statement 22 **Vive en Santo Domingo** becomes

32. Vive en Santo Domingo, según me dijeron.   2
      1

Spanish Vocatives

When followed by a vocative, an information question can end with a level juncture → instead of a fall ↓ .

INFORMATION QUESTION WITH VOCATIVE: /2 1 1 → 1 1 ↓/

33. ¿Dónde se encuentra la casa de correos, señor?   2
      1

Notice also that the intonation of the vocative **señor** in question 33 above falls, unlike English, where it usually rises.

      3
34. Where can I find the post office, sir?   2
      1

In 33 above a rise on **señor** would sound somewhat ingratiating and perhaps even overly friendly in Spanish, whereas a fall on *sir* in 34 would sound somewhat abrupt and officious in English.

Spanish Tag Questions

TAG QUESTIONS are actually short yes-or-no questions appended to statements either to request confirmation or simply to keep the lines of communication open. They are highly structured and rather complex in English: the word order is inverted, the same tense is maintained, the verb form is contracted if necessary, and the "polarity," so to speak, of affirmative and negative is reversed.

      3
35. I think he's gone too far, *don't you?* ↑   2
      1

      3
36. I don't agree with his policies, *do you?* ↑   2
      1

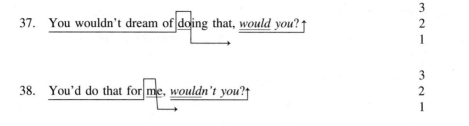

                                                                              3
37.   You wouldn't dream of doing that, *would you*?↑   2
                                                                              1

                                                                              3
38.   You'd do that for me, *wouldn't you*?↑   2
                                                                              1

In Spanish, although the intonation is almost the same, these questions are much simpler in their structure. The most common tag questions, of course, are ¿**verdad?** (anywhere) and ¿**no?** (anywhere except after negatives).

STATEMENTS WITH TAG QUESTION: /2 1 1 → 2 3 ↑ /

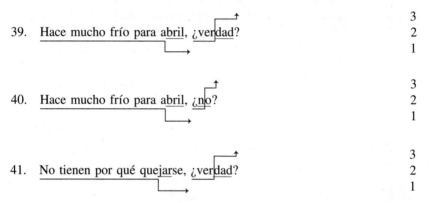

                                                                              3
39.   Hace mucho frío para abril, ¿verdad?   2
                                                                              1

                                                                              3
40.   Hace mucho frío para abril, ¿no?   2
                                                                              1

                                                                              3
41.   No tienen por qué quejarse, ¿verdad?   2
                                                                              1

Spanish Greetings

In Spanish, greetings are usually said with an emphatic level 3 on the prominent syllable—usually the last of the group.

GREETINGS: /2 3 1 ↓ /

                                                                              3
42.   Buenos días.   2
                                                                              1

                                                                              3
43.   ¿Qué tal?   2
                                                                              1

Thanking in Spanish

A similar intonation is also the normal one for saying *Thank you* in Spanish.

THANKING: /3 1 ↓ /

		3
44. Gra̲cias.		2
		1

Leave-Taking in Spanish

Leave-takings (or farewells) usually avoid pitch level 3 although the voice does not drop as far as it does for statements. Compare the farewell **Hasta mañana**

LEAVE-TAKING: /2 2 2 ↓ /

45. Hasta ma̱ñana.   2 *See you tomorrow.*

with the same sequence of words, which are now a mini-statement answering the question, **¿Cuánto tiempo dura el torneo?**

46. Hasta ma̱ñana.   2 *Until tomorrow.*
                             1

It is not uncommon for the same phrase to have two different meanings, conveyed entirely by the intonation.

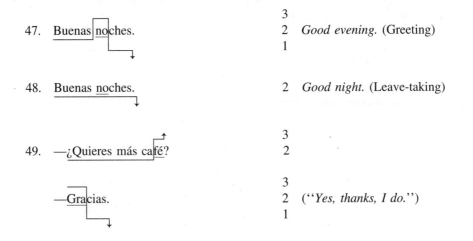

	3	
47. Buenas no̲ches.	2	*Good evening.* (Greeting)
	1	

48. Buenas no̲ches.   2 *Good night.* (Leave-taking)

	3	
49. —¿Quieres más ca̲fé?	2	
	3	
—Gra̲cias.	2	(*"Yes, thanks, I do."*)
	1	

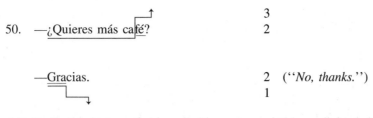

50. —¿Quieres más café?   3
                                              2

—Gracias.   2 (*"No, thanks."*)
                                              1

Admittedly this last **gracias** is probably accompanied by a slight shake of the head, or an upraised palm to signal a refusal, but this **gracias** said with the intonation /3 1 ↓ / of example 49 would be a strange way to refuse more coffee.

Spanish Commands

COMMANDS in Spanish are also said with a high pitch level, usually on the verb form itself.

COMMANDS: /3 2 1 ↓ /

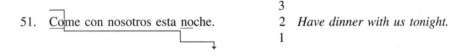

51. Come con nosotros esta noche.   3
                                              2 *Have dinner with us tonight.*
                                              1

In this particular example, if this were an ordinary statement conveying a friend's plans, it would not be said with such a high level.

52. —¿Qué va a hacer después de la reunión?

—Come con nosotros esta noche   2 *He's having dinner with us tonight.*
                                              1

Intonation Groups in Spanish Sentences

Before going on to longer sentences, with two or three breath groups in them, several observations should be made about both the role of juncture and stress in Spanish intonation. Punctuation in a written text (except for quotation marks) is usually a fairly reliable indication of where the pauses and thus terminal junctures are. A period normally corresponds to ↓ , a question mark in yes-or-no and tag questions corresponds to ↑ , and a comma, dash, colon, or semicolon, more often than not, to →. Obviously this is not always the case since information questions, for example, normally end with ↓ , despite the fact that they are questions. A ↑ is not necessary at the end of such utterances since the interrogative word (**cómo, quién, dónde**) at the beginning immediately signals that it is a question. Actually terminal junctures function in a similar way in both English and Spanish, although there are a few differences, which have been pointed out above.

In English the pitch usually rises on the stressed syllable near the end of the group (as in examples 1, 11, and 13). In fact, a general rule is that the heavier the stress, the higher the pitch. In Spanish, however, the pitch *drops* from 2 to 1 on the last stressed syllable of the group and stays there until the terminal juncture on the last syllable when it drops even a little more (as you see in examples 22 and 25). In emphatic versions the pitch rises from 2 to 3 on the last stressed syllable and drops down to 1 on the following unstressed syllables and stays there until the terminal juncture on the very last syllable where it drops even a little more (examples 24 and 27). So stress does correlate with pitch change in the two languages, but often in a completely different direction.

Following are examples of sentences with two or more breath groups. The English tendency is to drop the pitch of the voice at these internal pauses.

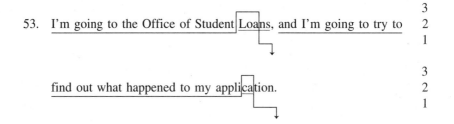

53. I'm going to the Office of Student Loans, and I'm going to try to   3 2 1

find out what happened to my application.   3 2 1

In Spanish, though, the pitch rises before these internal pauses.

STATEMENT WITH COORDINATED ELEMENTS: /2 2 2 ↑ 2 1 1 ↓/

54. Voy a la Oficina de la Decana, y voy a tratar de verla.   2 1

Likewise with subordinate clauses.

STATEMENT WITH SUBORDINATED ELEMENTS: /2 2 2 ↑ 2 1 1 ↓/

55. En cuanto comienza a llover a cántaros, parece que los   2

taxis desaparecen.   2 1

Often a long subject either at the beginning or end of the utterance requires a pause with a rise in pitch right before it.

LONG SUBJECTS: /2 2 2 ↑ 2 1 1 ↓/

56. El mismo tipo del paraguas rojo y el impermeable gris⌉   2

    esperaba en la parada de taxis.   2
                                            1

In English the pitch of the group tends to rise to 3 on the appropriate stressed syllable and then fall at the end of each item in an ENUMERATION.

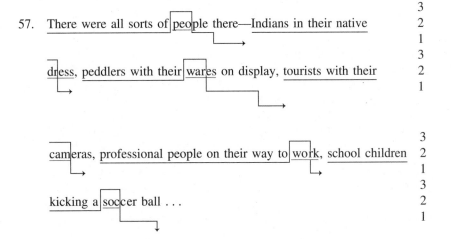

57. There were all sorts of people there—Indians in their native   3
                                                    2
                                                    1

dress, peddlers with their wares on display, tourists with their   3
                                                    2
                                                    1

cameras, professional people on their way to work, school children   3
                                                    2
                                                    1

kicking a soccer ball . . .   3
                                                    2
                                                    1

But in Spanish the pitch is fairly level with slight rises at these same points.

ENUMERATION: / 2 1 1 ↓ 2 2 2 ↑ 2 2 2 ↑ . . . 2 1 1 ↓/

58. Vamos a ver —una ensalada para comenzar,⌉ pan,⌉ carne   2
                                                    1
    para el plato principal,⌉ vino tinto para acompañarlo,⌉ flan de   2

    postre⌉ y café y aguardiente para rematar la comida.   2
                                                        1

This alternation of internal rises and falls in long sentences gives English an excited, animated sound to Spanish speakers, whereas the lack of this alternation gives Spanish a flatter, less emotional sound to English speakers—a contradiction to the stereotype of the ''cold, impersonal Anglo-Saxon'' and the ''lively, excitable Latin.''

In Summation

To review, there are several points where Spanish and English intonation differ that are particularly difficult for the English learner to master.

English easily puts sentence stress and pitch level 4 at any point in an emphatic utterance.

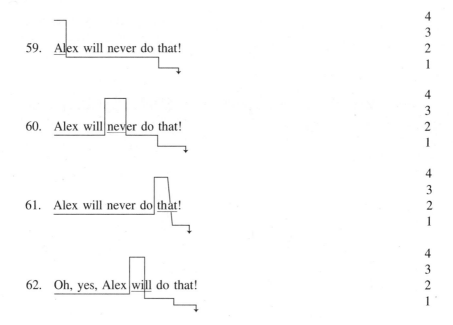

59. Alex will never do that!

60. Alex will never do that!

61. Alex will never do that!

62. Oh, yes, Alex will do that!

But typically in Spanish, the syntax must often be changed to show sentence stress since in emphatic utterances the element with sentence stress and pitch level 3 comes at or near the end.

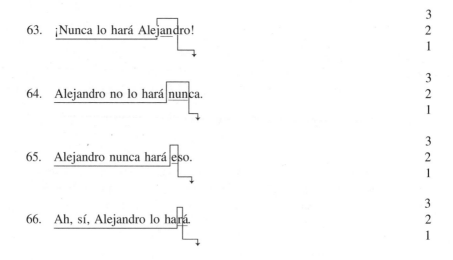

63. ¡Nunca lo hará Alejandro!

64. Alejandro no lo hará nunca.

65. Alejandro nunca hará eso.

66. Ah, sí, Alejandro lo hará.

Typically in English the voice falls before pauses that signal the end of subordinate clauses.

67. If I would've had the time, I would have included a lot of

   3
   2
   1

fancy graphics in my paper.

   3
   2
   1

In recent years, young speakers of General American English have begun using pitch rises in the first clause of a sentence with coordinate and subordinate clauses, in the elements of an enumeration, and even in complete statements.

68. I bought this new CD player, and I haven't been able to get it to

   2
   3

work right.

   2
   1

69. He had a CD ROM player, a scanner, a back-up tape drive, a laser

   3
   2
   4

printer, and the coolest screen saver.

   3
   2
   1

70. I went to the computer store in our mall (and . . .)

   3
   2
   1

This, coincidentally, is quite close to the proper Spanish intonation in subordinate clauses and enumerations.

71. Cuando regrese de las vacaciones, voy a organizar mis cosas

   2

de una vez por todas para el semestre.

   2
   1

72. Le compró a su hijo una camiseta a rayas azules y blancas,

   2

calcetines del mismo tipo y unos botines para fútbol de cuero

   2

de canguro.

   2
   1

Finally, English speakers can very easily lower the pitch of their voice in long yes-or-no questions because the syntax makes it immediately clear that the utterance is a question.

73.   Are there as many Spanish majors in the Department now as   2
     3
   there were back in the eighties when my bro ther started there?   2
     1

But a fall in pitch in the Spanish equivalent makes the utterance a statement rather than a question since the verb **hay**, like all Spanish verbs, is neutral to the concept of affirmative or negative.

74.   ¿Hay tantos especialistas en español en el departamento ahora   2

   como había en los ochenta cuando empezó sus estudios allí mi   2
     3
   her ma no?   2
     1
   (really meaning in Spanish *There are* . . . rather than
   Are there . . . ?)

To ask this question properly, the Spanish speaker must raise the pitch of his voice to level 2 or 3 on the last syllable **-no** and end the last vowel with a rising juncture ↑.

                                     3
75.   . . . her ma no?   2
     (now meaning *Are there . . . ?*)

To sum up, using your native English intonation while speaking Spanish will give your Spanish a foreign accent at best. At worst it can distort or completely change your intended meaning; make you sound annoyed, ingratiating, or disinterested when you don't mean to; or project impressions of you as an individual that may not be accurate and not at all the ones you intended to project.

Practice

A.

Read the following ORDINARY STATEMENTS *with the correct intonation:* /2 1 1 ↓ / *or* /2 2 1 ↓ /.

1. Mi tía ahora está trabajando.
2. Jaime habla quechua.
3. Quieren regresar a México.

4. La ciudad hispana más famosa por el béisbol es San Pedro de Macorís.
5. Tiene una docena de jugadores en las ligas mayores.

B.

Now read the same statements in Practice A as EMPHATIC STATEMENTS */2 3 1 ↓ / in response to the following utterances, which your instructor or a classmate will read. It may be appropriate to start your statement with* **No, . . .**

1. Llamé a tu tía pero no contestó. ¿Está enferma?
2. Jaime es de la sierra, y creo que habla aymará.
3. Su deseo es quedarse en Venezuela.
4. San Juan, Puerto Rico, ha contribuido muchísimo al deporte de béisbol.
5. Estás hablando de las ligas latinoamericanas, ¿no?

C.

Read the following ORDINARY INFORMATION QUESTIONS */2 1 1 ↓ / or /2 2 1 ↓ /.*

1. ¿Cuál es su apellido?
2. ¿Para dónde va?
3. ¿A qué hora comienza el partido?
4. ¿Con quién se casó tu hermana?
5. ¿Qué tal te gusta el vino rosado?

D.

Now repeat the same questions in Practice C as EMPHATIC INFORMATION QUESTIONS */2 3 1 ↓ / in response to the following utterances, to be read by your instructor or your classmates.*

1. Su nombre es María Concepción.
2. Permiso, permiso, abran paso.
3. Creo que el desfile, la banda y todo eso empieza a eso de la una y media.
4. Mi hermano sigue soltero. Pero, posiblemente algún día . . .
5. El vino tinto me da un dolor de cabeza; por eso, nunca lo tomo.

E.

Read the following YES-OR-NO QUESTIONS. *The most common intonation patterns are /2 2 2 ↑ / or /2 2 3 ↑ /. In some cases, however, the confirmation pattern /2 3 1 →/ may be more appropriate. If you use this one, explain why you did so instead of using one of the first two. For example,*

¿Está lloviendo?↑   or   ¿Está lloviendo?⌐   3
                                              2

The questions asked this way mean you are not sure what the weather is like and you want information about it. But if you say

¿Está llo|viendo?   3   2   1

it means that you are surprised, annoyed, or perhaps even doubt that your interlocutor is giving you the right information. Subtle, perhaps, but that's the way intonation works.

1. ¿Se han mudado del apartamento?
2. ¿Ya es la hora de salir de clase?
3. ¿Comienza el partido a las tres?
4. ¿María Concepción? ¿Estás seguro?
5. ¿Tienen un gobierno democrático?

F.

Read the following CHOICE QUESTIONS */2 2 2 ↑ 2 1 1 ↓/ or /2 2 3 ↑ 2 1 1 ↓/.*

1. ¿Juega para los Rojos o los Medias Rojas?
2. ¿Vive solo o tiene un compañero de casa?
3. ¿La capital de Bolivia es Sucre o La Paz?
4. ¿Aprendiste a manejar la computadora con Mac o con PC?
5. ¿Ese año fue más célebre O.J. o Michael Jordan?

G.

Read the following utterances, all with VOCATIVE */1 1 ↓/.*

1. No, señor.
2. Buenos días, profesora.
3. Estoy muy bien, Ricardo.
4. Hasta luego, mi amor.
5. Ahora todo está listo, doctora.

H.

Read the following utterances, all with TAG QUESTIONS */2 2 3 ↑/.*

1. Es impresionante, ¿no cree usted?
2. Todos están de acuerdo, ¿verdad?
3. Estos precios son módicos, ¿no?
4. La ciudad es más moderna de lo que pensabas, ¿verdad?
5. Es un lugar típico pero muy elegante a la vez, ¿no te parece?

I.

Read the following GREETINGS *and expressions of* THANKS /2 3 1 ↓ /.

1. ¡Hola!
2. ¡Buenas noches!
3. ¡Qué hubo! (*pronounced with only two syllables*, "Quiubo")
4. ¿Cómo te va?
5. ¡Felicidades! (*or* ¡Felicitaciones!)
6. ¡Muchísimas gracias!

J.

Read the following expressions of LEAVE-TAKING /2 2 2 ↓ /.

1. Adiós.
2. Hasta luego.
3. Buenas noches.
4. Hasta mañana.
5. Cuídate.
6. Que lo pase bien.

K.

Read the following COMMANDS /3 2 1 ↓ /.

1. Siéntate.
2. Dígame lo que quiere.
3. Pase enfrente del Monumento de la Independencia.
4. En la primera avenida doble a la izquierda.
5. Grábame la primera canción en la cara B.

L.

Read the following STATEMENTS WITH COORDINATED ELEMENTS /2 2 2 ↑ 2 1 1 ↓ /.
If you want to emphasize an element of the second clause you will, of course, use
/2 3 1 ↓ /. *Your listener will know immediately what is emphatic when you use pitch
level* /3/.

1. Voy a solicitar una beca, y también voy a pedir un préstamo.
2. El fútbol internacional es el deporte más popular, y todos los demás no tienen
   mucho público.
3. El fútbol es popular en los estadios, pero el estilo norteamericano está apareciendo
   cada vez más en la televisión.
4. No se aguanta a los niños; sin embargo, quiere ser maestra.
5. Tengo que estudiar para los exámenes; de modo que no voy a los bares este fin de
   semana.

M.

Read the following STATEMENTS WITH SUBORDINATED ELEMENTS. The intonation patterns and the instructions are the same as those for Practice L.

1. Aunque parece que lo sabe todo, en cuestiones de amor es un inocente.
2. Para que lo sepas, voy a necesitar el carro todos los días de la semana que viene.
3. Cuando se fue la luz, perdió todos los datos en su documento.
4. Después que leas esto, sabrás el motivo de todas mis quejas.
5. Si lo hubiera sabido, te habría ayudado con mucho gusto.

N.

Read the following STATEMENTS WITH LONG SUBJECTS. Follow the same instructions of Practices L and M. Remember to deal with emphatic elements if necessary.

1. El mismo chico descalzo y de la camiseta de los Cowboys de Dallas estaba vendiendo el diario en la esquina.
2. Cualquier mujer que se sienta ofendida y víctima del acoso sexual debería presentar una queja oficial al jefe del personal.
3. Desayunar solamente con dos tazas de café expreso y una copita de aguardiente no me parece muy saludable.
4. Los insuperables problemas políticos y socioeconómicos no dejan mucho lugar para el optimismo.
5. Los hispanos bilingües y monolingües de este barrio generalmente favorecen los programas que anuncian en español.

O.

Read the following statements with ENUMERATIONS. Follow the same instructions of Practices L, M, and N.

1. Fui a ver las pirámides, Guadalupe, las corridas, los templos, los mercados de los indios, el Ballet Folklórico y Chapultepec.
2. Tantas cosas que llevar: el pasaporte, la tarjeta de crédito, los boletos del avión, la billetera con identidad, la medicina, cheques de viajero y la lista de las direcciones de mis amigos.
3. ¡Qué curso! Hay que leer en voz alta en español, escuchar cassettes, escribir transcripciones fonéticas, dibujar cabezas vacías que no tienen cara y aprender de memoria un montón de datos lingüísticos.
4. Los idiomas indígenas eran el náhuatl, el maya, el arahuaco, el taíno, el quechua, el aymará, el guaraní y el mapuche.
5. Voy a llevar pantalones cortos, jeans, camisetas lisas, dos sudaderas, una cazadora, un anorak, un chaleco, dos gorras, ropa interior, tenis y calcetines.

P.

Read the following utterances, using the intonation that fits the context given for each one, as in the example below.

[Tu compañero(-a) de cuarto sigue haciéndote preguntas tontas mientras estás tratando de estudiar para un examen importante.]

—¡Hombre! (¡Mujer!) ¡No me fastidies con esas preguntas!

1. [Alguien te pregunta qué está haciendo tu amigo en este momento.]
   —Leonardo está viendo televisión.
2. [Quieres saber si tu amiga aprendió español en casa con la familia.]
   —¿Tus padres hablan español también?
3. [Te parece raro que tu amiga, aunque hispana, nunca haya hablado español en casa con la familia.]
   —¿Con tus padres hablabas inglés?
4. [Quieres saber la preferencia en deportes de tu nuevo amigo mexicano.]
   —¿Prefieres ver el fútbol regular o el norteamericano?
5. [Propones un "negocio" a un amigo.]
   —Tú me pasas el trabajo a la computadora, y yo hago imprimir el tuyo y el mío, y saco las fotocopias también. ¿De acuerdo?
6. [Estás un poco enojado(-a) con tu amigo, que quiere una cosa que ya le has negado varias veces.]
   —¿Cuántas veces tengo que decírtelo? ¡No!
7. [A las nueve tu invitada por fin llega al restaurante donde van ustedes a comer.]
   —Buenas noches, Amalia.
8. [Tu invitada lee el menú, y por lo visto los altos precios la sorprenden un poco, pero tú le dices . . .]
   —Pide lo que quieras.
9. [Ustedes salen del restaurante y el mesero les despide, diciendo . . .]
   —Buenas noches. Que vuelvan pronto.
10. [Tu invitada sigue tratando de suavizar la tremenda cuenta que acabas de pagar.]
    —Enrique, si hubiera sabido que las comidas aquí cuestan un ojo de la cara, habría propuesto otro lugar. Pero, de todos modos, gracias.

Q.

Two of you read the first minidialog. Then two more the next, and so forth.

1. —Dispense, señor, pero ¿por dónde se va para llegar a la estación de autobuses?
   —Siga por esta calle llegando a la segunda cuadra, en la esquina del banco doble a la derecha, vaya media cuadra más y a mano derecha la encuentra.
2. —¿No quieres ir? ¡Imposible! ¡Ya tengo las entradas!
   —Es que estoy bastante ocupado(-a), y además no me siento bien.

3. —Buenos días. ¿Cómo me le va, m'hijo?

—Lo más bien, 'mano. Déjeme contarle lo que me pasó recién.

4. —¿Y qué tal el examen?

—Malísimo. ¡El profesor debe de haberse puesto de acuerdo con el diablo!

5. —¿De qué preguntó más—del libro de texto o de las notas de clase?

—Del texto, sobre todo de los capítulos que no discutimos en la clase.

R.

Two of you read the following dialog in its entirety.

SEVERIANO: Hola, Anastasio, ¿qué haces por aquí?

ANASTASIO: Pues he venido a comprar unas cuantas cosas para la familia. ¿Y tú?

SEVERIANO: Voy al Ministerio de Gobernación porque tengo un asunto importante que resolver.

ANASTASIO: Y la familia, ¿qué tal?

SEVERIANO: Así, así. La menor con el sarampión y la mujer con sus benditas jaquecas. ¿Y los tuyos?

ANASTASIO: Regular. Tiburcio, el segundo, se cayó de un caballo y ahora anda con el brazo derecho enyesado. Con los niños nunca faltan problemas, ni siquiera cuando está uno de vacaciones.

SEVERIANO: A propósito, ¿cuándo regresan del veraneo?

ANASTASIO: En unas dos semanas, en cuanto abran la matrícula para las escuelas. Pero, me han dicho que piensas cambiar de empleo, ¿es cierto?

SEVERIANO: Sí, hombre. Casualmente a eso voy al ministerio. He sabido que necesitan un secretario y quiero ver si me nombran a mí.

ANASTASIO: ¿Es que no estás contento en la oficina de don Próspero?

SEVERIANO: Contento sí lo estoy. Don Próspero es muy bueno y siempre me ha tratado bien. Pero en el ministerio pagan mejor y no se trabaja tanto.

ANASTASIO: Comprendo. ¿Y tienes buenos padrinos que te ayuden a conseguir el puesto?

SEVERIANO: Ya lo creo. Nada menos que el cuñado de una prima de mi mujer. Él es tío de la esposa de un nieto del ministro.

ANASTASIO: Hombre, con semejante padrino es seguro que el puesto será tuyo.

SEVERIANO: Así lo espero. Pero, hablando de otra cosa, mira qué hombre más alto. Será un jugador de básquet, ¿no? Y ve a aquel viejito del bastón cómo se ha quedado al mirarlo. Parece que no ha visto nunca una persona de siete pies de altura.

ANASTASIO: Oyyyyy, el pobre no ve ni por dónde camina.

SEVERIANO: No se ha dado cuenta de que ya llegó a la esquina. ¡Cuidado, señor, cuidado con ese autobús!

ANASTASIO: ¡Hala, lo golpeó, lo golpeó! ¡Ayyy, mejor vamos a ayudarlo!

SEVERIANO: No, no, no, ya lo está ayudando a levantarse aquel policía. Parece que no fue nada serio. Está bien. Fue más el susto que otra cosa.

ANASTASIO: Bueno. Hasta la próxima. Mejor me voy porque si no, se me hace muy tarde, y la familia se preocupa.

SEVERIANO: Hasta luego.

ANASTASIO: Chau.

S.

Using conventional orthography, indicate the intonation contours of the following sentences. Use horizontal and vertical lines for the pitch levels, little arrows for terminal junctures, and numbers to the right for the levels. Then check your work in Appendix C.

1. ¿Cuándo tienen que comenzar?
2. Quiere sacar este vídeo por dos días.
3. ¿Cómo te va, hombre?
4. ¿Sabe usted el número de su apartamento?
5. Tengo que irme mañana **mismo**. *(emphatic)*
6. Adiós, señorita.
7. Antes que todos vengan, distribuya las sillas.
8. ¿Dónde dejo los **cassettes**? *(emphatic)*
9. ¿Lees *El Diario* o *El Universal*?
10. ¿Cómo me le va, Federico?
11. ¿Sabes si se puede comprarlos en aquella tienda también?
12. Llueve en el trópico todos los días, ¿verdad?

8

The Rhythm of Spanish

The last suprasegmental feature of Spanish to be taken up is RHYTHM, which depends mainly on the relative length of the stressed and the unstressed syllables. Although the feature of syllable length is not contrastive, functional, or phonemic in either Spanish or English, it is critical in the acquisition of a good accent since it is one of the two main elements of rhythm. Stress, which we have already dealt with, is the other one.

Just as with intonation, if you use the rhythm of English in speaking Spanish, you will retain a strong accent even though you handle all the segmental sounds and even the intonational or suprasegmental sounds perfectly. Before you got to your present stage in learning Spanish, you were probably struck by the fact that it seemed so fast when spoken by native speakers, at least as compared to English. Yet Spanish speakers have been known to make the very same comment about English. How can this be? Speakers of each language feel this way about the other language mainly because of the contrast in the two rhythms.

English: A Stress-Timed Language

English is known as a STRESS-TIMED LANGUAGE. This means that the flow and effect of the language are characterized by the recurrence and interplay of the primary, secondary, and tertiary stresses, with the weak-stressed syllables being squeezed in between. In English it takes roughly the same length of time to get from one primary-stressed syllable to the next in speaking at a steady overall tempo or rate of speed, whether there are few or many syllables in between. If there are few, you slow down; but if there are more you speed up on the syllables without primary stress. To do this, instead of changing your tongue position from one front or back vowel to the next, such as from /I/ to /o/ to /ɛ/ in the word *intonation*, you reduce the /o/ to /ə/, that is, the central vowel, *schwa*. Since this neutral vowel is pronounced in the center of your mouth, you are taking "a shortcut with your tongue," in a sense. If you went from /I/ to /o/ and back to /ɛ/, the word *intonation* would take longer to say because it would take more muscular effort of your lips and tongue. Try it this way. Now say it the normal way, by using /ə/ instead of /o/ in the second syllable. The last syllable of the word has the /ə/, too. And so would the last syllable of the word *intonational.* Thus this last five-syllable word has an /I/, an /ɛ/, and three /ə/'s and is a lot easier and faster to say this way than if it had an /I/, an /o/, an /ɛ/, an /ʌ/ (as in *shun*), and an /æ/ (as in *Al*).

This characteristic English rhythm, consisting of delaying over the heavy or primary stresses and compensatorily shortening the unstressed syllables by substituting /ə/ and sometimes /ɨ/ for other vowels, is sometimes termed ''galloping,'' and English just doesn't sound normal to us without it. We are really speaking of North American and British English, since many Asian and African native speakers of English do not have this same rhythm, thus making them somewhat difficult for North Americans to understand at first.

Take a sentence like, ''Jim's going on a picnic with his friends.'' Said exactly this way, the sentence has ten syllables. But you can easily add more syllables without creating a corresponding increase in the amount of time it takes to say the new sentence: ''My brother Jim's going on a picnic with his friends tomorrow.'' The sentence now has sixteen syllables, but the six extra syllables can be said in such a way that the new sentence doesn't take 60 percent more time to say it despite its having 60 percent more syllables. You can use /ə/ or /ɨ/ in *my,* in the last syllable of *brother*, and in the first and third syllables of *tomorrow.* Obviously it is not normal speech to say the second sentence in exactly the same length of time as the first (although you can quite easily do it). Nevertheless, the average speaker does not take 60 percent longer to say the second sentence just because it has 60 percent more syllables. You can experiment with a stop watch; the author took slightly less than two seconds to say the first one normally and about 2.5 seconds to say the second one normally, rather than 3.2 seconds.

This particular aspect of the English sound system forms the basis for the rhythm of traditional English verse—particularly popular or folk poetry—which is often written and most always read by the average person with a certain number of accents or beats or ''feet'' per line. The amateur reader tends to read most poetry with this type of rhythm. Children especially love to hear nursery rimes, limericks, stories like those found in the famous *Dr. Seuss* books, read to them in this fashion. Think of the famous '' 'Twas the night before Christmas, and all through the house. . . .'' In the popular mind, at least, this stress-timed rhythm is one of the essential ingredients of poetry. In fact, the average English speaker who is not trained in literary study and does not approach verse from a specialist's perspective is sometimes reluctant to believe that poetry without such rhythm is really poetry.

A well-known poem in American literature is Henry Wadsworth Longfellow's ''Paul Revere's Ride.'' In the following selection the heavy stressed syllables are marked with ´, and the number of syllables in each line appears on the right. Notice that, although each line has four primary stresses or beats or ''feet,'' the number of syllables varies between eight and twelve.

Lísten, my chíldren, and yóu shall héar	(9)
Of the mídnight ríde of Pául Revére,	(9)
On the éighteenth of Ápril, in Séventy-fíve;	(12)
Hárdly a mán is nów alíve	(8)
Who remémbers that fámous dáy and yéar.	(10)
He sáid to his fríend, 'If the Brítish márch	(10)
By lánd or séa from the tówn to-níght,	(9)
Hang a lántern alóft in the bélfrey árch	(11)
Of the Nórth Church tówer as a sígnal líght,	(10)
Óne, if by lánd, and twó, if by séa;	(9)
And Í on the ópposite shóre will bé,	(10)
Réady to ríde and spréad the alárm	(9)
Through évery Míddlesex víllage and fárm,	(10)
For the cóuntry fólk to be úp and to árm.'	(11)

Even though this is not necessarily the best or the only way to read this poem, the average English speaker almost always reads it that way and feels that this is the proper way to read it.

Notice that if, for some unknown reason, we wished to change the poem, we could add a few syllables here and there without disturbing the rhythm in the slightest. Suppose we took the first line and made it ''<u>Now</u> listen, my children, and you shall hear'' or ''<u>Now</u> listen, <u>all</u> my children, and you shall hear'' or even ''<u>Now</u> listen, <u>all</u> my <u>good</u> children, and you shall hear,'' the rhythm of four heavy stresses or beats would remain the same. We could also change the seventh line to ''By land or <u>by</u> sea from the town tonight,'' or ''By land or <u>by the</u> sea from the town tonight,'' or ''By <u>the</u> land or <u>by the</u> sea from the town tonight'' without altering the fundamental rhythm.

These syllables, of course, could only be added by shortening the time used to say them, which in turn would be done mainly by using /ə/ and /ɨ/ in place of the vowels that these added words would have when pronounced in isolation.

Spanish: A Syllable-Timed Language

Now let's look at Spanish, a SYLLABLE-TIMED LANGUAGE. This means that the flow and effect of the language are characterized much more by the number of *syllables* rather than by the number and location of the heavy STRESSES or beats. Thus, in Spanish it takes virtually proportionally longer to say an utterance of fifteen or twenty syllables than it does to say one of ten syllables. There is very little shortening of the unstressed syllables, since all vowels in all syllables are pronounced in just about the same length of time regardless of whether or not they are stressed, and the favorite unstressed vowels of English, /ə/ and /ɨ/, do not even exist in Spanish.

Instead of a ''galloping'' rhythm, Spanish has what might be termed impressionistically a legato or evenly connected rhythm. The Spanish version of our example sentence, **Jaime va a hacer un picnic con sus amigos**, has twelve syllables and the following rhythm: **Jai-me-va(a-a)ce-run-pic-nic-con-su-sa-mi-gos**. Normally in a conversational style the sequence **va a hacer** has only two syllables: **va-cer**. (Syllabication and how it affects vowels will be taken up in Chapters 13 and 18.) But if the Spanish speaker adds more words and syllables, as we did above in English, there will be a corresponding increase in the amount of time it takes to say the new sentence: **Mi hermano Jaime va a hacer un picnic con sus amigos mañana**. The sentence now has eighteen syllables as compared to twelve for the first, a 50 percent increase, almost as much as with our English example. **Mi** and **hermano** are fused to create just three syllables: **Miher-ma-no-Jai-me-va(a-a)ce-run-pic-nic-con-su-sa-mi-gos-ma-ña-na**. But a Spanish speaker took about two seconds to say the first sentence normally and slightly over three seconds to say the second one. Recall that the timings were slightly less than two and about 2.5 seconds for the author to say the English sentences. This difference may seem slight and trivial in these examples, but it is not hard to see how it could become quite noticeable in even a short series of utterances.

The main point, once again, is that syllable length fluctuates in English according to the stresses, but in Spanish syllable length is relatively uniform from stressed to unstressed syllables. If you carry over your typical "galloping" rhythm from a sentence like "He said that he knew it very well, that he was even sure of it, but that he really couldn't do much about it under the circumstances," to the equivalent Spanish sentence, **Dijo que lo sabía muy bien, que hasta estaba seguro de ello, pero que en realidad no podía remediarlo bajo esas circunstancias**, it will come out **Dijo que lo sabía muy bien, que hasta estaba seguro de ello, pero que en realidad no podía remediarlo bajo esas circunstancias**, instead of the correct and smooth **Dijo que lo sabía muy bien, ↑ que hasta estaba seguro de ello, ↑ pero que en realidad (↑) no podía remediarlo ↑ bajo esas circunstancias. ↓**

A Spanish speaker will probably say this Spanish sentence in four or five groups (three or four internal pauses or terminal junctures). He will say it with twelve stressed syllables rather than the six of the English version. Also these stresses will not be as heavy as they are in the incorrect Anglicized version of the sentence, and the thirty-three unstressed syllables in Spanish will be almost as long as the twelve stressed ones. And, most importantly, none of them will have the /ə/ and /ɨ/ that the English words *that, it, that, was, even, of, but, that, about, it, under, the, circumstances* do in their shortened syllables. Just as your galloping English rhythm does not sound right in the Spanish sentence, the legato rhythm of Spanish, with unstressed syllables of equal rather than shorter length, sounds unnatural in the English sentence.

It is interesting that this particular aspect of the Spanish sound system also forms the basis for the rhythm of Spanish verse, which is typically written and read in lines of a stipulated number of syllables rather than stresses or beats. Although the rhythm of Spanish poetry is also partially dependent on the stresses, it is not nearly as heavy and regular as that of popular English poetry. When you first heard Spanish poetry, you may have felt that it didn't particularly sound like poetry—even though it may have had the rhyme and the lyrical qualities that you associate with poetry. You may have wondered about the absence of the heavy beats of our stress-timed rhythm and even mistakenly tried to put them in as you read a piece of Spanish poetry.

One of the best known poems in Spanish literature is the *Coplas*[1] of Jorge Manrique, written in the late fifteenth century. In the following selection, the long lines all have eight syllables and the short lines four. Due to the rules and conventions of Spanish METRICS, when a line ends with an **aguda** word, another "psychological" or "ghost" syllable is counted, although not sounded.

> Recuerde el alma dormida,
> avive el seso y despierte
> contemplando
> cómo se pasa la vida,
> cómo se viene la muerte
> tan callando:
> cuán presto se va el placer (+ 1),
> cómo después, de acordado
> da dolor (+ 1),
> cómo a nuestro parecer (+ 1)
> cualquiera tiempo pasado
> fue mejor (+ 1).

When an uninitiated English speaker tries to read Spanish poetry, because of English rhythm he has a natural tendency to overemphasize the primary stresses in the poem and shorten the unstressed syllables. This is not only harder to maintain in Spanish, but it creates a very unpleasant effect to the Spanish ear. Observe now Longfellow's excellent translation of Manrique's *Coplas*.[2] Not only is the language equally moving, but this version is particularly skillful and interesting because Longfellow was able to maintain the same syllable count in each line in English that Manrique used in Spanish, although this is not a particular characteristic of English poetry. As you read this English rendition of the great Spanish poem, you may scarcely be able to keep from using your typical stress-timed rhythm of English and giving the long lines four beats or feet and the short ones two.

> O, let the soul her slumbers break,
> Let thought be quickened, and awake;
> Awake to see
> How soon this life is past and gone,
> And death comes softly stealing on,
> How silently!
>
> Swiftly our pleasures glide away,
> Our hearts recall the distant day
> With many sighs;
> The moments that are speeding fast
> We heed not, but the past—the past,
> More highly prize.

---

[1]Jorge Manrique, "A la muerte del maestro de Santiago don Rodrigo Manrique, su padre", *Las mil mejores poesías de la lengua castellana*, ed. José Bergua (Madrid: Ediciones Ibéricas, 1962), pp. 45–46.

[2]Henry Wadsworth Longfellow, "Coplas de Manrique," *The Poetical Works of Longfellow* (London: Oxford U. Press, 1961), p. 27.

The other main element of rhythm—stress—has already been dealt with extensively. English speakers, accustomed to their secondary and tertiary stresses, as well as primary and weak, carry them all over into Spanish at first. Not only does the use of all these varying degrees of stress cause a change in the syllable length, but it causes a "stopping-and-starting" effect rather than the steady even flow that characterizes Spanish.

You may still find it hard to believe that the rhythms of the two languages are really so different—perhaps because the rhythm of each language seems so apt for that particular language and fits its sounds and intonational patterns so well. But the difference between the two rhythms is most strikingly demonstrated when a speaker of one language carries his own rhythm over into the new language. Although rhythm is not phonemic or functional in the sense that it can control or change meaning, it is so important that you can never hope to achieve a satisfactory accent if you keep using your English rhythm.

Practice

A.

Your instructor will pronounce a series of Spanish words and phrases, all of which are part of a long sentence. Repeat them, maintaining the typical smooth, even, "legato" rhythm of Spanish. Remember the following: you do this by using only heavy and weak stresses and making the unstressed syllables just as long as the stressed ones. The "neutral" vowels /ə/ and /ɨ/ do not exist in Spanish, so be sure not to use them. Also remember that the time taken to say each utterance is increased proportionately as more syllables are added to it. Do not "squeeze" or shorten any syllables to work them in as you do in English.

1. *The resulting sentence is* **Habrá sido porque no te preparaste bien.** *The syllable that you will have most difficulty with is the second one of* **preparaste.** *Do not use* /ə/ *or* /ɨ/!

> bien / preparaste / te preparaste / te preparaste bien / no te preparaste
> bien // sido / habrá sido // Habrá sido porque no te preparaste bien.

2. *This sentence is* **Lo peor fue que apenas tuvimos una hora de tiempo para contestarlas todas.**

> todas / contestarlas todas / para contestarlas todas // hora / una hora / una
> hora de tiempo / una hora de tiempo para contestarlas todas // tuvimos /
> apenas tuvimos / apenas tuvimos una hora de tiempo para contestarlas
> todas // fue / peor / lo peor / lo peor fue // Lo peor fue que apenas tuvimos
> una hora de tiempo para contestarlas todas.

3. *This sentence is* **Empezando esta noche, me pongo a estudiar como un loco para el examen final y verás cómo saco una buena calificación.** *The syllables to be particularly careful of are the last one of* **examen,** *the first one of* **verás,** *and the*

second and third of **calificación**. *No /ə/ or /ɨ/! Also don't forget the terminal pitch rises* ↑ *after* **noche** *and* **final**. *And* <u>**saco**</u> *means* I'll get, *not* He/She got, *so be sure to put the stress on the first syllable.*

> calificación / buena calificación / una buena calificación / saco una buena calificación / cómo saco una buena calificación // verás / verás cómo saco una buena calificación // examen / examen final / el examen final / para el examen final // loco / un loco / estudiar como un loco / estudiar como un loco para el examen final / estudiar como un loco para el examen final y verás cómo saco una buena calificación // pongo / me pongo / me pongo a estudiar / me pongo a estudiar como un loco para el examen final y verás cómo saco una buena calificación // noche / esta noche / empezando esta noche / Empezando esta noche, me pongo a estudiar como un loco para el examen final y verás cómo saco una buena calificación.

B.

Practice the following dialog, being careful to achieve the proper rhythm by following all the tips given in the instructions above. Do it in its entirety or divide it any way your instructor decides.

HIPÓLITO: Y ¿qué tal el examen?

EUSTAQUIO: Malísimo. El profesor debe de haberse puesto de acuerdo con el diablo y nos hizo unas preguntas que ni Einstein hubiera podido contestar.

HIPÓLITO: Habrá sido porque no te preparaste bien.

EUSTAQUIO: ¡Qué va! Si me maté estudiando.

HIPÓLITO: ¿Cuántas preguntas había?

EUSTAQUIO: Sólo diez, pero ¡qué diez!

HIPÓLITO: ¿Largas o cortas de contestar?

EUSTAQUIO: Depende. Sobre las dos últimas se podría escribir un libro. Lo peor fue que apenas tuvimos una hora de tiempo para contestarlas todas.

HIPÓLITO: ¿De qué preguntó más, del libro de texto o de las notas de clase?

EUSTAQUIO: Del texto, sobre todo de los capítulos que casi no discutimos en la clase. Yo creo que ese profesor está empeñado en hacernos fracasar.

HIPÓLITO: Y los demás estudiantes, ¿qué piensan del examen?

EUSTAQUIO: No lo sé. No tuve tiempo de hablar con ninguno de ellos, pero la mayoría salieron con una cara muy triste.

HIPÓLITO: ¿Qué va a pasar ahora?

EUSTAQUIO: Pues nada. Por dicha que en los dos exámenes anteriores no salí tan mal. Empezando esta noche, me pongo a estudiar como un loco para el examen final y verás cómo saco una buena calificación.

HIPÓLITO: ¿Esta noche? Si es cuando tenemos la fiestecita en casa de Inés.

EUSTAQUIO: Caramba, se me había olvidado.

HIPÓLITO: Entonces no vendrás a la fiesta.
EUSTAQUIO: Eso jamás. Empezaré a estudiar mañana por la noche.

C.

*Read the following poem aloud, achieving the smooth syllable-timed rhythm of Spanish by avoiding the "galloping" effect of popular English poetry. Each line has eight syllables; thus certain adjacent vowels must be "telescoped" or pronounced differently than they would be in isolation. The problem of vowel combinations in Spanish poetry is complicated, and some of this material will be taken up in Chapter 18. But for now just remember that the vowels are pronounced the way they are to achieve the proper syllable count of eight for each line. Thus the e of se becomes more like i, the e's of oye and el are run together as one; the e of de also becomes more like i; the final o of **moribundo** becomes more like u; and so forth. Other cases of these same modifications are indicated by ⌢. Two cases, however, where the vowels must be pronounced separately are indicated by | in the text, and one case of complete elimination of the vowel is indicated by /.*

A un libro

En el medio de la noche
se͡ oye͡ el grito͡ agonizante
de͡ un dilapidado libro
moribundo͡ en el estante;

cubierta su piel de tierra,
su juventud ya reseca
como | una̸ hoja de͡ otoño,
como | una͡ antigua rueca;

pero͡ el grito͡ es persistente:
gime͡ y llora͡ en agonía
por el ojo dulce͡ y suave
que͡ en antaño le leía.

—Enrique Grönlund

9

Spanish Sounds Beyond the System

Paralanguage

There is another area of sounds so common that it is used every day by all speakers of all languages, regardless of their age, sex, social status, or educational level—PARA-LANGUAGE. As the prefix *para-* implies, this is an area beyond the regular sound system, that is, beyond the suprasegmentals we have just been practicing (stress, intonation, rhythm) and beyond the segmentals (vowels and consonants), which we will shortly take up.

Paralinguistic sounds are so numerous, so varied, and so individualized that they virtually defy precise systematic analysis and organization into classes, units, levels, degrees, and the kinds of categories that are frequently used in talking about the sound system of a language.

But we can relate paralanguage to the suprasegmentals and talk about such well-known vocal features as OVERLOUD (or SHOUTING), OVERSOFT, OVERHIGH (or SCREAMING, FALSETTO, SQUEAKING), OVERLOW, OVERTENSE (or RASPING), OVERFAST, OVERSLOW (or DRAWLING), CLIPPING, DEVOICING (or WHISPERING), BREAKING (or CRYING, LAUGHING, QUAVERING, TREMOLO, GLOTTAL STOPS), CHANTING, NASALIZING, and IMPLOSIVES (drawing the breath in to make sounds instead of expelling it, as in ingressive rather than egressive sounds, some of which are also called CLICKS).

Most of these features seem to be universal, that is, occur in all human languages, although with quite different functions and meaning, of course. For example, English speakers and Spanish speakers both make a voiceless bilabial click or kissing sound: drawing the air in sharply between the two lips, without phonation of any kind. In Mexico this sound can be used to call a waiter in a restaurant; in the United States to use it for this purpose would be extremely rude and perhaps even perilous, since we use it to attract dogs, not humans, to us.

Some speakers in both languages laugh by making ingressive or implosive sounds with their vocal bands: drawing the air in with accompanying phonation, potentially dangerous to one whose mouth is full of crumbs or liquid while performing this paralinguistic act. Others laugh by violently closing their vocal bands and expelling the air with accompanying phonation. The preferred method of laughter seems to depend on the speaker and is independent of his or her language. The meaning of each type of laugh is often exactly the same, although it may not be, depending on the accompanying circumstances. We all know that some laughs are giggles, and some are guffaws, and some are snickers, all depending on exactly what the "laugher" does with his vocal tract.

One of the most difficult tasks for the linguist is to separate these numerous and open-ended vocal paralinguistic manifestations from the DISCRETE, contrastive, and clearly analyzable features of the suprasegmental system—stress, intonation, and rhythm—since in any ordinary conversation in any language, they are virtually always present just as the systematic features are.

At best we can list and perhaps even classify some of the most common paralinguistic sounds in Spanish, indicate how they are used, and contrast them with their English counterparts. Obviously the best and perhaps the only way to learn them is to interact with native speakers, particularly in their own environment, observe their vocal manifestations, and begin to imitate them. To make them in one's own language is normal, natural, and unavoidable. But to make them in the foreign language, particularly in the classroom, requires a little imagination, some imitative ability, and perhaps even a bit of dramatic talent.

We can also approach these paralinguistic sounds from the point of view of their function as well as their physiology and articulation. Many are used to accompany our actions and help us express our emotions, such as laughing at something humorous or shouting in anger. These might be termed INTERJECTIONS. Others are purely imitative and are meant either to imitate or represent sounds around us: natural phenomena, man-made noises, animal cries, and so on. Imitating a slamming door or the bark of a dog are examples of such ONOMATOPOEIC SOUNDS. Some paralinguistic vocalizations substitute for individual words or may be specially modified words used to express ideas, such as semantic notions. For example, using two glottal stops in rapid succession, a short one and then an extended one—"U-uhhhhhhhhh"—means "No." We might call these SEMANTIC SIGNALS.

It is curious that for some of these paralinguistic vocalizations speakers are able to use sounds and sound combinations that do not normally exist in the phonological system of their language. In fact, some speakers find it difficult to make these very same sounds when they occur normally in a foreign language they are learning. For example, a violent voiceless velar affricate with lots of aspiration (and maybe even saliva) is made by English speakers, especially children, to represent the sound of a gun going off: "*Xkh, xkh, xkh!*" Yet we don't even have the written symbols to represent this velar sound properly in English because we have nothing close to it in North American English (although a similar sound exists in Scottish English, as in *Loch*). Most dialects of Spanish have no [š], as in English *she*, but, just as in English, Spanish speakers prolong this very sound to call for silence in a noisy room. English has the sequence [pt] at the end of a word, as in *swept*, but not at the beginning of a word. Yet most English speakers can easily say *Ptooey!* to represent spitting, for example. Spanish words do not ordinarily end in [m], yet Spanish speakers say **¡Pum!** to imitate a gunshot.

Following are some Spanish paralinguistic sounds with their English equivalents. Not all of these are known or common in all Hispanic countries.

Chart 6   Paralinguistic Sounds in Spanish

(1) INTERJECTIONS	
¡Ay!	*Ouch!*
¡Caramba!	*Oh, gosh (no)!* [indicating surprise or consternation]
¡Hala!	*Hey!, Wow!, Gee!* [indicating surprise or consternation, among many other things]
¡Juiiiiyyyy!	*Wow!* [indicating favorable surprise]
¡Ufff!	[grunting as you are lifting something heavy]
¡Upa! [said with a prolonged first syllable]	*Upsydaisy!* [said as you lift a child]
¡Vaya. . . !	*Wow! Great! What a . . . !*
[whistling]	*Booooo!* [particularly at athletic events]
(2) ONOMATOPOEIC SOUNDS	
¡Achís!	*Achoo!*
¡Cataplum!	*Crash!* [heavy objects falling to the floor, for example]
¡Guau, guau!	*Woof, woof! (Arf, arf!)*
¡Plaf!	*Slap!, Smack!, Crack!* [slap in the face or snapping of a stick]
¡Pum!	*Bang!* [gunshot]
¡Pum, pum, pum!	*Bang, bang, bang!* [pounding on door or desk]
¡Quiquiriquííííí!	*Cockadoodledoooo!*
¡Tángana!	*Slap! Smack! Bang! Smash!*
¡Toc, toc!	*Knock, knock!* [rapping on door]
Zumba, zumba.	*Buzzzzzz.* [insects]

(Continued)

(Continued)

(3) SEMANTIC SIGNALS	
Ahhhhh, sí.	*Oh, yes.* [indicating thoughtful agreement]
¡Arre, arre! [said with extra-high pitch and extra-loud on the first syllable]	*Giddyap!*
¿Eh?	*Huh?* [indicating that you have not heard]
Este. . . [said with a level juncture →]	*Er, uh. . .*
¡Misimisimisi! [said in a FALSETTO voice]	*Kitty, kitty, kitty!*
Queps [**Qué pues**, pronounced [képs] or even [kps]]	*Ya' know* [a filler expression to get some communicative feedback from your interlocutor]
¡Shhhh!	*Shhhhh!*
¡Sooooo! [said extra loud]	*Whoooa!*
Sssssssssss [one prolonged hiss]	*Shhhhhh! Be quiet!*
S-s-s-s-s-s [series of short hisses]	*Shhhhhh! Be quiet!* [or to attract someone's attention on the street or to get people in a group to be quiet to listen to one individual]
Tsk, tsk [voiceless alveolar CLICK with the blade of the tongue]	*No. You're wrong.* [often accompanied by the wagging of an upraised index finger]

You may be struck by the fact that some of these words and sounds do not sound to you, as an English speaker, very much like the noises or animals they are meant to imitate. A Spanish speaker, however, insisted to this author that **¡Zumba!** sounded a lot more like the noise of a bumblebee to him than *Buzzzzzz* did. Listen to a rooster and see if you really think he is crowing *Cockadoodledo!* rather than **¡Quiquiriquíííí!** Obviously bumblebees and roosters in Hispanic countries and in the United States or Canada sound exactly alike, but these paralinguistic sounds and words are cultural and linguistic conventions, often based on nursery rhymes, fairy and folk tales, and even on the words in the balloons you see in comic strips and cartoons rather than on phonetic reality.

When you are in a Hispanic country, you will immediately notice these and many other paralinguistic vocalizations. Using them in the appropriate way will give your Spanish flavor and authenticity.

Review and Discussion

1. Where does PARALANGUAGE fit into the Spanish sound system? Why?

2. What are some of the vocalizations you can produce by causing your vocal bands to "BREAK," or to open and close vigorously and rapidly, creating lots of phonation?

3. What types of vocalizations do you make in English with INGRESSIVE or IMPLOSIVE sounds?

4. What are INTERJECTIONS? Give a couple examples in both Spanish and English.

5. What are ONOMATOPOEIC sounds? Give a couple examples in both languages.

6. What are paralinguistic SEMANTIC SIGNALS? Give a couple examples in both languages.

7. How do you explain the fact that some of these PARALINGUISTIC vocalizations use sounds and sound patterns absent in the normal phonetic inventory of the language in question?

8. Can you give any examples of Spanish or English interjections, onomatopoeic sounds, and semantic signals not listed in this chapter?

9. Do you know any paralinguistic vocalizations in any language other than Spanish or English?

10. How do you explain the fact that onomatopoeic vocalizations meant to imitate exactly the same sound in the real world are sometimes different in the two languages?

10

Reviewing the Melody of Spanish (CHAPTERS 5–9)

Suprasegmentals

The intonational or prosodic or suprasegmental sounds of Spanish make up its melody. These melodic features include stress, pitch or intonation, rhythm, and even sounds beyond the system or paralanguage. You learned the basic melody of English long before you went to school. In fact, you learned it before you learned all the individual sounds, before you learned the grammatical patterns, and before you learned even a small portion of the words of the language that you now know. It is for this reason that learning the melody of Spanish is probably the last thing you will master in your study of this language. However, just as with English or any other language, using the right words, placed in the right grammatical constructions, is not enough to enable you to speak Spanish like a native. You must say all the syllables of your utterances with the right degree of loudness (stress), the right pitch (intonation), and the right length (rhythm).

Although it is theoretically possible to learn words and grammar in a foreign language from books in an artificial setting like the classroom, it is probably impossible to learn the suprasegmental features of Spanish without interacting directly with native speakers of the language. Listening to recordings is better than nothing, but it is only a first step in learning the sound system of the language through actual communication with its speakers.

Before we move on to vowels, consonants, and the orthographical system, let us review the basic components of the suprasegmental or melodic system of Spanish.

Stress

Stress, which controls meaning, is the linguistic function of the relative loudness of certain syllables. As you know by now, **Saco una buena calificación** means ''I'll get a good grade'' because the **sa-** of the first word is louder than the **-co**. If you reverse the volume of these two syllables, you are saying something quite different: **Sacó una buena calificación**, meaning ''She/He got a good grade.'' This very significant change in meaning is caused by the amplitude of the sound waves coming from your glottis as you pronounce the very first word of the sentence. Some language analysts say that your interlocutor will compensate for this and realize what you mean anyway. Yet in the right context, either meaning in this example could be appropriate. You cannot depend on your Spanish-speaking listener to come up with the right meaning every time if you do not know which syllables in the group to make louder. Fortunately Spanish has only louder and softer syllables whereas English has a system of four, rather than two, degrees of stress.

Pitch

Although pitch cannot control meaning on the word level, since Spanish is not a tone language like Thai, Chinese, or Vietnamese, you can create temporary confusion in your listener with the wrong intonation. If you say **¿Hay corridas en Puerto Rico?** with the /2 1 1 ↓/ pattern, your listener, if he is not from Puerto Rico or not familiar with this country, assumes you know what you are talking about and are stating the fact that Puerto Rico has bullfighting. Obviously he cannot see the question marks you are looking at on this page. But if he already knows there is no bullfighting in Puerto Rico, since what you say is really not a question but a statement, you can only imagine what he thinks of you for making this false assertion. However, if you simply raise the pitch of your voice slightly on the last syllable -**co**, /2 2 2 ↑/, you are now asking a question, seeking information about a country you obviously do not know.

In this particular case—a yes-or-no question—English has several possible intonation patterns that could be used. ''Are there bullfights in Puerto Rico?'' can be said with /2 2 3 ↑/, which is perhaps the normal one in General American. It can also be said with /2 3 1 ↓/, with the highest pitch on *bullfights* meaning, ''OK, they have lots of 'sports' in Puerto Rico, but how about this one?'' The opening ''Are there'' is a syntactic indicator of a question in English, and it is so strong that it overrides an intonational pattern that is actually more typical of statements. You might say that syntax in this case wins out over intonation. And, if you are from western and central Pennsylvania, you can even ask the question with the pattern /2 3 1 ↑/, meaning exactly what the first pattern /2 2 3 ↑/ means. If you use one of these alternate intonation patterns in English, with the correct syntax, your interlocutor will not be confused—as he would be in Spanish—about question versus statement, but he may think you mean a little bit more than you actually do with this question, or he may realize that you are from another dialect area of the United States.

Rhythm

Rhythm, like intonation, cannot determine the meaning of individual words as stress can. In fact, rhythm cannot even determine the meaning of larger syntactic groups as intonation can. It is subtler than stress and pitch in a sense because the wrong rhythm keeps reminding your interlocutor over and over that you are really not a native speaker of Spanish, although the other features of your Spanish may be fine. It may convey this message so consistently and stridently that occasionally his attention may wander from your message to your manner of speaking. And no one really wants this to happen while communicating in any language. It is even theoretically possible to sound "more Spanish" at times with the right rhythm and an occasional wrong vowel or consonant and even some wrong words. This is not common, of course, but some speakers, such as comedians gifted at mimicry, are able to achieve this strange effect. Rhythm, however, is also closely tied to the stress system of a language. The rhythm of Spanish is such that it helps you avoid the English weak vowels /ɨ/ and /ə/, which do not exist in Spanish and can easily blur important grammatical and lexical distinctions, as we will see later.

Paralanguage

Although paralanguage is not part of the linguistic system per se, it plays a major role in communicating effectively in the foreign language. To lend your Spanish an authentic ring, you can begin to use vocalizations the way native speakers do—particularly the interjections. Although they reflect universal emotions and attitudes, their makeup differs quite markedly from language to language. Only coincidentally can you expect an English interjection to be the same in Spanish. If you yell ¡**Ayyy!** when you catch your finger in a drawer, you will sound much more Spanish than if you yell "Ouch!" Obviously, at first you will do what is natural, but if you make the effort, you will surprise yourself at how in a Spanish-speaking environment you may suddenly blurt out interjections in Spanish rather than English. Together with what is called KINESICS, that is, body language, gestures, and facial expressions, the paralinguistic system and the linguistic system make up what is known as the "total package of human communication." Kinesics and paralanguage probably can be learned only in a Spanish-speaking environment, but the phonological part of the linguistic system at least, with proper analysis and practice, can be learned quite well in an artificial classroom setting like the one you are in now.

Practice

Write the answers to these questions. Then check your work in Appendix C.

1. Stress and pitch are segmental sound features.   TRUE/FALSE
2. Rhythm depends mainly on (a) the length of stressed and unstressed syllables; (b) the pitch of stressed and unstressed syllables; (c) the number of stressed syllables in an utterance.
3. The term *decibels* refers to a sound measurement also known as hertz or cycles per second.   TRUE/FALSE
4. Stress in both Spanish and English is important and often determines meaning, so we say that in these two languages stress is _____.
5. In the English sentence "Pittsburgh was at one time a steel town," the word *town* has a heavier stress than the word *steel*.   TRUE/FALSE

6. If you say the two words *blue* and *bird* together with a heavier stress on the first word, you are referring to _____.

7. To emphasize the word **la** (*her*) in Spanish, you give it a heavier stress.   TRUE/FALSE

8. A word, like a noun or verb, that can be said correctly in isolation is referred to in linguistics as _____.

9. The word **con** in Spanish is (a) often given a heavy stress; (b) never emphasized unless it is used with the word **sin**; (c) almost always unstressed because it is a simple preposition.

10. The Spanish expressions **porque** and **por qué** not only mean different things and are thus spelled differently but, with regard to suprasegmentals,

_____.

11. The Spanish word **ha**, from **haber**, (a) may have a heavy stress since it is a verb form; (b) is always pronounced exactly like the preposition **a**; (c) is never stressed because it has only one syllable.

12. Three Spanish terms to describe or classify Spanish words according to their stress patterns are _____, _____, and _____.

13. The Spanish word **regímenes** (*regimes* or *diets*) is unusual because (a) it is preantepenult-syllable stressed; (b) its stress is on the third syllable from the end; (c) its stress has shifted to a different syllable than the one stressed in the singular form.

14. The plural adjective **jóvenes** is in a different word-stress category from that of its singular form.   TRUE/FALSE

15. Seemingly simple and obvious Spanish words like **felicito, deposito,** and **burócrata** are often mispronounced by English speakers because _____.

16. All Spanish words that end in a vowel letter, **n**, or **s** (a) are stressed on the next-to-last syllable unless they have a written accent somewhere else; (b) change stress categories when pluralized; (c) have close and obvious counterparts in English.

17. There are no Spanish words where a stressed **i** or a stressed **u** is "silent," that is, represents no sound at all.   TRUE/FALSE

18. Pitch level /3/ in Spanish usually shows (a) emphasis; (b) anger; (c) uncertainty.

19. It is impossible to end a breath group without using one of the three terminal junctures.   TRUE/FALSE

20. The term _____ is the linguistic term for the name or title of the person that you actually say when you address him or her.

21. Terminal junctures always represent a slight change in pitch in exactly the same direction that the pitch has already taken.   TRUE/FALSE

22. Saying **Buenas noches** with the intonation pattern of /2 3 1 ↓ / means that (a) you are emphasizing **noches** to make your listener realize you don't think that the time of day is really **la tarde**; (b) you are trying to be particularly friendly; (c) you are greeting someone rather than bidding them farewell.

23. So-called "information questions" in Spanish almost always begin with a(n) _____ or perhaps a preposition and a(n) _____.

24. When people are talking, they often break long sentences up into breath groups, which are signalled in speech by (a) commas and semicolons; (b) terminal junctures and slight pauses; (c) the use of pitch level /3/.

25. English and Spanish both signal emphatic elements in exactly the same way in the stream of speech, that is, simply by raising the pitch level of the stressed element.   TRUE/FALSE

26. The favorite vowel of unstressed syllables in English is *schwa* [ə] because (a) English speakers simply like the sound of it; (b) in a way it represents "taking a shortcut" for the tongue in the mouth; (c) it has so many ways to be spelled.

27. English poetry is often referred to as "stress-timed"; Spanish poetry is referred to as _____.

28. If a native speaker of Spanish adds words and therefore syllables to any given utterance, (a) he must somehow try to squeeze in the new, unstressed syllables to reduce the extra amount of time it takes to say them; (b) he simply must use a terminal juncture, pause, and start a new utterance; (c) he will probably use proportionately more time to say the new utterance.

29. The metrical system of Spanish poetry often utilizes so-called "ghost" or unwritten and even unspoken syllables.   TRUE/FALSE

30. No paralinguistic expression in Spanish or English ever makes use of sounds not included in the normal phonetic inventory of both languages.   TRUE/FALSE

31. A Spanish-speaker "hears" a sneeze as the word _____.

32. Both Spanish speakers and English speakers use paralinguistic sounds when lifting something very heavy with both hands. The Spanish speaker says **¡Uffff!** and the English speaker *Uggghhh!* (a) to get in the right mood to perform physical exertion; (b) to signal anyone within hearing distance that physical assistance is needed; (c) to shut off the glottis, that is, the opening between the vocal bands, and create a column of air between that point and the diaphragm below the stomach, thereby allowing the speaker to tense his or her abdominal muscles and thus achieve the required exertion.

33. Spanish speakers, when they are temporarily at a loss for words, probably say **Este. . .** and English speakers in the same situation say *Er, uh* . . . because **Este** is a word that happens to have two instances of [e], the most frequently used sound in Spanish, and *Er, uh* . . . utilizes [ə], the most frequently used sound in English, both cases of what might be termed the "default" vowel.   TRUE/FALSE

11

Producing Speech Sounds: Articulation

In Chapter 4, ''Producing Speech Sounds: Phonation,'' we saw how sounds were produced mainly in the breathing passage: from the lungs up through the bronchial tubes, trachea, larynx, vocal bands, and glottis. This is known as the subglottal region of the vocal tract because it concerns the area that lies below the glottis, or opening between the vocal bands. The suprasegmental features of stress, pitch or intonation, and rhythm depend mainly on phonation and how the sound waves or frequencies reverberate in the resonance chambers, namely, the throat or pharynx, the mouth or oral cavity, and the nasal passages or nasal cavity. But now we will take a look at how the individual sounds are produced or articulated in the supraglottal region of the vocal tract, namely, the parts that lie above the glottis. This area is comprised of the lower or movable articulators and the upper or fixed articulators.

Segmental Sound Classes

The segmental or individual speech sounds can be divided into two basic groups, depending on how these articulators function with regard to the sound waves that are produced during phonation. CONSONANTS are produced or articulated if this airstream is stopped or impeded in any way, and VOWELS are produced or articulated if this airstream flows through the supraglottal part of the vocal tract freely and unimpeded. In some analyses of the Spanish sound system there is a third or intermediate category known as GLIDES or SEMI-CONSONANTS or SEMI-VOWELS, that is, sounds that seem to fit in neither of our two broad categories but form their own. In our analysis, however, some of these intermediate sounds will be considered to be consonants and the rest, vowels.

(Note: The numbers in Diagram 4 refer to the list in Chart 7 on page 98. The letter **a** refers to the lower movable articulators; the letter **b** to the upper fixed articulators.)

Diagram 4   Consonants: Points of Articulation

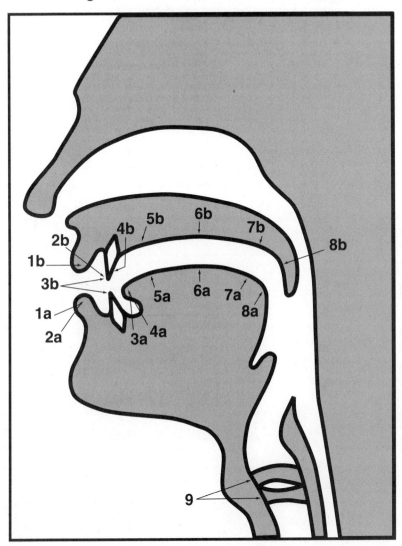

In Spanish there are nine places of articulation for consonants, depending on how the lower or movable articulators achieve what is known as MAXIMUM CLOSURE of the airstream with the upper or fixed articulators. The points of articulation for Diagram 4 are listed in Chart 7.

Chart 7   Points of Articulation for Spanish Consonants: I

Point of Articulation	(a) Lower Articulators	(b) Upper Articulators
1. BILABIAL	(a) lower lip	(b) upper lip
2. LABIO-DENTAL	(a) lower lip	(b) upper front teeth
3. INTERDENTAL	(a) tongue tip	(b) edges of upper and lower front teeth
4. DENTAL	(a) tongue tip	(b) edges or back of upper front teeth
5. ALVEOLAR	(a) tongue blade	(b) alveolar ridge
6. PALATAL	(a) middle tongue dorsum	(b) hard palate
7. VELAR	(a) rear tongue dorsum	(b) velum (soft palate)
1., 7. BILABIO-VELAR	(see 1 and 7 above)	
8. UVULAR	(a) rear tongue dorsum	(b) uvula
9. GLOTTAL	vocal bands (the concept of ''lower'' and ''upper'' does not apply here)	

A further description with examples from Spanish and English, and other languages (where they exist), follows in Chart 8.

Chart 8   Points of Articulation for Spanish Consonants: II

Point of Articulation	Description
1. BILABIAL	The lower lip (a) presses against or slightly touches the upper lip (b): [m] as in **más** or *mass*; [b] as in **bueno** or *boy*.

(Continued)

(Continued)

2. LABIO-DENTAL	The lower lip **(a)** presses against or slightly touches the upper front teeth **(b)**: [f] as in **feliz** or *fender.*
3. INTERDENTAL	The tip or blade of the tongue **(a)** protrudes slightly between the upper and lower front teeth **(b)**: [θ] as in the Castilian pronunciation of **zapato** or English *think*; [ð] as in the Castilian pronunciation of **juzgar** or English *there.*
4. DENTAL	The tip or blade of the tongue **(a)** presses against the inside surface of the upper front teeth or slightly touches the lower edge or the back of the upper front teeth **(b)**: [d] as in **Diga**. There are no purely dental sounds in most dialects of English. Some speakers in New York City and environs have a dental [d] in words like *these, them, that.*
5. ALVEOLAR	The tip or blade of the tongue **(a)** presses against or slightly touches the alveolar ridge (the gum ridge behind the upper front teeth) **(b)**: [l] as in **luna** or *loony*; [n] as in **nota** or *noble*; [s] as in **sí** or *seem.*
6. PALATAL	The blade or dorsum of the tongue **(a)** presses against or slightly touches the hard palate **(b)**: [ñ] as in **año**; [ŷ] as in **¡yo!** English has no "palatal *n*", and the English sound that corresponds most closely to [ŷ], [ǰ], is actually articulated farther forward on the palate. Thus, in some analyses of both Spanish and English another place or point of articulation is recognized: ALVEOLO-PALATAL, the area that includes the back of the alveolar ridge and the very front of the arch of the palate. In the interests of simplicity, although we analyze Spanish sounds like [ṅ] and [ĉ]—as in the word **ancho**—as alveolo-palatal rather than purely palatal, we do not include a separate alveolo-palatal section on the charts.

(Continued)

(*Continued*)

7. VELAR	The back of the tongue **(a)** presses against or slightly touches the velum or soft palate **(b)**: [k] as in **calle** or *card*; [ŋ] as in **estanco** or *sing*; [x] as in **jardín** in most dialects of Spanish. This sound does not exist in North American English.
1.,7. BILABIO-VELAR	This is actually a double place of articulation, since one movable articulator approaches one fixed articulator at the one point and another movable articulator approaches a fixed articulator at another point at the same time. The lower lip **(a)** approaches the upper lip **(b)**, as both are extended, and at the same time the back of the tongue **(a)** is raised to approach the velum **(b)**: [w] as in **hueso** or *way*.
8. UVULAR	The back of the tongue **(a)** slightly touches the uvula **(b)**, which vibrates from the pressure of the air being forced through: [R] as in **rico** as it is pronounced by some Puerto Ricans. This is the same sound heard in French **rouge** *red* and German **rot** *red*. English does not have uvular sounds.
9. GLOTTAL	The air rubs on the vocal bands themselves as it goes through. Although all voiced sounds are really ''glottal'' in the sense that the vocal bands are a vital part of the articulation, here we will use this term just to describe the voiceless [h] as in **jardín**, as pronounced in certain dialects of Spanish, or as in *help*. For [h] the air merely rubs against the vocal bands with friction, but they are not tense enough to vibrate as they do for all voiced sounds.

Chart 9 outlines the seven manners of articulation for consonants in Spanish (with examples in English, too).

Chart 9   Manners of Articulation for Spanish Consonants

Manner of Articulation	Description
1. STOP (also called OCCLUSIVE)	The airstream is stopped briefly and then abruptly released with a small explosion: [p] as in **pasar** or *span*; [t] as in **tomar** or *stone*; [k] as in **¿Cómo?** or *scold*.
2. FRICATIVE	The airstream, without being stopped, is forced through a narrow opening with resulting friction. If the opening is wide (horizontal) and flat, the sound is a SLIT FRICATIVE: [f] as in **frío** or *fender*. If the opening is small, round, and somewhat elongated from front to back, the sound is a GROOVE FRICATIVE: [s] as in **señor** or *send*. These grooved sounds are also called SIBILANTS, or ''whistled'' sounds.
3. AFFRICATE (STOP + FRICATIVE)	The airstream is stopped first as with a stop, but instead of being released abruptly with an explosion, it is released with the friction of a fricative: [ĉ] as in **chiflado** or *chicken*.
4. NASAL	The velum is lowered, and the airstream passes out through the nasal passage with great resonance: [m] as in **miembro** or *member*.
5. LATERAL	The oral cavity is closed off in the middle by the tongue, and the airstream escapes on either or both sides of it: [l] as in **libro** or *lily*.
6. TAP (also FLAP)	The tip of the tongue, under tension, strikes the alveolar ridge once as the airstream passes through: [r] as in **caro**. English also has a tap, but it is spelled with *t* or *d*: *water*, *raider*.

(Continued)

(*Continued*)

7. TRILL	The tip of the tongue, under even greater tension, strikes the alveolar ridge. The airstream forces the tongue tip back, but the muscular effort of the tongue pushes the tongue tip forward against the alveolar ridge several times in rapid succession: [r̄] as in **carro**. Sometimes the dorsum of the tongue strikes the velum or both the velum and the uvula in this fashion: [R] in **rico** as said by some speakers in Puerto Rico. North American English has no trills, although some speakers of British and Scottish English trill their *r*'s in various words.

Thus the consonants can be classified and arranged on a CHART, showing these three meaningful ways of producing or articulating sounds: PLACE or POINT OF ARTICULATION (from left to right on the chart), MANNER OF ARTICULATION (top to bottom), and FUNCTION OF THE VOCAL BANDS, that is, VOICING or lack of it (shown in the chart by the position of the symbols in the little boxes—VOICELESS consonants in the upper left, VOICED in the lower right). In Chart 10 on page 103, only the meaningful or distinctive consonants of all Spanish dialects are shown—no single speaker makes all of these distinctions. For example, the voiceless interdental fricative [θ] (as in **cinco** or **zorro**) is used only in Castilian (peninsular Spanish), and the voiced palatal lateral [l̃] (as in **llamar**) is distinctive only in certain parts of Spain and the Andes region of South America. Also most speakers from the Caribbean area have the glottal [h] rather than the velar [x] in words like **gente** and **jota**. This is the reason for the parentheses around these three consonants on the chart. Most dialects of American Spanish, all of which, of course, lack [θ], have either 18 or 19 distinctive consonant sounds. The technical term for such a contrastive sound is PHONEME, which will be explained in detail in Chapter 12, ''Contrasting the Sounds of Spanish.''

Vowels

In the case of vowels, the determining factor, rather than place and manner of articulation, is the position of the tongue because it determines the size and shape of the main resonance chamber, the mouth or oral cavity. Since there is no contact between the upper and lower articulators, the airstream in the production of vowels is not blocked or impeded

Chart 10   Consonant Phonemes of Spanish: Summary
Points of Articulation

(handwritten: Puntos)

MANNERS OF ARTICULATION	bilabial	labio-dental	inter-dental	dental	alveolar	palatal	velar	bilabio-velar	glottal
STOPS *(oclusiva)*	p *(sorda)* / b *(sonora)*			t / d			k / g		
FRICATIVES		f	(θ)		s	y	x / w		(h)
AFFRICATES *(Africada)*						ĉ			
NASALS *(nasal)*	m *(sonoro)*				n	ñ			
LATERALS *(Lateral)*					l	(l̃)			
TAP *(toque)*					r				
TRILL *(trino)*					r̄				

(handwritten "el" in left margin beside STOPS)

in any significant way. For Spanish we recognize three vertical positions of the tongue: HIGH, where the front or back of the tongue is raised and thus close to the palate or velum; MID, where it is about half raised (or lowered from the palate or velum); and LOW, where it lies very low in the mouth. We also recognize three horizontal positions on a front-to-back axis: FRONT, where the highest part of the tongue, the blade, is fairly close to the alveolar ridge; CENTRAL, where it is in the center of the oral cavity; and BACK, where the highest part of the tongue, now the dorsum, is fairly close to the velum.

This creates a two-dimensional system to classify the five meaningful vowels in Spanish.

1. HIGH FRONT: [i] as in **piso**
2. MID FRONT: [e] as in **peso**
3. LOW CENTRAL: [a] as in **paso**
4. MID BACK: [o] as in **poso**
5. HIGH BACK: [u] as in **puso**

The vowels of Spanish can then be placed in a traditional configuration in phonetics referred to as the vowel ''triangle.''

Chart 11   Spanish Vowels: The Triangle

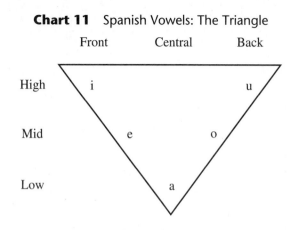

These five vowels can be shown on a regular rectangular chart as well.

Chart 12   Spanish Vowels: The Grid

	anterior Front	Central	Back
High	i		u
Mid	e		o
Low		a	

As you can see from Diagrams 5 and 6, which follow, the vowel positions in either of these charts are a rough representation of a side cross-section view of the area in the mouth where the air flows through between the tongue and the alveolar ridge, palate, or velum.

Diagram 5   Tongue Positions for [i] and [u] in Spanish

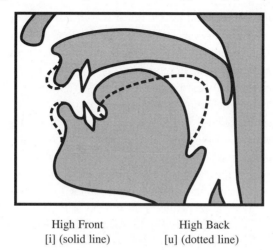

High Front   High Back
[i] (solid line)   [u] (dotted line)

Diagram 6   Tongue Positions for [i] and [a] in Spanish

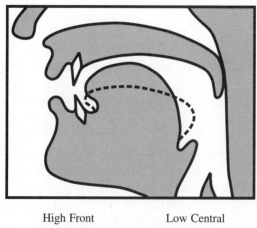

High Front   Low Central
[i] (solid line)   [a] (dotted line)

Spanish has the simplest vowel system of any of the languages commonly studied by North Americans. In other languages, like French and German, additional features make vowel articulation more varied and complex. In Spanish and English the production of these extra features is automatic and below the level of awareness, but in French and German, for example, they must be controlled by the speaker because they are significant in determining meaning.

Lip-Rounding for Vowels

LIP-ROUNDING (indicated by a [¨] over the vowel) versus LIP-SPREADING is very important in French and German, and although this feature exists in Spanish and English, too, it happens automatically and below the level of awareness of the speaker. When the tongue pulls back for [o], as in **mono**, or the [U], as in *put*, the lips automatically round. When the tongue goes forward for [i], as in **sí**, or [I], as in *sit*, the lips spread slightly. But in languages like French and German, lip-rounding or lip-spreading and tongue position are independent of each other. In French, to pronounce the vowel [i] in the word **vie** [vi] *life*, the tongue moves forward and the lips spread; to pronounce the vowel [u] in the word **vous** [vu] *you*, the tongue retracts and the lips round. But for the vowel [ü] in the word **vu** *seen*, the tongue moves forward as in **vie**, but at the same time the lips round as for **vous**. Most English speakers, at first at least, cannot do this and make **vu** sound like **vous**, as in the nonexistent **déjà "vous"* [vu] instead of the correct **déjà vu** [vü].

The same feature of independent lip-rounding exists in German, and English speakers typically say **"shane"** or **"shurn"** for **schön** [šön] *beautiful* since it is so unnatural for them to round their lips while their tongue is forward in the mouth. Fortunately Spanish and English work exactly the same with regard to this feature: lip-rounding automatically accompanies only the back vowels: [o] in both languages (**mono**, *obey*) and [u] in Spanish (**su**) and [U] in English (*put*).

Nasalization of Vowels

NASALIZATION (indicated by a [˜] over the vowel) is contrastive in French and Portuguese where it can determine the difference between two mid front vowels [ɛ] and [ɛ̃], thus creating the contrast in French of **fait** *made* with **fin** *end*. Nasalization also occurs in both Spanish and English, but, unlike the situation in French and Portuguese, it is not contrastive and happens below the level of awareness of the speaker. Just as you probably have never realized that the first vowel of the word *monkey* in English is nasalized, the Spanish speaker is unaware of the same fact in the word **mono**. Because nasal and oral vowels are produced automatically, unconsciously, and thus REDUNDANTLY by Spanish speakers and English speakers and, are in fact, even impossible to avoid in many cases, we do not indicate them in phonetic transcription in this book.

Vowel Length

LENGTH or duration (indicated by a [:] after the vowel, showing that it is a LONG VOWEL) was also contrastive in Spanish's ancestor language, Latin, as it is now in German, where it can determine the difference between the two low central vowels [a] and [a:], thus creating a contrast between **Stadt** *city* and **Staat** *state*. Lengthened and regular or short vowels occur regularly and noticeably in English—and to a much lesser extent in some dialects of Spanish—but, as with lip-rounding and nasalization, the phenomenon in these two languages is redundant and below the level of awareness. The English speaker automatically lengthens all vowels before voiced consonants—*cup* versus *cub, mate* versus *made, pick* versus *pig*, and so forth. Many Mexicans automatically shorten the final unstressed vowel, particularly between two voiceless consonants. In fact, in some cases it is so short that it almost disappears—**"accident's," "coch's," "graci's,"** and so forth. In this last case, however, we *do* mark this phenomenon in phonetic transcription (to be taken up in Chapter 14) because it is an interesting and identifying feature of certain dialects of Spanish, unlike the normal long and short vowels of English, which, since they occur automatically, tell us nothing about the dialect of English being spoken.

Glides

The final aspect of the production of speech sounds, mentioned earlier in this chapter, concerns GLIDES (also called SEMI-CONSONANTS or SEMI-VOWELS). In some languages it is difficult to decide whether these sounds are really consonants or vowels; sometimes, in fact, they are both. In English, for example, the palatal glide [y] functions more as a consonant at the beginning of a word or syllable, as in *yes* /yɛs/ or *lawyer* /loyər/, and more as a vowel at the end of a word or syllable, as in *say* /sɛy/ or *aim* /ɛym/. The same problem arises in Spanish, but with even more ramifications. In our analysis we consider both the palatal glide [i̯], as in **si̯ete** and **sei̯s**, and the velar glide [u̯], as in **bu̯eno** and **cau̯sa**, to be vowel sounds. The corresponding sounds [y], as in **yeso**, and [w], as in **hueso**, are considered to be consonant sounds.

Acoustic Phonetics

Thus far we have been discussing speech sounds from purely a production or articulatory point of view, that is, how they are actually made in the vocal tract. Also of great importance in linguistic theory and analysis—although not as useful in language learning and teaching—is ACOUSTIC PHONETICS, where the sounds are analyzed according to the sound waves themselves: their acoustic and auditory properties. Sound is made up of waves that travel through the air at a speed of 1,100 feet per second. These waves are created by the vibrations caused by the movement of the vocal bands and their further modification in the resonance chambers. The field of acoustic phonetics utilizes sophisticated electronic devices, such as the spectrograph, which can produce on a television screen and on paper images of the sound waves and their various properties, such as their frequency and amplitude. Acoustic phonetics is also important in a wide range of professions: music, physics, engineering, architecture, audiology, cybernetics, telecommunications, and medicine.

The findings of acoustic phonetics has led in the past to quite different ways of classifying sounds, based in part on how and where they are produced in the vocal tract, but also on how they are perceived and interpreted by the human ear. In this book, however, we confine our analysis to the more traditional manner of classifying sounds —called ''place and manner of articulation''—since, although it undeniably has certain shortcomings and disadvantages, it is much less complicated and can be quickly mastered and utilized by you, the student, to analyze the sounds of Spanish and pronounce them correctly.

Review and Discussion

1. What are the upper or fixed articulators? How about the lower or movable articulators?

2. What are the three most important parameters (dimensions, factors, elements) for the classification of Spanish consonants as presented here?

3. If you visualize a stylized cutaway cross-section of the vocal tract of a human face, which conventionally looks to the left or "west," how many places of articulation (points of maximum closure) can you name, starting from the right or "east," the direction of the outgoing airstream? Go in order if you can.

4. What are the stop consonants of English? Give examples of words that begin with stops. Now for Spanish.

5. What is slightly different about the manner of articulation known as affricate, as compared with the other manners? Give two affricate sounds from any language(s).

6. Do we have a tap sound in English, too? If so, give an example. How about trills?

7. Why do we "shift gears," or change the parameters of analysis, when we go from the classification of consonants to that of vowels? Explain.

8. What is the vowel triangle? Does it work as well for English as for Spanish? Prove it.

9. In an effort to simplify the phonetic analysis and transcription of Spanish, a couple of vowel features are dispensed with and never marked in transcription in this book. What are they, and what is the justification for this decision?

10. Are there any problems or disadvantages with our analysis of sounds, or does it all come out neatly?

12

Contrasting the Sounds
of Spanish

The human speech apparatus can produce an infinite variety of sounds, and only a relatively small number of them is ever used in any one language. A baby begins by making dozens of these sounds but gradually learns only those which it hears and which in turn it can use to elicit desired responses. When the child finally has complete control over the sound system of his or her language, he/she has narrowed the range of important sounds considerably—down to somewhere between fifteen and fifty.

Phonetics and Phonetic Transcription

We have already taken up the study of these sounds for Spanish and to a certain extent for English, too, in several ways. In PHYSIOLOGICAL PHONETICS (discussed in Chapter 4) we studied the entire human speech mechanism, the breathing and voicing apparatus. In ARTICULATORY PHONETICS (discussed in Chapter 11) we studied the way sounds are produced in the vocal bands, the resonance chambers, and the articulators. Diagrams 5 and 6, presented in the previous chapter, are called ARTICULATORY or FACIAL DIAGRAMS, and a three-way description of the sounds by their place and manner of articulation and the function of the vocal bands is an ARTICULATORY DESCRIPTION.

As we saw in the last chapter, the findings of ACOUSTIC PHONETICS, the study of the sound waves themselves, their transmission, and their reception, is important in a wide range of professions. Linguists, however—particularly phoneticians and phonologists—are most interested in how these sounds are produced in the human vocal tract and how they determine meaning. Linguists have created symbols to represent these sounds, but unfortunately there is no standard set of such symbols used by all in the way that English speakers, for example, use the same letters and numbers in conventional writing. Each phonetician or group of phoneticians uses his or her own system, and others who read their studies must constantly translate or TRANSLITERATE the unfamiliar symbols into their own familiar ones. Fortunately, there is a fairly large common body of symbols that all phoneticians use. So, although the symbols you find in this book are not exactly the same as those found in any other book, the majority of them are common and used by other Spanish phoneticians and phonologists. You have already seen phonetic symbols in your English dictionary in the word entries themselves and perhaps in a list either at the bottom of the page, in the introductory material of the book, or perhaps even on the inside of one of the covers.

Regular letters of the Roman or Latin alphabet have been used in our book wherever possible with some exceptions. Even many of the familiar letters must be modified in a way probably new to you simply because there are many more sounds in language than there are separate letters to represent them. For example, there is only one lower case Roman *n* letter available to us, yet Spanish in our analysis has five *n* sounds, so in this book you will see the following symbols to represent them: [n], [ṇ], [ǹ], [ñ], and [ŋ]. Square brackets, [ ], as you have guessed by now, indicate that the enclosed symbols are phonetic, meaning that they represent the articulated sound. Most of the symbols are lower case Roman letters, and some are upper case or capitals, which are *never* used in phonetics for proper names or to begin sentences the way they are in regular writing. Sometimes Greek letters are used—like [θ]—and sometimes letters are combined—like [æ]. Many letters must be modified with a variety of small marks, called DIACRITICS, which are placed under or over the letters, as for three of the *n*'s above: [ṇ], [ǹ], [ñ].

There are several other notation conventions that you need to know and begin to use, and they are summarized in the following chart. All of the new material found there will be taken up and explained shortly.

Chart 13   Forms of Linguistic Notation

Symbol	Purpose	Example
Regular letters of the alphabet	Normal text	You are now reading normal text. Puede ser en español también.
Boldface type	Spanish words, phrases, and sentences in English text	The Spanish word **jamás** is **aguda** with regard to its stress pattern. **con o sin leche** **Vive en Santo Domingo.**
Italic type	English words in normal text	The English word *bluebird* has a heavier stress on *blue* than on *bird.*

Chart 13 Forms of Linguistic Notation (Continued)

Symbol	Purpose	Example
Italic type (continued)	Also English glosses	**Régimen** also means *diet.*
	Also English words emphasized in the text	Capital letters are *never* used to begin a phonetic transcription.
	Also letters of the alphabet cited in the text	Spanish has five *n*'s in its phonetic inventory.
Letters between brackets: [ ]	Phonetic symbols	The five *n*'s are [n], [ṇ], [ǹ], [ñ], and [ŋ].
Letters between slash bars: / /	Phonemic symbols	But there are only two *n* phonemes: /n/ and /ñ/.
Quotation marks: " "	Special uses with which you are already familiar	Spanish is reputed to be an "easy" language.
		Some wag once said, "A language is just a dialect that had a strong army and navy in the past."

Redundancy in Phonetics

A few decades ago some linguists felt that although phonetic transcription of speech was useful and even essential for some types of work, it could at times be cumbersome and unnecessarily detailed. Many fine distinctions that the phoneticians recognized were redundant in the sense that they happened automatically and beyond the control and awareness of the native speaker. For example, in both Spanish and English all vowels between nasal consonants are also nasalized and should theoretically be represented by a different symbol than the one used for non-nasalized or oral vowels. Thus, the first syllables of both the words **mono** and *monkey* contain nasalized vowels and theoretically should be represented as [mõ-no] and [mÃŋ-kÌy], respectively. Yet since no speaker of either language can avoid nasalizing the first vowels in these words, we ignore this redundant feature and simply transcribe the words as [mó-no] and [mʌŋ-kÌy].

Functional Phonetics

As linguists studied a greater number of languages more and more closely, they came to the realization that some sound varieties that could be heard and consciously made were not nearly as important as others, that sounds could be grouped into families or functional groups, and, most important, that it was the sound family or functional group as a whole that determined meaning and was represented in the writing system. This concept is perhaps best illustrated in a language like Spanish where the writing system, although not perfect, is quite good at representing these sound families or functional groups—certainly better than in English. Although there are five Spanish *n* sounds, as we saw above, there are only two regular Spanish letters: **n** and **ñ**, and, not coincidentally, two Spanish *n* families or functional groups: /n/ and /ñ/.

Returning to English for a moment, the letter *t* really represents several sounds, which we pronounce at different times, according to their position in the word. At the beginning of a word like *top* the *t* has a little puff of air right after it. If you place the back of your hand or a tissue a few inches from your lips as you pronounce the word, you can feel on your hand or see by the moving tissue the accompanying breath or aspiration. This aspirated word-initial *t* then can be represented with the phonetic symbol [tʰ].

However, if you pronounce the word *stop*, you notice now that there is not nearly as much breath as with the [tʰ] in *top*. This is because in English *t* after *s* is unaspirated since the air has momentarily gone out of your mouth to produce the preceding *s*. This plain or unaspirated *t* can then be represented phonetically with a [t].

If you pronounce the word *water*, you notice that the *t* now does not have the puff of air that it did at the beginning of *top* nor does the tongue really seem to shut off the air flow as it does in both *top* and *stop*. Instead the tip of the tongue quickly strikes the alveolar ridge and returns to its original position. This is normal in English words where *t* comes between vowels, the first one of which is stressed: *butter*, *litter*, *daughter,* and so on. This *t* sound is known as a tap or flap and can be represented with a [t̂].

Finally if you pronounce the word *get*, you notice now that this *t* has no aspiration like the [tʰ] in *top* (unless you make a deliberate and somewhat unnatural effort to give it some), nor does the tongue tip quickly return to its original position like the [t̂] in *water*. Instead it remains quite tight against the alveolar ridge, waiting for the next sound. This is known as an unreleased *t* and can be represented phonetically with [t-].

Thus in American English there are at least four different varieties of *t,* varieties which are not only articulated in different ways in the mouth but which sound noticeably different to us once we really pay attention to them—as in the words *top*, *stop*, *water*, and *get*. Yet as we speak we rarely make any conscious effort to choose from among these four sounds. We pronounce them automatically according to their position in the word, the surrounding sounds, and the nearby stresses. All this is known as the PHONETIC ENVIRONMENT.

Let's return for a moment to the first word, *top*. If you place your tongue in the same position as you do for the first sound in the word, [tʰ], but allow your vocal bands to start vibrating immediately, you produce a very different consonant, *d*, and a strange word, *dop. This word may possibly mean something now to some speakers of the language or it may possibly mean something someday to all speakers of the language, but, at any rate, it certainly does not mean *top*. Thus the difference betweeen *top* and *dop* is enough to cause native speakers of English to accept the fact that there is something fundamentally different about [tʰ] and [dʰ]. This difference can change or destroy meaning. We also show this difference through the use of different letters of the alphabet, *t* and *d*, although in English these spelling differences in general are less reliable than the criterion of meaning change.

We are beginning to see that the [dʰ] of *dop* is somehow "more different" from the [tʰ] of *top* than the [t] of *stop* or the [t-] of *get* is. To prove this, do a quick experiment with the word *top*. If you can, try to pronounce it with the *unaspirated* [t] of the word *stop*. This may be difficult at first because you are so used to aspirating your word-initial *t*'s. The *top* with [t] instead of the normal [tʰ] sounds "funny," but you must agree that it doesn't sound as "funny" as *top* would with the initial sound [dʰ]. In fact, *top* with a [t] is still *top*, but *not* with a [dʰ].

Now pronounce the word *get* with these three *t*'s in succession: [t], [tʰ], and [t-]. The first one is a bit hard, but the word still sounds okay. The second one sounds exaggerated, emphatic, and perhaps "British," but is still *get*. The third one, of course, is the common one. But if you continue the experiment by substituting any form of *d*, the word is now just plain wrong: *ged*.

The Phoneme

In this illustration we have been dealing with the most important concept in phonology, the PHONEME. In most positions in a word no variety of *t* can be replaced by any variety of *d* without changing the meaning or creating a nonexistent word like *dop*. Thus, all four varieties of *t* belong to one family or class of *t* sounds, now referred to as the phoneme /t/, which is written between slash bars. All varieties of *d* likewise belong to the phoneme /d/. These two phonemes are distinctive sounds in English and many other languages—including, of course, Spanish—as well because their use changes the meaning or perhaps creates a meaningless form.

All speakers of English know this—perhaps without knowing they know it—but it can quickly be demonstrated to them or learners of the language by a technique that will be used a great deal in our analysis. Pairs of words differing only by the sound in question that prove this—like *tip-dip*, *bitter-bidder* (for many speakers), *lit-lid*—are called MINIMAL PAIRS. By using this testing technique of finding minimal pairs, we can begin to pick out the distinctive or meaningful sounds of English first and later Spanish. It should be emphasized that speakers of these languages already know what the distinctive sounds of their language are without ever thinking consciously about such things as minimal pairs, but the test is valuable for pedagogical purposes, particularly to convince the new learner of the language about the function of sounds in the new language.

We can quickly show anyone that English has two similar sets of phonemes: /p/ and /b/, and /k/ and /g/, by citing such minimal pairs as *pill-bill, ripping-ribbing, cup-cub* and *cold-gold, meeker-meager, flak-flag.* The fact that the spelling in these examples differs, too, is not the crucial factor—particularly in a language like English, which has such irregular and inconsistent spelling. For example, the words *rough* and *huff* form a minimal pair showing the phonemic status of /r/ and /h/. The fact that *-ough* and *-uff* are two different ways of spelling the sequence /ʌf/ is due to the English writing system, which is actually several hundred years "out of date." Such inconsistencies—which also exist in Spanish but to a much lesser extent—have forced linguists and lexicographers (dictionary makers) to resort to phonetic and phonemic transcriptions to indicate the sounds accurately and consistently.

All sounds can be referred to as PHONES. If we want to represent contrastive and functional families of phones that serve to distinguish meaning, we write them in slash bars and refer to them as PHONEMES: /p/, /b/, /t /, /d/, /k/, /g/, for example. To save space sometimes we can write a group of phonemes all together with only one set of slash bars: /p b t d k g/, which means exactly the same thing as the group in the previous sentence. However, if the phones in question are variants or just family members of the same phoneme—like four of the *n*'s of Spanish or the four *t*'s of English—we write them in square brackets and refer to them as ALLOPHONES: [n], [n̥], [ñ], [ŋ]; [tʰ], [t], [t̂], [t-]. Of course, we can also write these sets as [n n̥ ñ ŋ] and [tʰ t t̂ t-].

The phoneme is not an easy concept to grasp at first, and phonologists are not even in complete agreement as to its exact nature and behavior. But all agree that phonemes determine meaning in language, that they are realized in different ways (called "allophones" by some) according to their position in the word, and that, even though these allophones are not contrastive, if we put them in the wrong place, the resulting word usually does not sound quite right, at least not the same as a native speaker from your dialect area would say it. For example, if someone says in English [tip-] for [tʰip-], it sounds odd, perhaps even foreign, although we know exactly what it means. And if a Venezuelan visiting Argentina says **pan** as [paŋ] (with the final sound of the English word *sing*) instead of [pan] (with the final sound of the English word *sin*), the Argentinians know, of course, that he means *bread*, but that's not the way they say it.

The phoneme actually is an abstraction, but a very convenient one in linguistics. We cannot really pronounce phonemes (although we can spell them); we can only pronounce *allophones.* In any language the number of phonemes is obviously far lower than the number of allophones. In General American English there are 33 or 34; in General American Spanish there are 23 or 24; French has 33; German has 28; Italian has 27; Russian has 41. These numbers, of course, vary somewhat from dialect to dialect in all languages.

Minimal Pairs

Although the use of minimal pairs is the best and quickest way to determine or show whether two sounds in a language are phonemic or not, minimal pairs for certain sound contrasts are difficult to find because words containing them may be few in number and not very common. For example, in English /š/ (as in *she*) and /ž/ (as in *measure*) are phonemes, but there are few minimal pairs to show this. All native speakers of English, of course, already know that *she* with a /ž/ is wrong and that *measure* with /š/ is likewise wrong. But to demonstrate this fact to a foreign learner of English who perhaps cannot even hear the difference between the two sounds at first, it is most convincing to find a minimal pair. One is *Aleutian-illusion,* although some native speakers of English might object at first because they mistakenly feel that the vowel sounds at the beginning of each word are different (actually both are [ə]). Another is *Aleutian-allusion*, although many native speakers of English do not know the word *allusion*. Another one is *tressure-treasure*, but the first word—a type of figure in a coat of arms—is unfamiliar to almost every speaker of English who is not also a specialist in heraldry. And when we deal with a foreign language the task of finding minimal pairs can be even more difficult.

Phonetic Similarity

Because of these difficulties, linguists often rely first on another preliminary technique for finding phonemes in the language under study. They find the phones (sounds) that are phonetically similar. Although the concept of PHONETIC SIMILARITY can be somewhat arbitrary, we can take it to mean that *two* of the three crucial factors in sound analysis— place of articulation, manner of articulation, and voicing or lack of it—are the same. (Check the consonants in Chart 10 in the last chapter and note its three dimensions or parameters: the horizontal rows, the vertical columns, and the opposite corners of each individual compartment.) Once this is determined, the linguist tallies the distribution of these phones to begin to determine whether or not they are allophones of the same phoneme or different phonemes. As we have seen, allophones are most often pronounced by native speakers automatically according to certain factors, the main one being phonetic environment. This was demonstrated with the English /t/ phoneme and its four allophones: [tʰ t t̂ t-]. Your choice of which one to pronounce is virtually obligatory, involuntary, automatic, and below the level of your awareness. But the choice between [t-] and [d-] is different: this choice is optional, voluntary, and deliberate. Do you want to say *right* or *ride*? You must make this choice consciously because you are now dealing with /t/ versus /d/, a phonemic contrast.

The fact that you choose the allophone according to the phonetic environment without realizing it is very useful to the linguist. This means that she/he can determine or predict in advance the distribution of the allophones in question by determining the phonetic environment. Thus you as a student can be shown beforehand which allophone to use in Spanish once you know the surrounding sounds, namely, the phonetic environment. The native speaker of Spanish does it automatically; you, as a learner, must first think about it, but with practice it can become automatic with you, too, in your efforts to sound like a native speaker of Spanish.

The "Elsewhere" Convention

Turning now to Spanish, we find a phone [d], which is a voiced dental *stop*, and another one [ḏ], a voiced dental or interdental *fricative*. In English we have two phones very similar to these. Although English [d] is actually alveolar rather than dental, as it is in Spanish, and [ḏ], due to convention, is transcribed [ð], for all practical purposes we are dealing with the same two sounds in both languages. But in English the two are contrastive or phonemic and occur frequently in exactly the same phonetic environment. We can never substitute one for the other without changing or destroying the meaning: *dare* is not *there*, *riding* is not *writhing*, and *load* is not *loathe*. But in Spanish these two sounds never occur naturally in the same environment: [d] occurs at the beginning of a breath group, for example, after a pause, as in **Dígame**, after /l/, as in **falda**, and after /n/, as in **anda**; [ḏ] occurs between vowels, as in **lado** or **pide**, after /b/, as in **abdomen**, after /g/, as in **amígdalas**, after /r/, as in **pierde**, and after /s/, as the second *d* in **desde**. Notice that for [d] we listed only three environments whereas for [ḏ] we have listed five, and we could have listed even more had we listed all five vowels separately instead of saying between vowels. This leads to another crucial concept in phonology, namely ELSEWHERE.

The "elsewhere" convention means simply that we first list the allophone with the fewest phonetic environments—[d] in this case—and its environments. Then we list the other allophone—[ḏ] in this case—and say that its phonetic environments are all the others in the language not already included in our initial statement—that is, elsewhere. Suppose you gave a class party, but that of your twenty classmates you invited only eighteen of them. You were terrified that the two you refused to invite would come anyway. So, to take extra precautions, you posted a bouncer at the door of your apartment with strict instructions to exclude only these two. Which would be more efficient—to give your bouncer a list of the names of the eighteen who were invited and have him get out the names of all twenty classmates as they came to your door and check them against the long list, or simply give him the names of the two unwanted members and have him let everyone else in? The "elsewhere" convention in linguistics, if not in social events, simply puts exceptions first and the so-called normal or regular items last.

However, you must not take this analogy too far. Although the second allophone listed is probably more statistically frequent, it is not necessarily the basic or the real one or the so-called right one. As a matter of fact, in our analysis the allophone stop [d], although listed first as the exception and although less frequent than the other allophone, fricative [ḏ], is nonetheless considered more basic and fundamental than [ḏ] for reasons to be explained later.

Complementary Distribution

Knowing now what we do about the Spanish /d/ phoneme, we can set up a table of its distributional pattern according to its allophones and their phonetic environments.

Chart 14   Distribution of Spanish /d/

	After a Pause (Phrase-Initial)	After /l/	After/n/	"Elsewhere"
[d]	+	+	+	−
[đ]	−	−	−	+

Examples for [d] in the first three boxes on the first line are **Dígame, falda,** and **andar**; for [đ] in the last box on the second line are **cada, lodo, pierde, amígdalas.**

Even if the linguist did not find out the true story about Spanish /d/ through his search to find minimal pairs, such a pattern as we see in Chart 14 would lead him to suspect that these two phones, [d] and [đ], since they never seem to occur in the same environment, must be allophones of the same phoneme, namely /d/. This works, of course, only if the data are complete. Other assumptions must be made. For example, the unlikely, but re-motely possible coincidence that the sounds are really contrastive and phonemic and through completely random happenstance just never happen to occur in the same environment must be discounted. The linguist must also assume that, since no minimal pairs based on a supposed contrast between these two sounds can be found, a native speaker would recognize any word with the wrong allophone as the same word—although with an unusual sound. The word **lado,** pronounced [lá-do] with a stop [d] instead of [lá-đo] with a fricative [đ], would still mean *side*, but no native speaker would actually say it this way naturally. This means that if you, as a learner of Spanish, say [lá-do], although recognizable to a native speaker, it sounds odd or foreign, which is certainly not your aim when you speak Spanish. Likewise if you said [fál-đa] with a fricative [đ] instead of [fál-da] with a stop [d], for *skirt*, you're still saying *skirt*, but not the way Spanish speakers say it.

However, if you say [fál-ta] for *skirt*, communication could temporarily break down since, as you know, you are saying the word for *lack* or *mistake* rather than *skirt*. Why? Now you have not merely used the wrong *allophone* of /d/; you have crossed a phonemic boundary and used /t/ instead. This is a more serious error, as you might expect, based on the presumption that being understood and sounding odd or different is still better than not being understood at all.

Chart 14 shows a pattern of non-occurrence in the same position or the same phonetic environment, a situation known in linguistics as COMPLEMENTARY DISTRIBUTION. We can set up such a pattern for /t/ in English.

Chart 15   Distribution of English /t/

	After /s/	Between vowels, the first one of which is stressed	Word-final	Elsewhere
[t]	+	−	−	−
[t̂]	−	+	−	−
[t-]	−	−	+	−
[tʰ]	−	−	−	+

Example for [t] in the first box on the first line is *stop*; for [t̂] in the second box on the second line, *water*; for [t-] in the third box on the third line, *get*; and for [tʰ] in the last box on the fourth line, *top, deter, until, pertain.*

You will notice that one environment we have frequently talked about with regard to English /t/ seems to be missing above—namely ''word-initial.'' Why? Because there are at least two other environments for the aspirated [tʰ] in English: within a word before a stressed vowel, as in *deter*, and within a word after a consonant, as in *until* or *pertain*. Thus we are making use of the ''elsewhere'' convention to avoid complicating our chart by listing more environments than really need to be listed. It is simply convenient to talk about word-initial aspirated *t* in English, but ''word-initial'' is only one of several possible environments for this sound.

Free Variation

It would be nice and simple if allophones of the same phoneme always occurred in different, mutually exclusive environments, creating complementary distribution. But unfortunately, although most do most of the time, some occasionally do not. For example, in English, to show emphasis, you can use an aspirated [tʰ] rather than an unreleased [t-] at the end of a word at the end of a breath group: *Well, that's what you get!* Although the unreleased [t-] is much more common here, the aspirated [tʰ] is also possible.

As you might expect, exactly the same thing can happen in Spanish. The consonant /y/ has two allophones in Spanish: an affricate [ŷ], almost like the first sound in English *jet*, and a fricative [y], almost like the first sound in *yet*. The same Spanish speaker, for no reason apparent to you, may say **yo** with either sound, and, of course, with no change in meaning or even emphasis. When such a situation occurs, as with the varieties of English

/t/ and of Spanish /y/, we say that some of these allophones are occasionally in FREE or NON-FUNCTIONAL VARIATION rather than complementary distribution. This occurrence is random or determined by unknown or unimportant extralinguistic factors—such as style or attitude—rather than phonetic environment.

Actually native speakers in each case rarely realize when they are using allophones in free variation and usually do not even know why they do it when it is pointed out to them. However, foreigners learning the other language often notice this immediately and try to figure out why it is being done and whether they should do it, too. One mistaken reaction is that one of the two pronunciations is really incorrect or colloquial at best; another one is that it is dialectal. The phenomenon of free variation is far less common than complementary distribution, but when it occurs it is usually noticeable to the observant student. We will point out free variation in Spanish where it occurs and attempt to offer some explanation for its occurrence. Once again, the phenomenon, although interesting, is usually not critical since it is merely allophonic, *not* phonemic.

The statement of the properties of a phoneme and where its various allophones occur can be made in the form of a phonological rule or formula. Although these rules may seem unusual at first, they are really quite simple and straightforward when you become familiar with the use of each symbol.

Chart 16   Components of a Phonological Rule

/ / represents the phoneme in question (see the /d/ rule below).
→ means "is realized as" or "becomes."
[ ] represents an allophone.
/ means "in the environment of."
{ } to the left of the above diagonal enclose allophones, and { } to the right of the diagonal enclose the phonemes that form the phonetic environment. When two allophones occur in { } to the left of the diagonal one over the other, this shows free variation, often stylistically determined. In this case the top one shows the allophone that tends to be used in what we will call "careful," slower, or more formal speech and the lower one shows the allophone most often used in what we will call "casual," rapid, or more informal speech.
‖ represents the pause before and after the phonemic phrase or breath group, that is, one of its boundaries.

Chart 16 Components of a Phonological Rule (Continued)

represents a word boundary.
+ represents a morpheme (grammatical unit of meaning) boundary.
– represents a syllable boundary.
___ shows where the allophone in question occurs.
Ø represents silence, that is, the phoneme is omitted.
[ ] enclose the entire rule or formula.

Thus the following rule shows the distribution of the /d/ phoneme in Spanish.

$$/d/ \rightarrow \left[\begin{array}{l} [d] \Big/ \left\{ \begin{array}{l} \| \\ /l/ \\ /n/ \end{array} \right\} \underline{\quad} \\ \left\{ \begin{array}{l} [ð] \\ [Ø] \end{array} \right\} \Big/ \underline{\quad\quad} \# \\ [ð] \quad \text{elsewhere} \end{array} \right]$$

This rule says the following: the phoneme /d/ is realized as the stop [d] allophone in the following environments: after a pause ‖ , as in the ABSOLUTE-INITIAL position, after an /l/, and after an /n/, as **Dígame, falda,** and **anda.** It is realized either as a fricative [ð] in careful speech at the end of a word, or as [Ø] or silence in casual speech at the end of a word, as **verdad.** So it can be omitted completely: [ber-ðá]. This, of course, is free variation. It is realized as a fricative [ð] in all other positions, that is, *elsewhere*, as in **lado, pide, amígdalas,** and **pierde.** In Chapter 22 we will see even more possible cases of /d/ in the elsewhere position.

Remember that the braces { } to the left of the diagonal indicate free variation, that is, *either* allophone can be used in the environment indicated, although there are some guidelines for which one. But the braces to the right of the diagonal indicate that the allophones to the left occur in *all* these environments. So stop [d] must be used (1) after a pause ‖ *and* (2) after /l/ *and* (3) after /n/.

Once the symbols are learned, you can see that the rule is not only a concise description of the behavior of the phoneme, but also a convenient device for quick review of its allophonic distribution. These rules are not meant to be learned for their own sake, but instead to be used as a reminder of where speakers of General American Spanish use the various allophones of a phoneme. Thus, this is also a recommendation for you, a learner of Spanish, to do the same.

Phonemes and Allophones

To repeat, as you learn Spanish, you must make all the *phonemic* distinctions in the language or communication may temporarily break down, and ensuing confusion or embarrassment can result. The author recalls using the word **panales** (*honeycombs*) instead of **pañales** (*diapers*) in a conversation with a father-to-be from Colombia and the humor and embarrassment that followed this linguistic slipup. The two nasals /n/ and /ñ/ are phonemic in Spanish and not interchangeable. Nor can you point out how ''in the know'' or ''up on things'' someone is by saying **Está enterrado** instead of **enterado** because you have now put the poor individual in his grave; /r/ and /r̄/ are also phonemic in Spanish. You have surely heard foreign learners of English make similar embarrassing errors by inadvertently crossing phonemic boundaries.

But what about the allophones? Is stop [d] good enough in words like **lado, pierde, Estados Unidos**? Not if you want to do more than communicate in Spanish; that is, not if you want to sound like a native speaker. And if the Spanish speaker wants to sound like a North American, he must aspirate his word-initial *t*'s even though he never aspirates any *t*'s anywhere in his own language. Although *top* is still *top* even with an unaspirated [t], it just doesn't sound right to us. The whole matter is further complicated by the fact that the phonemes and the allophones of the two languages, Spanish and English, are never exactly the same in either quality or distribution. Spanish [ŷ], as in **¡Yo!**, and English, [ǰ], as in *Joe*, are quite close from an articulatory and certainly auditory point of view and can be substituted for each other cross-linguistically with little reaction on the part of either listener. But in English the sounds [y] and [ǰ], because they are allophones of different phonemes /y/ and /ǰ/ (now with slash bars), contrast as in *yellow-jello*, whereas in Spanish the corresponding sounds [y] and [ŷ] never contrast because they are just allophones of the same phoneme (thus no slash bars). The word **yo** can be said with either sound.

In each case there is a problem for the learner. When a Spanish speaker learns English, he must begin to make a meaningful distinction between two sounds that he has heretofore in his own language regarded as the same and that have occurred either automatically according to the phonetic environment (complementary distribution) or unpredictably (free variation). In both of these cases, the choice of the sounds is unimportant and below the level of the speaker's awareness; but this is not at all the case in the new language, English. Now if he uses one for the other, he risks an embarrassing error such as saying, ''My son is going to jail,'' when he means, ''My son is going to Yale.'' And you, as an English speaker learning Spanish, must get used to accepting either of these two sounds in a word like **yo** or **llamar** without attaching any special significance to one pronunciation or the other—since they are phonemes—as you have always done in English.

In the final analysis, a complete mastery of all the allophones of the foreign language, as well as the phonemes, is the essential goal of the learner who wishes to sound like a native speaker.

Review and Discussion

1. If a baby can make an infinite variety of sounds, why in just a couple of years can the child only make a couple dozen important ones?

2. Do all linguistics books use exactly the same phonetic symbols? Why or why not?

3. What is the meaning of the **boldface** type you frequently see in the textual passages of this book? How about *italics*? Square brackets [ ] ? Slash bars / / ?

4. In this book will we transcribe every Spanish sound that is known to exist? Why or why not? Other than nasalized vowels between nasal consonants, are there any other sounds you can think of in either Spanish or English that are produced automatically and obligatorily—completely below the level of awareness of the average speaker?

5. If you tried to tell a foreigner learning English where to use the aspirated [pʰ], the unaspirated [p], and the unreleased [p-], for example, how would you go about doing it? Would you try to make lists of common words, each of which is pronounced with one of the varieties of /p/? Why or why not?

6. What is the main difference between a phoneme and an allophone? This is actually a very hard question to answer without using examples from either Spanish or English to do so.

7. What is the meaning of an asterisk * before a word as it is used in this book? How about in a book on the history of the Spanish language? Could you show how you could use an asterisk in this way with people (personages) in past times rather than words in the language?

8. What's the quickest way to prove the existence of a phonemic contrast in any language? Can you do this for the vowels /a/ and /e/ in Spanish? How about /a/ and /ɛ/ in English. Hint: the word *pat* has neither of these vowels in it. You may have to check Charts 11 and 12 in Chapter 11 to get this one.

9. If you can't find two words to illustrate a phonemic contrast that you are pretty sure exists in Spanish or English, is such a contrast in doubt because you can't prove it? Explain.

10. There are several dozen sounds (phones) in Spanish, as there are in most languages. There are also thousands of words, making the task of finding the appropriate words to prove or disprove the phonemic contrast in question extremely daunting. Are there any shortcuts or preliminary steps you can take to prove what you want to prove?

11. Why give exceptions before the normal or the default sounds in phonology—the reverse of the way you may be used to hearing and stating rules? What is the name of this way of doing it?

12. What is complementary distribution? Free or non-functional variation? A definition is not much good without examples, so . . .

13. Is "rule" the only term to use to describe formulas, such as the one for Spanish /d/, which is shown in this chapter? Does a native speaker of Spanish approach or use these rules the same way you, as a student of Spanish, do? Why or why not?

14. When we say that [Ø] represents silence, what do we really mean? That the speaker actually stops talking? Can you think of any examples of this use of [Ø] in English?

13

Sound Groups in Spanish

Units of Language

When we talk about such terms as LETTERS, WORDS, SENTENCES, and PARAGRAPHS, we are talking about written symbols and groups. We determine and recognize these groups by visual rather than auditory criteria. Letters are special little black figures—either written or typed. *b* is a letter; ▼ is a symbol or sign, not a letter (at least not in English). Words are groups of these letters with spaces on either side of them, although occasionally we are not sure of the exact dimensions of a word since the criteria for determining words are a bit slippery and vague. *Bookcase* is definitely a word, and *run-in* maybe, but certainly not *wash-and-wear*.

Sentences are easier to determine: groups of words, the first of which begins with a large letter known as a CAPITAL and the last word of which is followed by a special small figure, known as a PUNCTUATION MARK. A paragraph is an even larger group—this time of sentences. Sometimes the paragraph is preceded by a blank space above it; sometimes its first word is moved or indented somewhat to the right of the left margin. Sometimes both of these devices are used, but at least one must be present so that we know we are dealing with a paragraph.

The definitions of these written groups are often arbitrary and occasionally inaccurate. But when it comes to sound groups, the parameters change and are fortunately easier to deal with.

Words in Spoken Spanish

In spoken English we can often pick out the words by little signals, like the aspirated [tʰ] at the beginning. Sometimes other features, which we will take up later, enable us to distinguish between such phrases as *Why choose?* and *white shoes*, or *syntax* and "*sin tax.*" In spoken Spanish, however, words are harder to pick out since their boundaries are rarely indicated in the stream of speech. This is one of the characteristics that makes you think Spanish sounds so fast when spoken by native speakers. Out of context and in isolation (admittedly a rare situation in real language use, but a possible one), there is absolutely no way that you can decide whether the sequence of sounds you have heard is **el hijo** or **elijo**, **un aparte** or **una parte**, . . . **la sabes** or . . . **las aves**. A child of a Spanish-speaking acquaintance of the author was surprised to find out at school when she began to learn to read and write that the word for *grapes* was **uvas** and not *suvas. Why? Because in her lifetime up to that point she probably had never heard the word in its singular form—only plural—and never alone but always in a phrase like **las uvas**, **tus uvas**, **más uvas**, and so forth. She divided up the sequence in her mind incorrectly, putting the **-s** from the end of the previous word at the beginning of the next word, **uvas**, just as you might mistakenly do with one of the Spanish phrases above. This simple anecdote illustrates one of most important concepts that you will deal with in learning the sound system of Spanish: LINKING. (More on this shortly.)

The lack of discernible word boundaries in spoken Spanish is best shown in a phonetic transcription. For example, the Spanish sentence **Los alumnos están en el aula** *The students are in the classroom* can be transcribed several ways: [lo sa lúm no ses tá ne ne láu̯ la] or perhaps [losalúmnosestáneneláu̯la] (which is really closest to the way it really sounds) or, as we will do it in this book, [lo-sa-lúm-no-ses-tá-ne-ne-láu̯-la], showing the syllable boundaries, but not, of course, word boundaries. We will shortly see several advantages to showing the syllable boundaries, not the least of which is that it is simply easier to read and to work with. At any rate, any one of the three ways above is a much better representation of the sentence **Los alumnos están en el aula** than these boldface letters are because of what we have already said about word boundaries in spoken Spanish. The word just does not have as much importance in spoken Spanish as the smaller group, the SYLLABLE, or the larger group, the PHONEMIC PHRASE (known also as the BREATH GROUP or the INTONATIONAL GROUP).

The Syllable in Spanish

The most basic group in phonetics, and the smallest, is the syllable. It, too, is sometimes difficult to define precisely, and its nature varies from one language to the next. Nevertheless, native speakers of any language seem intuitively to be able to figure out how many syllables a given utterance in their language has even if they have little idea of what a syllable really is and do not know exactly where the syllable boundaries are.

Approaching the problem from a physiological point of view, we might say that the syllable is the sound produced between two successive occurrences of muscular tension in the vocal tract and breathing apparatus. The syllable, then, might be regarded as a type of pulse. From an acoustic point of view, the syllable can be the stretch of sound which occurs between two successive depressions in the perceptibility of the stream of sound.

But the easiest way to define a syllable in Spanish is to approach it from a functional point of view: what is the nature of the sounds making up the syllable and how do they pattern? Certain combinations or sequences of segmental phonemes—vowels and consonants—are possible in Spanish, and others are not. Only certain sequences can begin a syllable, a few can end one, and the others must be divided to form the end of one syllable and the beginning of the next. Adjacent consonants in the breath group form a SEQUENCE, but only those in the *same syllable* form a CLUSTER. A handy rule-of-thumb, and more than just a coincidence, is the fact that any consonant sequence that cannot cluster to *begin* a word in Spanish cannot cluster to begin a syllable either. Thus, such words as **isla**, **perla**, and **hasta**, must be divided **is-la**, **per-la**, and **has-ta**, for the same reason that no Spanish word starts with *sl-, *rl-, or *st-. The same principle, however, does not hold for the *ends* of syllables and words. No Spanish word, for example, ends with *ns, but this cluster can end a syllable: **ins-tan-te**. Since at this point you are probably more familiar with Spanish words than syllables, you can rely on this knowledge and remember that no syllable can *begin* with a consonant cluster that cannot also begin a word. Thus an English speaker keying in text on a computer syllabicates *instant* at the end of a line as *in-stant*, based on the dictionary and even his word processor's hyphenation program. But a Spanish speaker keying in text syllabicates **instante** as **ins-tante** or perhaps **instan-te**, but never *in-stante** because *st- simply cannot begin a word or a syllable in Spanish.

Syllabication in Spanish

The rules for Spanish syllabication are quite clearcut and followed by every Spanish speaker who knows anything about spelling rules. Unfortunately, this is not true of English. This author's dictionary has the following syllabication of *travel* listed on successive lines: *tra-vel agency* and *trav-el agent*. The average educated English speaker must frequently rely on a dictionary or a word-processing hyphenation program to find these answers. Fortunately, this is never necessary in Spanish.

But SYLLABICATION has even greater importance for us than merely determining how we hyphenate words at the end of a line of text. The syllable often determines the phonetic environment, which as we know now, often in turn determines the quality of the individual sounds. Before going on to the five rules of Spanish syllabication, let's consider a few definitions.

An OPEN SYLLABLE is one that ends in a vowel (including the letter **y**, which sometimes represents the sound /i/ at the end of a word): **no, ma-no, re-ve-la, hoy**. A CLOSED SYLLABLE is one that ends in one or two consonants (excluding the letter **y**, which represents /i/ at the end of a word): **más, már-tir, im-por-tan-tes, trans-por-tan**.

A DIPHTHONG is a cluster of two vowels, one of which must be an unstressed /i/ or /u/, *fused* into a single syllable: **seis, hay, cau-sa, deu-da, sie-te, pio-jo, bue-no, muy**. If either the /í/ or the /ú/ is stressed, the sequence is *not* a diphthong but is composed of separate syllables, a situation called HIATUS: **mí-o, le-ís-te, ba-úl, con-ti-nú-a**. Don't forget that verbs, nouns, and adjectives are stressed in the stream of speech (refer to Chapter 6), so there are words containing a stressed /í/ that you might overlook because they do not have written accents. Thus a phrase like **Vi animales por todas partes** does not have a diphthong at the beginning since **vi** as a verb form has a stressed /í/: **Vi-a-ni-ma-les . . .** This opening sequence is exactly the same as that of the word **vía: ví-a** and not like that of **viaje: via-je**, which does have a diphthong because of the unstressed /i/ next to another vowel.

A TRIPHTHONG is a cluster of three vowels *fused* into a single syllable because the first and third vowels are any combination of unstressed /i/ and /u/: **es-tu-diáis, a-ve-ri-guáis, buey, Bioy** (proper name). Notice that the *middle* of the three vowels may be stressed and usually is, but as long as the /i/ and/or /u/ on either side of it has no stress, we have a triphthong. They are particularly common in Castilian Spanish because of the **vosotros** verb forms, which all end in **-is**, and, which, of course, are not used in American Spanish.

A SEMI-VOWEL is an unstressed /i/ or /u/ fused with an adjoining vowel in the same syllable, as in a diphthong or triphthong. The semi-vowel may come first: **sie-te, bue-no**, second: **seis, deu-da**; or first and last: **es-tu-diáis**.

A MONOPHTHONG is a syllable consisting of only a single vowel, as contrasted with diphthong and triphthong above.

Syllables are formed in Spanish in basically the same way in sound and in writing (within one word, at least). These rules are absolutely regular and followed in writing with great consistency by all educated speakers of the language. In the following abbreviated rules, **C** = any consonant *sound*; C̲ = the consonants /l/ or /r/; V = any vowel sound *except* an unstressed /i/ or /u/; V̲ = an unstressed /i/ or /u/. These rules refer only to the critical part of the syllable. There may be sounds or letters before or after the C or V, but they are irrelevant to the point where the syllable is divided.

Rules for Spanish Syllabication

1. **V-CV (or V-C̲V)**   This means that a single consonant sound between two vowels always starts the *next* syllable: **o-so, ma-no, o-la, o-ro, re-ve-la-do.** This shows how Spanish favors *open* syllables wherever possible. The letter combinations **ch, ll,** and **rr** are DIGRAPHS or pairs of letters that each represent only *one sound* and therefore are not separated: **ha-cha, ca-lle, pe-rro.** English has digraphs, too: *ch, ck, ph, sh, th,* for example.

2. **V-CCV**   The first possibility of two adjoining consonants between vowels or at the beginning of a word is a syllable-initial CLUSTER as long as they are one of the following 12 groups: **pl, pr, bl, br, tr, dr, cl** (/kl/ in sound), **cr** (/kr/ in sound), **gl, gr, fl, fr**. You will notice that the initial consonants are the six stops + **f**, that **l** /l/ or **r** /r/ is the second member of each cluster, and that **tl** and **dl** are missing from the stop groups.[1] Remember that these 12 syllable-initial consonant clusters are also the only possible *word-initial*

---

[1]The initial cluster **tl-** is possible only in the Spanish of Mexico, Guatemala, and El Salvador because of the many names and borrowed words from Nahuatl and other Meso-American languages: **Tlaxcala, Tlacotalpan, tlapalería.** No dialect of Spanish has the initial cluster ***dl-**.

consonant clusters in Spanish. Following are examples of each, both at the beginning of a word and within a word.

pl	pla-ya, a-pli-car	cl	cli-ma, bu-cle
pr	pro-bar, o-pri-mir	cr	cre-ma, la-cre
bl	blan-co, do-ble	gl	glo-ria, i-gle-sia
br	bri-sa, a-bre	gr	gris, a-grio
tr	tres, o-tro	fl	flor, chi-fla-do
dr	dra-ma, la-drar	fr	frí-o, co-fre

VC-CV   The second possibility of two adjoining consonants between vowels is a *sequence* of two consonants other than those above, which must be divided, one with each syllable. Notice that **s** is in this part of the rule and not above with the syllable-initial clusters. This means, of course, that no Spanish word begins with **sC** or **sC**, as we have in English with *spirit* or *slam*. Following are a few examples of divided consonant sequences, all necessarily within words.

r-l	per-la	r-s	Pér-si-co
b-t	ob-te-ner	b-y	ab-yec-to
c-c	lec-ción	t-b	fút-bol
n-d	gran-de	c-t	ac-to
s-f	es-fe-ra	s-c	es-ca-par

3.   **VC-CCV**   The first possibility of three adjoining consonants between vowels is a syllable-final consonant and a syllable-initial cluster, which must be one of the 12 in rule 2, above. The first consonant goes with the preceding vowel, and the next two start the next syllable. Here are some examples, all within words, of course.

m-br	hom-bre	m-bl	a-sam-ble-a
m-pr	siem-pre	m-pl	sim-ple
l-fr	Al-fre-do	l-dr	sal-drá
n-cl	an-cla	n-tr	en-trar
s-pr	des-pren-der	s-tr	as-tro

VCC-CV   The second possibility of three adjoining consonants between vowels is a syllable-final cluster and a single syllable-initial consonant. The second consonant in these syllable-final clusters is always /s/. The sound group /ks-/ in these cases is spelled with an **x**. Here are some examples, all within words, of course.

ns-p	trans-por-te	ns-t	ins-tan-te
x-p (/ks-p/)	ex-per-to	x-t (/ks-t/)	ex-tin-guir
rs-p	pers-pi-caz	ns-c	trans-cur-so

4.   **VCC-CCV**   The only possibility of four adjoining consonants between vowels is a syllable-final cluster and then a syllable-initial cluster, a relatively rare combination in Spanish. The second consonant of the first cluster is almost always /s/ (sometimes spelled

with an **x** and thus really /ks-/), and the second cluster is always one of the 12 we have already seen in rules 2 and 3: **pl, pr, bl,** and so on.

ns-pl   trans-plan-te   bs-tr   obs-truc-ción

5.   **V-V**   The first and by far most frequent possibility of two adjoining vowels is the hiatus situation, that is, each vowel in a separate syllable. Don't forget that **V** can also stand for a stressed /í/ or /ú/ as well as any /a/, /e/, or /o/. These five are the so-called ''strong'' vowels in Spanish. Here are some examples.

e-a	cre-a	o-e	po-e-ta
e-o	cre-o	o-a	clo-a-ca
a-e	ca-e	a-o	ca-os
e-í	le-í	í-e	rí-e
a-í	ca-í	í-a	dí-a
o-í	o-ís-te	í-o	mí-o
a-ú	ba-úl	ú-a	grú-a
e-ú	re-ú-ne	ú-e	gra-dú-e

VV, VV, VVV   The remaining vowel combinations consist of unstressed /i/ or /u/ —the semi-vowels (and thus ''weak'' vowels)—beside another vowel in the same syllable. If an /i/ or a /u/ occurs *before* a /u/ or an /i/, respectively, the first one is always the semi-vowel. Here are some examples, first of diphthongs, then triphthongs.

ia	via-je	ai	hay
ie	sie-te	ei	seis
io	pio-jo	oi	boi-na
ua	sua-ve	au	cau-sa
ue	bue-no	eu	deu-da
uo	cuo-ta	ou	(no common Spanish
iu	viu-da		words with
ui	rui-do		this diphthong)
iei	es-tu-diéis	uei	gra-duéis
uai	con-ti-nuáis	uau	guau-guau

Exceptions in Spanish Syllabication

There are a few minor exceptions to these basic rules of syllabication and also one apparent exception, which is really not one. There are some words with internal consonant sequences that are divided as above in speaking but differently in writing because of their structure. For example, all speakers say **sublevar** as **su-ble-var**, but, in writing at the end of a line, many divide it **sub-levar,** since they know this word has a common prefix **sub-**. The same is true of words like **bienestar, desagradable**, and **inoportuno**. In writing at the end of a line, they may divide them as **bien-estar, des-agradable,** and **in-oportuno** because of the obvious prefixes, but in speaking they are, as the rules above indicate, **bie-nestar, de-sagradable,** and **i-noportuno.** One common word with a **sub-** prefix, **sub-rayar** *to underline*, is at first an apparent exception since it is divided both in writing and in speaking **sub-rayar.** But this word is not really an example of **V-CCV**, as is **so-b<u>r</u>e**, for example, but really of **VC-CV.** This is because the first **r** of **subrayar** represents the *trill* phoneme /r̄/, not the *tap* phoneme /r/, which is the second member of the 12 clusters listed in rules 2, 3, and 4, above. Thus, there are a few exceptions to these rules of syllabication in written Spanish but none in the spoken language.

The Phonemic Phrase

After the syllable the next most important sound group is not the word, the clause, or the sentence, but rather the PHONEMIC PHRASE (also referred to as the BREATH GROUP or the INTONATION GROUP). It is the stream of sounds produced between two pauses no matter how slight. Each group, as we have seen, has a particular intonation pattern and ends with one of the three terminal junctures: ↑ → ↓ . Each Spanish speaker, just as you do, makes frequent pauses in his or her speech for a variety of reasons: to separate grammatical groups, to emphasize certain words, to think, to remember, to breathe, to swallow. But in Spanish all the sounds of the breath group are run together and pronounced *just as though they were in one single word.* As we have said, Spanish speakers do not normally observe word boundaries when they speak—as we often do in English—unless they have a very compelling reason to do so. Out of context there is just no way in Spanish to distinguish between the spoken phrases **la sabes** *you know it* and **las aves** *the birds.* Fortunately, as you might expect, it is rare for two such phrases to be confused in real language use, but many times you, as a student of Spanish, are stumped by unfamiliar words because you are not sure of their boundaries.

The first sound of the phonemic phrase, that is, the first sound after a pause, is called ABSOLUTE-INITIAL. (It could also be called GROUP-INITIAL or PHONEMIC PHRASE-INITIAL.) This is to distinguish it from syllable-initial, which we looked at above, and word-initial, which has some importance in Spanish phonology, but not nearly as much as syllable- or absolute-initial. This first position of the phonemic phrase is so important because several Spanish phonemes have different allophones whose occurrence depends on whether the phoneme occurs *within* the phonemic phrase or at the very beginning. For example, in the last chapter we saw that the phoneme /d/ was realized as a stop [d] after a pause (absolute-initial), after an /l/, and after an /n/, but as a fricative [ð] elsewhere, that is, everywhere except these first three environments, including, of course, between vowels. You should note that the *word* was never included as one of the determining environments. This means that the phrase **D<u>í</u>gale la verdad** has a stop [d]—*not* because it comes at the beginning of the word **diga** but because it comes at the beginning of the entire phonemic phrase or breath group as the absolute-initial. Also the word **verdad** has two fricative [ð]'s because the /d/ is not absolute-initial, not after an /l/, not after an /n/, but in the elsewhere position.

Let's change the phrase to **No le diga la verdad**. The /d/'s in the word **verdad** are the same. But now the initial /d/ of **diga** is a *fricative* [ð] rather than the stop [d] that it is in the affirmative command where the word **diga** started the group. The word **diga** means exactly the same thing to a Spanish speaker whether it has a stop [d] or a fricative [ð]. But he or she automatically chooses the correct allophone according to the phonetic environment, absolute-initial being one of the various positions that make it up. It means that **diga** with a fricative [ð] in **Dígale la verdad** sounds odd, and **diga** with a stop [d] in **No le diga la verdad** sounds odd. The meaning is the same, but it just doesn't sound right. Thus, you as a learner must do it the way Spanish speakers do to sound right, too.

Linking

The next important concept in looking at how sounds group together in Spanish is LINKING. This means that, because of the first rule of syllabication above—namely, that a single consonant between two vowels goes with the next vowel to start the syllable (**V-CV**), the same situation holds *between* words in the phonemic phrase as well as *within* words. So when a word ending in a consonant precedes a word beginning with a vowel—within the phonemic phrase, of course—linking (or **enlace**) occurs. Thus the phrase **el oro** is really pronounced [e-ló-ro], **el hombre** is really pronounced [e-lóm-bre], and **las aves** sounds just like **la sabes**: [la-sá-ßes]. Many phrases have a series of such linkings: **Los alumnos están en el aula para estudiar español** [lo-sa-lúm-no-ses-tá-ne-ne-láu-la-pa-ra-es-tu-ðiá-res-pa-ñól]. Once again you should now be able to understand the Spanish-speaking girl's mistaken notion that the word for *grapes* was *suvas. She had probably almost always heard the word with **enlace** almost every single time in her entire life.

Diphthongs

Not only does **enlace** occur within the phonemic phrase, but also DIPHTHONGS can occur across word boundaries as long as the /i/ or /u/ involved is unstressed. Thus the phrase **se imagina** [sei-ma-xí-na] has the same diphthong [ei] in it as the word **seis** [seis], the phrase **está usted** [es-táus-téð] has the same diphthong [au] as the word **causa** [káu-sa], and so forth. But if the /í/ or /ú/ is stressed we have hiatus or separate syllables: **caí** and **la isla** have the same sequence [a-í]. Despite the fact that **isla** does not have a written accent due to the rules of Spanish spelling, as a noun it still has a stressed /í/, which is clearly heard in the stream of speech. Likewise with **baúl** and **la uva**, both of which have the hiatus sequence [a-ú] despite the lack of a written accent on the noun **uva**.

The letter **h**, which represents silence or has no sound in Spanish (except when it occurs in the digraph **ch**), has no effect whatsoever on any of these combinations. **La hija** has the same sequence [a-í] at the word boundary as the words **la isla** have or **caí** has within the word. **Esta historia** has the same diphthong [ai] at the word boundary as the words **esta italiana** have or **Jaime** has within the word.

Syllabication of Identical Consonants

Except for **ll** and **rr**, digraphs representing just *one* sound, two identical consonant letters are divided because they represent identical consonant sounds that occur in separate syllables. Most of these sequences occur between words: **la-bon-dad-de. . .** , **el-li-bro, un-nom-bre, más-sua-ve,** although there are a few cases of **b-b** and **n-n** within words: **ob-vio** (**v** respresents /b/), **in-na-to.**

Marking Phonemic Phrases

The native speaker of Spanish pauses naturally without thinking about it, and these pauses, wherever they occur, form the boundaries of his or her phonemic phrases. If you are transcribing his or her speech phonetically, you should have no problem deciding where the phonemic phrases are because the native speaker decides this and reveals it quite clearly by the terminal junctures and pauses, however slight. But if you are speaking Spanish or transcribing a written passage for practice, you yourself must make the decisions as to where to make these pauses. In writing, punctuation is a fairly good indication of phonemic phrase boundaries. To be sure, native speakers often make pauses where there would be no written punctuation, and conversely they often do not make pauses where there would be written punctuation. But when you are working with a written text—as you will usually be doing for the practices in this book—and have no spoken Spanish to listen to, you can assume that almost every punctuation mark (except quotation marks and apostrophes) indicates a pause of some sort and thus the end of the phonemic phrase.

There will be other pauses, however, *not* marked by punctuation. Any native speaker often makes junctures and pauses between relatively long syntactic elements, such as between a subject and its predicate or between two clauses: **El hombre que les habló ayer ‖ es el nuevo jefe de la compañía petrolera** or **Vaya usted a la oficina ‖ y la encuentra en el pasillo.**

For **Practice B,** following, you should use conventional letters of the alphabet, hyphens for the syllables, accent marks for the primary stresses, and vertical lines ‖ for any pauses you decide to make. The last sentence in the previous paragraph should be marked as follows: **Vá-yaus-té-da-la-o-fi-cí-na ‖ y-la-en-cuén-tra-e-nel-pa-sí-llo.** This admittedly looks a little strange until you realize that you are showing the sentence as it is really pronounced with **enlace,** diphthongs between words, and all the primary stresses. However, this is not yet a real phonetic transcription; these will start in Chapter 15, and you will be given complete instructions on how to do them at that time.

Practice

A.

Using regular orthography, divide the following words into syllables with hyphens, according to speech. Do not divide any prefixes you see just because they are prefixes. Be sure to mark all the primary stresses by underlining the stressed vowel.

1. aborigen	15. país	29. subrayar
2. construcción	16. quebrar	30. ahí
3. buey	17. graduáis	31. hoyuelo
4. lechero	18. instruido	32. día
5. tranquilizar	19. subversión	33. institución
6. hay	20. inhumano	34. ahumado
7. desastroso	21. habituarse	35. corrió
8. paisano	22. caos	36. obviar
9. aún	23. transplante	37. poesía
10. caudillo	24. deuda	38. amarrar
11. innovación	25. extraordinario	39. oído
12. malograr	26. pasear	40. baúl
13. constante	27. aunque	
14. ahogar	28. homogeneidad	

B.

Using regular orthography, divide the following phrases and sentences into syllables with hyphens, and mark all the primary stresses by underlining the stressed vowel and identifying all pauses with ‖ . Handle any prefixes the same way you did in Practice A.

1. el animal
2. el hijo
3. la hija
4. la hijita
5. las hijas
6. hablan español
7. su ave
8. mi amigo
9. mis amigos
10. para este hijito
11. se veía muy bien
12. en Ecuador
13. son hombres
14. son nombres
15. las obras
16. las sobras
17. la odio
18. hable usted

19. la honra
20. por el amor a mi patria
21. La isla se halla en el Mediterráneo.
22. Las llamas van por las calles de Cuzco.
23. La chica delgada corrió tras el perro.
24. Tienes que subrayar todos los elementos interesantes.
25. El chícharo se cultiva mucho en Puerto Rico.
26. A mi hija no le gustan para nada las corridas de toros.
27. El búho estaba de mal humor y no quiso cantar.
28. Se prohíbe fijar carteles en estos muros de la ciudad.
29. El árbitro gritó en voz alta, "¡Rudeza innecesaria!"
30. Todos los miembros de nuestra clase se reúnen en esta aula en la planta baja.

C.

Answer the following questions briefly.

1. Which items in Practices A and B have diphthongs? Triphthongs? Don't forget that these vowel groups can occur across word boundaries, too, as long as there is not an intervening pause or juncture.
2. Which items have vowel sequences in hiatus (that is, separate syllables)? These, too, can occur across word boundaries.
3. How do you know that some of the examples in Practice B that you chose to answer question 2, above, really have a stressed /í/ or a stressed /ú/ when the **i** or **u** in question does not have a written accent?
4. Point out the cases of **enlace** or linking in Practice B.

14

Introducing the Vowels of Spanish

Classifying Vowels in Spanish

Vowels are distinguished from consonants by the fact that the airstream is not blocked or impeded by the upper and lower articulators. The quality of vowels is determined by the size and shape of the resonance chambers: the oral cavity (mouth) and the pharynx (throat). These shapes, in turn, are created by the position of the tongue on both a vertical axis and a horizontal axis (see Diagrams 5 and 6 in Chapter 11).

There are three vertical positions of the tongue: HIGH, where the front or back of the tongue is close to the palate or velum; MID, where it is about halfway down in the mouth; and LOW, where it is very low in the mouth. There are also three tongue positions on a front-to-back axis: FRONT, where the highest part of the tongue, the blade, is fairly close to the alveolar ridge; CENTRAL, where the highest part of the tongue is in the center of the oral cavity; and BACK, where the highest part of the tongue, the dorsum, is fairly close to the velum.

Thus, we can classify vowels in this two-dimensional fashion. In Spanish there are five meaningful or phonemic positions.

1. HIGH FRONT: /i/ as in **piso**
2. MID FRONT: /e/ as in **peso**
3. LOW CENTRAL: /a/ as in **paso**
4. MID BACK: /o/ as in **poso**
5. HIGH BACK: /u/ as in **puso**

These vowels can be plotted on a quadrangular grid.

Chart 17   Spanish Vowel Phonemes: The Grid

	Front	Central	Back
High	i		u
Mid	e		o
Low		a	

But it is most common in Spanish phonetics and phonology to represent them on what is traditionally called the vowel triangle.

Chart 18   Spanish Vowel Phonemes: The Triangle

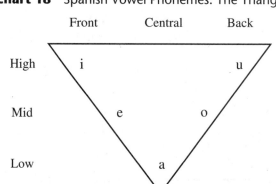

As you can see (refer again to Diagrams 5 and 6 in Chapter 11), the vowel positions in either of these two configurations are a rough approximation of the place in the mouth where the air flows through between the tongue and upper articulators, that is, the alveolar ridge, the palate, and the velum.

Classifying Vowels in English

The Spanish vocalic system is the simplest and most symmetrical of any of the languages commonly studied by North Americans. The vocalic system of American English is more varied and complicated than that of Spanish and must be represented on a quadrangular grid rather than a triangle because of the two additional central vowels and the two additional low vowels.

Chart 19   English Vowel Phonemes: The Grid

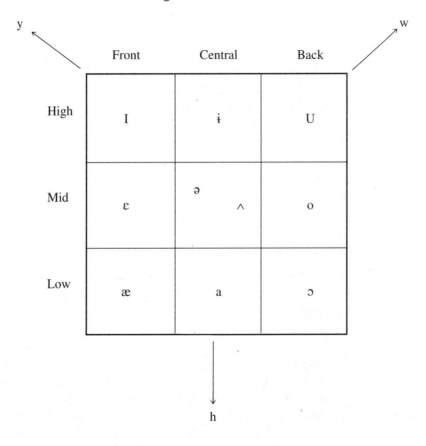

Some dialects of North American English have only nine vowel phonemes, lacking the contrast between /ɑ/ and /ɔ/, having the intermediate vowel /ɑ/ instead. These speakers pronounce *cot* and *caught* with the same vowel: /kɑt/, rather than as /kat/ and /kɔt/, respectively. Also you see the arrow representing the movement of the tongue to pronounce the three glides: /y/ (palatal), /w/ (velar), and /h/ (low), all of which function either as syllable-initial consonants or post-vocalic semi-vowels (the second element of a diphthong). Thus we have in North American English, depending on the dialect, the following vowels.

1. HIGH FRONT: /I/ as in *pit*
2. MID FRONT: /ɛ/ as in *pet*
3. LOW FRONT: /æ/ as in *pat*
4. HIGH CENTRAL: /ɨ/ as in the first syllable of *just a minute* or the last syllable of *bucket*
5. MID CENTRAL (UNSTRESSED): /ə/ as in the first syllable of *appear*
6. MID CENTRAL (STRESSED): /ʌ/ as in the adjective *just*
7. LOW CENTRAL: /a/ as in *pot*
8. HIGH BACK: /U/ as in *put*
9. MID BACK: /o/ as in the first syllable of *obey*
10. LOW BACK: /ɔ/ as in *bought* (as said by some speakers of eastern dialects of North American English)
11. HIGH FRONT GLIDE: /y/, the last sound in *say*
12. HIGH BACK GLIDE: /w/, the last sound in *now*
13. LOW CENTRAL GLIDE: /h/, the last sound in *paw* or the last sound in the pronunciation of *car* in the ''*r*-less'' dialects of English

The diphthongs (also called COMPLEX VOWEL NUCLEI) in North American English end in one of the three glides: /y/ as in *bee* /bIy/, *bay* /bɛy/, *buy* /bay/, *boy* /boy/; /w/ as in *new* /nUw/, *no* /now/, *now* /naw/ or /næw/; /h/ as in *paw* /pɔh/ or the Eastern ''*r*-less'' pronunciation of *poor* /pUh/, *pour* /poh/, *par* /pah/.

Vowels and Dialect Differences

As you might expect, not all dialects of English have all 40 possible combinations made up of these ten vowels plus the 30 vowel + glide diphthongs, or any number even close to it. But this rich vocalic system means that pronunciation differences between the dialects of English are due mainly to variations in the vowels and how they combine with the glides. In Spanish, however, dialectal differences are due mainly to consonantal variations—partly because Spanish has such a simple vowel system. As already shown, the Spanish vocalic system is much more uniform and symmetrical than that of any other language commonly studied by North Americans. There are a few minor vocalic variations, but only /i/ and /u/ have important allophones, a semi-vowel in each case. Some linguists recognize other vowel allophones, but these distinctions are minor, hard to perceive, and depend so much on phonetic environment that, just as Spanish speakers do, English speakers usually pronounce them automatically.

Vowel Modifications

As we saw in Chapter 11, there are several possible vowel modifications, a couple of which happen in certain dialects of Spanish. Lip-rounding, although functional and contrastive in a language like French or German, happens automatically in both Spanish and English. The back vowels /o/ and /u/ in both languages are rounded; the rest are not. Nasalization, although functional or contrastive in languages like French, Portuguese, and Polish, also happens automatically in Spanish and English. Any vowel between two nasal consonants in either language is automatically nasalized: **mono** [mõ-no], *monkey* [mÃŋ-kỉy]. The fact that such nasalization is automatic, is never contrastive, and is even below the level of awareness of the average Spanish and English speaker has led us to ignore it completely in our analysis and in the inventory of Spanish phones and thus in the phonetic transcriptions as well. Vowel length is important in a language like German where several LONG VOWELS are phonemically distinct from their short counterparts. In English, vowel length is automatic: all vowels are lengthened before voiced consonants: *mate-made, mace-maze*, and so on. In Spanish, however, vowel length, although never phonemic in any dialect, is a characteristic and identifying feature of certain ones.

Vowel Shortening and Devoicing in Spanish

Both VOWEL SHORTENING (or REDUCTION) and DEVOICING OF VOWELS (or "WHISPERED" VOWELS) are common in Mexican and Andean Spanish.

Vowel shortening is represented by the small superscribed letters and occurs in these dialects mainly with unstressed vowels, particularly those immediately before or after the main stress of the word: **posesiones** [po-s^e-si̯ó-nes], **ayudar** [a-y^u-ɖár], **las gallinas** [laz-ǵ^a-yí-n^{a}s]. These reduced vowels, however, although much shorter than normal ones, maintain their quality and are not really the same as the neutral unstressed schwa [ə] of English.

Devoiced or whispered vowels are represented by a small circle under the letter. Although the airstream passes through the characteristic vowel opening created by the configuration of the lips, tongue, and mouth, the vocal bands either vibrate not at all or only partially during the articulation of such a vowel. This usually happens in the unstressed syllable following the stress and particularly after or before a voiceless consonant: **pesos** [pé-sọs], **veinticinco** [béi̯ṇ-ti̯-síṇ-kọ], **suculenta** [su-ku-léṇ-ta̡], **ocho** [ó-ĉọ], **haces** [á-sẹs]. Sometimes vowel reduction and devoicing are combined: **gracias** [grá-si̯^{a}s], **accidente de coches** [ak-si-ɖéṇ-t^e-ɖe-kó-ĉ^{e}s].

Although both of these last two vowel modifications are heard in Mexico and the Andean countries, not all speakers use them and the speakers who use them do not do so all the time. If you hear them among Spanish speakers around you and decide to use them, too, be careful not to articulate the English unstressed vowel [ə], which is not the same as these reduced and devoiced vowels and does not exist in Spanish.

Despite the simplicity of the Spanish vocalic system, it contains two main pitfalls for English speakers, both of which naturally originate in features of the English vowel system.

In English, syllables almost never end with *stressed vowels*, but instead with a consonant or one of the three glides indicated above: /y w h/. Thus, the vowels that school teachers have traditionally called "long" are in reality complex vowel nuclei or diphthongs composed of vowel + glide (or semi-vowel). *No* has three phonemes or sounds: /nów/;

new likewise has three: /nÚw/; *bee* is really /bÍy/; and *bay* is /bɛ́y/; *sigh* is /sáy/; and so forth.

But in Spanish, stressed vowels very commonly end syllables: **no** /nó/; **tú** /tú/; **vi** /bí/; **ve** /bé/; and so forth. Unaccustomed to such patterns, you may tend to pronounce these Spanish words with the same complex vowel nuclei or diphthongs of English: */nów/, */tÚw/, */bÍy/, */bɛ́y/, and so forth. Not only does this sound wrong to the Spanish speaker, but the problem is further complicated by the fact that Spanish, too, has a few complex vowel nuclei or diphthongs, but *they are always represented in writing* and contrast with simple vowels. Spanish has both **le** /le/ *to him* and **ley** /léi/ *law*, both **pena** /péna/ *pain* and **peina** /péina/ *she combs*. Thus, there may be phonemic confusion as well as phonetic inaccuracy if the simple vowels in Spanish are not pronounced properly.

The other major problem, which is even more prevalent and critical, concerns *unstressed vowels* in Spanish. In English most unstressed syllables contain the neutral central vowels [ɨ] and [ə], both spelled with many different vowel letters or combinations thereof: *captain, atom, madam, porpoise, haven, muffin, marvelous, campus, luncheon,* and so on. So it is natural for you to have a tendency to use one or both of these vowels in Spanish unstressed syllables. This is unacceptable for two reasons. First, it sounds wrong, and, second, it may destroy a phonemic contrast such as those that exist in noun and adjective gender or verb tense endings: * /dəríə/ could be **daría** *I would give* or **diría** *I would say*, a logical substitution; * /miermánə/ could be **mi hermano** or **mi hermana**, leaving your interlocutor to guess at the sex of your sibling.

Both of these problems are serious ones for you as an English speaker learning the sound system of Spanish and will be dealt with repeatedly in the coming chapters.

15

The Low Vowel /a/ and the Mid Vowels /e/ and /o/

Allophone of /a/

The vowel /a/ in Spanish has one allophone [a], a low central oral vowel.

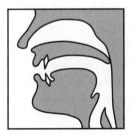

[a]

Description of /a/ Allophone

For [a] the velum is closed, as it is for all oral vowels, the mouth is quite open, and the lips are neither spread nor rounded but in an intermediate position. The tip of the tongue rests near the lower front teeth. The tongue body lies low and level in the mouth. Spanish [a] is similar to the English [a] in *hot* in most North American dialects, but it is somewhat more open, tenser, and shorter in duration.

Distribution of /a/

Since /a/ has only one allophone, the low central vowel [a], the rule is simple:

/a/ → [a]   **la casa, hasta**

There are no important dialectal variations of /a/ other than the reduction or devoicing explained in Chapter 14.

Contrasts with English

You must be careful to place your tongue low enough for unstressed Spanish [a] and avoid the English mid central vowel [ə] as in *[ká-sə] for **casa** or * [es-pə-ñól] for **español**. This is done by deliberately opening your mouth more, putting your tongue as low as possible in the mouth, and slightly prolonging this [a] sound. If you use a [ə], for example, for the first /a/ in the word **daría** *I would give*, your listener might mistake it for **diría** *I would say*, a logical possibility in the discourse. Or if you need a couple more **mesas**, it may sound like you need more time, namely a couple more months (**meses**).

Stressed /á/ in Spanish should not be too elongated, causing **casa** to have the same first vowel as *father* (as many textbooks mistakenly recommend) and come out as [ká:-sa]. (A colon in phonetics indicates lengthening of the previous sound.) As we pointed out in the previous chapter, a few dialects in the eastern United States (such as in western Pennsylvania, for example) make no distinction between *cot* and *caught*, or *body* and *bawdy,* using a low vowel /ɑ/, made with the tongue retracted somewhat from the central position, instead of /a/ and /ɔ/, respectively. Using this vowel in Spanish will blur the distinction between **hambre** and **hombre** or **casa** and **cosa**, for example.

Spelling of /a/

The Spanish phoneme /a/ is always spelled with either **a** or **ha**, as in **ala**, **van, animal, hablar, azahar**.

Allophone of /e/

The vowel /e/ in Spanish has one principal allophone, [e], a mid front oral vowel.[1]

For [e] the velum is closed since it is an oral vowel, and the lips are spread, as they are for all front vowels in Spanish. The tip of the tongue rests against the lower front teeth. The highest part of the tongue dorsum is in the front of the mouth. This [e] is slightly more closed than the vowel in English *let*—more like the *first* part of the English complex vowel nucleus (diphthong) in *ate*.

---

[1]In the first two editions of *Spanish Pronunciation*, we recognized a more open allophone of /e/, namely [ɛ], which Spanish speakers use automatically in a variety of phonetic environments, but mainly closed syllables, as in **ven, perla, usted**, and **enviar**. This sound is almost the same as the [ɛ] of French, as in **lait**, or of English, as in *let*. Our experience has subsequently shown that this allophone is virtually redundant in Spanish, and English speakers normally need pay no attention to the position of their tongue for it. Remember that the so-called "long a" in English, as in *late*, really has a vowel plus a glide, /lɛyt/, as opposed to the simple [ɛ] of *let* /lɛt/. In fact, in many years of teaching Spanish phonetics the author remembers only one individual—a native speaker of Hungarian—who seemed incapable of pronouncing anything but this more open [ɛ] in any syllable, closed or open, saying * [lɛ́-čɛ̨] for **leche**, * [ɛ̨-lɛ́-na] for **Elena**, and so forth.

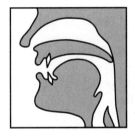

[e]

Distribution of /e/

Since /e/ has only one allophone in our analysis, the rule is

/e/ → [e]   es̠te̠, pe̠rla, compre̠nde̠s

Dialectal Variations of /e/

One dialectal variation is worthy of note. In the Caribbean area, particularly Cuba, the open allophone [ę], mentioned in footnote 1, is frequently used in open syllables: **peso** [pę́-so]. Also /e/ is frequently reduced and/or devoiced, as other vowels are, too. (See Chapter 14 for an explanation of these phenomena.)

Contrasts with English

Spanish [e] is not difficult for English speakers per se, even though it is more closed than the English [ɛ] of *let*. This means that to pronounce such words as **le, leche, lento, lerdo,** for example, the tongue is higher in the mouth—closer to the alveolar ridge—and it does not move or "glide up" until the next consonant is pronounced, as it almost always does in English. But to make English [ɛ] the tongue is lower to begin with and then moves either for the next consonant as it does in Spanish or for the following glide /y/, as in *let-late, red-raid, wren-rain,* and so forth.

Spanish has virtually the same diphthong that English does in words like *late, raid, rain, pain, they,* but in Spanish this sequence *is always represented in writing by* ei, as in **veinte, seis,** and **reino,** or **ey,** as in **ley** and **rey.** Thus Spanish has the following contrasts, which are difficult for the average English speaker both to perceive and to make: **¡Vente!** *Get over here!* versus **¡Veinte!** *Twenty!,* **reno** *reindeer* versus **reino** *kingdom,* **pena** *pain* versus **peina** *(he, she) combs,* **tenés** *you have* (**vos** form of **tener**) versus **tenéis** *you* (pl.) *have* (**vosotros** form of **tener**). This problem is most severe with stressed /é/, although it can occur with unstressed /e/, too, as in **penado** *convict* versus **peinado** *hair-do.* You must avoid saying, **¡Qué bueno!**, for example, as *[kʰέi̯-bu̯έi̯-no] instead of the correct [ké-ƀu̯é-no].

The main problem with unstressed /e/ in Spanish, is, as usual, the substitution of English [ə], which can blur important lexical and grammatical distinctions, such as the difference between **pesaron** and **pisaron** (different verbs), **ingleses** and **inglesas** (different gender), or **ayuden** and **ayudan** (different verb mood).

Spelling of /e/

The Spanish phoneme /e/ is always spelled with either **e** or **he**, as in **eso, ven, leche, helar, rehén.**

Allophone of /o/

The vowel /o/ in Spanish has one principal allophone, [o], a mid back oral vowel.

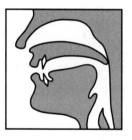

[o]

Description of /o/ Allophone

For [o] the velum is closed, and the lips are rounded. The highest part of the tongue dorsum is in the back of the mouth. This [o] is very similar to the *first* part of the English complex vowel nucleus (diphthong) in *boat*.

Distribution of /o/

As with /a/ and /e/ above, the rule is simple:

/o/ → [o]   <u>o</u>s<u>o</u>, <u>o</u>l<u>o</u>r<u>o</u>s<u>o</u>, h<u>o</u>spital

Dialectal Variations of /o/

In parts of Mexico, Colombia, and particularly Cuba, a final unstressed /o/ is often realized as [u], as in **caso** [ká-su]. This is done sporadically and usually causes no confusion since there are so few Spanish words that end in unstressed /u/ (like **espíritu** or **tribu**) that could be confused with counterparts ending in /o/. Also /o/ is frequently reduced and/or devoiced, as are other vowels.

Contrasts with English

The problems that English speakers have with Spanish /o/ are quite similar to those they have with /a/ and /e/. As usual, you must guard against using [ə] in the unstressed syllable, as in the second syllable of words like **preocupo, señorita, fósforo**, and so forth. Schwa [ə] can be pronounced with no movement of the lips or tongue, but for /o/ (Spanish or English) you must round your lips, retract your tongue, and be able to feel this movement in your lips, cheeks, and tongue.

With stressed /ó/ in Spanish the problem is almost exactly like that of the stressed /é/, except that in this case it is the velar glide /w/ that must be avoided rather than the palatal glide /y/. It is very difficult to find examples of "pure" /o/'s in English: those *not* followed by /w/, as in *note, cope, cone,* and so forth. One example frequently cited is the first syllable of the casual pronunciation, *gonna,* which is quite different from the syllable of the verb *go* itself. The so-called "long *o*" in English is really the diphthong /ow/. (The so-called "short *o*," of course, is not an /o/ at all, but an /a/, as in *not, cop,* and *con.*) Unlike the case with stressed Spanish /é/, where we have a fair number of words with the diphthong (**reino, veinte**), there are almost no Spanish words with the /ou/ diphthong (with a few exceptions like the family name **Alou),** although the sequence happens across word boundaries: **No unieron el país** [nóu̯-ni̯é-ro-nel-pa-ís]. Thus, while the incorrect use of your customary /ow/ diphthong in English for Spanish /o/ sounds very foreign, at least there is little chance of confusion with other words as there is with some of the other mispronunciations already discussed.

However, there is an additional problem with Spanish /o/, both stressed and unstressed, which is similar to the /a/ problem—the mistaken use of either /ɑ/, the intermediate vowel of some American English dialects (between /a/ and /ɔ/) or the low back /ɔ/ itself, thus causing confusion between **hambre** and **hombre, cantar** and **contar**, and so forth.

A related problem with /o/ is rooted in the English spelling system, and is perhaps even more troublesome than the others discussed so far. Very often the letter **o** in English really represents the sound /a/, rather than mythical "short *o*," as in *hospital, conversation, monstrous, operation, responsibility, opportunity,* and literally hundreds of other examples. Many of these words, fortunately for you as you learn Spanish vocabulary but unfortunately as you learn the sound system, are matched by close Spanish cognates: **hospital, conversación, monstruoso, operación, responsabilidad, oportunidad**, and so forth.

Therefore you may have a tendency to say *[a-pər-tu-ni-đáđ] rather than the correct [o-por-tu-ni-đáđ].

Spelling of /o/

The Spanish phoneme /o/ is always spelled with either **o** or **ho**, as in **ola, mano, honra, ahora**.

Practice

A.

Your instructor will read one of the Spanish words in each numbered sequence, switching randomly from one column to the next. Identify which word has been read by indicating the column. If your instructor wishes, give the meaning, too.

a	b	c
posar	pesar	pisar

*(Your instructor reads **pesar**.) The answer is **b. pesar** to weigh; to distress*

	a	b	c
1.	esta	este	esto
2.	le	ley	
3.	vasito	besito	visito
4.	reno	reino	
5.	emito	omito	humito
6.	pena	peina	
7.	pasaron	pesaron	pisaron
8.	ves	veis	
9.	preposición	proposición	
10.	vente	veinte	

B.

*Your instructor will read one word or phrase in each numbered sequence, choosing at random. Identify the language by saying just **español** if the word is Spanish, but if it is English, say **inglés** and give the corresponding Spanish word. Don't look at your books for this one; it will spoil the fun. For example,*

no   *no*

*(Your instructor reads **no**.) You say **español**.*

pe   *pay*

(The instructor reads pay.*) You say* **inglés,** *and then* **pe**.

1. dé   *day*
2. lo   *low*
3. va   *bah*
4. me   *may*
5. do   *dough*
6. papa   *papa*
7. fe   *Fay*
8. habló   *a blow*
9. qué   *Kay*
10. ve   *bay*
11. yo (*with* [ŷ])   *Joe*
12. pe   *pay*
13. jaló   *hello*
14. se   *say*
15. lana   *Lana*
16. no   *no*
17. le   *lay*
18. polo   *polo*
19. mama   *mama*
20. so   *sew*

C.

Pronounce the following Spanish words, either by repeating after your instructor or reading them directly. Remember to avoid [ə] *in all unstressed syllables; be careful not to elongate a stressed* /á/ *(as in* father*); make sure that you do not turn stressed* /é/ *and stressed* /ó/ *into the diphthongs* /ɛy/ *and* /ow/, *respectively, unless the Spanish word really has a diphthong in it.*

1. oloroso
2. bebé
3. acá
4. peinado
5. preparaste
6. oportunidad
7. conversación
8. fósforo
9. dólar
10. mesas
11. monopolio
12. barceloneses
13. vente
14. don Quijote
15. fiestecita
16. salieron
17. colorado
18. señorita
19. español
20. próspero
21. producto
22. sonoro
23. ayuden
24. preocupa
25. lisonjeará
26. ministerio
27. Honduras
28. vapor
29. ingleses
30. doctor
31. derecho
32. paseará
33. oficial
34. operación
35. coméis
36. honrado

37. oficina	42. verás	47. nota
38. nene	43. coloreó	48. golpeó
39. monstruo	44. examen	49. caramba
40. meses	45. reno	50. Medinaceli
41. hospital	46. veis	

D.

Read or repeat the following Spanish sentences, being particularly careful of the pronunciation of /a e o/. Remember—you should be able to feel some unfamiliar muscular movements in your tongue, lips, and cheeks, because, when you pronounce Spanish correctly, you are opening and closing your mouth more vigorously than you do in English.

1. ¡Qué bueno, Honorato!
2. Celebrarán Santo Tomás quizás.
3. Papá y Álvaro van a la Habana.
4. Se pasearán todas por estas calles.
5. Casualmente a eso voy al Ministerio.
6. Habrá sido porque no te preparaste bien.
7. Ana buscará la lana, pero no la encontrará.
8. Hablará a mi mamá cuando vuelva de la oficina.
9. El joven notó un olor a óleo cuando pasó por el Prado.
10. La muchacha va a pasar por acá mañana por la mañana.
11. ¿Y tienes buenos padrinos que te ayuden a conseguir el puesto?
12. El coro cantó primero y luego el cura habló lenta y solemnemente.
13. Se cayó de un caballo y ahora anda con el brazo derecho enyesado.
14. Conversaba conmigo en la oficina cuando estaba procesando el texto en su ordenador.
15. Recuerden ustedes que las perlas no parecen valiosas, pero sí lo son.
16. Yo creo que he visto unos ojos como los que he pintado en esta leyenda.
17. Mi primo hermano vivió mucho tiempo en la ciudad de Colón en Panamá.
18. El doctor se quedó en el hospital para operar a la víctima del accidente de coches.
19. Nada menos que el cuñado de una prima de mi mujer. Él es tío de la esposa de un nieto del Ministro.
20. Vente para acá, Amalia. ¿No te he dicho veinte mil veces que no exageres tanto?

E.

Prepare a brief presentation in writing, but one that you will deliver orally to the class. It should be no more than a dozen or so sentences. Mark in advance all the cases of /a e o/ in your presentation so that you will be aware of them when you speak. Be sure to avoid [ə], don't make stressed /á/ too long, and so forth. And don't forget stress and intonation! Some suggestions: **La historia de mi vida en dos minutos, Mi carrera en la universidad, Lo que me gusta más (menos) de mi compañero(-a) de cuarto (casa),** *or* **Mi familia**. *Then ask your classmates for some constructive feedback, namely, "How did I do with /*a e o/?"

F.

This is the first real *phonetic transcription you have been asked to do. Even though we have studied only a few of the segmental phonemes of Spanish so far, all the transcription answers in Appendix C will be given entirely in correct transcription. That means you will at first see lots of unfamiliar symbols. But only those studied so far will be underlined, and they are the ones you are supposed to know at any given point. So, since we have studied only /*a e o/ *up to this point, a transcription for a sentence like* **Esta historia es interesante** *will look like this:* [és-ta͜is-tó-ri̯a-é-si̯n̩-te-re̯-sán̩-te]. *Naturally, as we go along, more and more symbols will be underlined in the Answer Key transcriptions. When we get to consonants in Chapter 21, the ground rules will change a bit, but more on that when the time comes. In the meantime be sure to include all the stresses on the appropriate vowels. Unless intonation contours are specifically requested, do not put them in, but indicate all pauses with vertical lines* ‖ : [bá-ya͜us-té-ða-la-o-fi-sí-na ‖ i-la-en̩-ku̯én̩-tra-e-nel-pa-sí-yo].

1. Papá va a la Habana para hablarle a Arnaldo Arana.
2. Álvaro está alegre y quizás va a acompañar a papá cuando vaya.
3. Buscarán recuerdos para toda la familia.
4. El doctor que busco no está en su consultorio, es decir, su oficina, sino en el hospital.
5. Pronto lo tomó.
6. El Congreso de Honduras completó todo lo posible.
7. En el trópico lo humillaron, quitándole el oro y el fósforo que robó.
8. ¿Vive usted en Panamá?
9. ¿Ves lo que hacen?
10. ¿En qué curso piensas hacer ese trabajo?
11. Pienso hacerlo en esta clase.
12. El hombre y sus parientes viven en el otro pueblo.
13. ¿Viste la estatua de don Quijote en la calle Medinaceli?
14. Creo que se llama así el estado de Colorado por el color de la tierra.
15. Recuerden ustedes que las perlas no parecen valiosas, pero el rey las quiere para pagar las deudas en Europa.

16

The High Vowel /i/

Allophones of /i/

The vowel /i/ in Spanish has three allophones: [i], a high front oral vowel; [i̯], a high front oral semi-vowel (or glide); and [y], a voiced palatal slit fricative consonant.[1]

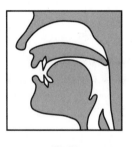

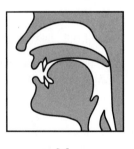

[i] [i̯]   [y]

Description of /i/ Allophones

For [i] the velum is closed, and the lips are spread. The tip of the tongue rests against the lower front teeth. The highest part of the tongue dorsum is in the front of the mouth and very close to the alveolar ridge and front palate. This Spanish [i] is more closed than the vowel in English *sit*; it is more like the *first* part of the English complex vowel nucleus (diphthong) in *seat*.

---

[1]In strict structuralist theory, [y] is really an allophone of the consonant phoneme /y/, creating here what might be called "phonemic replacement." In generative theory, where there are no allophones, [y] is the result of a rule called "glide spirantization" by Cressey, *Spanish Phonology and Morphology,* p. 82, which turns /i/ into [y] at one point in the derivation. Thus, although strictly speaking [y] cannot be an allophone of /i/ in either of these theories, we will view it as such for purposes of simplicity in this book since our approach is more ITEM AND ARRANGEMENT than ITEM AND PROCESS.

For [i̯] everything is almost the same as for [i], except that the sound is much shorter in duration. The tongue is always in the process of going up from a lower vowel or going down to one. It is shorter and higher than the English glide /y/, heard at the end of *bee, bay, buy, boy.*

The tongue position for [y] is similar to that of both these vowel sounds except that the tongue body comes so close to the ALVEOLO-PALATAL region that there is often slight friction or mild turbulence, changing the sound into a true consonant (see note 1).

Distribution of /i/

There are two rules for /i/, the first one being for a stressed /í/:

$$/í/ \rightarrow [i] \qquad \textbf{f\underline{i}no, o\underline{í}, ped\underline{i}mos}$$

This means that a stressed /í/ in Spanish has only one allophone, [i], which can occur in a variety of environments: V̲C **ir** [ír], CV̲C **fin** [fín], CV̲ **sí** [sí], CV̲-V **vía** [bí-a], V-V̲-V **oía** [o-í-a], V-V̲ **huí** [u-í], CV-V̲C **leíste** [le-ís-te]. Notice that in some cases stressed [í], like all stressed vowels, does *not* have a written accent because of the rules of Spanish spelling (see Chapter 31): **fino, pedimos**, **ir, fin,** and so on.

But the rule for *unstressed* /ĭ/ is the most extensive and complex we have dealt with so far and will be explained below and illustrated by abundant examples (see page 152). Notice that the unstressed /i/ is marked in the rule with a superscribed DIACRITIC mark: /ĭ/. This is just to call your attention to the fact is that is *unstressed*. In phonetic transcription this will not be done, however, since the lack of any mark over any vowel symbol will in itself mean that it is unstressed. A few more points to note. A symbol like /V₁/ is called a CONDITION of the rule, which will be explained under the rule itself. Also two allophones within braces to the left of the diagonal show free or non-functional variation, often stylistically or attitudinally determined. In other words, the first or top one is most common in careful (slow) speech and the second or lower one in casual (rapid) speech. The ___ mark indicates where the allophone in question goes.

When /ĭ/ is unstresssed, it is realized either as the full vowel [i], the semi-vowel [i̯], or the consonant [y], depending on its phonetic environment, on the location of various boundaries (morpheme, word, phrase), and stylistic considerations (careful or slow speech).

When /ĭ/ is bounded by a consonant and a different vowel, CV̲V₁, as you can see in the first section of the rule on page 152, it is the semi-vowel [i̯], as in **v̲iaje** [bi̯á-xe], **s̲iete**, and so forth. This is also true when /ĭ/ follows the low and mid vowels, V₂ V̲, as in **hay̲** [ái̯], **se̲is, rey̲.**

When /ĭ/ is between vowels, V-V̲V, it is realized as [y], as in **rey̲es** [r̄é-yes], or **ley̲ó**, as compared with **sal̲ió** [sa-li̯ó], for example. This also happens in the few cases where it occurs at the beginning of a word before a vowel, #V̲V, as in **h̲ielo** [yé-lo], as compared with **c̲ierro** (from the verb **cerrar**) [si̯é-r̄o], for example.

$$
/\breve{\imath}/ \;\rightarrow\;
\begin{bmatrix}
[\underset{\cdot}{\imath}] & \Big/ \left\{\begin{array}{l} /C/\underline{\quad}/V_1/ \\ /V_2/\underline{\quad} \end{array}\right\} & \text{viaje, siete, piojo, viuda} \\[2mm]
 & & \text{hay, seis, boina} \\[4mm]
[y] & \Big/ \left\{\begin{array}{l} /V/ \\ \# \end{array}\right\} \underline{\quad} /V/ & \text{leyes, leyó} \\[2mm]
 & & \text{hielo, hierba} \\[6mm]
\left\{\begin{array}{l} [i] \\ [y] \end{array}\right\} & \Big/ \left\{\begin{array}{l} /V_3/ \\ \| \end{array}\right\} \underline{\quad} \# /V_1/ & \text{Pablo y Enrique} \\[2mm]
 & & \text{Y además} \\[6mm]
\left\{\begin{array}{l} [i] \\ [\underset{\cdot}{\imath}] \end{array}\right\} & \Big/ \left\{\begin{array}{l} /V_3/\; \# \underline{\quad} \\ \underline{\quad} + (\#)\, /V_1/ \end{array}\right\} & \text{la hijita, la invitó, lo importante} \\[2mm]
 & & \text{fió, guiamos; mi amigo, mi universidad} \\[6mm]
\left\{\begin{array}{l} [\underset{\cdot}{\imath}] \\ [y] \end{array}\right\} & \Big/ /V_2/ \underline{\quad} \# /V_1/ & \text{hoy es viernes, ley opresiva} \\[4mm]
[i] & \text{elsewhere} & \text{interés, pintar, cursi, flúido}
\end{bmatrix}
$$

Conditions: $/V_1/$ is only /a e o u/ since [$\underset{\cdot}{\imath}$] does not precede /i/.

$/V_2/$ is only /a e o/ since [$\underset{\cdot}{\imath}$] does not follow /i/ or /u/.

\# is a word boundary.

$/V_3/$ is a full vowel, not a semi-vowel.

$\|$ is a phonemic phrase boundary, meaning a pause.

$+$ is a MORPHEME (grammatical unit) boundary.

$+ (\#)$ means that there is always a morpheme boundary here and maybe a word boundary, too.

When /ĭ/ is between vowels, the second of which starts a word, $V_3 \; \underline{V}\#V$, as in **Pablo y Enrique**, it remains [i] in careful speech: [pá-ɓlo-i-en-r̄í-ke], but becomes [y] in casual or rapid speech: [pá-ɓlo-yen-r̄í-ke]. The same thing happens when /ĭ/ is between a pause and a word that begins with a vowel, $\| \; \underline{V}\#V$, as in **Y además**: [i-a-ɗe-más] (careful) or [ya-ɗe-más] (casual).

When /ĭ/ begins a word after a full vowel, $V_3 \; \#\underline{V}$, it remains [i] in careful speech: **la invitó** [la-im-bi-tó]. This also happens when it precedes a vowel either at a morpheme boundary, $\underline{V}+V_1$, within a word, as in **fió** [fi-ó], or at word boundary, $\underline{V}\#V_1$, as in **mi amigo** [mi-a-mí-ɣo]. But in casual speech in these cases it becomes [$\underset{\cdot}{\imath}$]: [fi̯ó], [mi̯a-mí-ɣo].

Notice that a phrase like **mi amigo** can have either the full vowel [i] or the semi-vowel [i̯], depending on the speed and style of speech, because a *word boundary* is involved. But the word **Miami** can have *only* the semi-vowel [i̯] because there is no word boundary. In other words, **Miami** fits only in the slot at the very top of the rule, giving it only one possible pronunciation. Likewise with **fió** and **dio**. **Fió** has two pronunciations: a careful one with [i] and a rapid one with [i̯]. This is because native speakers know, in most cases without even realizing it, that **fi-** is the root of the verb **fiar** *to trust* and thus can be separated syllabically. But the only part of the root of the verb **dar** left in the preterit is **d-**. The **-io** is the ending and thus stays together as a diphthong. This fact is further revealed in the Spanish system of written accents, which is based on careful speech. **Fió**, as a ''sometimes'' two-syllable word, has a written accent as do all **aguda** (last-syllable stressed) words ending in a vowel, such as **pisó, firmó, silbó, habló. Dio**, because of its diphthong, is just a one-syllable word matched by none other in Spanish and thus has no written accent.

When /i/ ends a word after a vowel and precedes a word beginning with a vowel, $V_2\underline{V}\#V$, as in **hoy es**, we again have two choices—a careful one [i̯], and a casual one [y]: [ói̯-es] or [ó-yes].

Unstressed /í/ in all other positions (elsewhere) is just [i]: C$\underline{V}$ **cursi** [kúr-si], C$\underline{V}$C **pintar** [piṇ-tár], $\underline{V}$C **interés** [iṇ-te-rés]. It is also [i] in a few words in Spanish where unstressed /i/ follows a stressed /ú/, V-$\underline{V}$, as in **flúido** [flú-i-ɗo].

The vowel /i/ has no important dialectal variations in Spanish other than the reduction and devoicing that can happen with all vowels (already explained in Chapter 14).

Contrasts with English

The difficulties English speakers have with /i/ in Spanish are virtually the same as those already discussed for the mid vowels /e/ and /o/. Schwa [ə] or barred *i* [ɨ] must never be used for unstressed /i/, as in **aspirina** *[as-pə-rí-na] or *[as-pɨ-rí-na] rather than [as-pi-rí-na].

Just as with stressed /é/ and /ó/, English speakers have a tendency to follow stressed /í/ with a glide, just as they do in English in words like *see, read, keep*, and so forth. Although there is no diphthong *[ii̯] in Spanish to create confusion as there is with [e] versus [ei̯], the sequence is foreign-sounding in such examples as **sí, sin,** and **viví**. Also, English /I/ of *sin* is lower than the Spanish [i] of **sin** and cannot be substituted for it.

The Spanish semi-vowel [i̯] presents some problems, particularly in cognate words. The Spanish pattern of C$\underline{i}$V, that is, consonant + semi-vowel [i̯] + vowel as in **viaje, tiene, diario**, occurs mainly in English with /u/ as the vowel after the /y/ glide: *few, coupon, beauty, future,* and so forth. Thus in borrowed Spanish words English speakers separate the diphthongs that have vowels other than /u/: *fiesta* /fɨyéstə/, *patio* /pǽtɨyò/, and so forth. This hiatus pronunciation, while acceptable in English, is not in Spanish: **tiempo** is [tiém-po] rather than *[tⁱi-yém-po], **adiós** is [a-ɗiós] rather than *[a-dɨ-yós], and so forth.

Spelling of /i/

The Spanish phoneme /i/ is spelled in several different ways. It is spelled with a **y** in the word **y**, when unstressed, following another vowel at the end of a word, as in **hay, ley, hoy**, and in a few proper names of non-Spanish origin, as in **Ypoá, Yrigoyen**. Elsewhere it is spelled either with **i**, as in **isla, vino, tiene, paisano, cursi**, and with **hi**, as in **hijo, prohibir, ahí, hielo, hierba**.

Practice

A.

Your instructor will read one of the Spanish words in each numbered sequence, switching randomly from one column to the next. Identify which word has been read by indicating the column. If your instructor wishes, give the meaning, too. (This is exactly the same activity as you did in Practice A in Chapter 15.)

	a	b	c
1.	penar	pinar	
2.	pesado	pisado	
3.	emito	imito	omito
4.	pidiendo	pudiendo	
5.	descante	discante	
6.	fisión	fusión	
7.	seseo	siseo	
8.	remar	rimar	
9.	legar	ligar	lugar
10.	peñita	piñita	

B.

*Your instructor will read one word or phrase in each numbered sequence, choosing at random. Identify the language by saying **español** if the word is Spanish, but if it is English, say **inglés** and give the corresponding Spanish word. (This, too, is just like Practice B in Chapter 15. So don't look at your books for this one either.)*

1.	mí	*me*
2.	ti	*tea*
3.	ni	*knee*
4.	sí	*see*
5.	vi	*bee*
6.	di	*Dee*

7. linda   *Linda*
8. sin   *seen*
9. bis   *Beese*
10. Cid   *seethe*
11. mil   *meal*
12. ir   *ear*

C.

Pronounce the following Spanish words, either by repeating after your instructor or reading them directly. Remember to avoid [ə] and [ɨ] in all unstressed syllables; make sure that you do not turn stressed /í/ into the diphthong /Iy/; keep your tongue high enough so that the Spanish [i] of **sin** *doesn't sound as open as the English [I] of* sin; *and do not separate the diphthongs in cognate words like* **fiesta** *with hiatus.*

1. salir
2. imperio
3. adivinar
4. circo
5. fiesta
6. ágil
7. ministro
8. inteligente
9. imaginarse
10. Diego
11. individuo
12. frágil
13. patio
14. salí
15. sutileza
16. alergia
17. interno
18. firmar
19. sin
20. pies
21. mexicano
22. Dios
23. preferir
24. hábil
25. ministerio
26. Lili
27. ciudad
28. diplomático
29. siesta
30. cristal
31. Bolivia
32. siempre
33. intenso
34. civil
35. hemorragia
36. ir
37. civilización
38. adiós
39. Mario
40. interior
41. rápido
42. mil
43. calificación
44. tiempo
45. sarampión
46. aspirina
47. invitar
48. solicitar
49. viví
50. disgusto

D.

Read or repeat the following Spanish sentences, being particularly careful of the pronunciation of /i/. Remember that for a word like **sin** *your tongue should be higher in the mouth than it is for the /I/ of the English word* sin; *for* **sí** *you should not move your tongue as you do for the English word* see *until you get to the next sound; for a word like* **aspirina** *keep your tongue forward for unstressed /í/ (no [ə] or [ɨ] in Spanish); and for a word like* **patio** *do not turn the semi-vowel [i̯] into a syllabic [i] when* *it forms part of a diphthong with another vowel—***patio** *has two syllables, not three like English* patio.

1. Leí la ley.
2. ¿Leíste tú las leyes?
3. Ignacio es un paisano mío.
4. En esta ciudad hay más de mil taxis.
5. Hola, Anastasio. ¿Qué haces por aquí?
6. Me dormí y perdí el hilo de la conversación.
7. ¡Qué barbaridad! ¡Qué tiempo! ¡Taxi! ¡Taxi!
8. Si tienes sarampión, no deberías tomar aspirina.
9. Pero, Hipólito, no puede conseguir uno ni de milagro.
10. Durante la fiesta todos pasaron mucho tiempo en el patio.
11. Los internados internacionales son de lo más interesante.
12. Visité las islas Filipinas y naturalmente su capital Manila.
13. La mayoría de los estudiantes salieron con una cara muy triste.
14. Lo importante es que viene a la ciudad a ayudarle en la farmacia.
15. Vivíamos en el mismo país, Bolivia, hace dieciséis o diecisiete años.
16. Los incas eran interesantes por su civilización y su imperio también.
17. Los inquilinos trataron de influir al dueño a no aumentar el alquiler.
18. No puedes sacar buenas calificaciones si pasas tanto tiempo en las fiestas.
19. ¡Dios mío! Diez preguntas, pero sobre las dos últimas se podría escribir un libro.
20. Indicó que en el avión el indio sufrió una hemorragia nasal increíblemente sangrienta.

E.

Prepare a brief presentation in writing (10–12 sentences), but one that you will deliver orally to the class. Mark in advance all the cases of /i/ so that you will be aware of them when you speak. By now you should be on to the trouble spots with /i/. If you didn't make a presentation for Chapter 15, your instructor may let you use the one you prepared for that chapter now, since you can be sure there will be plenty of /i/'s in it. Ask your classmates for constructive feedback, mainly for /i/'s, but, if your instructor wishes, you can get some for /a e o/, stress, and intonation, too.

F.

Make a phonetic transcription of the following sentences. So far we have studied the vowels /a e o i/, so these are the ones to watch for in particular. Don't forget the stresses. Do not include intonation contours, but use ‖ *to indicate the pauses, that is, where terminal junctures would go if you were doing intonation.*

1. Ignacio es un paisano mío.
2. Vivíamos en el mismo país, Bolivia, hace dieciséis o diecisiete años.

3. Y eso es cómo se interesó en los asuntos de mi amigo Zoilo.
4. Y lo importante es que viene a la ciudad a ayudarle en la farmacia.
5. Estoy seguro de la pronunciación de palabras como **alergia, energía, hemorragia** y **melodía** cuando veo las tildes, es decir, los acentos escritos.

17

The High Vowel /u/

Allophone of /u/

The vowel /u/ in Spanish has three allophones: [u], a high back oral vowel; [u̯], a high back oral semi-vowel (or glide); and [w], a voiced, bilabio-velar slit fricative consonant.[1]

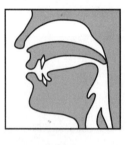

[u] [u̯]

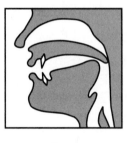

[w]

Description of /u/ Allophones

For [u] the velum is closed, and the lips are very rounded or pursed. The highest part of the tongue dorsum is in the back of the mouth and very close to the velum. This Spanish [u] is more closed than the vowel in English *soot*; it is more like the *first* part of the English complex vowel nucleus (diphthong) in *suit*.

For [u̯] everything is almost the same as for [u], except that the sound is much shorter in duration. The tongue is always in the process of going up from a lower vowel or going down to one. It is shorter and higher than the English /w/ heard at the end of *cow, blue, low*.

---

[1]Virtually the same theoretical problem exists here with the /u/ as we saw in the last chapter with /i/, with a few differences, which we will ignore. Again, as with [y], /y/, and /i/, [w] is really an allophone of the consonant phoneme /w/. But, since we are following neither strict structuralism nor generative phonology in our analysis, we will view it also as an allophone of /u/.

The tongue position for [w] is similar to that of both these vowel sounds except that the tongue body comes so close to the velar region that there is often slight friction or mild turbulence, changing the sound into a true consonant (see note 1).

Distribution of /u/

There are two rules for /u/, the first one being for a stressed /ú/:

$$/ú/ \rightarrow [u] \quad \text{p\underline{u}so, tab\underline{ú}, \underline{ú}ltimo, virt\underline{u}d}$$

This means that a stressed /ú/ in Spanish has one allophone, [u], which can occur in a variety of environments: **V̱C ¡uf!** [úf], **C̱V̱C justo** [xús-to], **C̱V̱ tú** [tú], **C̱V̱-V actúa** [ak-tú-a], **CV-V̱ urutaú** [u-ru-ta-ú],[2] **V-V̱C aún** [a-ún]. Although stressed /ú/ theoretically can occur in the environment **V-V̱-V**, there are no words with this pattern in Spanish, although there are hypothetical phrases, such as **siete u ocho** [sie̯-te-ú-ó-ĉo], where, for some reason, the word *or* might be stressed. Notice that in many cases stressed [ú], like all stressed vowels, occurs *without* a written accent because of the rules of Spanish spelling (see Chapter 31): **puso, virtud, justo**, and so on.

But the rule for *unstressed* /ŭ/ is just as extensive and complex as the one we saw in the last chapter for unstressed /ĭ/. Fortunately the /ŭ/ rule parallels the /ĭ/ rule quite closely, with just a few differences. Also unstressed /ŭ/ will be marked in our discussion and in the rule with a superscribed diacritic so you will be aware that it is unstressed. However, in phonetic transcription this will not be done; a [u] with no mark over it will mean in itself that it is unstressed. Just as with the rule in the last chapter, there are "conditions," indicated by viritually the same symbols. Remember that a choice of allophones to the left of the diagonal indicates non-functional variation based on the style of speech: slow speech first (above) and rapid speech below.

When /ŭ/ is unstressed, it is realized either as the full vowel [u], the semi-vowel [u̯], or the consonant [w], depending on its phonetic environment, on the location of various boundaries (morpheme, word, phrase), and stylistic considerations (careful or slow speech).

When /ŭ/ is bounded by a consonant and a different vowel, $CV̱V_1$, as you can see in the first section of the rule on page 160, it is the semi-vowel [u̯], as in **s̱uave, c̱uesta**. This is also true when /ŭ/ follows the low and mid vowels, $V_2V̱$, as in **ca̱usa, de̱uda**.

When /ŭ/ is between vowels, the second of which starts a word, $V_3V̱\#V$, as in **siete u ocho** it remains [u] in careful speech: [sie̯-te-u-ó-ĉo], but becomes [w] in casual or rapid

---

[2]No Spanish words fit this pattern; **urutaú** is a borrowing from Guaraní and is a type of owl found in Argentina and Paraguay.

speech: [sié-te-wó-ĉo]. The same thing happens with /ŭ/ is between a pause and a word that begins with a vowel, ‖ V̱ # V, as in **u̱ horas** [u-ó-ras] (careful) or [wó-ras] (casual).

$$
/ŭ/ \rightarrow
\begin{bmatrix}
[u̯] & \Big/ \begin{Bmatrix} /C/ \_\_ /V_1/ \\ /V_2/ \_\_ \end{Bmatrix} & \text{suave, cuesta, cuota, suizo} \\
& & \text{causa, deuda} \\
\begin{Bmatrix} [u] \\ [w] \end{Bmatrix} \Big/ \begin{Bmatrix} /V_3/ \\ ‖ \end{Bmatrix} \_\_ \# /V_1/ & & \text{siete u̱ ocho} \\
& & \text{u̱ horas} \\
\begin{Bmatrix} [u] \\ [u̯] \end{Bmatrix} \Big/ \begin{Bmatrix} /V_3/ \# \_\_ \\ \_\_ + (\#) /V_1/ \end{Bmatrix} & & \text{la u̱niversidad, se u̱nió, mi u̱niversidad, lo u̱nió} \\
& & \text{constru̱iste; su̱ ave, su̱ enemigo, su̱ hijo} \\
\begin{Bmatrix} [u̯] \\ [w] \end{Bmatrix} \Big/ /V_2/ \_\_ \# /V_1/ & & \text{Bernabeu̱ es un estadio.} \\
[u] \quad \text{elsewhere} & & \text{su̱perior, ju̱ntar, tribu̱}
\end{bmatrix}
$$

Conditions: /V₁/ is only /a e o i/ since [u̯] does not precede /u/.

/V₂/ is only /a e o/ since [u̯] does not follow /i/ or /u/.

\# is a word boundary.

/V₃/ is a full vowel, not a semi-vowel.

‖ is a phonemic phrase boundary: a pause, for example.

+ is a morpheme (grammatical unit) boundary.

+ (#) is a morpheme boundary here and sometimes a word
      boundary, too.

When /ŭ/ begins a word after a full vowel, V₃ # V̱, it remains [u] in careful speech: **la universidad** [la-u-ni-βer-si-ɖáɖ]. This also happens when it precedes a vowel either at a morpheme boundary, V̱+V₁, within a word, as in **construiste** [kons-tru-ís-te] or at a word boundary, V̱#V₁, as in **su̱ hijo** [su-í-xo]. But in casual speech in these cases it becomes [u̯]: [kons-tru̯ís-te], [su̯í-xo]. Notice that a phrase like **su̱ hijo** can have either the full vowel [u] or the semi-vowel [u̯], depending on the speed and style of speech because a *word boundary* is involved. But the word **su̱izo** can have *only* the semi-vowel [u̯] because there is no word boundary. In other words, **su̱izo** fits *only* in the slot at the very top of the rule, giving it only one possible pronunciation, but **su̱ hijo** fits in the part of the rule that has two possible pronunciations. Further evidence of the fact that words like **hu̱ir** and **construir** have "double" pronunciations—a careful one with a full vowel [u] and a casual one with a semi-vowel [u̯]—is the fact that words like **hu̱iste** and **construiste**, despite the official rules of Spanish orthography, still have written accents in some dictionaries: **huíste**. The accents show that the **u** and the **i** form separate syllables, and the **í** must be accented just as the **í** of **mío** or **oí** is accented. But notice that a word like **fu̱iste** never has a written accent since there is no possibility—in any style of pronunciation—of separating the **u** and the **i** in this word, as there is in **hu̱iste**, whether written this way or **huíste**.

When /ŭ/ ends a word after a vowel and precedes a word beginning with a vowel, V₂V̱#V, as in **Bernabeu̱ es un estadio**, again we have two choices—a careful one [u̯], and a casual one [w]: [ber-na-þéu̯-e-su-nes-tá-ɗi̯o] or [ber-na-þé-we. . .]. There are almost no Spanish words (just proper names like the name of the Madrid soccer stadium) that end in a /Vu/ diphthong.

Unstressed /ŭ/ in all other positions (elsewhere) is just [u]: CV̱ **tribu̱** [trí-þu], CV̱C **ju̱ntar** [xun̪-tár], V̱C **u̱rgente** [ur-xén̪-te].

The vowel /u/ has no important dialectal variations in Spanish other than the reduction and devoicing that can happen with all vowels.

Contrasts with English

The difficulties English speakers have with /u/ in Spanish are virtually the same as those already discussed for the mid vowels /e/ and /o/ and the other high vowel /i/. Schwa [ə] or barred [ɨ] must never be used for unstressed /u/, as in **suspenso**.

Just as with stressed /é/, /ó/, and /í/, English speakers have a tendency to follow stressed /ú/ with a glide, just as they do in English in words like *sue, rude, tune,* and so forth. Although there is no diphthong *[uu̯] in Spanish to create confusion as there is with [e] versus [ei̯], the sequence is foreign-sounding in **tú, según,** and so on.

Some dialects of English use /ɨw/ instead of /Úw/, as in *food, two, you,* and, although there is virtually no chance for phonemic confusion in Spanish, this sequence is also foreign-sounding.

English /U/, as in *soot* and *look,* is lower than Spanish [u] and cannot be substituted for it. The Spanish word **sus** does not have the complex vowel nucleus of English *sues,* and its [u] is much higher than the /U/ of *soot.*

The Spanish semi-vowel [u̯] is higher and more closed than English /w/ in post-vocalic position as in *cow, how.* Thus the first syllables of the Spanish words **causa** and **jaula** have a shorter, tenser sound than *cow* and *how.* Also many southern and eastern dialects of American English have a different diphthong in these words: /æw/ instead of /aw/. Since the vowel /æ/ does not even exist in Spanish, such pronuncations as *[kǽu̯-sa] for **causa** and *[ǽu̯ŋ-ke] for **aunque** sound strange although they are usually understood.

The Spanish semi-vowel [u̯] presents other problems, too, for you, as an English speaker. In Spanish the pattern of [Cu̯V], as in **cuando, bueno, cuota,** is quite common with all consonants. However, in English the corresponding pattern of /CwV/ has certain restrictions. C is practically always /k/, /s/, or /t/, as in *quit, sweater,* or *twice.* There are a few words with /d/—*dwell*—and a few borrowings from other languages with /g/: *Gwendolyn* or /p/: *puerile, Pueblo (Indians).* In some borrowings many English speakers break the diphthong with a full vowel /u/ and say in English /pu-wé-blo/ for *Pueblo* or /ru-wán-da/ for the country *Rwanda.* Thus such Spanish words as **bueno, chueca, luego, llueve, mueca, nuera, pues** are often mispronounced with the bisyllabic sequence *[Cu-V. . .] instead of the correct monosyllabic and diphthongal [Cu̯V. . .]: [ĉu̯é-ka], [mu̯é-ka], [yu̯é-þe], and so forth. This is even done in Spanish words that have the same combination as English—/tw/, for example. Thus **situado** is mispronounced as *[si-ĉu-wá-do] or *[si-ĉɨ-wá-do] instead of the correct three-syllable pronunciation of [si-tu̯á-ɖo]. (The reason for [ĉ] instead of [t] will be taken up in Chapter 29.)

Another problem for English speakers also has to do with dividing diphthongs into hiatal combinations. For some reason not entirely clear, English speakers often pronounce **deuda** as *[de-ú-ɖa] rather than [déu̯-ɖa], and **aunque** as *[a-úŋ-ke] rather than [áu̯ŋ-ke] even though most dialects of English have the diphthong /aw/, which corresponds closely to Spanish [au̯].

The final problem involving /u/ has a markedly lexical rather than phonetic aspect. Many English words spelled with *u* are pronounced with a /yu/ or even a /yɨ/, depending on where the stress is: *fume, particular, peculiar, popular, ridiculous*. Many English speakers carry this pronunciation over into all Spanish cognate words of this type and improperly add an intrusive [i̯]: *[r̄i-ɖí-ki̯u-lo] instead of saying the correct [r̄i-ɖí-ku-lo]. This pattern is so strong that it has created one of the most common mispronunciations in Spanish: *[pe-lí-ki̯u-la] for **película** instead of [pe-lí-ku-la], despite the fact that few English speakers even know the scientific Latinism *pellicular* 'covered with a thin membrane or film'. This mispronunciation probably can be attributed to analogy with similar words that do exist.

Spelling of /u/

The Spanish phoneme /u/ is spelled in several different ways. It is spelled with a **u**, as in **u, último, unir, luna, ombú, tribu, causa, suave**; with an **hu**, as in **humo, ahumar, rehusar, huida**; and with a **ü**, as in **vergüenza, lingüista**. The letter **u** does *not* represent any sound at all when it occurs in the four combations **gue** [ge], **gui** [gi], **que** [ke], and **qui** [ki], as in **guerra, guitarra, queso,** and **quitar**. It is merely an orthographic device that automatically follows **q** and follows **g** before **e** or **i** to show that the consonant represented by **g** is the phoneme /g/ and not the phoneme /x/, as in **gente** and **gitano**. Thus there is *no* /u/ *sound anywhere* in the verbs **querer** or **seguir**, for example. This particular use of the letter **u** also shows up in derived and related forms: **larguísimo** (from **largo**), **llegué** (from **llegar**), **Dieguito** (from **Diego**). If there really is a /u/ between **g** and **e** or **i**, it is represented by the letter **ü** with a dieresis over it: **averigüé** [a-ƀe-ri-ǵu̯é] or **argüimos** [ar-ǵu̯í-mos].

Practice

A.

Your instructor will read one of the Spanish words in each numbered sequence, switching randomly from one column to the next. Identify which word has been read by indicating the column. If your instructor wishes, give the meaning, too.

	a	b	c
1.	troncar	truncar	
2.	lechar	luchar	
3.	vocal	bucal	
4.	acosar	acusar	
5.	motilar	mutilar	
6.	amito	omito	humito
7.	sección	succión	
8.	plomero	plumero	
9.	perito	porito	purito
10.	anhelar	anular	
11.	sociedad	suciedad	
12.	soplico	suplico	

B.

Your instructor will read one word or phrase in each numbered sequence, choosing at random. Identify the language by saying **español** *if the word is Spanish, but if it is English, say* **inglés** *and give the corresponding Spanish word. And, of course, don't look at your books.*

1.	luz	*loose*
2.	su	*sue*
3.	tú	*two*
4.	según	*Say "goon".*
5.	mus	*moose*
6.	tabú	*taboo*
7.	yugo	*You go!*
8.	cu	*coo*
9.	Lucas	*Lucas*
10.	numen	*new men*
11.	¿jugo?	*Who go?*
12.	tul	*tool*
13.	u	*Ooh!*
14.	¿muro?	*"Moo dough"?*
15.	junta	*junta*
16.	tuna	*tuna*
17.	bu	*Boo!*
18.	dúo	*duo*

C.

Pronounce the following Spanish words, either by repeating after your instructor or reading them directly. Remember to avoid [ə] and [ɨ] in all unstressed syllables; make sure that you do not turn stressed /ú/ into the diphthong /Uw/; keep your tongue high enough so that the Spanish [u] of **sus** *doesn't sound as open as the English [U] of* soot*; make sure that the [CǔV] combination in Spanish stays diphthongal and mono-syllabic, as in* **situado***; and be careful not to insert the semi-vowel [ɨ̯] where it doesn't belong in cognates like* **ridículo.**

1. anular	21. baúl	41. tripulación
2. insinuar	22. luz	42. mueca
3. ocupado	23. ridicularizar	43. calcular
4. puntualidad	24. chueco	44. minutero
5. brújula	25. musical	45. saludar
6. suciedad	26. deuda	46. trueno
7. automóvil	27. figúrese	47. puridad
8. pubertad	28. documento	48. mula
9. ruana	29. insinúo	49. Cuba
10. graduamos	30. puntual	50. buró
11. acusar	31. reuma	51. popular
12. furioso	32. particular	52. regular
13. situado	33. simular	53. entumecido
14. llueve	34. adular	54. mutuo
15. verduras	35. útil	55. puntuación
16. fluorita	36. inundación	56. cura
17. ayudando	37. pútrido	57. afortunado
18. desocupado	38. título	58. bucal
19. hondureño	39. turno	59. museo
20. Europa	40. película	60. continuo

D.

Read or repeat the following Spanish sentences, being particularly careful of the pronunciation of /u/. Remember that for a word like **sus***, your tongue should be higher in the mouth than it is for the [U] of the English word* soot*; for* **tú** *you should not move your tongue as you do for the English word* two *until you get to the next sound; for a word like* **plumero** *keep your tongue back for the unstressed /ǔ/ (no [ə] or [ɨ] in Spanish); and in a word like* **mueca** *keep the [CǔV] combination together as one syllable; and be careful not to insert [ɨ̯] in cognate words like* **ocupado**.

1. Hugo, vamos a tomar el auto tuyo.
2. Se veía tan augusto, presuntuoso y triunfal.
3. ¿Tuviste tú que hacerlo después de la película?
4. Estoy seguro que ese trabajo no es ridículo ni duro.
5. Mi abuelo rehusó hacer el acuerdo aunque todo era gratuito.
6. Cuidado, aquí hubo un accidente de guaguas hace unos días.
7. Las uvas tenían un color purpúreo aunque todavía era agosto.
8. Los deudores formaron un grupo para actuar más eficazmente.
9. Su pronunciación de la **u** con la úvula producía un ruido extraño.
10. Estamos autorizados para incluir el costo anual de la graduación también.
11. El país no estaba muy unido hasta que lo unieron las amenazas continuas.
12. La viuda sufrió de una reuma cruel que fue la causa de su invalidez últimamente.
13. Umberto llevaba su antiguo uniforme a la antigua usanza a pesar de la humedad.
14. La junta yugoeslava consideró un triunfo la tregua que resultó durante la guerra de autonomía.
15. El circuito dañado causó un ruido tremendo y la explosión resultante ahumó por completo el cuarto.
16. El gaucho rehusó usar el caucho en sus esfuerzos para enjaular la yegua porque creía que era cruel.
17. Sus sucursales europeas, después de la guerra, tenían tantas deudas que casi estaban en la ruina.
18. Nos reunimos aquí en esta aula de la universidad para continuar nuestros estudios, los cuales no son gratuitos.
19. El cura estaba un poco preocupado porque todavía no había visitado todos los monumentos de la ciudad.
20. Pronuncia las siguientes palabras útiles, teniendo mucho cuidado con la **u**: atún, betún, azul, gandul, sur, ataúd, esclavitud, cruz, avestruz.

E.

Prepare a brief presentation to be delivered orally to the class. Mark in advance all the cases of /u/ so that you will be aware of them when you speak. Ask your classmates for constructive feedback, mainly for /u/'s, but, if your instructor wishes, for all the vowels, stress, and intonation, too.

F.

Make a phonetic transcription of the following sentences. So far we have studied all five vowel phonemes, so these symbols are the ones to watch for in particular. Remember, too, the semi-vowels [i̯] and [u̯], and don't forget the stresses. Do not include intonation contours, but use ‖ to indicate the pauses, that is, where terminal junctures would go if you were marking intonation.

1. Aunque no sea la causa de la deuda, lo humilla mucho.
2. La película aún es en el Cine Europa.
3. Vamos a tomar el auto, Hugo.
4. Bueno, puse el agua aquí, y ahora huele a humo.
5. Cuidado, aquí hubo un accidente de guaguas hace unos días.
6. ¿Cuántos quieres? ¿Siete u ocho?
7. Pues, Eusebio, no es ni bueno ni fuerte ni suave ni útil.

18

Vowel Combinations in Spanish

Morphophonemic Vowel Changes

In all languages the sounds of a given word or MORPHEME (grammatical unit of meaning) very often are changed, modified, or even eliminated when the word or morpheme is juxtaposed with certain other words or morphemes. For example, in English when the word *won't* /wównt/ precedes the word *you* /yÚw/ in normal conversation, the final /t/ of *won't*, which is alveolar, and the initial /y/ of *you*, which is palatal, combine in a sense and turn into a third sound /č/, also palatal: /wównčÛw/ or perhaps even /wównĉǯ/ in faster speech. In virtually any style of speech in Spanish when the word **la** /la/ precedes the word **abuela** /abuéla/, the unstressed /a/ of **la** disappears or combines with the /a/ of **abuela**, giving /labuéla/. Such changes are referred to in linguistic terminology as MORPHOPHONEMIC CHANGES because the phonemic shape or structure of the morphemes and words is altered when they come in contact with each other.

It is somewhat ironic that, although the Spanish vocalic system with only five vowel phonemes, /a e i o u/, is one of the simplest and most symmetrical of any language North Americans commonly study, the modifications produced when these vowels come in contact with each other are quite varied and complex.

These resulting morphophonemic changes in Spanish vowels are determined by four main factors: (1) style of speech (either slow or fast)[1]; (2) stress; (3) word and morpheme boundaries; and (4) the nature of the vowels themselves, front or back, for example.

---

[1]These two styles correspond closely to those proposed by James Harris, *Spanish Phonology* (1969), p. 7, and described with terminology from music as **andante** and **allegretto**. He recognizes two others, **largo** and **presto**, which we will not use in our analysis. He defines each style as follows: 1. **Largo**: very slow, deliberate, overprecise; 2. **Andante**: moderately slow, careful, but natural; 3. **Allegretto**: moderately fast, casual, colloquial; 4. **Presto**: very fast, completely unguarded. Although any one speaker might easily switch among two or more styles in the same discourse or even same sentence, vowel combinations in our analysis will be presented separately for just style 2, careful, and style 3, casual.

Vowel Modifications in Spanish

Contiguous (adjoining) vowels undergo five different types of modifications in Spanish, although the first one is rare in casual speech. As you go through these modifications, keep in mind the four governing factors: style, stress, boundaries, and vowel type.

1. SEPARATED.   There can be a complete break between the two vowels. Often this break is a sound known as *glottal stop*, represented in phonetics as [ʔ], a symbol occasionally mistaken for a question mark. The vocal bands catch abruptly—like the sounds you make to warn an infant not to touch something: *Uh-uh-uh-uh-uhhhhhh!* This sound is also heard in words like *cotton* and *button* or in the pronunciation in some British dialects of *bottle* (''*bott'l''*) or ''Ya go' a mome', guv?'' (''You got a moment, gov?''). This sound is even a segmental phoneme in some languages like German or Arabic. In North American English, however, we use it as a paralinguistic sound to indicate attitude, emotion, emphasis: ''No, it's my *only* [mây ʔ ównlĺy] one!!!'' or sometimes just to show word boundaries, as in *the owl* [ðə̆ ʔ áwl]. Many English speakers feel for some reason that this sound is appropriate to separate Spanish words that might otherwise run together (which is what they really should do): **No sé nada de esto** * [de ʔ és-to] or **Va a comer** *[vá ʔ a-ko-mér]. But glottal stops are almost never used in Spanish and then only in the slowest, most unnatural style for great emphasis and effect.

2. LINKED.   In either style, careful or casual, this is the proper modification to link adjoining vowels that are in separate syllables. There is no pause or glottal stop, but rather a smooth unbroken transition between the two vowels. The vocal bands never stop vibrating even though the muscular action in the vocal tract is creating separate syllables. Thus the above expressions are pronounced in slow, careful speech: [de-és-to] or [bá-a-ko-mér].

In the following vowel combinations, the vowels are LINKED in separate syllables with no pause in the stream of sound. There is no glottal break of any kind between them.

In careful and casual speech, two contiguous identical vowels, both of which are stressed, are linked in separate syllables, as in **Va Ana** [bá-á-na], **Dé esto** [dé-és-to], **Vi islas** [bí-ís-las], **No odio** [nó-ó-ɖio], **Tú únicamente** [tú-ú-ni-ka-mén̩-te]. You will remember from Chapter 6, ''Stress in Spanish,'' that verb forms (**va**, **dé**, **vi**, and **odio**), nouns and pronouns (**Ana**, **esto**, **islas**, and **tú**), negative words (**no**), and the first element of **-mente** adverbs always carry a heavy stress in the stream of speech, whether shown with written accents or not. The fact that some of these stresses are represented by written accents is a feature of the Spanish spelling system and is not in itself a determining factor in the pronunciation of vowel combinations. Note also that this particular combination virtually always involves a *word boundary*.

In careful speech only, when only *one* of two contiguous identical vowels is stressed, they are still both linked in separate syllables. It doesn't matter whether the stressed vowel comes first: **va Anita** [bá-a-ní-ta], **hablé español** [a-ɸlé-es-pa-ñól], **di indicios** [dí-in-dísịos], **yo honré** [yó-on-r̄é], **tú usaste** [tú-u-sás-te], or second: **la abre** [la-á-ɓre], **de esto** [de-és-to], **mi hija** [mi-í-xa], **lo otro** [lo-ó-tro], **tu único** [tu-ú-ni-ko]. This same phenomenon now can also occur within a word, although mainly with /e/ and /o/: **cree** [kré-e], **creemos** [kre-é-mos], **moho** [mó-o], **alcohol** [al-ko-ól]. Once again, verbs, nouns, and pronouns carry heavy stresses in the stream of speech—regardless of the presence of a written accent—and the letter **h**, as you can see, has no effect on any of this.

In both styles of speech—careful and casual—the so-called strong vowels coming together also produce linked separate syllables, within or between words. The strong vowels are /a e o/, stressed /í/, and stressed /ú/. Obviously the only remaining vowels are the two weak vowels: unstressed /ĭ/ and unstressed /ŭ/, which, as you learned in the last two chapters, usually turn into the semi-vowels [i̯] and [u̯], respectively, in these positions. Thus, in this case, they are in the *same* syllable and *not* linked. Examples of linked strong vowels, one of which is stressed, occurring within words are **vía** [bí-a], **país** [pa-ís], **leíste** [le-ís-te], **ríe** [r̄í-e], **creo** [kré-o], **poeta** [po-é-ta], **crear** [kre-ár], **cae** [ká-e], **caos** [ká-os], **toalla** [to-á-ya]. Examples of linked strong vowels, one of which is stressed, occurring between words are **vi animales** [bí-a-ni-má-les], **la isla** [la-ís-la], **me iba** [me-í-ɓa], **pedí el dinero** [pe-ɖí-eḷ-di-né-ro], **hablé alemán** [a-ɓlé-a-le-mán], **lo habla** [lo-á-ɓla]. Examples of linked strong vowels, neither of which is stressed, occurring within words are **leoncitos** [le-on-sí-tos], **poetisa** [po-e-tí-sa], **ahorita** [a-o-rí-ta], **toallero** [to-a-yé-ro]. Examples of linked strong vowels, neither of which is stressed, occurring between words are **le hablamos** [le-a-ɓlá-mos], **la esposa** [la-es-pó-sa], **lo amamos** [lo-a-má-mos], **la envidian** [la-em-bí-ɖi̯an]. Everything said in the previous paragraphs about forms stressed in the stream of speech, the use of written accents, and the letter **h** holds here, too.

There are cases where unstressed /ĭ/ and unstressed /ŭ/, however, retain their value as full vowels and do *not* turn into semi-vowels to create diphthongs when they are next to the strong vowels /a e o/. This, as we saw in the last two chapters, can happen only when we are dealing with morpheme boundaries (+) and word boundaries (#). In careful speech the unstressed /ĭ/ and unstressed /ŭ/ retain their respective value as full vowels when such a boundary separates them from the vowel: **fió** [fi-ó] (**fi-** is the verb root), **mi amigo** [mi-a-mí-ǵo], **graduar** [gra-ɖu-ár] (**gradu-** is the verb root), **su amigo** [su-a-mí-ǵo], **lo invitaron** [lo-im-bi-tá-ron], **la universidad** [la-u-ni-ɓer-si-ɖáɖ]. Notice that three of the four factors mentioned at the beginning of this chapter are in operation here: speech style (careful), stress (none), and boundaries.

3.   FUSED.   The term FUSED means forming a diphthong or a cluster of two vowels in a *single* syllable. And, of course, it can also mean forming a triphthong or a cluster of three vowels in a single syllable. One element of a fused group or diphthong (or triphthong) is *always* an unstressed /ĭ/ or an unstressed /ŭ/, realized as the semi-vowels [i̯] and [u̯], respectively. Examples of stressed syllabic full vowels in a diphthong or triphthong occurring within words are **seis** [séi̯s], **siete** [si̯é-te], **causa** [káu̯-sa], **bueno** [bu̯é-no], **buey** [bu̯éi̯]. Examples of stressed syllabic full vowels in a diphthong or triphthong occurring between words are **hablé inglés** [a-ɓléi̯n-glés], **mi héroe** [mi̯é-ro-e], **da usted** [dáu̯s-téɖ],

su época [sų́-po-ka], **estudió historia** [es-tú-ɟi̯ói̯s-tó-ri̯a]. Examples of unstressed syllabic full vowels in a diphthong or triphthong occurring within words are **peinar** [pei̯-nár], **fiestecita** [fi̯es-te-sí-ta], **causar** [kau̯-sár], **buenísimo** [bu̯e-ní-si-mo]. Examples of unstressed syllabic full vowels in a diphthong or triphthong occurring between words are **le informaron** [lei̯m-for-má-ron], **mi error** [mi̯e-r̄ór], **la universidad** [lau̯-ni-ƀer-si-ɖáɖ], **su enemigo** [sų̯e-ne-mí-ǥo], **antigua historia** [an̯-tí-ǥu̯ai̯s-tó-ri̯a].

Words and phrases with boundaries can contain fused vowel combinations that sound just like the fused diphthongs within words in *rapid speech*: **mi amigo** can have the same diphthong as **Miami** [mi̯a-]. But in *slow speech* **mi amigo** can have linked vowels: [mi-a-] whereas in slow speech **Miami** still has the [mi̯a-] diphthong because there is no word boundary. Likewise with **fió** and **dio**. **Fió** in rapid speech has a fused combination: [fi̯ó], but in slow speech is [fi-ó] because of the morpheme boundary between the root **fi-** and the ending **ó**. But **dio** has only one pronunciation in both styles: [di̯ó] because the root is just **d-** and the ending **-io** stays together. **Fió** has a written accent because the rules for written accents in Spanish are based on slow speech, and in this style **fió** is a bisyllabic word ending in a vowel and stressed on the last syllable. So it has an accent for the same reason **pisó, pasó, habló**, and hundreds of other such words in Spanish do. But **dio** has only one syllable even in slow speech, and one-syllable words in Spanish have written accents only when there is another word pronounced the same way: **mi/mí, tu/tú, se/sé**. There is no other word **dio** in standard speech.

4.   ELIMINATED.   When two vowels come together—particularly in rapid speech—one is often eliminated (or elided). Once again we must take into account the nature of the vowels themselves, whether or not they are stressed, and whether or not there is a word boundary present.

Let's take the case of identical vowels, as when the same two vowels come together, in the word **creer** or the phrase **mi hija**, for example. If both of the vowels are unstressed, in *both* careful and casual speech, one drops out or is eliminated: **creeré** [kre-ré], **lo omitieron** [lo-mi-ti̯e-ron]. Only in very slow, formal, and emphatic speech would both unstressed vowels remain.

If you recall, when one of the two like vowels is stressed, in careful speech they both remain in separate syllables but linked (see "Linked," above). But in *rapid* or *casual* speech, the unstressed one drops out or is eliminated, regardless of the presence of boundaries: **cree** [kré], **alcohol** [al-kól], **hablé español** [a-ƀlés-pa-ñól], **la abre** [lá-ƀre]. Notice once again that many stressed vowels in Spanish do not have written accents because of the spelling rules of the language. Remember that this elimination of the unstressed vowel next to the same stressed vowel would sound strange in slow speech; a speaker is usually speaking quite rapidly when he or she does this.

There are other cases of vowel loss, and now the phenomenon is dependent on *all four* factors: style of speech, stress, boundaries, and nature of the vowels themselves. Visualize the Spanish vowel triangle, /a/ is at the bottom—really on neither side but in the middle. /e/ is midway up in the front below /i/, and /o/ is midway up in the back below

/u/. (See Chart 18 in Chapter 14 if necessary.) Thus in *rapid speech only* (factor 1) an *unstressed* vowel (factor 2), at the end of a word before another word beginning with a vowel (factor 3), is eliminated in the following cases: /ă/ before any of the other four vowels, /ĕ/ *only* before /i/, and /ŏ/ *only* before /u/ (factor 4). Factor 4 needs further explanation. This vowel loss happens only when the vowel comes before a higher vowel *on the same side of the vowel triangle*. Visualize the vowel triangle once again—/ă/ drops before any vowel simply because the other four are higher and /ă/ is on the same side of the triangle as all the others, being at the low central point of the triangle. /ĕ/ drops *only* before /i/ because /i/ is the only higher vowel on the same side of the triangle, and /ŏ/ drops *only* before /u/ for the same reason.

Here are some examples where the unstressed vowel drops out *only* in rapid speech, *only* at word boundaries, and *only* in the cases described above. /ă/ drops before any vowel: **la esposa** [les-pó-sa], **la hembra** [lém-bra], **la irlandesa** [lir-lan̦-dé-sa], **la hija** [lí-xa], **la oficina** [lo-fi-sí-na], **la otra** [ló-tra], **la universidad** [lu-ni-βer-si-ɗáɗ], **la última** [lúl-ti-ma]. Remember that you must be speaking fairly fast to do this; it sounds forced and strange in slow speech. Also there must be a word boundary present. Under no circumstances can the unstressed vowel in these cases drop out if it is *within* a word: *[kér] is incorrect for **caer** in any style of speech, and likewise with *[mís] for **maíz**, or *[búl] for **baúl**.

/ĕ/ drops *only* before /i/: **me iba** [mí-βa], **me imagino** [mi-ma-xí-no], but not *[lís-te] for **leíste**, because this is within a word. /ŏ/ drops *only* before /u/: **tengo uno** [téŋ-gú-no], **lo unieron** [lu-ni̯é-ron].

5.   REPLACED.   Many linguists refer to this as VOWEL RAISING because the most typical cases are an unstressed /ĕ/ being ''raised'' to /i/ and an unstressed /ŏ/ being ''raised'' to /u/ (picture the vowel triangle again). However, we include two more slightly different cases, so we prefer the term REPLACED. For this particular phenomenon three of the four factors are operative: (1) style, (2) stress, and (4) nature of the vowels. Factor 3, boundaries, is not important here.

In rapid speech when either of the *unstressed* mid vowels /ĕ/ or /ŏ/ come next to any of the other three vowels, whether *they* are stressed or not, whether within a word or between words, the /ĕ/ and /ŏ/ raise to or are replaced by the semi-vowels [i̯] and [u̯], respectively: **peor** [pi̯ór], **no encontró** [nói̯ŋ-kon̦-tró], **pasear** [pa-si̯ár], **cae** [kái̯], **toalla** [tu̯á-ya], **pero ahora** [pe-ru̯a-ó-ra], **lo importante** [lu̯im-por-tán-te]. If both /ĕ/ and /ŏ/ come next to each other, although either vowel can be replaced, it is most common for the first one to be replaced or raised: **lo encontró** [lu̯eŋ-kon̦-tró] rather than [loi̯ŋ-kon̦-tró], **se ofrece** [si̯o-fré-se] rather than [seu̯-fré-se]. This explains why some marginally educated Spanish speakers spell a word like **trae** as *tray, which is exactly how they pronounce it (replacing /ĕ/ with [i̯]). It should be pointed out that, while this spelling is incorrect, the pronunciation is not and is common among educated speakers when speaking rapidly. Notice that the /ó/ of **no encontró** cannot be modified because it is stressed, unlike the /ŏ/ of **lo encontró**.

The last case of vowel replacement is the change of the semi-vowels [i̯] and [u̯] to the consonants [y] and [w], respectively. We have seen examples of both of these replacements in Chapters 16 and 17. They happen when either of the two semi-vowels comes between two vowels within a word: **leyes** [lé-yes]; at the beginning of a word followed by another vowel: **hierba** [yér-ƀa], **huelo** [wé-lo]; between two vowels at a word boundary: **Pablo y Enrique** [pá-ƀlo-yen-r̄í-ke], **siete u ocho** [si̯é-te-wó-ĉo], **hoy es viernes** [ó-yez-ƀi̯ér-nes], **Bernabeu es un estadio** [ber-na-bé-we-su-nes-tá-đi̯o]; or between a pause and a vowel at a word boundary: **Y además** [ya-đe-más], **huir** [wír].[2]

Special Cases

The word **muy**, as an adjective qualifier, can be stressed or unstressed (see the categories of stressed words in Chapter 6). When it is unstressed, the /u/ is realized as a semi-vowel [u̯]: [mu̯i]. When the word is stressed, there are two possible pronunciations, depending on whether the stress is on the /i/ or the /u/. In slow speech **muy alto** can be pronounced [mu̯í-ál-to], but in rapid speech the stress can shift back to the /u/, causing the semi-vowel [i̯] to be replaced by [y]: [mú-yál-to] or just linked vowels: [mú-i-ál-to].

Similar to **muy** with regard to stress shift are a few words like **océano.** Many speakers shift the stress in this word to change it from an **esdrújula** (third-from-last syllable stressed) word to a **llana** (next-to-last syllable stressed) word: from [o-sé-a-no] to [o-se-á-no]. Some speakers even replace the now unstressed [e] of **oceano** with [i̯], saying [o-si̯á-no]. Slightly different is the common expression **¡Qué hubo!** "Hi, how ya doin'?", heard throughout Mexico, Central America, and northern South America. This phrase is virtually always heard with stress loss on **Qué** and replacement of the resulting unstressed [e] by [i̯]: [ki̯ú-ƀo].

Phrases like **la oficina** or **la esposa** have three possible pronunciations—with regard to the vowels—depending on the style and speed of speech: in careful speech LINKED [la-o-fi-sí-na] [la-es-pó-sa], and in rapid speech REPLACED [lau̯-fi-sí-na] [lai̯s-pó-sa] or ELIMINATED [lo-fi-sí-na] [les-pó-sa]. Whether the pronunciation is replaced or eliminated depends to a certain extent on the individual speaker, as well as the style of speech since the complete elimination of the unstressed vowel occurs only in very rapid, casual, colloquial speech.

Following are some formulaic rules for these modifications. Remember once again that a choice of pronunciations in the brackets to the left of the diagonals is still the same: careful speech above, rapid speech below.

---

[2]There is actually one more vowel modification—LENGTHENED—where two equal vowels, one of which is stressed, combine in the same syllable into one long one: **de él** becomes [dé:l] as well as [dél] with elimination in rapid speech and [de-él] with linked vowels in slow speech. However, the difference between the lengthened [dé:l] and the linked [de-él] is very slight, and we have chosen to eliminate the modification "lengthened" to avoid further complicating an already very complex aspect of Spanish phonology.

Chart 20   Modification of Identical Vowels in Spanish

Both stressed	$/\acute{V}_1\ \acute{V}_1/ \rightarrow [\acute{V}_1\text{–}\acute{V}_1]$	**dé esto** [dé-és-to]
Both unstressed	$/\breve{V}_1\ \breve{V}_1/ \rightarrow [\breve{V}_1]$	**de español** [des-pa-ñól]
First stressed, second unstressed	$/\acute{V}_1\ \breve{V}_1/ \rightarrow \left\{ \begin{array}{c} [\acute{V}_1\text{–}\breve{V}_1] \\[6pt] [\acute{V}_1] \end{array} \right\}$	**dé el dinero** [dé-e̦l-di-né-ro] [dé̦l-di-né-ro]
First unstressed, second stressed	$/\breve{V}_1\ \acute{V}_1/ \rightarrow \left\{ \begin{array}{c} [\breve{V}_1\text{–}\acute{V}_1] \\[6pt] [\acute{V}_1] \end{array} \right\}$	**de esto** [de-és-to] [dés-to]

$/V_1\text{–}V_1/$ or $[V_1\text{–}V_1]$ means that both vowels are the same. **Dé** has a stress because it is a verb; the written accent reflects this. The preposition **de** never has a stress. **Esto** has a stress because it is a demonstrative pronoun, but it has no written accent because there is no other **esto**. The article **el** never has a stress.

Modification of Different Vowels

The rules for all stressed vowels are not shown because they are so simple: each stressed vowel has only one allophone. The rules for unstressed /ǐ/ and /ǔ/ are found in Chapters 16 and 17, respectively. Thus here we give only the rules for unstressed /a e o/ when they are found next to other vowels. The only exceptions occur when the vowel by itself is a word: **a** *to,* **e** *and,* **o** *or,* and **u** *or,* all of which are explained after each rule.

$$ /\breve{a}/ \rightarrow \left[\left\{ \begin{array}{c} [a] \\ [\emptyset] \end{array} \right\} \Big/ \ \underline{\quad} \ \#/V/ \right] \qquad \begin{array}{l} \textbf{la esposa} \ [\text{la-es-pó-sa}] \ [\text{les-pó-sa}] \\ \textbf{la única} \ [\text{la-ú-ni-ka}] \ [\text{lú-ni-ka}] \end{array} $$

As you know by now, # represents a word boundary. As you can see, it doesn't matter whether word-final /a/ precedes a stressed or unstressed vowel, and it doesn't matter what the vowel is. One exception to this rule is the word **a**. In this case unstressed /ǎ/ cannot be eliminated in any style of speech because this would blur an important grammatical distinction. The unstressed /ǎ/ must remain in **Habló a Eduardo** ''She spoke to Edward'' to avoid having the utterance sound instead like **Habló Eduardo** ''Edward spoke.''

$$/\verb|ĕ|/ \rightarrow \begin{bmatrix} \begin{Bmatrix} [e] \\ [\underline{i}] \end{Bmatrix} \Big/ \begin{Bmatrix} \underline{\quad} /V_1/ \\ /V_1/ \underline{\quad} \end{Bmatrix} \\ \\ \begin{Bmatrix} [e] \\ [\emptyset] \end{Bmatrix} \Big/ \underline{\quad} \# /i/ \end{bmatrix}$$

teatro	[te-á-tro] [ti̯á-tro]
la esposa	[la-es-pó-sa] [lai̯s-pó-sa]
me iba	[me-í-ɸa] [mí-ɸa]
me imagino	[mei̯-ma-xí-no] [mi-ma-xí-no]

/V₁/ is /a o u/

Unstressed /ĕ/ can be replaced in rapid speech by [i̯] before or after a stressed or unstressed /a o u/ (which is what V₁ means in the rule) within or between words. It can be completely eliminated in rapid speech before a stressed or unstressed vowel, but *only* in word-final position—thus the symbol # in the rule above. We also find the same exception that we found with unstressed /ă/.

Unstressed /ĕ/ can also be the word **e** *and*, which is used before words beginning with an /i/, in phrases such as **Fernando e Isabel, padres e hijos**, and so forth. In this case, the unstressed /ĕ/ cannot be eliminated in any style of speech because this would blur a grammatical distinction. It would make, for example, **español e inglés** *Spanish and English*, for example, sound like **español inglés** *"English Spanish"* (?) or *"an English-style Spaniard"*(?).

$$/\verb|ŏ|/ \rightarrow \begin{bmatrix} \begin{Bmatrix} [o] \\ [\underline{u}] \end{Bmatrix} \Big/ \begin{Bmatrix} \underline{\quad} /V_1/ \\ /V_1/ \underline{\quad} \end{Bmatrix} \\ \\ \begin{Bmatrix} [o] \\ [\emptyset] \end{Bmatrix} \Big/ \underline{\quad} \# /u/ \end{bmatrix}$$

toalla	[to-á-ya] [tu̯á-ya]
la oficina	[la-o-fi-sí-na] [lau̯-fi-sí-na]
lo único	[lo-ú-ni-ko] [lú-ni-ko]
lo humillaron	[lou̯-mi-yá-ron] [lu-mi-yá-ron]

/V₁/ is /e a i/

Unstressed /ŏ/ can be replaced in rapid speech by [u̯] before or after a stressed or unstressed /e a i/ (which is what V₁ means in the rule) within or between words. It can be completely eliminated in rapid speech before a stressed or unstressed vowel, but *only* in word-final position—thus the symbol # in the rule above. We also find the same exception that we found with unstressed /ă/ and /ĕ/. Unstressed /ŏ/ can also be the word **o** *or*. In this case, the unstressed /ŏ/ cannot be eliminated in any style of speech because this would blur a grammatical distinction, making **animal o humano** *animal or human*, for example, sound like **animal humano** *human animal*.

For the most part, these vowel modifications are not geographically determined. The raising of /e/ and /o/ to /i/ and /u/, respectively, is widely done among rural speakers all over Spanish America but is also done by educated speakers in virtually every dialect area, mainly in rapid speech. It is particularly common in Mexico and Central America among all speakers.

The problems that you, as English speakers, have with Spanish vowel combinations are basically the same as those that are common with individual vowels, all of which have been presented in detail in previous chapters.

The following chart presents no new information but is intended to be used as a handy summary of the various modifications, which are accompanied by examples. Only the vowels in question are transcribed. The modification SEPARATED is not shown.

Chart 21 Types of Vowel Combinations in Spanish: Summary

Vowels Involved	LINKED	FUSED	ELIMINATED	REPLACED
Identical vowels, both stressed $/\acute{V}_1\ \acute{V}_1/$	*(careful and rapid speech)* **dé esto** [é-é] **vi islas** [í-í]			
Identical vowels, both unstressed $/\breve{V}_1\ \breve{V}_1/$			*(careful and rapid speech)* **creeré** [e] **la abriré** [a]	
Identical vowels, one of which is stressed $/\acute{V}_1\ \breve{V}_1/$ $/\breve{V}_1\ \acute{V}_1/$	*(careful speech)* **cree** [é-e] **alcohol** [o-ó]		*(rapid speech)* **cree** [é] **alcohol** [ó]	
Strong vowels: stressed /a e o/ and stressed /í ú/ with other vowels	*(careful and rapid speech)* **vía** [í-a] **país** [a-í] **caer** [a-é] **caótico** [a-ó] **oí** [o-í] **creo** [é-o] **poeta** [o-é] **baúl** [a-ú] **grúa** [ú-a] **ahora** [a-ó]			
Unstressed /a e o/ before higher vowels (*at word boundaries*)	*(careful speech)* **la hijita** [a-i] **la esposa** [a-e] **la oficina** [a-o] **la universidad** [a-u] **me imagino** [e-i] **lo único** [o-ú]		*(rapid speech)* **la hijita** [i] **la esposa** [e] **la oficina** [o] **la universidad** [u] **me imagino** [i] **lo único** [ú]	

Environment	careful speech	careful and rapid speech	rapid speech
Unstressed /e o/ with other vowels (elsewhere: not before higher vowels)		pasear [e-á] le hablamos [e-a] poeta [o-é] pero ahora [o-a]	pasear [i̯á] le hablamos [i̯a] poeta [u̯é] pero ahora [u̯a]
Weak vowels: unstressed /i u/ between other vowels or between pauses and other vowels (at boundaries)	dicho y hecho [o-i-é] muy alto [ú-i-á] siete u ocho [e-u-ó] y además [i-a] huir [u-í]	muy alto [u̯i-á] hoy es viernes [oi̯-e]	dicho y hecho [o-yé] muy alto [u-yá] siete u ocho [e-wó] y además [ya] huir [wí] hoy es viernes [ó-ye]
Weak vowels: unstressed /i u/ with other vowels (at boundaries)	me imagino [e-i] mi amigo [i-a] su amigo [u-a] fió [i-ó]		me imagino [ei̯] mi amigo [i̯a] su amigo [u̯a] fió [i̯ó]
Weak vowels: unstressed /i u/ with other vowels (elsewhere: no boundaries)		seis [éi̯] Miami [i̯á] suave [u̯á] causa [áu̯] ruido [u̯í] dio [i̯ó] deuda [éu̯]	

Practice

A.

Say the following phrases and sentences, either by repeating after your instructor or reading them directly. Most of the contiguous vowels in all these items are LINKED *in separate syllables. But do* not *separate them with pauses or glottal stops—keep your vocal bands vibrating for all the vowel transitions. Use* careful *speech throughout. If your instructor wishes, indicate where the* linked *vowels are. If an item contains more than one set of linked vowels, this is indicated in parentheses after the item.*

1. Es otro país.
2. ¿Leíste la descripción de la carestía de energía? (3)
3. No habla nunca de lo íntimo. (2)
4. Su hijo no está en este momento. (3)
5. La uva es la base de muchas comidas interesantes.
6. Lo útil a veces no se ve al principio. (2)
7. La hembra del mosquito no tiene otro nombre. (2)
8. Hablé alemán de niña.
9. Mi padre habló alemán conmigo. (2)
10. Lo hecho hecho está. (3)
11. El tipo ríe a grandes carcajadas. (2)
12. Vi otros del mismo tipo.
13. Olí humo en el piso. (2)
14. Los camiones necesitan grúas para ese tipo de trabajo. (2)
15. ¿Tú observas el búho en el árbol? (3)
16. Vi islas desde la canoa. (2)
17. Estudié esto a más no poder. (2)
18. Va Ana para reclutar a la Alta, porque la Alta es buena jugadora de básquet. (3)
19. Mucho alcohol daña el hígado. (3)
20. Tú únicamente sabes la cosa.

B.

Say the following phrases and sentences. Most of the contiguous vowels in all these items are FUSED *in the same syllable (diphthongs or triphthongs). Since they are all within words, it doesn't matter whether the speech is* careful *or* rapid. *If your instructor wishes, indicate where the* fused *vowels are. More than one diphthong and/or triphthong in an item is indicated in parentheses.*

1. Es un paisano nuestro. (2)
2. La reina no se peina; tiene peinadora. (4)
3. Nunca lleva boina porque no le sienta bien con su peinado. (4)

4. No conozco la causa de su manía.
5. ¿Tienes muchas deudas? (2)
6. Necesita ir a la farmacia para conseguir medicinas para sus alergias. (2)
7. Vi la película *El piano* en Miami. (2)
8. **Homogeneidad** es una palabra bien difícil de pronunciar. (3)
9. ¡Fui a ver *La fiestecita* siete veces! (3)
10. ¿Vosotros estudiáis varias materias en el mismo semestre? (3)
11. Los perros siempre tienen piojos. (3)
12. ¿Por eso dicen ''Guau, guau''? (2)
13. ¿Vio? No fue toro, fue buey. (4)
14. Piura no es una ciudad pequeña. (2)
15. Aunque está muy reumático, no tiene mucho cuidado. (5)
16. Oigamos lo que están tocando en el patio. (2)
17. Cuando llueve, no sale sin ruana. (3)
18. Si os graduáis, no tendréis que seguir pagando la cuota mensual. (4)
19. Suavecito, es muaré y se daña fácilmente. (2)
20. ¡Mujer! Hace tiempitos que no te veo. ¡Qué fiesta!, ¿no? (2)

C.

Say the following phrases and sentences. Most of the contiguous vowels in all these items are either identical unstressed vowels, identical vowels with only one of them stressed, or unstressed /a e o/ in word-final position before a higher vowel. Since the speech is to be rapid, *one of them should be* ELIMINATED. *Remember that if you speak too slowly, eliminating these vowels won't sound right. Two or more cases of eliminated vowels are indicated.*

1. Leí un artículo sobre los efectos del alcoholismo.
2. Va a hablar exactamente sobre lo que vamos a leer. (2) [How do you think the *three* unstressed /a/'s at the beginning should be handled in rapid speech?]
3. Sssssssss. Habla Álvaro.
4. Habla a Álvaro. [In this case there are two unstressed /a/'s, followed by one stressed one, but there is a slight problem. How do you solve it?]
5. El azahar huele bien.
6. Uno no puede depender del azar.
7. ¿Son dos palabras distintas—el azar y el azahar? [Why should **azahar** be pronounced differently in this sentence than in 5 above?]
8. Mi hijito querido, no te creerán. (2)
9. En Colombia se oye mucho la frase, ''¿Cómo me le va, m'hijo?'' [The spelling gives this one away.]
10. Entiende español, pero no entiende esto. (2)
11. Hablé español siempre con nuestro obrero. (2)

12. No odiamos al hombre por lo que escribió en su último libro. (2)
13. Yo sí lo odio.
14. —¿La abre? —No, pero seguramente la abrirá. (2)
15. La entrada no cuesta tanto.
16. La universidad cobra demasiado por eso.
17. Pregunta en la oficina no más.
18. Me era fácil creerlo. (2)
19. La hacienda era enorme. (2)
20. Era menos pintoresco, pero de igual utilidad.
21. Con la abundancia de fruta hermosa y suculenta... (3)
22. Lo único que sé es que ahora tengo uno. (3)
23. —Oye, chico. ¿Tienes la hora?
24. —¿Me le parezco un reloj?

D.

Say the following phrases and sentences. Most of the contiguous vowels in all these items are either unstressed /ĕ ŏ/ next to other vowels or unstressed /ĭ ŭ/, all in positions where they are REPLACED by [i̯ u̯ y w], respectively. This has to be rapid speech, too. As usual, two or more cases are indicated.

1. Perdón, pero creo que **chao** se escribe con **u** al final, ¿no?
2. Los cohetes caerán dentro de poco. (2)
3. Mami, ¿por qué no se escribe **cae** con **y griega**?
4. Estaban rodeadas de un enorme patio. (2)
5. Se habla siempre de lo íntimo. (2)
6. Hombre, lo hecho hecho está. (2)
7. Lo hablan siempre.
8. León, el teatro este año es peor que nunca. (5)
9. Siempre lo hablamos de niños.
10. No sabía que estaban enfermos, pero sí lo están.
11. Niño u hombre, tiene que hacerlo. (2)
12. Grau era un dramaturgo muy conocido.

E.

Say the following items in CAREFUL (SLOW) speech.

1. Bilbao es una ciudad del norte de España.
2. Solía ayudar a mi tío y a sus empleados.
3. Estudia algo pero no sé exactamente qué.
4. Le interesaba la historia de la marcha triunfal de Aníbal.
5. A veces la leche se transforma en mantequilla y en queso.
6. ¡Leoncitos a mí!

7. Estudió historia antigua cuando estaba en la universidad.
8. Pero de igual utilidad eran los cerdos.
9. No quería beber el alcohol porque era malo para el hígado.
10. Estudié eso pero no lo aprendí.
11. Sabe él que la cosa no puede menos que empeorar.
12. Sí, hay animales—siete u ocho.

F.

Say the following items in CASUAL *(RAPID) speech.*

1. Bilbao es una ciudad famosa por su bacalao.
2. Mi hijo tiene mucha dificultad con la historia—no le entra.
3. —León, ¿qué estás madurando allí?
4. Y además la carne de vaca es una parte imprescindible de nuestra dieta.
5. Pero era muy productivo, y por fin se instaló aquí.
6. No estudió mucho cuando estaba en la universidad.
7. Siempre hay animales en el zoológico.
8. Sabe él que la cosa no puede menos de empeorar.
9. Lo abrió y no encontró nada.
10. Eran animales que en otras partes no veía sino muertos y preparados para la mesa en la cocina.
11. Te engañó cuando te dijo que no podía ir a Honduras.
12. Pablo y Eduardo vieron lo horrible de la situación.
13. Me honraron cuando me invitaron al teatro para ver esa obra.
14. Llevaba su antiguo uniforme a la antigua usanza.
15. En este momento todo mi interés está en este libro de español.

G.

Conduct a brief dialog (a few minutes) with a classmate, who is supposed to be a visiting Spanish speaker unfamiliar with your town and campus. Tell her/him about the three most important or interesting places to see. As you go along, she/he will ask questions since she/he has to decide which one to see first. The rest of the class should pay particular attention to the vowel combinations and give you both some constructive feedback.

H.

Make a phonetic transcription of the following sentences. Do not include intonation contours, but use ‖ *to indicate the pauses. Watch particularly for vowel combinations. Assume that someone is reading these items, using* careful *speech.*

1. La ama con toda su alma.
2. No creo que los poetas se paseen por esta avenida.

3. Me siento ahogado.
4. Me imagino que te ibas a la Unión.
5. Quería dieciséis o diecisiete, pero no hay aquí más que quince.
6. Pienso que es de Ecuador.
7. Su ave es suave.
8. Y eso no es yeso.
9. Si entras, lo sientes en seguida.
10. Sabe él que la cosa no puede menos que empeorar.

I.

Now transcribe the same sentences, but this time assume that the individual is using rapid *speech. This will make a difference in most of the sentences. In some there are even a couple of possible right ways of doing it. These will be indicated in Appendix C.*

19

Reviewing the Vowels of Spanish (CHAPTERS 14–18)

The best way to show the vowel phonemes of Spanish is the conventional vowel triangle.

Chart 22   Spanish Vowel Phonemes: The Triangle

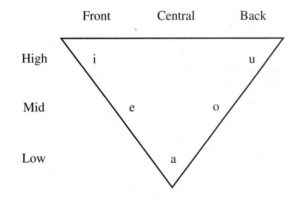

The quadrangle, however, is better to show the vowel allophones of Spanish, and bear in mind that [y] and [w], although considered allophones of /i/ and /u/, respectively, are really consonants (see note 1 in Chapter 16). [y] is a voiced, palatal slit fricative, and [w] is a voiced, bilabio-velar slit fricative. This will be explained further in Chapter 23.

Chart 23 Spanish Vowel Allophones: The Grid

	Front	Central	Back
High	y i̯ i		w u̯ u
Mid	e		o
Low		a	

Oral vowels are produced when the airstream flows freely from the larynx through two cavities: the pharynx (throat) and the oral cavity, whose size and shape is formed by the lips and tongue. Nasal vowels are produced when the airstream flows through the pharynx and the nasal cavity. However, since nasal vowels are produced completely automatically—redundantly in Spanish—we have chosen to eliminate them from our analysis. We could not do that for languages like French, Portuguese, or Polish, where nasal vowels are functional. That is, they contrast with their oral counterparts.

Although the dialects of Spanish are determined—at least as far as sounds are concerned—mainly by consonants rather than vowels, there are some interesting dialectal vowel modifications. The two most important ones are vowel shortening or reduction and vowel devoicing or whispering. Both are extremely common in Mexican and Andean Spanish. The vowels most likely to undergo these modifications are found in unstressed syllables, near the end of the word, and particularly after or between voiceless consonants: **muchas gracias, un accidente de coches, un bloc para apuntes, un hecho importante.**

English speakers typically have two main problems with Spanish vowels: one with unstressed vowels, the other with stressed. As you recall, most unstressed syllables in English contain one or the other of the two mid central vowels, [ə] and [ɨ]—both absent in Spanish. Not only do these vowels sound foreign in Spanish, but their use can blur important grammatical distinctions, such as adjective gender and verb endings as well as lexical distinctions, such as the difference between words. These vowels can be avoided in Spanish if you make a concerted effort to move your jaws, lips, and tongue properly as you go from one of the five Spanish vowels to the other. You should be able to feel these movements in your face if you are pronouncing the Spanish vowels properly. This is not true in English because we avoid these extreme movements by ''cheating'' in a sense with the two mid central vowels, mentioned above, which can be pronounced with relatively little movement of the lips and jaws. In fact, this is so true that if you speak Spanish properly for quite a while after an extended period of *not* speaking Spanish, your jaw muscles will be somewhat tired at first. Also if your face is sunburned, speaking Spanish will have a more noticeable effect on your tender skin than English because of the more extreme movements in pronouncing the five vowels, none of which occurs right in the middle, as schwa, for example, does in English.

The second problem involves Spanish stressed vowels. Almost no word ends in English with a ''pure'' stressed vowel, that is, one without one of the three glides, /y w h/ or a consonant after it. Although you may think at first that words like *no, two, see, say,* and *bah* end in vowels, they actually end in one of these glides, and the vowels, therefore, are the first part of diphthongs. Spanish, however, has no such restrictions, and the Spanish words **no, tú, sí, sé**, and **va** do end in ''pure'' vowels, that is, unaccompanied by glides or semi-vowels. Spanish, of course, does have some word-final diphthongs, but they are always represented in writing: **rey, voy, hay, Grau**. The English word *ray* has virtually the same diphthong that the Spanish word **rey** does; likewise with *rain* and **reino**. But Spanish contrasts **reino** *kingdom* with **reno** *reindeer,* and English has no word with exactly the same syllable as Spanish **re-**. *Rain* also has the diphthong [ɛy], but *wren* has just an [ɛ] which is considerably more open (the tongue is lower) than the Spanish [e] in open syllables like **re-**. Spanish has **pena** with a more closed [e] and **peina** with the [ei̯] diphthong. Saying **pena** with the [ɛ] of *pen* is not correct, nor is saying it with the [ɛy] of *pain* correct. This problem of simple vowel versus diphthong is an everpresent one for the English speaker learning Spanish, although perhaps not as severe as the use of [ə] in unstressed syllables.

Other than the two points mentioned above, the Spanish vowels /a e o/ have no other particular problems for English speakers. The high vowels /i u/, however, each present some difficulties in COGNATE words. You may have a tendency to separate the Spanish diphthongs starting with [i̯], particularly in Spanish words that have similar counterparts in English, saying **pati-o* instead of **patio**, because of *patio*, or **ti-empo* instead of **tiempo** because of the use of *Tiempo* in English for various products or **fi-esta* instead of **fiesta** for the same reason. In the case of /u/, English-speakers have a tendency to insert a palatal glide /y/ ([i̯] in Spanish) in cognate words: **miuseo* instead of **museo**, **regiular* instead of **regular**, and the common **película*, probably through analogy with words like *ridiculous, perpendicular, particular.*

Practice

A.

The following English words, all of which have appeared somewhere in the last six chapters, have Spanish cognates or Spanish words with virtually the same sound structure. Give the Spanish word if you can; otherwise repeat it after your instructor. More than one Spanish word may fit. An example of cognate words is animal–**animal**.

An example of non-cognate words with similar sound structures is rain–**reino** *or* **reina** (*but* not **reno**!).

1. possessions	35. accident	69. construct
2. "pesos"	36. circus	70. sues
3. succulent	37. agile	71. situated
4. no	38. energy	72. linguist
5. two	39. individual	73. mutilate
6. bee	40. patio	74. society
7. bay	41. allergy	75. loose
8. pain	42. internal	76. Yugo
9. spirit	43. sin	77. insinuate
10. preoccupy	44. Mexican	78. occupied
11. "señorita"	45. American	79. punctuality
12. "hombre"	46. diplomatic	80. communicate
13. hospital	47. "siesta"	81. automobile
14. responsibility	48. Bolivia	82. furious
15. Bah!	49. discrete	83. Europe
16. low	50. civil	84. musical
17. papa	51. Chile	85. document
18. Joe	52. hemorrhage	86. particular
19. "don Quijote"	53. civilization	87. simulate
20. Colorado	54. merit	88. adulate
21. prosperous	55. Mario	89. regularize
22. vapor	56. Linda	90. title
23. doctor	57. mill	91. turn
24. official	58. meal	92. authorize
25. chocolate	59. iris	93. circular
26. exam	60. solicit	94. mule
27. note	61. "Diablo"	95. popular
28. "Caramba!"	62. disgust	96. mutual
29. boy	63. taboo	97. humiliate
30. invite	64. suave	98. chaotic
31. firm	65. cause	99. alcohol
32. aspirin	66. Swiss	100. unique
33. "Adios!"	67. debt	
34. Tiempo	68. "junta"	

B.

Write the answers to these questions and check them in Appendix C.

1. With regard to vowels, "high" refers to the vertical position of the tongue.   TRUE/FALSE

2. Three vowels that do not exist in Spanish are (*give the phonetic symbols*) _____, _____, and _____

3. Complex vowel nuclei in North American English can also be referred to as diphthongs.   TRUE/FALSE

4. One feature of vowel pronunciation that is *not* phonemic or functional in Spanish or English is (a) lip-rounding; (b) height; (c) position on a front-to-back axis.

5. "Whispered" vowels are also referred to as _____ vowels.

6. One of the main problems that English speakers have with Spanish vowels are the "whispered" vowels.   TRUE/FALSE

7. If you don't pronounce the unstressed vowel of Spanish **mesas** properly, it may sound like (a) **masas**; (b) **mesa**; (c) **meses**.

8. Spanish /a/ is always spelled with **a** or **ha**.   TRUE/FALSE

9. English [ɛ] is (a) more closed than Spanish [e]; (b) always followed by a glide; (c) pronounced with the tongue slightly lower in the mouth.

10. You should always know when a Spanish word has the diphthong [ei̯] because

_____.

11. The so-called "short *o*" of English, as in *not, cop,* and *con,* is really not an /o/ at all but an /a/.   TRUE/FALSE

12. Spanish [i̯] is different from [i] because the former is a _____ whereas the latter is a full vowel.

13. Stressed /í/ in Spanish has (a) two allophones; (b) a semi-vowel after it in most cases; (c) only one allophone.

14. When you see a little subscribed numeral in a phonological rule, it calls your attention to something that is called a _____ of the rule.

15. Casual or rapid speech, while we recognize that it happens in Spanish, is meant to be avoided by a foreigner like you learning the language.   TRUE/FALSE

16. The symbol ‖ in Spanish phonology and phonetics represents (a) a pause; (b) a morpheme boundary; (c) a diphthong: two vowels in one syllable.

17. A word like **miasma** *putrescent pollution* and a phrase like **mi asma** *my asthma* can only be distinguished from each other by context, but never by their sounds, like *aboard* and *a board* in English.   TRUE/FALSE

18. The [I] in the English word *mill* is different from the [i] in the Spanish word **mil** because (a) the tongue is lower in the mouth when it is pronounced; (b) it has a palatal glide after it; (c) it is much longer in duration.

19. The Spanish phoneme /i/ is spelled with the letters _____, _____, and _____.

20. Unstressed /ŭ/ often carries the little curved mark above it (a) just to point out the fact that it is unstressed; (b) because it is occasionally nasalized; (c) because it always precedes a word or morpheme boundary.

21. Unstressed /ŭ/ can be realized as a [w] in several phonetic environments, one of which is _____.

22. Unstressed /ŭ/ can never be realized as the semi-vowel [u̯] when it comes as the first sound in a word.   TRUE/FALSE

23. Some dialects of North American English have the low front vowel _____ *(give the phonetic symbol)* in the diphthong of words like *how, now, brown,* and *cow.*

24. The pattern of [CU̯V] occurs widely in Spanish with a variety of consonants, but its distribution is much more restricted in English.   TRUE/FALSE

25. The word **deuda** (a) has three syllables; (b) has a diphthong; (c) has a hiatus.

26. The word **seguir** has no /u/ phoneme in any of its forms.   TRUE/FALSE

27. Words like **vergüenza** and **lingüista** have a dieresis ¨ (a) to show that the /u/ and the following vowel form separate syllables; (b) to show that they really have a /u/ sound in them; (c) as a carry-over from Latin orthography.

28. Three factors that govern the pronunciation of Spanish vowels in combination with each other are _____, _____, and _____.

29. One feature that can completely separate vowels next to each other is called a glottal stop.   TRUE/FALSE

30. An unstressed /ǐ/ or unstressed /ǔ/ before another vowel can retain its status as a full vowel, that is, not turn into a semi-vowel, when it occurs _____.

31. Diphthongs cannot occur between words, only within them.   TRUE/FALSE

32. An eliminated vowel (a) must be unstressed; (b) may be stressed; (c) must be a mid or low vowel.

33. Eliminated vowels sometimes sound strange in _____ speech.

34. An unstressed mid vowel can be eliminated at word boundaries only before a high vowel on the same side of the vowel triangle.   TRUE/FALSE

35. Mid vowels, when replaced in rapid speech, are usually done so (a) only before a low vowel; (b) next to any of the other three vowels anywhere; (c) only before high vowels.

36. Can you give a Spanish phrase that might have three different pronunciations, depending on the style of speech, with regard to the vowels which combine at the boundary of the two words? _____

20

Introducing the Consonants of Spanish

As we have already seen, consonants are sounded when the airstream is stopped or impeded in some way in the upper vocal tract or supraglottal cavities: from the vocal bands up and out to the lips. There are three meaningful ways of classifying consonants in Spanish: PLACE OF ARTICULATION—bilabial, labio-dental, interdental (Spain only), dental, alveolar, palatal, velar, bilabio-velar, glottal (some dialects only); MANNER OF ARTICULATION—stops, fricatives, affricates, nasals, laterals, tap, trill; and FUNCTION OF VOCAL BANDS—voicing or the lack of it.

In Chapter 11 (see Chart 10) we saw how a chart could be made showing all three dimensions: place or point of articulation across the top (roughly analogous to the points as they are actually found in the vocal tract of an individual looking to the left), manner of articulation from top to bottom, and voicing by the position of the consonant in the compartment—voiceless sounds in the upper left, voiced in the lower right.

Spanish Dialectal Differences

Vowels play a major role in determining the dialects of English; in Spanish, however, dialectal variations depend mainly on the consonants, particularly /s/ (and /θ/), /y/ (and /ʎ/), /x/ (or /h/), /ĉ/, and /r̄/. For example, American Spanish does not have the /s/–/θ/ contrast, since it lacks the /θ/ phoneme (as in English _theme_): **sierra** and **cierra** are pronounced exactly alike. In Spain, however, most speakers distinguish these words and many others like them because of the /θ/ phoneme of Castilian Spanish. The palatal /y/ has a wide variety of realizations and in some dialects contrasts with /ʎ/ (almost like the consonant sound in English _million_). Most speakers of American Spanish and many in Spain pronounce **haya** and **halla** exactly alike. However, many speakers on both sides of the Atlantic distinguish these words and dozens like them because of the palatal /ʎ/ phoneme (spelled with **ll**).

Central Americans, Caribbean speakers, and many from the northern coastal regions of South America, as well as speakers from southern Spain, pronounce such words as

jardín and **gente** with a glottal /h/ (as in English _hand_). Others in Spanish America and throughout Spain pronounce them with a velar /x/ (as in the Scottish _Loch_). Many speakers in these same areas of Spanish America and also in southern Spain pronounce words like **chico** and **leche** with a fricative [š] (as in English _sheep_) rather than the affricate [ĉ] (as in English _cheap_) used by speakers everywhere else. In many parts of Spanish America the voiced alveolar trilled phoneme /r̄/ is not trilled or even voiced but pronounced in a variety of ways that will be taken up in Chapter 28.

Syllable-Final Consonant Modifications

All dialects of Spanish show great consonantal modifications in the syllable-final position. These modifications, unlike the ones mentioned above, are fairly uniform from dialect to dialect, but contrast greatly with the behavior of similar consonants in similar positions in English. We can show this position as VC̲ (#)-C for within a word (**cos̲ta**) or at the end of a word before a consonant (**los̲-tiempos**) and as VC̲# for the end of a word before a pause (**más̲**). This representation, of course, ignores consonants that appear in other positions, such as at the beginning of the syllable in question or in subsequent syllables. As you know, if the consonant at the end of the word is followed by another word beginning with a vowel, the consonant in question is no longer in syllable-final position, but is now in syllable-_initial_ position because of **enlace** or linking. The phrase **los ama** is really composed of three open syllables: **lo-s̲a-ma**, and thus the consonant /s/, although at the end of a word, is not in syllable-final position as it is in **los̲-tiem-pos**.

One of the main reasons for consonant modifications in syllable-final position in Spanish is the fact that the speech organs get ready for the next consonant a bit too soon—''in a hurry,'' so to speak—and thus modify the first consonant accordingly. The phoneme /s/ is normally realized as a voiceless [s] in syllable-initial position: **sesenta** [se-sén̦-ta]. But if /s/ occurs in a word or phrase immediately before a voiced _consonant_, rather than a vowel, as in **los̲ mis̲mos̲ días̲**, it is quite often realized as a voiced [z] instead: [loz-míz-moz-ð̦í-as]. This is because the vocal bands start vibrating in advance for the [m]'s of **mismos** and the [ð̦] of **días**, and this vibration turns the previous [s] into [z].

Assimilation

This phenomenon, known as ASSIMILATION, is extremely common in all dialects of Spanish and in many other languages, too. One sound undergoes a change when it comes in contact with another; that is, it _assimilates_ to or becomes more like the neighboring sound. The example of **los̲ mis̲mos̲ días̲** illustrates one kind of assimilation, namely RE-GRESSIVE ASSIMILATION, which is by far the most common type in Spanish. The term _regressive_ means ''backwards'' in a sense—the following sound influences the preceding one.

A less common form in Spanish is PROGRESSIVE ASSIMILATION, just the opposite: the first or preceding sound influences the second or following sound. An example of this is what happens to the /b/ in the word **hombre**. More often than not, /b/ in Spanish is realized as a fricative [β] rather than as a stop [b]. Thus the words **lobo, obra, esbelto** all have fricative [β]'s. But a preceding nasal sound—always [m]—causes the /b/ to be realized as a stop [b], rather than a fricative, giving us [óm-bre] for **hombre**, as opposed to [ló-βo] for **lobo.** In this case, unlike the example of **los mismos días**, the first sound [m] works ''forward'' on the following sound, giving [b] rather than [β].

English is rich in examples of progressive assimilation. The regular plural of nouns is determined by this phenomenon: /s/ follows most of the voiceless consonants as in *cup-cups, cat-cats, pick-picks, cuff-cuffs,* and /z/ follows most of the voiced consonants as in *cub-cubs* (really pronounced with a /z/: /kʌbz/), *bid-bids* (again, really with a /z/), *pig-pigs, groove-grooves*. In other words, the voicelessness or the voicing of the consonant at the end of the noun is carried over to the plural ending. The same progressive assimilation is shown in the third-person singular of the present tense of regular English verbs: *talk-talks, laugh-laughs,* for example, for /s/, and *stab-stabs, live-lives* for /z/.

In Spanish regressive and progressive assimilation happen readily across word boundaries as well as within words, as we have seen in **los mismos días**. English also often assimilates within words: *raspberry* (with a /z/), but not normally between words (that is, at the end of one word preceding another one): *this berry* (with an /s/). This is just another illustration of a concept first introduced to you in Chapter 13: word boundaries in Spanish pronunciation are far less important than syllable and intonation-group boundaries.

There are other important differences between the behavior of consonants in Spanish and in English. Spanish has fewer consonants to begin with, and their distribution is much more restricted. English words can begin with as many as three consonants: *spray, split, sclerosis, scream,* and end with as many as four: *texts* (/teksts/), *sixths* (/siksθs/). In Spanish the maximum number of consonants in a word-initial cluster is two (remember the groups /pr pl br bl/, etc.). And there are very few Spanish words that end with a consonant cluster (**bíceps** is an example of this unusual pattern). Almost no Spanish words end in the single consonants /p t k b g/, and many speakers even leave them out of the words where they do occur, saying [yór] for the last word of **Nueva York,** or [ber-mú] for **vermut** *(vermouth).*

The Phonological Rule

Remember also the essential elements of phonological rules like the following.

$$
/d/ \rightarrow
\left[
\begin{array}{l}
[d] \Big/ \left\{\begin{array}{l} \| \\ /l/ \\ /n/ \end{array}\right\} \underline{\quad} \\[2em]
\left\{\begin{array}{l} [ð] \\ [\varnothing] \end{array}\right\} \Big/ \underline{\quad} \# \\[2em]
[ð] \text{ elsewhere}
\end{array}
\right.
\quad
\begin{array}{l}
\textbf{Dígame, falda, anda} \\[2em]
\textbf{verdad} \\[2em]
\textbf{lado, pide, amígdalas, pierde}
\end{array}
$$

This rule says the following: the phoneme /d/ is realized as the stop [d] allophone in the following environments: after a pause ‖ , as in the ABSOLUTE-INITIAL position (**Dí-game**), after an /l/ (**falda**), and after an /n/ (**anda**). (This, by the way, is an example of progressive assimilation, since the preceding sounds influence the following /d/.) The phoneme /d/ is also realized either as a fricative [đ] in careful speech at the end of a word, or as [ø]. In casual speech at the end of a word it may be realized as silence, that is, omitted completely: **verdad** [ber-đá]. (This, of course, is free variation.) And it is realized as a fricative [đ] in all other positions, that is, *elsewhere*, as in **lado, pide, amígdalas, pierde**.

Remember that the braces (''pointy parentheses'') to the left of the diagonal indicate free variation; that is, *either* allophone can be used in the environment indicated, although there are usually some guidelines for which one. But the braces to the right of the diagonal indicate that the allophones to the left occur in *all* these environments. So stop [d] must be used (1) after a pause *and* (2) after /l/ *and* (3) after /n/.

Phonological rules like this will be presented for each consonant; in some cases there will be two or three rules for the consonant in question to show how it is pronounced in different dialects of Spanish.

You will also have to keep in mind several important concepts from previous chapters, such as LINKING (**enlace**), the SYLLABLE, the PHONEMIC PHRASE (or BREATH GROUP or INTONATIONAL GROUP), CONSONANT CLUSTER, OPEN versus CLOSED SYLLABLES, ABSO-LUTE-INITIAL position, and the ELSEWHERE concept. If you are still unsure of these terms, check them again in Appendix A before going on to the next chapter.

21

The Voiceless Consonants /p t k/

Allophone of /p/

The consonant /p/ in Spanish has only one allophone [p], a voiceless bilabial stop, shown in the diagram.

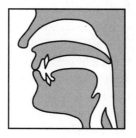

[p]

Description of the /p/ Allophone

For [p] the two lips press together to stop the airstream, which is then released abruptly *without* aspiration: there is no puff of air because voicing for the following sound begins almost immediately.

Distribution of /p/

Although /p/ has only the above allophone, it occasionally drops out completely. This is shown by the following rule.

$$/p/ \rightarrow \left[\begin{matrix} \left\{ \begin{matrix} [p] \\ [\varnothing] \end{matrix} \right\} \Big/ \begin{matrix} \text{in } \textbf{séptimo,} \\ \textbf{se(p)tiembre, etc.} \end{matrix} \\ [p] \quad \text{elsewhere} \end{matrix} \right] \quad \textbf{pasa, tapa, hampa}$$

/p/, since it is implosive and sometimes unreleased in syllable-final position, weakens and even disappears, particularly in the rapid pronunciation of words having to do with the number **siete: séptimo, septiembre, septimazo.** Alternate spellings, such as **sétimo** and **setiembre**—the latter being virtually standard now throughout the Hispanic world—reflect this pronunciation.

Dialectal Variations of /p/

One interesting dialectal variation with /p/ occurs sporadically throughout the Hispanic world, namely the substitution of /k/ for /p/ in the syllable-final position within a word. **Pepsi Cola** comes out [pék-si-kó-la], and natives of Bogotá, Colombia, talk about their evening stroll down Seventh Avenue as **dar un septimazo** [sek-ti-má-so] (*"hitting the Big 7"*).

Contrasts with English

The most important and most obvious contrast with English is the fact that /p/ is always unaspirated in Spanish. In English, however, /p/ is aspirated in word-initial position (*port*) or within a word before a heavy stress (*apart, important*), unreleased at the end of a word (*cup*), and unaspirated elsewhere (*upper, hamper, sport*). Aspirating /p/ in Spanish—as you do in English—helps to create a foreign accent even though, just as in English, it doesn't affect meaning. The main strategy for avoiding this aspiration in Spanish is to purse your lips and release them almost simultaneously with the sound for the following vowel or consonant. The main reason for aspiration of /p/ in English is the fact that the following sound is articulated with what is called "delayed voicing": vocal band vibration. This slight time lapse allows the air to accumulate in your mouth and come out with a puff or with aspiration following the release of your lips. If you time the release of your lips to coincide with the vibration of your vocal bands, you will avoid aspiration.

There is another problem regarding the pronunciation of Spanish /p/ for English speakers. Since, as we described above, the voicing for the following vowel occurs just a split second after the release of the lips, this often causes English speakers to perceive /p/ as /b/. **Paño** sounds like **baño**, **pista** sounds like **vista**, and so forth. However, with Spanish /b/ the voicing slightly *precedes* the release of the lips whereas with /p/ it slightly follows it. This confusion of /p/ and /b/ is aided, of course, by the lack of aspiration with Spanish /p/, which the English speaker expects to hear at first.

Spelling of /p/

/p/ is spelled everywhere in Spanish with **p: pasa, tapa, hampa.** The letter **p** occurs in the traditional spelling of some scientific and specialized words like **psicología** and

psiquiatra, but there is no /p/ sound in them. As we said, words having to do with the number **siete** are often spelled without **p**, reflecting a common pronunciation: **setiembre, sétimo.** This pronunciation has existed for decades and is the subject of a humorous anecdote about one of Spain's greatest philosophers and writers, Miguel de Unamuno (1864–1936). A proofreader corrected Unamuno's spelling of **setiembre** by writing in the margin of the manuscript: "**Ojo. Septiembre.**" "*Take note* (literally *eye*). *Septiembre.*" Unamuno, crossed out the correction and wrote, "**Oído. ¡Setiembre!**" "*Listen* (literally *ear*). *Setiembre!*"

Allophones of /t/

The consonant /t/ in Spanish has one principal allophone: [t], a voiceless dental stop, shown in the first diagram below. It also has a voiced dental fricative: [ɖ], shown in the second diagram.

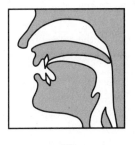

[t]

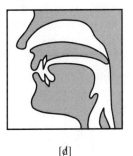

[ɖ]

Description of the /t/ Allophones

For [t] the tongue tip presses against the back of the upper front teeth to stop the airstream, which is then released abruptly *without* aspiration: there is no puff of air because voicing for the following sound begins almost immediately. Thus [t], just like [p], is unaspirated and the following voicing is virtually simultaneous. For [ɖ] the tongue tip is placed very lightly against either the back or the edges of the upper front teeth. The airstream, rather than being stopped, continues steadily through the horizontal slit formed by the tongue tip and teeth. The vocal bands vibrate to create voicing.

Distribution of /t/

Although /t/ in the vast majority of cases has only the voiceless allophone shown and described above, it is occasionally voiced and realized as a voiced fricative [ɖ], particularly before a voiced consonant. This is shown by the following rule.

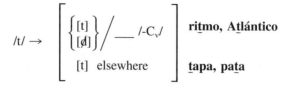

/-C$_v$/ is any voiced consonant that starts a new syllable.

This realization of /t/ as [đ] can also be viewed as a type of phonemic replacement or NEUTRALIZATION. This means that occasionally phonemes lose their contrastive property in certain positions. Although /t/ and /d/ clearly contrast at the beginning of a syllable or word, as in **moto-modo** or **tomar-domar**, either one can occur with no change in meaning at the end of a syllable before a voiced consonant. Thus the word **atlas** can be pronounced either [át-las] or [áđ-las], and most native speakers are unaware of these two different pronunciations, reacting to them as though they were the same. Phonemic neutralization happens in English, too. Although /s/ and /z/ are clearly distinctive, as in *sue-zoo* or *fussy-fuzzy*, either phoneme can be used in such words as *citizen* or *partisan* or the name *Clemson,* with no change in meaning.[1]

Take careful note of one seemingly small detail in the rule above. The /-C$_v$/ environment in which the neutralization of /t/ and /d/ takes place is a following syllable-*initial* consonant, thus the hyphen (-) before the C. This means that /t/ is syllable-*final* and not the first part of the syllable-initial cluster /tr/ (as in **tres**). Even though /r/ is voiced, [đ] cannot occur here because /t/ is not syllable-final in words like **tres** and **trepar**, but rather syllable-initial. Spanish speakers may say **ritmo** as [r̄ít-mo] or [r̄íđ-mo], but *no* Spanish speaker says **otro** as *[ó-đro] instead of [ó-tro] for the reason just explained.

Dialectal Variations of /t/

There are no important dialectal variations of /t/.

Contrasts with English

The most important and obvious contrast with English is the same feature that we mentioned above with [p], the lack of aspiration with Spanish [t]. In English /t/ is aspirated in word-initial position (*take*) or within a word before a heavy stress (*deter, until*); it is a flap or tap within a word between a heavy-stressed vowel and a weak-stressed one (*water, butter, Plato*); it is unreleased at the end of a word (*hot*); and it is unaspirated after /s/ (*stake*). Aspiration of /t/ is just as foreign sounding as aspiration of /p/, and the technique for avoiding it is basically the same. Press the tip of your tongue firmly against the back of your upper front teeth and release it almost simultaneously with the sound for the

---

[1]It is a theoretical matter of no great pedagogical importance whether in Spanish the phoneme /t/ is *replaced* by the phoneme /d/ in these situations or whether it, too, has the same voiced allophone that the /d/ phoneme does, thus creating "phonemic overlap." This same "problem" exists with other phonemes in Spanish, particularly the nasals and laterals. Our approach toward them will be the same as it is for /t/–/d/ and /k/–/g/.

following vowel or consonant. If you do this, you will avoid the buildup of air in your mouth that causes aspiration with /t/ in English at the beginning of a word or before a stress within a word. So, although /t/, just like /p/, is considered voiceless, the subsequent voicing almost coincides with the release of both consonants in Spanish.

Another problem for English speakers is the same as that of /p/. The timing of the voicing with /t/, plus the lack of aspiration, may make it sound like /d/ to you. **Tía** may sound like **día, teja** like **deja**, and so forth. Just as with /b/ in Spanish, the vocal bands vibrate slightly *before* /d/ is sounded whereas with /t/ they vibrate almost immediately afterward, allowing no time for the puff of air known as aspiration.

The final problem with /t/ comes from the fact that Spanish /t/ is dental, not alveolar as it is in English. Also English /t/ in the intervocalic position within a word after a heavy stress is flapped: [ɾ], as in *water, butter, Plato*. Spanish has exactly the same sound, but it is an /r/, not a /t/, and is spelled with **r**. If you pronounce Spanish /t/ in this situation as a flap, it will make **moto** *motorscooter* sound like **moro** *Moor (North African)*, **foto** *photo* sound like **foro** *forum,* and **meta** *goal* sound like **mera** *mere*. Spanish /t/ in these words is *exactly like* the /t/ in **tomar, tía,** and so forth.

Spelling of /t/

/t/ is spelled everywhere in Spanish with **t**: **tomar, pata, hasta, antes.**

Allophones of /k/

The consonant /k/ in Spanish has one principal allophone: [k], a voiceless velar stop, shown in the first diagram below. It also has a voiced velar fricative: [ǥ], shown in the second diagram.

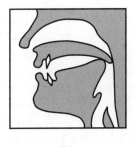

[k]

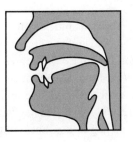

[ǥ]

Description of the /k/ Allophones

For [k] the tongue dorsum presses against the velum to stop the airstream, which is then released abruptly *without* aspiration: the puff of air that accompanies /p t k/ in English in some positions. Again the subsequent voicing is almost simultaneous with the release of the tongue dorsum for [k]. For [ǵ] the back of the tongue is placed very lightly against or very close to the velum. The airstream, rather than being stopped, continues steadily through the horizontal slit formed by the tongue dorsum and the velum. The vocal bands vibrate to create voicing.

Distribution of /k/

Although /k/ in the vast majority of cases has only the voiceless allophone shown and described above, it is occasionally voiced and realized as a voiced fricative [ǵ], particularly before a voiced consonant. Unlike the situation with /t/, which voices only before voiced consonants, /k/ voices before any consonant, voiced or unvoiced. This is shown by the following rule.

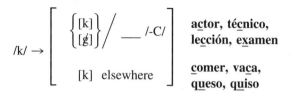

/-C/ is any consonant that starts a new syllable.

This realization of /k/ as a fricative [ǵ] is another example of phonemic replacement, overlap, or neutralization, already explained above with /t/ (see Note 1). The pronunciation happens mainly in rapid speech, but speakers are unaware of the difference. In some areas the voiced sound predominates: for example, most Peruvians call their city Tacna [tág-na].

The same little detail that we saw in the rule for /t/ is to be noted here, too. The hyphen before /-C/ in the rule condition means that the realization of /k/ as [ǵ] takes place only when this consonant represented by C is syllable-*initial*, thus putting /k/ in the syllable-*final* position. Even though both /l/ and /r/ are voiced, /k/ cannot voice when it is the first part of the two syllable-initial clusters /kl/ (as in **clima**) or /kr/ (as in **crema**). /k/ voices to [ǵ] only when it is syllable-final. Spanish speakers may say **técnico** as either [ték-ni-ko] or [tég-ni-ko], but *no* Spanish speaker says *[cî-ǵle] instead of [cî-kle] for **chicle** or *[se-ǵré-to] instead of [se-kré-to] for **secreto** for the reason just explained.

Most Spanish speakers eliminate /k/ at the end of foreign words, because they are not used to this pattern since no native Spanish word ends in /k/. **Nueva York** is [nué-βa-yór]; **coñac** is [ko-ñá]. Many Spanish speakers in rapid speech also eliminate /k/ in syllable-final position, saying [do-tór] for **doctor**, [tá-si] for **taxi**, [au̯-sí-li̯o] for **auxilio**, and [e-sá-men] for **examen**. But the same speakers in careful speech may pronounce the /k/, saying [dok-tór], [ták-si], and so forth.

Dialectal Variations of /k/

Many speakers of peninsular Spanish (Castilian) in rapid speech substitute /θ/ (as in *think*) for /k/ in the syllable-final position before /t/, saying [koṇ-táθ-to] for **contacto** or [aṡ-péθ-to] for **aspecto**. This pronunciation is common even among educated speakers.

Contrasts with English

English speakers have the same two problems with /k/ that we have already seen with /p/ and /t/: aspiration of word-initial /k/ and the inability to distinguish between /k/ and /g/ in the stream of speech. Unlike the /k/ of English *calm,* the /k/ of Spanish **cama** has no aspiration. The formula for success is the same: press the dorsum of your tongue firmly against the velum and release it just a split second before the following sound, thereby avoiding the accumulation of air known as aspiration. And, as with /b/ and /d/, Spanish /g/ has pre-voicing: the vocal bands start vibrating a fraction of a second *before* the tongue is released for /g/, and they start vibrating a fraction of a second *after* the release for /k/, thus differentiating between **cama** and **gama**, **callo** and **gallo**, and so forth.

For Spanish /b d g/ at the beginning of a word, you should feel the vibrations of your vocal bands in your neck, throat, mouth, cheeks, and nose *before* these consonants are articulated. This sensation of vibration is *totally absent* with /p t k/, as is the puff of air that accompanies them in English. This unwanted aspiration is extremely noticeable to Spanish speakers and can give your Spanish a definite English sound.

Spelling of /k/

The spelling of Spanish /k/ is a bit more complicated than that of /p/ or /t/. Three different letter combinations are used: **k** in a handful of foreign words like **kiosco, kiló-metro, kerosén, Nueva York**; **qu** before /e/ and /i/ in all native Spanish words, as in **queso, quiso, busqué, poquito**; and **c** everywhere else, as in **casa, cosa, cuna, frac, finca, técnico**. As you know, this creates one type of a large group of Spanish verbs known as orthographical-changing verbs. This particular spelling point and others will be taken up in Chapter 31.

Practice

A.

Your instructor will read each of the following three-word groups once or twice as he/she prefers. After each group, pick out the one word that is different from the other two. There are four possibilities: "first," "second," "third," or "all the same." For example, if your instructor reads **pan van van,** *you say "first." Or* **van pan van,**

1. paca paca paca	11. di ti di
2. daba daba taba	12. ganas canas ganas
3. cala gala cala	13. pez pez vez
4. van van van	14. teja teja teja
5. tanza tanza danza	15. goza cosa cosa
6. gordura cordura gordura	16. boca boca boca
7. prisa brisa brisa	17. tomar domar tomar
8. dé dé te	18. codo codo godo
9. coma goma coma	19. pesar besar besar
10. beca beca beca	20. dan tan tan

B.

Your instructor will read each Spanish word. Repeat the word, and give its meaning if your instructor wishes. Then say the so-called ''opposite'' word, and give the meaning if asked. ''Opposite'' means **b** *for* **p** *and vice versa,* **d** *for* **t** *and vice versa,* **g** *for* **c** *(or* **qu***) and vice versa. For example, your instructor says* **pesar.** *You also say* **pesar,** *and, if asked, give the meaning—to weigh. Then say* **besar,** *and, if asked, give the meaning—to kiss. Or your instructor says* **goza.** *You also say* **goza,** *and, if asked, give the meaning—she/he enjoys. Then say* **cosa,** *and, if asked, give the meaning— thing. Don't forget that all these words are in the vocabulary at the end of this book.*

1. callo	11. domar
2. bala	12. paz
3. tomar	13. gato
4. ganso	14. vender
5. vino	15. pino
6. pista	16. cosa
7. panal	17. penado
8. cama	18. velar
9. tía	19. gana
10. pan	20. té

C.

Read the following words, first the English, then the Spanish. You will obviously aspirate /p t k/ in the first word in each pair because it is English; but be careful not to aspirate the /p t k/ in the corresponding Spanish word. The words are not necessarily related to each other in meaning; they simply have similar patterns of /p t k/.

1. *pot*	pata	3. *Kay*	qué
2. *take*	teja	4. *tome*	tomo

5. *panel*	pana	13. *impel*	imprimir
6. *con*	cana	14. *deteriorate*	deteriorar
7. *apart*	aparte	15. *incredible*	increíble
8. *until*	entero	16. *poker*	póquer
9. *occur*	ocurre	17. *tennis*	tenis
10. *tip-off*	tipo	18. *case*	queso
11. *penalty*	pena	19. *pistol*	pistola
12. *cola*	cola	20. *two*	tú

D.

Read or repeat the following Spanish sentences, being particularly careful with the pronunciation of /p t k/.

1. Me canso mucho.
2. Pásame la sal, Paco.
3. Té helado, por favor.
4. Con este calor, es necesario tomarlo.
5. ¿Cómo se dice eso en portugués?
6. ¡Pégale fuerte, Carlos!
7. ¿Tan rico es tu tío Teófilo?
8. Págale en seguida, y en pesetas, por favor.
9. Pero, Pablo, ¿no se usan pesos en este país?
10. Coca Cola para él y un café con una copita de coñac para mí.
11. ¿Qué quieres, Cristóbal?
12. Camilo Pascual Pérez, un pícher de mucho control.
13. Paulina va a pasar las vacaciones en Panamá con sus papás.
14. Papá, permíteme pelar las papas para la comida.
15. Teodoro, ¿cuántas veces te he dicho que no tomes té con tenedor?
16. Quico, no comes carne con cuchara sino con tenedor.
17. ¡Caramba, Quico, cuando comes carne con cuchara en vez de tenedor, te creen loco!
18. ¿Tienes que ir a Texas o a Nueva York a principios de agosto?
19. ¿Cuestan mucho esas cositas de plata?
20. Pablo, no permitas que Pedro te pague con esas pesetas porque va a costarnos mucho cambiarlas por pesos.

E.

Now for some practice with /p t k/ as you speak Spanish on your own rather than just read something written for you. Your instructor can provide a map of the Americas and of Europe or perhaps just sketch a rough one on the board, or maybe you can visualize one. See if you can name countries or states or cities whose names start with or contain /p t k/ and say something in Spanish about each one: **Perú es el país de los incas. Texas está en el sur de nuestro país. Pittsburgo es una ciudad de Pensilvania.** *Or your instructor can help you out with some creative prodding:* **¿Cuál es el estado cuya capital es Sacramento?** *Answer, of course:* **California es el estado cuya capital es Sacramento.** *Or* **¿Qué país comparte la península ibérica con España?** *Answer:* **Portugal comparte la península ibérica con España.** *The name of the game is to avoid aspiration with /p t k/ and not confuse these phonemes with their counterparts /b d g/.*

F.

Make a phonetic transcription of the following sentences. Now in the Answer Key we stop underlining vowels and start underlining just the consonants as we go along, chapter by chapter, until we have finished all the consonants. In some items you are not asked to put in the intonation contours, so in these use vertical lines ‖ to indicate pauses, and mark all the stresses with ´. In others, however, you are asked to put in intonation contours, so in these items, instead of ‖ to indicate pauses, use the terminal junctures: → ↑ ↓ , and, of course, continue to mark the stresses. Also if more than one allophone is possible, this will be indicated in Appendix C. This is careful speech.

1. Pablo, quiero tomar una taza de té.   [*intonation, too*]
2. Tomás, ¿a ti te gusta más el jugo de naranja o la Coca Cola?   [*intonation, too*]
3. El semestre de la escuela elemental comienza a principios de setiembre.
4. Quiso comprar un litro de kerosén, pero naturalmente el kiosco no tenía estas cosas.
5. ¿Podría tomar un poquito de queso?   [*intonation, too*]
6. Busqué un técnico para que me ayudara con la confección del atlas.

22

The Voiced Consonants /b d g/

Allophones of /b/

The consonant /b/ in Spanish has two principal allophones: [b], a voiced bilabial stop, and [ꞵ], a voiced bilabial slit fricative. Some speakers occasionally use a third allophone: [v], a voiced labio-dental slit fricative.

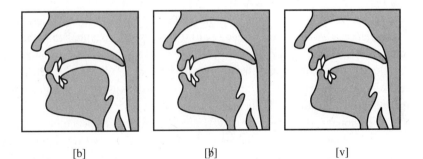

[b]   [ꞵ]   [v]

Description of /b/ Allophones

For [b] the two lips press together to stop the airstream, which is then released abruptly without aspiration. The vocal bands start vibrating a split second before the release of the lips and continue throughout the release. This means that [b] is slightly pre-voiced and clearly distinguished from [p], which is a voiceless bilabial stop.

For [ꞵ] the two lips touch very slightly—as they do when you prepare to blow out a match—but not enough to keep the airstream from continuing steadily through the horizontal slit they form. The vocal bands vibrate throughout.

For [v] the lower lip lightly touches the edge of the upper front teeth, and the airstream, without stopping, passes through the horizontal slit formed by the lip and teeth. The vocal bands vibrate throughout, distinguishing [v] from [f].

Distribution of /b/

The rule for /b/ shows another variation, namely the complete omission of the phoneme in certain circumstances.

$$
\text{/b/} \rightarrow
\begin{bmatrix}
[\text{b}] & / \begin{Bmatrix} \| \\ \text{/N/} \end{Bmatrix} \text{—} \\[2ex]
\begin{Bmatrix} [\beta] \\ [\emptyset] \end{Bmatrix} / \begin{Bmatrix} \text{/ob(C)-C/} \\ \text{/sub(C)-C/} \end{Bmatrix} \\[2ex]
[\beta] \quad \text{elsewhere}
\end{bmatrix}
\qquad
\begin{array}{l}
\underline{v}oy, \underline{b}aile \\
hom\underline{b}re, en\underline{v}iar, \\
un \underline{b}aile \\[1ex]
o\underline{b}jeto, o\underline{b}stáculo, \\
su(\underline{b})stituir \\[1ex]
yo \underline{v}oy, el \underline{b}aile, lo\underline{b}o
\end{array}
$$

/N/ is a nasal phoneme (/m/ or /n/).

/-C/ is any consonant that starts a new syllable.

The stop [b] occurs in the absolute-initial position, that is after a pause ‖ as in **voy** [bói̯], and also after a nasal, which is either /m/, as in **hombre** [óm-bre], or /n/, as in **enviar** [em-bi̯ár]. This sequence of sounds, /N/ + /b/, can occur within a word (**hombre, enviar**) or between words (**álbum bonito, un buen día, un vaso**). And regardless of the spelling, the sequence is *always* pronounced [m-b]. REGRESSIVE ASSIMILATION (the second sound influences the first) to the bilabial /b/ causes the nasal /N/ to be realized as [m], and PROGRESSIVE ASSIMILATION (the first sound influences the second) causes the /b/ to be realized as a stop [b]. This is sometimes referred to as MUTUAL ASSIMILATION because of the reciprocal direction of influence.

The phoneme /b/ is realized as a fricative [β] in careful speech in words with **ob-** and **sub-** prefixes or beginning syllables if the /b/ is at the end of the syllable (**objeto, subjuntivo**) or near it (**obstáculo, substituir**). But the /b/ drops completely in these cases in rapid speech. Thus the words are either [oβ-xé-to] or [o-xé-to], [suβ-xun̯-tí-βo] or [su-xun̯-tí-βo], [oβs-tá-ku-lo] or [os-tá-ku-lo], [suβs-ti-tu̯ír] or [sus-ti-tu̯ír], depending on the style of speech. These pronunciations are reflected in the spelling of some of these words. The common spelling of **oscuro** shows that speakers virtually always say it this way in any style of speech. **Obscuro** is not only an old-fashioned spelling, but represents a stilted and artificial pronunciation. But both spellings are still used for words like **su(b)stituir** and **su(b)scribir**, showing that some speakers still pronounce a /b/ in these words in careful speech.

Everywhere else the phoneme /b/ is realized as a fricative [β]. This includes a wide variety of environments: between vowels, as in **yo voy** [yó-βói̯], **lobo, lavar, la vaca, ella baila**; after /l/, as in **alba** [ál-βa], **el baile**; after /r/, as in **árbol** [ár-βol], **color verde**; after /s/, as in **esbelto** [ez-βél̯-to], **nosotros vamos, los bailes**; and even after /b/ itself, as in **obvio** [óβ-βi̯o].

This means that the same word beginning with a /b/ can have two different pronunciations, depending on whether it follows a pause or a nasal or occurs elsewhere. For example, the verb **bailar** has a stop [b] in the affirmative command **Baile** [bái̯-le] because it is in the absolute-initial position of the breath group, or in the phrase **Juan baila** [xu̯ám-bái̯-la] because it follows a nasal. But the same verb has a fricative [ƀ] in the negative command **No baile** [nó-ƀái̯-le] because the phoneme is no longer *absolute*-initial (although it is still word-initial), or in the phrase **María baila** [ma-rí-a-ƀái̯-la] for the same reason. The word-initial /b/ is now between vowels, that is, in the elsewhere position. The noun **vaso** has a stop [b] in the phrase **un vaso** [um-bá-so] because /b/ follows a nasal, but a fricative [ƀ] in the phrase **el vaso** [el-ƀá-so] because it does not; it, too, is in the elsewhere position.

Dialectal Variations of /b/

There is one important geographical dialectal variation of the phoneme /b/. In northern Central America and Colombia many speakers pronounce an occlusive [b] where one would expect a fricative [ƀ]: after certain consonants, particularly at the beginning of a word (**árbol, las vacas, el vino**), and after the semi-vowels [i̯] and [u̯] (**el rey volvió**). Thus a speaker from Bogotá may say **Es bueno** as [éz-bu̯é-no] whereas a speaker from Mexico City or Buenos Aires always says [éz-ƀu̯é-no]. However, you, as a learner of Spanish, should make an effort to use the fricative [ƀ] in these and other similar words and phrases since it is correct everywhere in the Spanish-speaking world whereas an occlusive [b] might sound unnatural to many Spanish speakers.

Contrasts with English

There are two reasons for the sporadic occurrence of labio-dental [v] in Spanish. It is in free variation with [ƀ] and occurs below the level of consciousness of the speakers, who never correlate their pronunciation with the written form. **Haber** and **a ver** might both be pronounced [a-ƀér] at times and [a-vér] at other times.

The use of labio-dental [v] is also an example of linguistic HYPER-CORRECTION, that is, the result of a misguided effort by educated native speakers to show that they know how a given word is spelled. Such speakers make an attempt to use [v] in words spelled with **v** and [b] or [ƀ] in words spelled with **b** because they feel it is more cultured and correct, but even they are rarely able to do it consistently. This is somewhat akin to native speakers of English pronouncing the word *often* with a /t/ in it, perhaps to show that they know the word is spelled with a *t*, or perhaps because they have been influenced by other speakers. At any rate, anyone learning English can be well advised to make *often* rime with *soften*, with no /t/ in either. Likewise, a foreigner would be well advised never to try to pronounce [v] in Spanish simply because [v] and [ƀ] are *not* phonemic or contrastive in any dialect of Spanish, despite the existence of apparent minimal pairs like **tuvo** and **tubo**, or **votar** and **botar**. These pairs of words are pronounced exactly alike in normal speech in all dialects of Spanish. This fact shows up when Spanish speakers learn English or French where /v/ and /b/ *are* phonemic. They inevitably confuse *very* with *berry* or *TV* with *TB* in English or **voir** *to see* with **boire** *to drink* in French. The fact that **viene** is spelled with a **v** in Spanish and **bien** with a **b** is an orthographic tradition carried down from Latin (where there was a phonemic difference) and in no way reflects a real contrast today.

Spelling of /b/

/b/ is spelled with either **b** or **v** in Spanish: **bala, iba, también, vale, uva, invitar**. The spelling is determined by Latin tradition and never by phonemic considerations as it often is in English. The Spanish Royal Academy of the Language in the past century recommended that school children be taught to distinguish the two sounds in speaking, but abandoned the campaign early in the twentieth century, admitting the futility of the endeavor. Educated speakers of Spanish everywhere still occasionally confuse **b** and **v** in spelling, much the way North Americans occasionally mix up *ei* and *ie* in words like *receive* and *believe*.

Allophones of /d/

The consonant /d/ in Spanish has two principal allophones: [d], a voiced dental stop, and [ɖ], a voiced dental slit fricative.

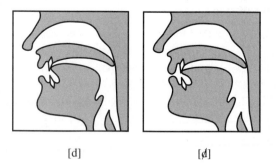

[d]   [ɖ]

Description of /d/ Allophones

For [d] the tip of the tongue presses against the back of the upper front teeth to stop the airstream, which is then released abruptly without aspiration. The vocal bands start vibrating a split second before the release of the tongue and continue throughout the release. This means that [d] is slightly pre-voiced and clearly distinguished from [t], which is a voiceless dental stop.

For [đ] the tip of the tongue is placed very lightly against either the back or the edges of the upper front teeth. The airstream, rather than being stopped, continues steadily through the horizontal slit formed by the tongue tip and the teeth. Sometimes [đ] is inter-dental, since the tongue can touch the edges of both the upper and lower front teeth at the same time, like the English /ð/ of *there*.

Distribution of /d/

The rule for /d/ shows another variation, namely the complete omission of the pho-neme, i.e., "phonetic zero," [Ø], in certain circumstances.

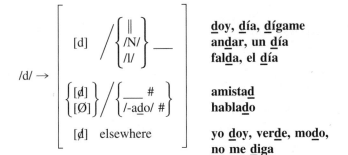

doy, día, dígame
andar, un día
falda, el día

amistad
hablado

yo doy, verde, modo,
no me diga

/N/ is a nasal phoneme (/n/).

is the end of a word.

Just as /b/ does, the phoneme /d/ has a pattern of partial complementary distribution with some free variation. The stop [d] occurs in the absolute-initial position, that is, after a pause ‖ , as in **doy** [dói̯] and also after a nasal, which is always /n/, as in **andar** [an̪-dár]. Regressive assimilation to the dental /d/ causes the preceding nasal /N/ to be realized as a dental [n̪], and progressive assimilation causes the following /d/ to be realized as a stop [d]. The same thing happens in the sequence /l-d/, as in **falda** [fál̪-da]. The dental /d/ causes the preceding lateral /l/ to be realized as a dental [l̪], and progressive assimilation causes the following /d/ to be realized as a stop [d]. Just as with /b/, this is another case of mutual assimilation.

/d/ has two possible realizations when it occurs at the end of a word or in the word-ending sequence of /-ado/. In careful speech the /d/ is retained: **amistad** [a-mis-táđ], **ha-blado** [a-ɓlá-đo], but in rapid speech many speakers eliminate the /d/ completely in these cases, saying [a-mis-tá], [a-ɓlá-o].

In very rapid speech some speakers even eliminate /d/ in other word-final sequences, such as [bó-a] for **boda** and [ná-a] or even [ná] for **nada**. However, these pronunciations are considered incorrect by other speakers, who eliminate /d/ only in the cases shown in the rule above.

Just as with /b/, a single word beginning with /d/ can have two different pronunciations, depending on whether it follows a pause, a nasal, or /l/, or if it occurs elsewhere. For example, the verb **decir** has a stop [d] in the affirmative command **Dígame** [dí-g̶a-me] because it is in the absolute-initial position of the breath group, or in the phrase **Juan dice** [xu̜án̩-dí-se] because it follows a nasal, or in the phrase **Raúl dice** [r̄a-úl̩-dí-se] because it follows /l/. But the same verb has a fricative [d̶] in the negative command **No me diga** [nó-me-d̶í-g̶a] because the phoneme is no longer *absolute*-initial (although still word-initial), or in the phrase **María dice** [ma-rí-a-d̶í-se] for the same reason. The first /d/ is now between vowels, that is, in the elsewhere position. The noun **día** has a stop [d] in the phrase **un día** [un̩-dí-a] because it follows a nasal or in **el día** [el̩-dí-a] because it now follows an /l/, but a fricative [d̶] in the phrase **los días** [loz-d̶í-as] because it is now in the elsewhere position.

Dialectal Variations of /d/

There is one important geographical dialectal variation of the phoneme /d/. In northern Central America and Colombia many speakers pronounce an occlusive [d] where one would expect a fricative [d̶]: after certain consonants, particularly at the beginning of a word (**pardo, desde, los días, la dama**). Thus a speaker from Bogotá may say **Es de aquí** [éz-de-a-kí] whereas a speaker from Mexico City or Buenos Aires always says [éz-d̶e-a-kí]. However, you, as a learner of Spanish, should make an effort to use the fricative [d̶] in these and other similar words and phrases since it is correct everywhere in the Spanish-speaking world, whereas an occlusive [d] might sound unnatural to many Spanish speakers.

In Spain and Mexico word-final /d/ is occasionally devoiced to [θ] (as in *think*), particularly at the end of the phonemic group: **Pase usted** [pá-se̜us-téθ].

Contrasts with English /d/

You as an English speaker have another problem with Spanish /d/, not unlike the same problem encountered with /t/, particularly within a word. You will recall that English /t/ is usually flapped in the intervocalic position after a heavy stress: *water, butter, Plato*. Exactly the same thing happens with /d/: *muddy, ladder, trading*. Some linguists even analyze this tap or flap sound [t̂] as being the same in all these words, saying that many English speakers do not distinguish in rapid speech between *latter* and *ladder, bitter* and *bidder*, and so forth. The English speakers who do distinguish these pairs then also have a voiced tap or flap [d̂]. At any rate, either of these sounds is the equivalent of Spanish /r/, a different phoneme. Spanish /d/ is *never* flapped in these situations, and if you do so, you will make **todo** sound like **toro**, **modo** sound like **moro**, **mida** *measure* sound like **mira**, and so forth. At first, it is best for you to exaggerate Spanish [d̶] and pronounce it as interdentally as you pronounce the /ð/ of *father*. Even though this English sound is really more interdental and more forceful than Spanish [d̶], its conscious use will keep you from your natural tendency to pronounce the tap [ĭ] (or [d̂]), which will always be confused with Spanish /r/.

Also you must avoid aspirating the Spanish /d/ in word-initial position or at the beginning of stressed syllables within a word as you do in English. Just as with /t/ this aspiration does not affect meaning in Spanish, but it sounds strange. Usually this aspiration can be avoided simply by making the /d/ dental instead of alveolar, as it is in English.

Spelling of /d/

/d/ is spelled with **d** everywhere in Spanish: **dí̱a, na̱da, aṉda, faḻda, usteḏ.**

Allophones of /g/

The consonant /g/ in Spanish has two principal allophones: [g], a voiced velar stop, and [g̷], a voiced velar slit fricative.

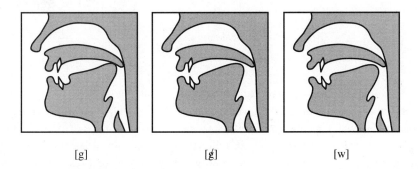

[g]   [g̷]   [w]

Description of /g/ Allophones

For [g] the dorsum or back of the tongue presses against the velum to stop the airstream, which is then released abruptly without aspiration. The vocal bands start vibrating a split second before the release of the tongue and continue throughout the release. This means that [g], just as its counterparts [b] and [d], is slightly pre-voiced. This clearly distinguishes it from [k], which is a voiceless velar stop.

For [g̷] the back of the tongue is placed very lightly against or very close to the velum. The airstream, rather than being stopped, continues steadily through the horizontal slit formed by the tongue dorsum and the velum. This is practically the same sound heard in a very rapid and relaxed pronunciation of *sugar* or *beggar* in English.

Sometimes the sequence [gu̯] or [g̷u̯] is replaced by [w], which we have already seen in Chapter 17 in connection with the vowel /u/. The tongue position for [w] is similar to that for [u] and [u̯], except that the tongue body comes so close to the velum that there is often slight friction or mild turbulence, justifying the analysis of this sound as a true consonant.

Distribution of /g/

The rule for /g/ shows these various realizations.

$$
/g/ \rightarrow
\begin{bmatrix}
[g] \quad \Big/ \left\{ \begin{matrix} \| \\ /N/ \end{matrix} \right\} \underline{\quad} & \begin{matrix} \text{ganó, gato} \\ \text{tengo, un gato} \end{matrix} \\[2em]
\left\{ \begin{matrix} [g] \\ [\varnothing] \end{matrix} \right\} \Big/ \left\{ \begin{matrix} \| \\ /N/ \end{matrix} \right\} \underline{\quad} /uV/ & \begin{matrix} \text{guapo} \\ \text{un guapo} \end{matrix} \\[2em]
\left\{ \begin{matrix} [\acute{g}] \\ [\varnothing] \end{matrix} \right\} \Big/ \left\{ \begin{matrix} /C_1/ \\ /V/ \end{matrix} \right\} \underline{\quad} /uV/ & \begin{matrix} \text{el guardia} \\ \text{la guardia} \end{matrix} \\[2em]
[\acute{g}] \qquad \text{elsewhere} & \text{lo ganó, los ganó}
\end{bmatrix}
$$

/N/ is a nasal phoneme (/n/).

/C₁/ is any consonant but /n/.

Just as /b/ and /d/ do, /g/ has a pattern of partial complementary distribution with some free variation. The stop [g] occurs in the absolute-initial position, that is, after a pause ‖ , as in **Ganó** [ga-nó], and also after a nasal, which is always /n/, as in **tengo** [téŋ-go]. Regressive assimilation to the velar /g/ causes the preceding nasal /N/ to be realized as a velar [ŋ], and progressive assimilation causes the following /g/ to be realized as a stop [g].

Just as with /b/ and /d/, the same word beginning with /g/ can have two different pronunciations, depending on whether it follows a pause or a nasal, or occurs elsewhere. For example, the verb **ganar** has a stop [g] in the phrase **Ganó el premio** [ga-nó . . .] because it is in the absolute-initial position of the breath group, or in the phrase **Juan ganó el premio** [xu̯áŋ-ga-nó . . .] because it follows a nasal. But the same verb has a fricative [ǵ] in the phrase **Lo ganó** [lo-ǵa-nó] because the phoneme is no longer *absolute*-initial (although still word-initial). The noun **gato** can have either a stop [g] or a fricative [ǵ], depending on whether the phrase is just **gato** or **un gato** (both [g]) or **el gato** or **los gatos** (both [ǵ]) for the same reasons.

/gu/ and /w/

A /g/ coming before a diphthong composed of /u/ + any vowel, as in **guapo, un guapo, la guapa, el guapo, los guapos**, can actually disappear with many speakers in rapid speech. In this case, as we saw back in Chapter 17 (on the vowel /u/), the [u] is replaced by the consonant [w], and /g/ will be realized according to the rule: an occlusive [g] after a pause or /n/: **Guapo** [gu̯á-po] or [wá-po], **un guapo** [uŋ-gu̯á-po] or [uŋ-wá-po], and a fricative [ǵ] after vowels and other consonants: **la guapa** [la-ǵu̯á-pa] or [la-wá-pa],

el guapo [el-ǵṵá-po] or [el-wá-po], **los guapos** [loz-ǵṵá-pos] or [loz-wá-pos]. This means that in rapid speech a phrase like **la guagua** *the bus* can have four possible pronunciations, all of which are so close to each other that native speakers of Spanish are probably not aware of them, although native speakers of English are: [la-ǵṵá-ǵṵa], [la-wá-ǵṵa], [la-ǵṵá-wa], or [la-wá-wa].

Some native speakers can distinguish, for example, between the two phrases: **degüellas** [de-ǵṵé-yas] *you behead* and **de huellas** [de-wé-yas] *from tracks (prints),* thus justifying the consideration of /w/ as a separate phoneme and not just a realization of /gu/. However, when learning English, Spanish speakers usually pronounce the latter sequence in *w* words and names like *when, while, William, Washington.* Although /w/ and /gw/ are clearly distinctive in English, there are only a few minimal pairs to show it: *when-Gwen, win-Guinn.*

Dialectal Variations of /g/

The same geographical dialectal variation that we saw with /b/ and /d/ also exists with /g/. In northern Central America and Colombia many speakers pronounce an occlusive [g] where one would expect a fricative [ǵ]: after certain consonants, particularly at the beginning of a word (**algo, largo, los gatos, ciudad grande**). Thus a speaker from Bogotá may say **Es grande** [éz-grán-de] whereas a speaker from Mexico City or Buenos Aires always says [éz-ǵrán̩-de]. However, you, as a learner of Spanish, should make an effort to use the fricative [ǵ] in these and other similar words and phrases since it is correct everywhere in the Spanish-speaking world, whereas an occlusive [g] might sound unnatural to many Spanish speakers.

Contrasts with English

Fricative [ǵ], although not nearly as common in English as in Spanish, does exist in rapid or relaxed speech in such words as *sugar* and *beggar.*

Spelling of /g/

/g/ is spelled with **gu** before /e/ and /i/: **guerra, llegué, guitarra, Dieguito,** and with **g** everywhere else: **gato, hago, tengo, gusano, dogma.** Just as with **qu** for /k/ before /e/ and /i/, the use of **gu** before the front vowels also creates a large class of orthographical-changing verbs, which will be taken up in Chapter 31.

Practice

A.

Repeat or say the noun alone *first, then say it with the* definite article, *and then with the* indefinite article. *For example,* **gato, el gato, un gato.** **Gato** *alone has a stop* [g] *because /g/ follows a pause.* **El gato**, *however, has a fricative* [g̃] *because /g/ does not follow a pause or a nasal.* **Un gato** *has a stop* [g] *because /g/ follows a nasal. Then put any one of these three in an original Spanish sentence, being careful of the pronunciation of the initial sound of the noun:* **"Gato" es el nombre de un animal doméstico** *or* **El gato quiere salir** *or* **Mi compañero de casa quiere un gato.** *Remember that all these items are in the end vocabulary of this book.*

1. baile	4. botella	7. banco
2. doctor	5. derecho	8. día
3. grupo	6. gusto	9. guante

B.

Repeat or say the verb alone *first. Then say it in* any tense *in* any person *with a* noun object. *Then say it again, but this time converting the noun to an* object pronoun. *Be sure to pronounce the correct allophone of /b d g/. For example* **ganar** [g]; **Gané** [g] **el premio**; **Lo gané** [g̃] **la semana pasada.**

1. bailar	4. vender	7. visitar
2. dar	5. decir	8. dudar
3. guiar	6. guardar	9. gastar

C.

Use each verb in the imperfect *tense in an original sentence. For example* **vivir**: **Vivía con mis abuelos entonces.**

1. bailar	4. visitar
2. beber	5. enviar
3. estudiar	6. invitar

D.

Use each verb in the present perfect *tense in an original sentence. For example* **estudiar**: **He estudiado este libro cada día de esta semana.**

1. comer	4. beber
2. ir	5. salir
3. hablar	6. tardar

E.

Your instructor will say the following words, all containing intervocalic /d/ or /r/. You repeat the word and then say the "opposite" word, meaning that for a word with an intervocalic /d/, like **mide,** *you will give the corresponding word with an intervocalic /r/— * **mire** *in this case. Or vice versa:* **todo** *for* **toro,** *for example.*

1. moro	4. mido	7. lloro	10. sera
2. cada	5. loro	8. todo	11. yodo
3. hablada	6. oda	9. codo	12. uniros

F.

*Repeat or say the following items, being careful to pronounce the correct allophone of /*b d g/.

1. Vuelva usted mañana.
2. Dígame la verdad, por favor.
3. Busco gangas.
4. Véalo.
5. Sí, ya lo veo.
6. ¿Eres de Colorado?
7. Habla de un modo gangoso.
8. En Madrid todos los días tomaba un café cortado.   [*No one in Madrid would use a /d/ in the word* **cortado** *with this meaning. If you did, try it again.*]
9. Volvió a Bolivia.
10. Un banco venezolano nos envió los documentos.
11. El fútbol es un deporte que se juega en todo el mundo.
12. Venda usted ambos, y en seguida.
13. ¡Ay, daría el brazo derecho por ser ambidextro!
14. ¿Toros los días? ¿No quieres decir ''todos los días''?
15. Este lugar está muy sucio. Bota esas botellas y lava los vasos.
16. La verdad es que el pobre está tomado.
17. ¿Sabes que **estaros** y **uniros** son palabras posibles, pero no son las que quieres decir? Lo que quieres decir es **Estados Unidos.**
18. Con ese dolor deberías buscar un doctor sin vacilar.
19. Siempre me fascinaba el modo moro de comer con los dedos.
20. No me gusta el sistema de guaguas que tienen en esa ciudad.

G.

Improvise a short narrative in Spanish (six to ten sentences), following the instructions given.

1. Use the present perfect, which will give you practice in saying words ending in **-ado** and **-ido.**

2. Use the imperfect, which will give you practice in saying words ending in **-aba** unless you deliberately pick all **-er** and **-ir** verbs, so be sure to include some **-ar** verbs.

3. Give someone a brief set of instructions with both affirmative and negative commands. Use these verbs and others (preferably beginning with **b-** or **v-**, **d-**, and **g-**, of course): **bailar, beber, ir, vender, vivir, ver, viajar, venir, dar, decir, despertar, ganar, grabar, guardar**.

H.

Make a phonetic transcription of the following sentences. Remember that you are now responsible for stress, intonation, syllable division, vowels, and the allophones of the following consonants (which are underlined in the Answer Key): /p t k b d g/. Put in the intonation contours when requested. Otherwise use ‖ for pauses. Mark all stresses in any case. This is rapid speech.

1. ¿Viene Benito a verte el sábado?   [*intonation, too*]
2. No, ¡qué va! Va a visitar a Pablo, que vive en Venezuela.
3. Víctor fue al banco a cambiar un cheque para comprar el boleto.
4. Eduardo me dijo que Reinaldo le debía mucho dinero.
5. Cuando me vio, me preguntó dónde andaba Reinaldo en estos días.   [*intonation, too*]
6. Le respondí que no sabía nada, pero era evidente que no me creía.
7. Quería fugarse de la aldea pero no estaba segura que pudiera completar la maniobra con éxito.
8. Le gritaron: —¡Guardia! ¡Venga! ¡Venga!   [*intonation, too*]
9. Compré el vestido porque me gusta el color negro y porque además era una gran ganga.
10. Hemos tardado ya demasiado tiempo. ¡Date prisa! ¡Acaba ya!

23

The Voiced Consonants
/y/ and /w/

Allophones of /y/

The consonant /y/ in Spanish has two principal allophones: [ŷ], a voiced palatal affricate (like the consonant sounds in English *judge*), and [y], a voiced palatal slit fricative (as in English *yes*). Some speakers use a third allophone: [ž], a voiced palatal groove fricative (as in English *measure*).

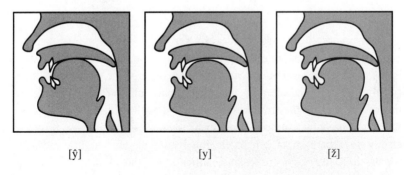

| [ŷ] | [y] | [ž] |

Description of /y/ Allophones

For [ŷ] the tongue tip rests against the inside of the lower front teeth. The dorsum humps up and makes extensive contact with the palate. This contact momentarily stops the airstream, as with a stop. But the dorsum then quickly relaxes its contact, forming a slight opening between itself and the palate, and the airstream passes through this opening as in a fricative. Spanish [ŷ] is very similar to English [ǰ], but the latter sound is really alveolo-palatal and thus the tongue tip and blade are raised to touch the alveolar ridge and the front region of the palate. Spanish [ŷ], less full and noisy in its acoustic effect, is like any affricate, namely a stop + a fricative, pronounced at almost the same time.

For [y] the tongue tip also rests against the lower front teeth. The dorsum humps up but *without* making complete contact with the palate. Thus the airstream, as with any fricative, keeps flowing through the slit formed by the tongue and palate and can be prolonged. There is slight audible friction unlike with the English /y/ of *yes*, which has none. For this reason English /y/ is often analyzed as a glide, but Spanish /y/ has more consonantal properties.

For [ž], which is heard in other languages, such as English (*measure*), French (**Jacques**), Portuguese (**Janeiro**), the tongue assumes almost the same position as for both [š] (as in English *she*) and [y], except that the sides of the tongue dorsum touch the sides of the palate and upper back teeth, leaving a round opening in the middle. The airstream keeps passing through the groove formed by the tongue dorsum and front region of the palate. Thus [ž] is completely fricative and can be prolonged as long as the airstream lasts.

Distribution of /y/

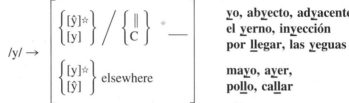

☆ is the more prevalent allophone in all speech styles.

This phonological rule is the first one you have seen with an indication of preference in the cases of free variation. Most speakers most of the time use the affricate allophone [ŷ] after a pause and after any consonant, particularly /l/ and /n/. However, it is by no means rare to hear the fricative allophone [y] in these same situations nor is it incorrect for you to pronounce it here. Most speakers most of the time use this latter allophone [y] elsewhere—that is, between vowels. But again you may well hear the affricate [ŷ] in these words, too. Most Spanish speakers, particularly if they do not know a language where the two sounds are contrastive (as in English *yet* versus *jet*), not only are not aware of which allophone they are using at any given time, but frequently cannot even hear the difference between the two when it is brought into their awareness. English speakers, of course, hear it immediately and often attach some special significance to one pronunciation or the other, which is totally lacking in Spanish. To sum up, you, as an English speaker, can say a sentence like **Yo nací en mayo** with any combination of [y] and [ŷ], although if you say it as [ŷó-na-sí-em-má-yo], you will be saying it the way the majority of speakers of General American Spanish say it frequently in ordinary conversation.

The [y] sound is also heard exclusively at the beginning of words that are spelled with **hie-**: **hierba, hielo, hiena**. This is because these words actually begin with the vowel /i/, and the vowel allophone in this case is [y], the same sound that can also be an allophone of the consonant /y/. Thus virtually all Spanish speakers can contrast **yerro** *I wander, err* with **hierro** *iron*, the first word being pronounced [ŷé-r̄o] or [žé-r̄o], and the second [yé-r̄o]. Although words spelled with **y** or **ll** can also be pronounced with [y] by all Spanish speakers, words spelled with **hie-** are rarely pronounced with [ŷ] or [ž], since they are considered as starting with the vowel /i/ rather than the consonant /y/.

Dialectal Variations of /y/

The /y/ phoneme has two interesting dialectal phenomena. The first, called **yeísmo** (literally **y**-*ing* or **y**-*ism*), is characteristic of most dialects of Spanish, including those of both American Spanish and peninsular Spanish. This means that the lateral phoneme /l̃/, the palatal *l*, always spelled with **ll**, is absent; the phoneme /y/ is used instead. Thus most speakers of American Spanish and many speakers of peninsular Spanish or Castilian (particularly in Madrid and throughout southern Spain) do not distinguish in sound such hypothetical pairs as **hay̲a** (subjunctive of **haber**) and **halla** (*she/he finds*) or between **cay̲ó** (*she/he fell*) and **calló** (*she/he was quiet*). In most dialects on both sides of the Atlantic the first two words are pronounced either as [á-ya] or [á-ŷa] (as discussed in the previous section) and the second pair either as [ka-yó] or [ka-ŷó]. But in many highland areas of South America—parts of Colombia, Peru, Ecuador, and Bolivia—and also Paraguay and throughout central and northern Spain, the lateral palatal /l̃/ is used in words spelled with an **ll**. Thus, these speakers, who are *not* **yeísta** in their speech, pronounce **halla** *she/he finds* as [á-l̃a] and **calló** *she/he was quiet* as [ka-l̃ó], distinguishing them from **hay̲a** and **cay̲ó**, respectively. This usage is called **lleísmo** (literally *double-llíng* or *double-llism)* and will be discussed further in Chapter 27.

The other phenomenon involving /y/ is called **žeísmo** (literally **ž**-*ing* or **ž**-*ism*), which means pronouncing the voiced palatal groove fricative [ž] (as in *measure*), instead of the palatal slit fricative [y], used by the majority of Spanish speakers. Although this sound [ž] is heard sporadically in Spain and throughout Spanish America, it is most common in Costa Rica, parts of Colombia, and in most of Argentina and Uruguay. In fact, when Spanish speakers who do not use the sound hear it, they assume that the user is from the River Plate area—Argentina or Uruguay.

Remember, however, that even in Argentina, as in all areas of the Spanish-speaking world, words beginning with **hie-** do not have this groove fricative [ž]. **Yerba**, pronounced [žér-ƀa], is the name of the herb used to brew one of the nation's favorite beverages, **yerba mate**, a type of strong tea, but the term for ordinary lawn grass is **hierba**, always pronounced [yér-ƀa]. The spelling shows that one word begins with a consonant, the other with a vowel.

An interesting variety of **žeísmo,** very common among female speakers in Argentina, is the devoicing of [ž] to [š] (as in *she*). This variation, which was first documented in the 1940s, is one of the only sound features in Spanish characteristic of one sex—the others being a few intonational patterns. Thus as you listen to a Buenos Aires couple, you may well hear the man say [ká-že] and the woman [ká-še] for *street*.

Contrasts with English /y/

Both Spanish fricatives [y] and [ž] have almost exact equivalents in English, as in the words *yolk* and *measure,* respectively. Spanish affricate [ŷ], however, is slightly different, having somewhat less friction and turbulence than its English counterpart [ǰ]. These two sounds are close enough, though, that you can use the English one anywhere in place of Spanish [ŷ].

Spelling of /y/

Spanish /y/ is spelled with **y: y̱a, y̱acer, hoy̱uelo, cay̱ó**. In the **yeísta** dialects—where palatal [l̃] is absent as a phoneme—/y/ is also spelled with **ll: ḻlama, haḻlar, poḻlo, aḻlí, caḻló**.

Allophone of /w/

The consonant /w/ has only one allophone: [w], a voiced bilabio-velar slit fricative.

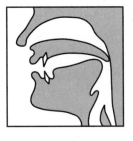

[w]

Description of /w/ Allophone

The back of the tongue comes almost as close to the velum as it does for [g̶] but at the same time the lips are rounded as for the vowel /u/. The consonant [w] is almost the same as the vowels [u] and [u̯], except that the tongue body comes so close to the velar region that there is often slight friction or mild turbulence, one characteristic of a consonant as opposed to a vowel.

Distribution and Dialectal Variations of /w/

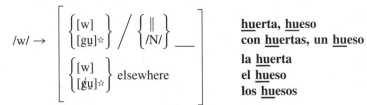

$$/\text{w}/ \rightarrow \left[\begin{array}{l} \left\{ \begin{array}{l} [\text{w}] \\ [\text{gu̯}] ☆ \end{array} \right\} \Big/ \left\{ \begin{array}{l} \| \\ /\text{N}/ \end{array} \right\} \underline{\quad} \\ \\ \left\{ \begin{array}{l} [\text{w}] \\ [\text{g̶u̯}] ☆ \end{array} \right\} \text{elsewhere} \end{array} \right]$$

huerta, hueso
con huertas, un hueso

la huerta
el hueso
los huesos

☆ is considered by some speakers to be substandard.

Sometimes, as you can see by the preceding rule, [w] is replaced by the sequence [gu̯] or [g̶u̯], the choice between these two sequences depending on whether or not there is a pause or a nasal preceding /w/. Thus the word **huerta** is pronounced either [wér-ta] or [gu̯ér-ta], the latter having a stop [g] since /g/ follows a pause. **Un hueso** is pronounced either [uŋ-wé-so] or [uŋ-gu̯é-so] since /g/ follows a nasal. However, the phrase **la huerta** is either [la-wér-ta] or [la-g̶u̯ér-ta], and the phrase **los huesos** is either [loz-wé-sos] or [loz-g̶u̯é-sos] since in both cases /g/ is now in the elsewhere position, that is, not after a pause or a nasal. Some speakers can distinguish between the two phrases: **de huellas** [de-wé-yas] *from tracks (prints)* and **degüellas** [de-g̶u̯é-yas] *you behead,* thus justifying the consideration of /w/ as a separate phoneme and not just a realization of /gu/. Also many of these speakers feel that the pronunciation with /g/ is substandard or incorrect, but nonetheless it is widely used in rapid conversation throughout the Spanish-speaking world even by educated speakers. This might be regarded as a phenomenon of social rather than geographical dialect.[1] Most Spanish speakers, regardless of whether they are able to distinguish between words with /gu/ and those with /w/ or how they feel about the correctness of the /g/ pronunciation in such words as **huerta** and **hueso**, are unable to make this distinction when learning a language like English where the sequences are distinctive, as in *when-Gwen* or *win-Guinn*. They usually start words like *when, while, William, Washington* with a /g/.

This phenomenon is revealed not only by Spanish speakers' pronunciation of certain English words but also words from other languages that have had some influence on Spanish, like Arabic or Nahuatl. For example, the Arabic word for river bed is *wadi* and appears in many Spanish place names spelled and pronounced with a /g/: **Guadiana, Guadalquivir, Guadalcanal, Guadalajara**. Many Spanish words borrowed from Nahuatl not only have a double pronunciation, as indicated by the phonological rule above, but an official double spelling as well: **guarache** or **huarache** *sandal,* **mariguana** or **marihuana** *marijuana,* **güero** or **huero** *blond, American,* **güipil** or **huipil** *embroidered dress worn by Indian women in Mexico.* For a time the Spanish Royal Academy tried to promulgate **güisqui** as the official spelling of the English word *whiskey.* **Guachimán** is one of the standard words for *watchman.* And in the Hispanic cities where the stores still exist, the name *Woolworth* is pronounced [gúl-g̶ort].

Spelling of /w/

/w/ is spelled with **w** (or **wh**) in a few foreign words and names: **wáter, Wáshington, whisky**, and with **hu-** elsewhere: **huarache, hueso, huerta, huipil**. In many foreign

---

[1]An example is the title of a novel by Argentine writer, Benito Lynch (1885–1952), *El inglés de los güesos* (lit. "The Englishman of the Bones," referring to an archaeologist). This spelling of the word **huesos** represents the Indians' so-called incorrect pronunciation [gu̯é-sos] rather than [wé-sos]. This is an example of EYE DIALECT, in which an incorrect spelling is meant to represent slang or even the substandard pronunciation of an uneducated individual. Examples in English are "sez" for *says* or "wimmin" for *women*. But in both the Spanish and English examples, the eye dialect spelling is actually a fairly accurate phonetic representation of standard correct speech. Many educated Spanish speakers says **huesos** as "güesos" in given circumstances, and "sez" is the only way to say *says* in English.

borrowings where /w/ precedes a vowel the **hu-** is replaced by **gu-** (before /a/): **guarache** or **gü-** (before /e/ and /i/): **güero, güipil.** Also /w/ frequently replaces /gu/ when it precedes a vowel in native Spanish words: **agua, antiguo, guagua.**

Practice

A.

Your instructor will read the following three-word groups, each one once or twice as she/he prefers. Some words will have two consecutive vowels, like **veo** *or* **lees,** *and others will have an intervocalic /y/, like* **bello** *or* **leyes.** *After each group, pick out the one word that is different from the other two. There are four possibilities: "first," "second," "third," or "all the same." For example, if your instructor reads* **veo bello bello,** *you say "first." For* **bello veo bello,** *you say "second." For* **veo veo bello,** *you say "third." For* **bello bello bello,** *you say "all the same."*

1. brío brillo brillo	11. sombrilla sombría sombría
2. bella vea vea	12. cerilla cerilla cerilla
3. pilló pilló pió	13. creó creyó creó
4. Lillo Lillo Lillo	14. bello bello veo
5. sea sella sella	15. pía pilla pía
6. milla milla mía	16. leyes lees leyes
7. ea ea ella	17. tía tía tía
8. trillo trío trillo	18. villa vía vía
9. tía tilla tía	19. Lillo lío lío
10. vía vía vía	20. peón pellón peón

B.

Your instructor will read each Spanish word. Repeat the word, and give its meaning if your instructor wishes. Then say the so-called "opposite" word, and give the meaning if asked. "Opposite" means that for a word with an intervocalic /y/, like **bello,** *give the corresponding word with two consecutive vowels—* **veo** *in this case. Or vice versa:* **leyes** *for* **lees,** *for example. Remember that all these words are defined in the end vocabulary.*

1. pió	9. vea
2. Lillo	10. creó
3. sella	11. brío
4. pellón	12. leyes
5. vía	13. cerilla
6. sería	14. ella
7. trillo	15. pilló
8. milla	16. sombría

C.

Read or repeat the following Spanish sentences. Your instructor will indicate how she/he wants you to pronounce /y/, that is, with [y], [ŷ], *or* [ž], *and also whether to use* /gu/ *in place of* /w/.

1. Es hueco.
2. El pájaro pió de pura alegría.
3. Huelo algo.
4. Sí, esos huevos huelen mal. Bótalos.
5. Sella el sobre, por favor.
6. Sea lo que sea, no lo sello.
7. Un huerto huele mejor que una huerta. ¿Sabes por qué?
8. ¿Sabes qué haces para que no huela un pez muerto?
9. —¿Cúbrelo de yerbabuena?   —No. Tápale las narices.
10. La Real Academia insistía en que la palabra *whiskey* se escribiera **güisqui**.
11. La hembra del caballo se llama **yegua**.
12. Juanillo lloró cuando le pusieron la inyección.
13. Yo lloro cuando me ponen yodo.
14. Las llamas viven en la sierra, no en el llano.
15. El masajista entró a la gramilla con un cubo de hielo.
16. Las huacas generalmente son artefactos y tumbas que a veces contienen huesos.
17. El gallo no tiene interés en los huevos de la gallina.
18. En los cursos de derecho, lees las leyes constantemente.
19. El gayo pilló los huevos del nido del gorrión.
20. Pero recién dijiste que el gallo no tiene interés en los huevos.
21. No, ¡qué va! Esta vez estoy hablando de un pájaro, el **gayo**, que se escribe con **y griega. Gallo** es un ave, y se escribe con **doble ele**. Pero se comprende tu error porque pronunciamos las dos palabras de un modo exactamente igual.
22. Cada dedo tiene una yema, y cada huevo tiene una yema. ¿Ya entiendes?
23. El argentino le dijo al guía: ''Por favor, mi esposa y yo queremos ver el Valle de los Caídos''.
24. El guía castellano contestó: ''Ya, ya, señor, llegaremos, llegaremos''.
25. Pero la esposa del argentino proclamó: ''Ya es tarde para ir allá y además está lloviendo''.
26. —¿Se cayó?   —Claro, no podía hablar.   —No, no, digo, ¿perdió pie?   —Sí, y se calló después porque perdió el sentido.
27. No, te confundiste. La hierba se encuentra en la cancha de fútbol—es gramilla. La yerba se encuentra en el mate, y se toma con una bombilla.
28. El hiato se usa mucho en los versos yámbicos.
29. Hmmmmmm. Eso tiene que ver con la yod, ¿no?
30. Claro, y supongo que encima sabes que estas frases te dan mucha práctica con el yeísmo.

D.

Check the end vocabulary or your dictionary, and find five or six words containing **y, ll,** *or* **hie,** *but words that have either exact or near homophones (words that sound alike). For example, take* **cayó** *she/he fell and* **calló** *she/he was quiet (both pronounced* [ka-yó]) *or perhaps* **hieno** *hay (pronounced only* [yé-no]) *and* **lleno** *full (pronounced* [yé-no] *or* [ŷé-no] *or* [žé-no]). *Be prepared to define, explain, or say a few things about these words in Spanish.*

E.

Make a phonetic transcription of the following sentences. Remember that you are now responsible for stress, intonation, syllable division, vowels, and all allophones of the following consonants (underlined in the Answer Key): /p t k b d g y w/. *Use* [w] *for* /w/, *and either* [y] *or* [ŷ] *for* /y/, *depending on the phonetic environment as shown in the rule on p. 216. Show all stresses, and put in intonation contours when requested, otherwise* ‖ *for pauses. This is* careful speech.

1. Llámame después de llegar.   [*intonation, too*]
2. Llénala con agua, y pronto se convertirá en hielo.
3. Las llamas ya no habitan esta parte del valle, ¿sabes?   [*intonation, too*]
4. Los huaqueros, con sus huaraches, cubrieron las huellas de los huesos.
5. ¿Dijiste que la gramilla se usa para hacer yerba mate?   [*intonation, too*]
6. No, la gramilla es hierba, pero creo que los gauchos confundían la palabra y empezaron a llamar la hierba especial yerba.
7. Si la llave ya no está en el llavero, ¿dónde se halla?   [*intonation, too*]
8. En México llaman a los americanos **hueros** o **güeros** a pesar de que no todos somos rubios.

24

The Voiceless Consonants /s/ and /θ/

Allophones of /s/ and /θ/

The consonant /s/ in Spanish has two principal allophones: [s], a voiceless corono- or dorso-alveolar[1] groove fricative, and [z], a voiced corono- or dorso-alveolar groove fricative, shown in the first diagram below.[2] Some dialects have as the two principal allophones [ṣ], a voiceless apico-dental[3] groove fricative, and [ẓ], a voiced apico-dental groove fricative, shown in the second diagram. Other dialects have as the two principal allophones [ś], a voiceless apico-alveolar groove fricative, and [ż], a voiced apico-alveolar groove fricative, shown in the third diagram. The consonant /θ/ is absent from American Spanish but is a phoneme in Castilian Spanish and has two principal allophones: [θ], a voiceless, interdental slit fricative, and [ð], a voiced, interdental slit fricative, shown in the fourth diagram. Many dialects also have a third allophone, a palatalized s, [sʲ], which is a voiceless corono-alveolar or prepalatal palatalized groove fricative, impossible to show in a facial diagram. Most dialects have an additional /s/ allophone: [h], a voiceless glottal slit fricative, not depicted below for reasons explained in Note 2.

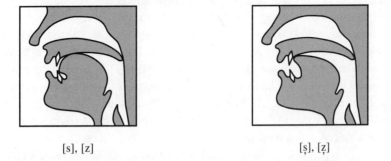

[s], [z]   [ṣ], [ẓ]

---

[1]*Corono-* (from *coronal*) refers to the blade of the tongue, the area immediately behind the tip. *Dorso-* (from *dorsal*) refers to the top or dorsum of the tongue.

[2]The voicing or vibration of the vocal bands, which distinguishes [z], [ẓ], [ż], and [ð] from their voiceless counterparts [s], [ṣ], [ś], and [θ], respectively, is not represented in these facial diagrams, which show only the supraglottal (above the larynx) articulators. Thus the glottal [h], to be discussed later in this chapter, cannot be represented either.

[3]*Apico-* (from *apical*) refers to the tip or apex of the tongue.

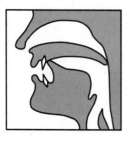

[ś], [ż]

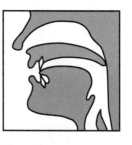

[θ], [ð]

Description of /s/ and /θ/ Allophones

The standard (or default) *s* of General American Spanish is the corono- or dorso-alveolar convex groove fricative [s], along with its voiced allophone [z] (see the first facial diagram on page 223). This, and all other groove fricatives, are known as SIBILANTS, since the resultant sound is a type of hissing or whistling. For this [s] and [z] the tongue tip rests lightly against or near the *lower* front teeth. The groove through which the airstream flows, is in the tongue blade or the foreward part of the tongue back or dorsum. The tongue has a convex (humped up) shape. Unless otherwise specified, all future references to /s/ in Spanish will be to this [s].

Another *s*, heard in Mexico and the Andean region of South America, is known as the dental *s* (see the second facial diagram on page 223). The tongue is relatively flat, and the tip presses against the back of the *upper* front teeth with a considerable amount of tension. The groove through which the airstream flows is in the tongue tip itself. This [ş] also has a voiced counterpart [ẓ].

The third type of *s*, heard in central Colombia and parts of Bolivia, is also the predominant one in Castilian Spanish and is heard throughout central and northern Spain. This [ś] is known by a variety of names: the apico-alveolar *s*, the retroflex *s*, **la s castellana**, **la s espesa** (*the "thick" s*), and even **la s gorda** (*the "fat" s*). The first two terms describe the way it is articulated, the third indicates its main area of occurrence in Spanish, and the last two describe its acoustic effect, similar to English [š] (as in *she*). The tongue tip is at right angles with the alveolar ridge or is even turned back (retroflexed) slightly as it touches the alveolar ridge (see the left diagram above). The tongue has a concave (hollowed out) shape. To achieve this tongue position, the lower jaw is thrust slightly forward. This [ś], too, has a voiced counterpart [ż].

Another type of /s/ is the so-called palatalized *s*, [sʲ], which occurs before the front vowel /i/, as in **si̲e̲te** or **nac̲i̲ón**, due to regressive assimilation. As the tongue produces the standard dorso-alveolar convex [s], the tongue body almost simultaneously rises slightly, creating a very slight *i*-like sound, similar to the truly palatal [š], as in English *she*. Since it never occurs before any sound but /i/, there is no voiced variety due to regressive assimilation to a following voiced consonant, as there is with the other varieties of /s/.

The final sound is the *theta* or so-called *th*-sound. For [θ] the tongue tip is placed between the upper and lower front teeth (see the right diagram, facing page), or sometimes lightly against the back of the upper front teeth, as in English *think*. The tongue body is relatively flat. It is distinguished from all varieties of /s/, which are *groove* fricatives or sibilants, by the fact that the airstream flows through a horizontal slit created by the tongue tip and the teeth, making [θ] a *slit* fricative. It, too, has a voiced counterpart [ð], as in English *this*. This sound is absent in American Spanish, but is a phoneme in Castilian Spanish, where it is spelled with **z** and with **c** before **e** and **i** and contrasts with /s/, as in **ca̱za** [ká-θa] (*hunting*) versus **ca̱sa** [ká-ṡa] (*house*), **ce̱rrar** [θe-r̄ár] (*to close*) versus **se̱rrar** [ṡe-r̄ár] (*to saw*), or **ci̱ma** [θí-ma] (*top, summit*) versus **si̱ma** [ṡí-ma] (*pit, abyss*). However, in all dialects of American Spanish, the words in each of these pairs are pronounced exactly alike—with /s/—and are thus homophones, distinguished only by context.

This American Spanish mode, known as SESEO (literally, *s-ing*), is the standard pronunciation in all Spanish dialects of the Western hemisphere and among speakers of all educational and socio-economic levels. The Castilian mode of contrasting the two sounds /s/ and /θ/ has no standard name but is sometimes called DISTINCIÓN (literally, DISTINC- *TION*). It is the so-called official pronunciation in Spain, taught in schools, used on radio and television, and is the norm among most speakers in central and northern Spain and also among many speakers in southern Spain. This pronunciation is sometimes mistakenly referred to as CECEO, a quite different phenomenon, which will be taken up in the section on dialectal variations.

Distribution of /s/ and /θ/

Following is the rule for /s/ in General American Spanish.

$$/s/ \rightarrow \begin{bmatrix} \begin{Bmatrix} [s] \\ [z] \end{Bmatrix} \Big/ \underline{\quad} \ /C_1/ \\[2ex] \begin{Bmatrix} [s] \\ [z] \\ [h] \\ [\emptyset] \end{Bmatrix} \Big/ \underline{\quad} \ /\bar{r}/ \\[2ex] [s] \quad \text{elsewhere} \end{bmatrix}$$

mismo, las manzanas, hallazgo,
los gatos, desde, es de

Israel
los ricos

sala casa, hasta, las peras,
busca, zapato, caza, vez

/C$_1$/ is any voiced consonant but /r̄/.

The realization of /s/ before any voiced consonant except /r̄/ is often determined by regressive assimilation; that is, the voicing of the following consonant causes /s/ also to be voiced and thus realized as [z]. This is particularly true in rapid speech. Words and phrases like **mismo** and **los gatos** are pronounced [mís-mo] and [los-ǵa-tos], respectively, in careful speech, but [míz-mo] and [loz-ǵá-tos] in rapid speech. When /s/ precedes the trilled consonant /r̄/, there are four possibilities depending on speech style and degree of emphasis. Since considerable muscular effort is required to pronounce this trill, the faster one speaks the greater likelihood there is of /s/ modification. In the slowest speech, it is fairly easy to pronounce [s] before [r̄], but when one is speaking fast, /s/ undergoes regressive assimilation [z], aspiration [h], or complete deletion [Ø], giving four possible pronunciations of a phrase like **Los recuerdo**: [los-r̄e-kу̧ér-đo], [loz-r̄e . . .], [loh-r̄e . . .], or [lo-r̄e . . .]. This often causes a corresponding modification of /r̄/ itself, and this will be taken up in Chapter 28.

In **distinción** usage in Spain the phoneme /θ/ is also affected by regressive assimilation (just as /s/) and is realized as a voiced interdental slit fricative [ð] before voiced consonants: **hallazgo** [a-yáð-ǵo], **gozne** [góð-ne], **en vez de** [em-béð-đe].

Dialectal Variations of /s/

One of the most important differences between American Spanish and Castilian (or standard peninsular Spanish) is the fact that the former has no /θ/ phoneme, using /s/ instead in words spelled not only with **s** but also **z, ce,** and **ci**. However, many speakers in southern Spain—the area known as Andalucía—also use **seseo**, rather than **distinción**, the so-called official or standard mode of Spain. Spanish Americans, since they never hear /θ/, are consistent in their use of /s/ in all these words: **sol, zapato, sino, cine, sello, cena,** and so forth. Such Castilian minimal pairs as **cierra-sierra, cepa-sepa, vez-ves** are simply homophones for them. However, these **seseante** Andalusians, who hear **distinción** all around them—often in school, usually on the radio and on television, in the movies, and in announcements in transportation centers—occasionally pronounce the interdental /θ/.[4] This may be due to hypercorrection or some attitudinal or stylistic reasons. Occasionally it is due to uncertainty as to how a word is spelled. For example, a menu in a Seville restaurant may list the well-known Spanish soup as **gazpacho** or **gaspacho**, and the waiter may say [gaθ-pá-ĉo] or [gas-pá-ĉo] or both, depending on different sociolinguistic factors, such as the speech of the patron he is serving, for example. These occasional slips or variations are normal in the speech of Spaniards who use **seseo** but are unknown among Spanish Americans, since the latter never hear /θ/ in their linguistic environment (unless they run into a Spaniard or see a movie or TV program made in Spain).

Seseo is widely accepted in Spain (even with the occasional slips or variations mentioned) and given little attention. However, there is a related phenomenon in southern

---

[4]This is true of Andalusians but not of Canary Islanders, natives of the seven Spanish islands off the northwest coast of Africa. Their speech, which is remarkably like Caribbean Spanish (Cuba, Puerto Rico, Dominican Republic, Venezuela), is also **seseante**. They are completely consistent—like Spanish Americans—in their use of /s/ in words that mainland Spaniards pronounce with /θ/.

Spain known as **ceceo**, which is not widely accepted and is actually considered by many to be incorrect and characteristic of rural uneducated speech. **Ceceo** means *lisping*, or pronouncing /θ/ in place of /s/, exactly what lisping is in English. Although **ceceo** speakers favor the interdental /θ/, they occasionally pronounce /s/, but many times in the wrong place, that is, where /θ/ would be used by speakers of standard Castilian. Usually, both ca**s**a and ca**z**a are pronounced [ká-θa], both **ves** and **vez** pronounced [béθ], and so forth. Thus a sentence like **S̲everiano s̲alió a comprar̲s̲e un par de z̲apatos̲** might come out [θe-β̞e-ri̠á-no-θa-li̠ó-a-kom-prár-θeu̯m-pár-ð̞e-θa-pá-toh], with the final /s/ being aspirated. The same speaker, for undetermined reasons, might also pronounce any one of the four words **S̲everiano, s̲alió, comprar̲s̲e, z̲apatos̲** with [s] on any given occasion, but a **seseo** speaker from either side of the Atlantic would replace every instance of [θ] with [s]. A **distinción** speaker from Madrid or Bilbao would say [s̠e-β̞e-ri̠á-no-s̠a-li̠ó-a-kom-prár-s̠eu̯m-pár-ð̞e-θa-pá-tos̠], distinguishing throughout words with /θ/ and /s/ and using the apico-alveolar [s̠] for the latter phoneme. Thus, **ceceo** is either the absence of the /s/ phoneme or its sporadic occurrence in the so-called wrong places—from the point of view of a speaker of standard Castilian.

In summation, **seseo** is the norm for American Spanish—and thus also the norm used in this book—and is heard in southern Spain and the Canary Islands and is accepted all over Spain, even by speakers who do not use it. **Distinción** is the norm for Spain, used by all speakers in central and northern Spain and many in southern Spain as well. **Ceceo** is non-standard and heard mainly in southern Spain. This dialectal **ceceo** should not be confused with children's **ceceo** or lisping, which seems to occur at an early age in children in many languages, including both Spanish and English, then disappearing after a brief period of childhood.

The dental [s̩] and [z̩] are used widely in Mexico and the Andean regions of Ecuador, Peru, and Bolivia. These sharp prominent *s*'s are also heard in some dialects of American English, such as in and around New York City, parts of New Jersey, and northeastern Pennsylvania.

As we have said, most, but not all, speakers of Castilian Spanish in central and northern Spain use the apico-alveolar [s̠]. This particular sibilant also exists in two areas of Spanish America: the Colombian provinces of Caldas and Antioquia and a small region of south central Bolivia. It is also heard in many areas of the United States, including coastal Massachusetts and the Atlantic and Gulf Coast regions of the South, from North Carolina to Texas.

Another dialectal variation of /s/ is heard in Ecuador, where /s/ is realized as dental [z̩] at the end of a word that precedes a word beginning with a vowel. This is most common with a modifier before the modified word. For example, the word **lo̲z̲ano** is pronounced with a dental [s̩], [lo-s̩á-no], because the /s/ comes between vowels *within* a word, but the phrase **lo̲s̲ animales** is pronounced [lo-z̩a-ni-má-les̩] because the /s/ is now *word-final* before a vowel. The word **ma̲s̲aje** is pronounced [ma-s̩á-xe], but the phrase **má̲s̲ ajo** is [má-z̩á-xo], for the same reasons.

In Costa Rica and Colombia /s/ is sporadically voiced to [z] both within a word and word-final before a vowel, as in **preṣente** [pre-zén̦-te] or **loș hijos** [lo-zí-hos].

The palatalized [sʲ], sounding almost like [š] and occuring mainly before /i/, is heard in Cuba, Mexico, Argentina, and Andalusia. It varies in its sociolinguistic role, however. In Argentina it is more common in male than female speech and thought by many educated Argentinians to be a mark of the lesser educated, such as the **compadre**, or *tough street guy*. Yet it is used by educated public figures, like Cuba's Fidel Castro, as well as Buenos Aires street vendors, who shout ''**¡Salió *La Nación*!**''[sʲ] "Read all about it in the latest edition of *Nación*!" [one of the leading daily papers of Buenos Aires].

But the major dialectal variation of /s/ is referred to variously as /s/ deletion, /s/ aspiration, or, as we call it to include both these phenomena, /s/ modification. This particular feature is widespread on both sides of the Atlantic and even predominates in the Spanish-American coastal areas: Cuba, Puerto Rico, Dominican Republic, Panama, northern Venezuela and northern Colombia, the Pacific coast of Ecuador and Peru, most of Chile, Argentina, and Uruguay, and, of course, the areas in the continental United States where Cuban Americans (Florida), Puerto Ricans, and Dominicans live (the metropolitan areas of New York, Connecticut, New Jersey, as well as Washington, DC, Philadelphia, and numerous cities and towns of eastern Pennsylvania). It is also common throughout Andalusia in Spain and the Canary Islands. A syllable-final /s/, that is, one coming at the end of a syllable either before a consonant or a pause is either aspirated to a voiceless glottal [h] or eliminated entirely. This elimination is represented by [Ø] in an explanation or a rule, but by the absence of any symbol in transcription. Thus, in Puerto Rico, **¿cómo eṣtá?** may be pronounced [kó-mo-eh-tá] or even [kó-mo-e-tá]. Occasionally the /s/ is modified in any word-final position, even before a vowel. Thus, **Loș he visto** may be pronounced [lo-he-ɸíh-to]. This can also happen within a word when /s/ comes at the end of a morpheme, particularly in the word **noṣotros**: [no-hó-troh].

This /s/ modification—aspiration or elimination—is extremely common in these areas even among educated speakers, particularly in rapid conversation. In fact, a prominent [s] or [z] in these environments can sound affected and stilted, even effeminate for a man, although these reactions would be toward native speakers, not Americans speaking Spanish. An analogous case for English would be the scrupulous pronunciation of the velar [ŋ] in all *-ing* words, even in rapid pronunciation: "Do you need the phone now? I'm going /gówiŋ/ to surf the Internet for a while," rather than the more natural "I'm 'gonna' surf the Internet for a while."

/s/ modification is slightly different from area to area. In the Caribbean, coastal South America, and southern Spain, for example, /s/ is modified in rapid conversation in syllable-final position, whether the /s/ is followed by another consonant or a pause, that is, absolute-final position. But in Argentina, /s/ is usually retained before a pause. Thus a Cuban might say **loș gatoș** as [loh-ǵá-toh] or even [lo-ǵá-to] whereas an Argentinian would say [loh-ǵá-tos].

Following is the /s/ modification rule for most such speakers.

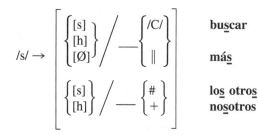

/C/ is any consonant.

‖ is a pause, or a phonemic phrase boundary.

\# is a word boundary.

\+ is a morpheme boundary.

A few remarks about this rule. The consonant in the first part of the rule necessarily begins a new syllable because of the syllable structure rules in Spanish, thus making the preceding /s/ syllable-final. The realization of /s/ in the /s/-modification dialects is also determined by style and speech. Most speakers can pronounce /s/ as [s] in slow, careful speech, but modify it as they speak faster. In the case of word and morpheme boundaries, complete omission is not a possibility since deleting the /s/ of **los** in the phrase **los otros** would make it sound like **lo otro**, something completely different. Likewise **nosotros** with complete /s/ deletion would sound like **no otro**, a different phrase. But the aspiration of /s/ to [h] prevents this interpretation.

Contrasts with English

Since American English has the same two common /s/ articulations as General American Spanish, the corono- or dorso-alveolar [s] and [z], you will have no trouble pronouncing them. However, you may mistakenly substitute [z] for [s] in word-initial and word-medial intervocalic position, particularly in cognate words, saying *[r̄ó-za] instead of [r̄ó-sa] for **rosa** or *[pre-zéṇ-te] instead of [pre-séṇ-te], for **presente**, for example. This is another case of the native language interfering with the foreign language. The English words *rose* and *present* influence your pronunciation of their Spanish counterparts. There are literally dozens of such words that you will have to remember to pronounce with [s] rather than [z]. Also the letter *s* frequently represents /z/ in English: *busy, observe, compose*, and the letters *z* or *zz* almost always do: *zest, hazard, fuzzy, buzzing,* causing you to pronounce a [z] in Spanish words spelled with *s* and *z*: **residencia, Isabel, mozo, zapato**. Actually, Spanish does have a [z] sound, but only in syllable-final position before a voiced consonant, as in **mismo, isla, rasgar, asno**, due, of course, to regressive assimilation. Spanish never uses [z] in word-initial position, and rarely in word-medial intervocalic position (with only the dialectal exceptions mentioned above). Thus you should avoid the voiced sibilant [z] in Spanish in all but syllable-final position. Here it can actually help you distinguish between words and phrases that are distinguished by Spanish speakers, not by [s] versus [z], as you can do, but by the following consonants: **este** [és-te] versus **es de** [éz-ɖe] , **rascar** [ɾas-kár] *to scratch* versus **rasgar** [ɾaz-ǵár] *to tear*, **las pecas** [las-pé-kas] *the freckles* versus **las becas** [laz-ƀé-kas] *the scholarships.* This, of course, is because /s/ and /z/ are phonemic in English, but merely allophonic and predictable in Spanish.

Another possible difficulty concerns /s/ and /θ/, the latter phoneme being characteristic of Castilian Spanish only. American students who learn Castilian Spanish rarely master the correct use of /θ/ and mix it up with /s/ (just as some Spaniards from southern Spain do), saying things like **En esa ciudad hacía mucho calor** [e-né-sa-sįu-ɖá-ɖa-θí-a-mú-ĉo-ka-lór]. Unless you can be completely consistent and use these two phonemes the way Spaniards do (and the way you do in your own English), it is best to drop /θ/ completely and use **seseo** (only /s/). This may cause a few spelling problems at first—you may forget whether the word is *ofisio or **oficio**—but this a minor problem which Spanish American school children face everyday as they learn to spell their own language and which they overcome without too much trouble. **Seseo** is used by five or six times as many Spanish speakers as **distinción** and is also accepted by the latter. Thus it is the pronunciation mode we recommend for American students of Spanish unless they have a compelling reason to learn **distinción**.

Spelling of /s/ and /θ/

/s/ is spelled in all forms of Spanish with the letter **s**: **sala, casa, sentarse, ese, sí, insistir, sol, oso, su, usual, más, rasgo, isla, mismo**. In American Spanish it is also spelled with **c** before **e** and **i**: **centro, hace, cinco, pacífico**; and also with **z**: **zapato, caza, zorro, mozo, zurdo, dulzura, paz, hallazgo**. There are only a handful of words and names where /s/ is spelled with **z** before **e** and **i**: **zeta, zigzaguear, Zedillo, Zendejas**.

/s/ is also spelled with **x** in many common words: between vowels, such as **taxi, exacto**; preceding a consonant: **extraño, expansión**; and at the beginning of a handful of specialized words: **xenofobia, xilófono**. In Mexico /s/ is also spelled with **x** in many Indian names: **Xochimilco, Tlaxcala, Taxco**.

However, Castilian Spanish has the phoneme /θ/, always spelled with **c** before **e** and **i**: **centro, cinco**; and with **z** elsewhere: **zapato, vez**. /s/ is spelled only with **s**. Thus in Castilian, words like **sierra-cierra, ves-vez** are minimal pairs—the first word in each pair having /s/ and the second /θ/. But in American Spanish these are pairs of homophones pronounced exactly alike, like *seed* and *cede* in English.

Practice

A.

Your instructor will read each Spanish word or phrase. Repeat it, and give its meaning if the instructor wishes. Then say the so-called "opposite" word or phrase, and give the meaning if asked. "Opposite" means a word with /b/ for /p/, /d/ for /t/, or /g/ for /k/, or vice versa. For example, your instructor says **rascar**. *You also say* **rascar**, *and, if asked, give the meaning*—to scratch. *Then say* **rasgar**, *and, if asked, give the meaning*—to tear. *Or if your instructor says* **las becas**, *you also say* **las becas** *and, if asked, give the meaning*, the scholarships. *Then say* **las pecas**, *and, if asked, give the meaning*—the freckles.

1. esposo	11. ¿dices "boca"?
2. de este	12. los godos
3. los huevos	13. este
4. es vaca	14. los paños
5. tienes pecas	15. no es cordura
6. rascar	16. desde
7. esbozo	17. los codos
8. es de aquí	18. ¿dónde están los baños?
9. ¿quieres pesarlo?	19. ¿necesitas velarlo?
10. es gancho	20. este aquí

B.

Your instructor or a classmate will read the English word or phrase. You then say the corresponding Spanish word or phrase with an [s]. *For example, if you hear* president, *you then say* **presidente**. *Don't forget that, unlike the English words, none of the Spanish words have* [z]. *So then where does* [z] *occur in Spanish?*

1. president	13. compromise	25. Jesus
2. pose	14. physical	26. tranquilize
3. vocalize	15. phrase	27. Casanova
4. rose	16. zoology	28. Isabel
5. residence	17. reside	29. paralyze
6. proposal	18. visit	30. music
7. present	19. harmonize	31. Venezuela
8. Kansas	20. Mesoamerica	32. emphasize
9. observe	21. reason	33. imposition
10. reservation	22. resign	34. horizon
11. Zapotec	23. resist	35. Zorro
12. zigzag	24. sterilize	36. Tarzan

C.

Read the following Spanish sentences. In this practice, it is important that you read rather than repeat since the spelling of /s/ is an important issue, too. Some of these Spanish words do have [z]. *Do you know why?*

1. Es de este país.
2. Va a visitar Venezuela.
3. Este aquí no vale nada.
4. El esposo hizo un esbozo.
5. Todos los huevos tienen yema.
6. Esta taza está reservada para mí.
7. No, el Kansas City famoso no está en Kansas.
8. La gordura no tiene nada que ver con la cordura.
9. —¿Dónde están los paños?   —No, qué va. Los *baños*.
10. Los suevos habitaban el territorio al norte de los godos.
11. No hay rosa sin espinas. Por eso, cuidado con no rozarlas.
12. El presidente quiso visitar a los alumnos en sus residencias.
13. Isabel no quería posar porque veía que el resultado sería absurdo.
14. Los cazadores tratan de fomentar la preservación del territorio de caza.
15. La expresión para hablar con mucha animación es: "Hablar hasta por los codos."
16. La zeta es una letra del alfabeto; creo que la seta tiene que ver con los hongos.
17. En el béisbol, los lanzadores zurdos tienen una ventaja al tirar la pelota a un bateador zurdo.
18. Hay un famoso chiste que tiene que ver con el seseo andaluz.
19. En un lugar de Andalucía, cuyo nombre no quiero mencionar, un norteamericano le preguntó al campesino: "¿Aquí puedo cazar?"
20. El campesino, que era seseante también, se alegró porque creía que el yanqui había propuesto matrimonio con Susana, su hija soltera. (¿Comprendes?)

D.

Make a phonetic transcription of the following sentences. Remember that you are now responsible for all the suprasegmentals, all the vowels, and all the allophones of the following consonants (underlined in the Answer Key): /p t k b d g y w s/. Since /θ/ is used only in Castilian Spanish, it will not be used in these transcriptions. Follow the same procedure for stress and intonation as in previous chapters. The speech style will be indicated in each case, and this will determine which allophones you should use in your transcription.

1. Oímos una voz misteriosa en la residencia.   [*rapid speech; intonation*]
2. Observé que al tipo no le gustaba el chorizo en su paella.   [*careful speech*]
3. Algo me rozó el brazo.   [*careful speech; intonation*]
4. El presidente mismo salió de su oficina sin zapatos.   [*rapid speech*]
5. ¿Hay una gran diferencia entre jugo y zumo?   [*careful speech; intonation*]
6. Un refrán para la persona que no es capaz de esperar es: "No se ganó Zamora en una hora".   [*careful speech*]

7. Se fueron a la isla para gozar de muchas diversiones, pero se transformaron en asnos.   [*rapid speech*]

8. Husmeaba las rosas y pensaba en los días cuando llegaron los aztecas a esas regiones.   [*careful speech*]

9. Zorro no hacía la señal de la cruz sino de la letra Z.   [*rapid speech; intonation*]

10. —¿Zorro? ¿Qué es? ¿Un animal? —¡No, *bobo*! ¡Era un personaje conocido de la *televisión*!   [*rapid speech; intonation*]

25

The Voiceless Consonants
/ĉ f x (h)/

Allophones of /ĉ/

The consonant /ĉ/ has one principal allophone in Spanish: [ĉ], a voiceless alveolo-palatal affricate, shown in the first diagram below. Some dialects have another allophone, [š], a voiceless palatal groove fricative (as in English *she*), shown in the second diagram.

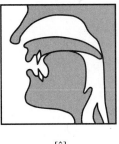

[ĉ]

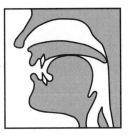

[š]

Description of /ĉ/Allophones

For [ĉ] the blade and tip of the tongue rise and touch the alveolar ridge and the front part of the palate, hence the term ALVEOLO-PALATAL. The sides of the tongue dorsum touch the sides of the palate and the upper back teeth, leaving an opening in the middle. The contact of the tongue blade with the alveolo-palatal region momentarily stops the airstream, as with a stop. But the blade then quickly relaxes its contact, forming a round opening between itself and the front palate, and the airstream passes through this groove as in a fricative. [ĉ], like any affricate then, is a stop + fricative, pronounced almost simultaneously.

For [š] the tongue assumes almost the same position as for [ĉ], except that the tongue blade never touches the front palate. The airstream keeps passing through the groove formed between the tongue dorsum and the front palate. [š] is completely fricative whereas [ĉ] has a slight stop first, making it an affricate.

Distribution and Dialectal Variations of /ĉ/

In most dialects of Spanish, /ĉ/ has only one allophone.

/ĉ/ → [ĉ]   **chico, muchacho**

In some Caribbean countries, such as Panama, Cuba, and Puerto Rico, the fricative [š] is used in free variation with the affricate [ĉ]: **noche** [nó-še]. This is also true of Andalucía in Spain, where the [š] predominates with many speakers.

Contrasts with English

[ĉ] represents no problem for English speakers learning Spanish since it is exactly the same in both languages. (English phoneticians, however, prefer the symbol [č].)

Spelling of /ĉ/

The phoneme /ĉ/ is spelled with **ch** everywhere: **chico, muchacho, leche. Ch** is one of the three digraphs (two letters representing one sound) in Spanish, along with **ll** and **rr**. Currently most dictionaries, lexical studies, and textbook vocabularies have a separate section for words beginning with **ch**, placing **charlar**, for example, after **cuna** for this reason. However, the Spanish Royal Academy, in line with a recommendation from UNESCO (United Nations Educational, Scientific, and Cultural Organization) about standardizing world orthographical practices, recently proposed that **ch** words be included in the **c** section of lexical works, as they are in other languages, placing **charlar** between **cenar** and **cine**, for example. All their works published after 1998 will follow this new system. It is not certain how widely this will be followed by other publishers in the future.

Allophones of /f/

The consonant /f/ has one principal allophone: [f], a voiceless labio-dental slit fricative, shown in the first diagram below. Some dialects have another allophone, [φ], a voiceless bilabial slit fricative shown in the second diagram.

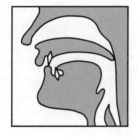

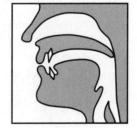

[f]   [φ]

Description of /f/ Allophones

For [f] the lower lip lightly touches the edge of the upper front teeth. The airstream, without stopping, passes through the slit formed by the lip and teeth.

For [ɸ] the two lips almost touch, and the airstream, without stopping, passes through the slit formed between them. The place and manner of articulation are the same as [β], except that there is no voicing.

Distribution and Dialectal Variations of /f/

The phoneme /f/ has only one allophone in most dialects.

/f/ → [f]   **fuerte, ga̲fas**

Many speakers in Central America and the Andean region of South America have another allophone, a bilabial [ɸ] (the voiceless counterpart of [β]), which is in free variation with the labio-dental [f]. This is particularly common before /ue/, as in **fuerte** [ɸu̯ér-te] or **fuera** [ɸu̯é-ra]. Some speakers even use a velar [x] before /ue/—[xu̯ér-te] or [xu̯é-ra]— although this is considered substandard by many educated speakers.

Contrasts with English

[f] represents no problem for English speakers learning Spanish since it is exactly the same in both languages.

Spelling of /f/

The phoneme /f/ is spelled with **f** everywhere: **flor, ga̲fas**.

Allophones of /x (h)/

The consonant /x/, known in Spanish as **jota**, has two principal allophones: [x], a voiceless velar slit fricative, shown in the first diagram below, and [ç], a voiceless palatal slit fricative, shown in the second diagram. Some speakers of General American Spanish have a corresponding phoneme /h/, which has three allophones, the principal one being [h], a voiceless glottal slit fricative, which cannot be shown on a facial diagram, plus both [ç] and [x]. Speakers of Castilian Spanish have another allophone of /x/: [X], a voiceless velar or uvular trill, shown in the third diagram.

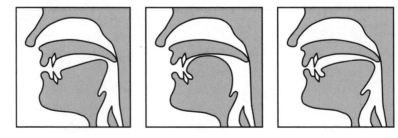

[x]   [ç]   [X]

Description of /x (h)/ Allophones

For [x] the back of the tongue is placed lightly against or very close to the velum. The airstream, rather than being stopped, passes between the tongue and the velum, creating audible friction. This sound does not exist in American English, but it is heard in Scottish English, as in *Lo**ch** Ness*; in German, as in **machen**; in Yiddish, as in **chutzpah**; and in Russian, as in **Kharkov** or **khorosho**.

The articulation of [ç] is almost the same as that of [y] except that there is more friction and no voicing. The tongue dorsum humps up, almost touching the palate, and the airstream keeps passing through the slit. The sound is heard in German, as in **ich,** and many speakers of English have it in words beginning with *hu-*, like *human, humid, humility*, and it thus can contrast with [y], as in *Hugh-you*.

The glottal [h] is actually articulated more like a vowel than a consonant. The speech organs are neutral, that is, they assume the position of the next sound, usually a vowel. However, since [h] is voiceless, the airstream passes through the glottis with friction but without creating vibrations. The vocal bands begin vibrating for the following vowel, which is always voiced, of course.

For [X] the back of the tongue is placed against or very close to the very back of the velum or the uvula. The air is pushed through with enough force to make the uvula and back of the velum vibrate, thus creating a trill. The sound is harsher than that of the purely fricative [x].

Distribution and Dialectal Variations of /x (h)/

In many dialects of American Spanish, such as those of Mexico, the Andean region, and the Southern Cone (Chile, Argentina, Uruguay), /x/ has two allophones: [x] and [ç]. The latter sound, articulated farther forward in the mouth than the velar [x], often precedes the front vowels /i/ and /e/: **girar** [çi-rár], **gente** [çén̦-te]. [x], articulated farther back in the mouth, usually precedes the central vowel /a/ and the back vowels /o/ and /u/: **jardín** [xar-ɖín], **joya** [xó-ya], **jugar** [xu-ǵár]. Thus these two allophones are determined by *regressive* assimilation, that is, the first sound becomes more like the second sound.

The /x/ rule for these speakers, then, would be as follows.

$$/x/ \rightarrow \left[\begin{matrix} \left\{ \begin{matrix} [ç] \\ [x] \end{matrix} \right\} / \underline{\quad} \left\{ \begin{matrix} /i/ \\ /e/ \end{matrix} \right\} \\ [x] \ \text{elsewhere} \end{matrix} \right]$$

gitano, jinete, general, mujer

jabón, baja, joven, hijo, jurar, Jujuy, reloj

In other dialects of American Spanish, such as those of Central America, Colombia, the Caribbean, and Caribbean speakers in the U.S., the palatal sound is occasionally heard but the glottal [h] is the predominant allophone: [hi-rár], [hén̦-te], [har-ɖín], [hó-ya], [hu-ǵár]. In such dialects, then, the phoneme itself is best analyzed as /h/ rather than /x/. This explains why our consonant charts have the phoneme (/h/) in parentheses, indicating that any given dialect of Spanish has *either* /x/ *or* /h/ as a phoneme, but not both.

The /h/ rule for these speakers, then, would be as follows, with the same examples as given above for the /x/ rule.

$$
\text{/h/} \rightarrow \left[\begin{array}{l} \left\{ \begin{array}{l} [\varsigma] \\ [h] \end{array} \right\} \Big/ \underline{\quad} \left\{ \begin{array}{l} /i/ \\ /e/ \end{array} \right\} \\ [h] \quad \text{elsewhere} \end{array} \right]
$$

In Castilian Spanish /x/ is realized either as the purely fricative velar sound [x] or the strong, harsh-sounding velar or even uvular trill [X]. In fact, this sound, along with the interdental /θ/, is one of main features that enable Spanish Americans to recognize a speaker from central or northern Spain. This sound is a close equivalent to trilled *r* sounds of both French, as in **rouge**, or German, as in **recht**, although these sounds are normally voiced whereas [X] is always voiceless.

Contrasts with English

Spanish **jota**, the voiceless velar fricative [x], however, does not exist in American English and most other dialects of English, and thus is a potential problem for English-speaking students of Spanish. Not only is the sound a new one, but it strikes many English speakers as being somewhat unpleasant. Sometimes they pronounce the closest English sound—the velar /k/—instead. These two sounds, however, are phonemic in Spanish, and **baja**, for example, if pronounced with a /k/, comes out **vaca**. Thus many English speakers prefer [h] and [ç], both of which are acceptable substitutes for [x] in Spanish. Going to the opposite extreme, many American students who study in Spain are struck by the strong velar or uvular trill [X] of Castilian Spanish and adopt it immediately. This sound is noticeable to Spanish Americans since they do not use it themselves. Thus American students should base their decision on which variety of **jota** they use on where they will be using Spanish.

Spelling of /x (h)/

The phoneme /x/ (or /h/) is spelled in two principal ways—with **j** in all phonetic environments: **jardín, bajo, jefe, mujer, jinete, ají, jota, ajo, jurar, cejudo, reloj**; with **g** before /e/ and /i/: **gente, dirige, gitano, agitar**. The fact that **g** before the other vowels represents the voiced phoneme /g/ causes spelling changes in many Spanish verbs. For example, in verbs ending in **-ger** and **-gir**, all forms that end in **-o** or **-a** are spelled with **j**: **dirigir** but **dirijo, escoger** but **escoja**.

/x/ is also spelled with the letter **x** in Indian words and names, mainly in Mexico: **mexicano, México, Oaxaca, Xococo**. The name of the country itself and its derivatives are spelled with **j** only in Spain: **Méjico, mejicano**, and so forth.

Practice

A.

Your instructor will read each Spanish word or phrase. Repeat it, and give its meaning if the instructor wishes. Then say the so-called ''opposite'' word or phrase, and give the meaning if asked. ''Opposite'' means a word with /x/ (or /h/) for /k/, or vice versa. For example, your instructor says **carro**. *You also say* **carro**, *and, if asked, give the meaning—car. Then say* **jarro**, *and, if asked, give the meaning—jar. Or if your instructor says* **baja**. *You also say* **baja**, *and, if asked, give the meaning,* short. *Then say* **vaca**, *and, if asked, give the meaning—cow.*

1.	jama	11.	jornada
2.	toco	12.	joya
3.	Baco	13.	loca
4.	jareta	14.	ceja
5.	laja	15.	cota
6.	quema	16.	paca
7.	cota	17.	bajo
8.	jurar	18.	faja
9.	faca	19.	jarro
10.	moco	20.	gema

B.

Read or repeat the following Spanish sentences. Use either the velar [x] *or the glottal* [h] *for the* **jota**, *according to the wishes of your instructor. Or perhaps even the strong* [X] *if he/she wishes. Use* [ĉ] *for /ĉ/ and* [f] *for /f/.*

1. Oh, esa mujer es genial.
2. Hacía frío y por eso prendió el fuego.
3. El general fue con su mujer a Ginebra.
4. La palabra **cochino** no sólo se refiere a los chanchos.
5. En mi país preferimos decir **elegir** en vez de **escoger.**
6. Se dice que los norteamericanos son flojos en geografía.
7. Los gitanos viven en ese barrio donde ves algunas rejas.
8. En la Argentina el carro usa como combustible la **nafta.**
9. Me hacen falta gafas para leer una transcripción fonética.
10. En España dicen **pijama,** pero en México dicen **piyama.**
11. Fue elegido alcalde o de Oaxaca o de Guanajuato. No recuerdo.
12. La mujer estaba en el jardín recogiendo las flores para la fiesta.
13. El chocolate de los aztecas era muy fuerte y mucho menos dulce.
14. La teoría es que Baco era tan bajo por haber ingerido tanto vino.

15. Pero **charlatán** ahora significa mucho más que un individuo a quien le gusta charlar.

16. En Puerto Rico, dicen ''¡qué facha!'' para el aspecto general de una persona, pero **facha** en la Argentina es **cara**.

C.

Make up one or two Spanish sentences with each of the following words, or, if your instructor prefers, define them in Spanish.

1. familia
2. freír
3. fumar

4. chiste
5. chico
6. chisme

7. jactarse
8. juez
9. gimnasio

D.

Make a phonetic transcription of the following sentences. Remember that you are now responsible for all the suprasegmentals, all the vowels, and all the allophones of the following consonants (underlined in the Answer Key): /p t k b d g y w s ĉ f x/. Follow the same procedure for stress and intonation as in previous chapters. The speech style is indicated in each case so you can decide which allophones to use in your transcription.

1. Hicieron construir una reja para proteger el jardín.   [*careful*]
2. Su nombre oficial es Francisco, pero lo llaman Pancho.   [*rapid; intonation*]
3. ¿Salchicha? ¡No, quiero *chorizo*! ¡Es totalmente diferente!   [*rapid; intonation*]
4. Sí, es confuso, la cocina es la estufa, que se encuentra en la cocina.   [*careful*]
5. **Blasfemia** es el sustantivo, pero **blasfemar** es el verbo.   [*careful; intonation*]
6. Las palabras **fuera**, **fuerte** y **fuego** no se pronuncian con **jota** sino con **f**.   [*careful*]
7. En México, ¿qué prefieren decir? **¿Chico** o **pequeño?**   [*careful; intonation*]
8. Ese chisme es chabacano y chocante. Pero, Zoilo, ¡cuéntame más, por favor!   [*rapid*]

26

The Nasal Consonants /m n ñ/

Allophones of /m n ñ/

The consonant /m/ has one principal allophone in Spanish: [m], a voiced bilabial nasal, shown in the first diagram below. The consonant /n/ has seven allophones in American Spanish: [m], described above and shown in the first diagram; [ɱ], a voiced labio-dental nasal, shown in the second diagram; [n̪], a voiced dental nasal, shown in the third diagram; [n], a voiced alveolar nasal, shown in the the fourth diagram; [ñ], a voiced alveolo-palatal nasal, shown in the fifth diagram; [ñ], a voiced palatal nasal, shown in the sixth diagram; and [ŋ], a voiced velar nasal, shown in the seventh diagram (next page).[1] The consonant /ñ/ has one allophone: [ñ], described above and shown in the sixth diagram.

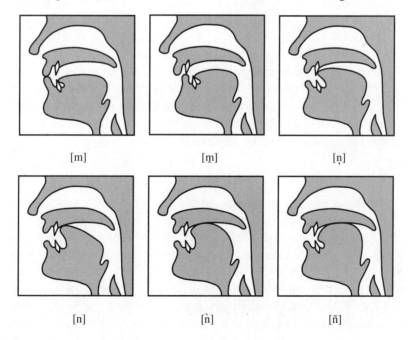

[m]	[ɱ]	[n̪]
[n]	[ñ]	[ñ]

[1]In Castilian Spanish /n/ has another allophone: [n̪], a voiced interdental nasal, which, since it precedes only the interdental /θ/, as in **incierto**, is not heard in American Spanish and thus not practiced in this book. English has the same sound in *tenth*.

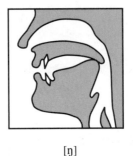

[ŋ]

Description of /m n ñ/ Allophones

Each of these nasal allophones is HOMORGANIC with a non-nasal, that is, they are articulated in exactly the same place in the vocal tract, usually due to regressive assimilation. The main difference between the nasal sounds and their oral (non-nasal) counterparts is the fact that for the former the velum is open (see any of the diagrams above), allowing the airstream to pass through and resonate in the nasal as well as the oral cavity.

For [m] the lips press together just as they do for the stops [p] and [b]. For [m̩] the lower lip presses against the edge of the upper front teeth as it does for the slit fricatives [f] and [v]. However, since these last two sounds are fricative, the lip touches the teeth lightly, but for the nasal counterpart [m̩] it presses firmly, forcing the air out through the nostrils. For [n̪] the tip of the tongue is placed against the back of the upper front teeth, as it is for the stops [t] and [d]. For [n] the tongue tip is placed against the alveolar ridge as it is for the lateral [l] or the tap [r]. For [ǹ] the tongue tip is placed a bit farther back on the alveolar ridge where the palate begins, hence the term ALVEOLO-PALATAL. This is the same place of articulation for the affricate [ĉ]. For [ñ] the tongue dorsum humps up and makes extensive contact with the palate as it does for the first part of the palatal affricate [ŷ]. For this last sound the tongue is quickly released, but for [ñ] it remains pressed against the palate as the air escapes through the nostrils. For [ŋ] the tongue dorsum presses against the velum as it does for the stops [k] and [g].

Distribution of /m n ñ/

There are three nasal phonemes in Spanish, which contrast and distinguish meaning within a word between vowels, as in **cama** *bed*, **ca̲na** *a (single) gray hair*, **caña** *reed, cane,* or **doma** *he/she tames,* **do̲na** *he/she donates,* **do̲ña** *lady* (title of respect used with a woman's first name). Yet elsewhere these three phonemes never contrast. Only /n/ occurs naturally at the end of a word in Spanish (**pa̲n, habla̲n**). /ñ/ never occurs here, and /m/ is replaced by /n/ in natural speech—**álbu̲m** [ál-ƀun]. The plural of this word even has /n/, although written with **m**—**álbume̲s**: [ál-ƀu-nes]. Only a few Spanish words begin with /ñ/—**ñandú, ño̲ño**. And these three nasal phonemes never contrast in syllable-final position before a consonant. Rather, they NEUTRALIZE, and the resulting allophones are realized automatically according to the point of articulation of the following consonant, due, of course, to regressive assimilation. To show this we can use "P.A." to represent consonant point of articulation, that is, bilabial, labio-dental, dental, and so on. This enables us to give a shortened or streamlined /n/ rule in which the various syllable-final nasal articulations are homorganic with the following consonants and do not have to be listed individually—although we have provided examples below.

/m/ → [m]   **más, ca_m_a, ha_m_pa, ho_m_bre**

/ñ/ → [ñ]   **ñandú, ba_ñ_o**

$$
/n/ \rightarrow \begin{bmatrix} [N^{P.A.}] \Big/ \underline{\quad} /C/ & \text{(see examples below)} \\ \left.\begin{cases} [n] \\ [\eta] \end{cases}\right\} \Big/ \underline{\quad} \# \begin{cases} V \\ \| \end{cases} & \begin{array}{l} \textbf{u\underline{n} amor} \\ \textbf{pa\underline{n}} \end{array} \\ [n] \quad \text{elsewhere} & \textbf{\underline{n}o, ma\underline{n}o} \end{bmatrix}
$$

$[N^{P.A.}]$ represents the nasal allophones homorganic with the following consonants.

Examples of $N^{P.A.}$:

[m] (bilabial), as in **ha_m_pa, ho_m_bre, u_n_ peso, e_n_viar, u_n_ vaso**

[m̦] (labio-dental), as in **e_n_fermo, u_n_ farol**

[n̦] (dental), as in **a_n_tes, u_n_ tigre, a_n_dar, u_n_ día**

[n] (alveolar), as in **la_n_za, u_n_ suéter, i_n_nato, u_n_ negro, u_n_ libro,
    e_n_redar, u_n_ rato**

[ñ̦] (alveolo-palatal), as in **a_n_cho, u_n_ chico**

[ñ] (palatal), as in **i_n_yección, u_n_ yerno, co_n_ hielo, u_n_ ñandú, co_n_ llave**

[ŋ] (velar), as in **esta_n_co, u_n_ carro, te_n_go, u_n_ gato, mo_n_ja, u_n_ jarro, u_n_ hueso**

As you can see, the nasal allophones cover almost the entire range of possibilities in the upper articulators, from the outer edge of the vocal tract (the two lips) to nearly as far back as the upper articulators go (the velum). The rule could be detailed, giving all the allophones in the environment of each possible following sound, but the above way is a more succinct way of doing exactly the same thing.

Some speakers occasionally depart from this process of regressive assimilation when /n/ precedes /m/ and pronounce the first nasal as an alveolar [n] instead of bilabial [m], as in **conmigo** [kon-mí-ǵo], rather than the expected [kom-mí-ǵo]. This is an example of another process, called DISSIMILATION, the opposite of *assimilation*. In the latter case, the speaker attempts to make one sound like another one next to it, but in dissimilation the speaker attempts to make one sound *unlike* one near or next to it. Another example of dissimilation in Spanish is the diminutive ending **-ico**, which Costa Ricans, particularly, use instead of **-ito** to alter nouns with a /t/ at the end, thus avoiding two /t/'s in close proximity. They say **perrito**, but **gatico**, **librito** but **zapatico** because of the /t/'s in **gato**

and **zapato**. The process exists in English, too. For example, some Americans say "*chim-
ley*" instead of *chimney*, to prevent two nasals from coming together. And all English
speakers say *February* without the first /r/ to avoid the combination of two /r/'s so close
together—a slightly different type of dissimilation.

There is one more wrinkle to the /n/ rule. Speakers in the Caribbean region, including
U.S. mainland Puerto Ricans and Cuban Americans, in Central America, in the Andean
region of South America, and also in southern Spain pronounce either an ordinary alveolar
[n] or a velar [ŋ], as in English *sing*, at the end of a word when it precedes a word beginning
with a vowel or a pause. Thus the phrase **en español** is pronounced either [e-nes-pa-ñól]
or [e-ŋes-pa-ñól]. Although the rule implies that the alveolar [n] is characteristic of more
careful speech and the velar [ŋ] of rapid speech, the situation is not that simple with word-
final /n/. The same speaker may vary back and forth between these two pronunciations,
often in the same speech style, thus producing true free variation, in which it is almost
impossible to predict which allophone will occur.

Such speakers, if the discourse demands it, can distinguish between such minimal
pairs as **enojas** *you annoy* [e-nó-xas] and **en hojas** *on leaves, pages* [e-ŋó-xas] or **enaguas**
petticoat, slip [e-ná-g̣uas] and **en aguas** *in waters* [e-ŋá-g̣uas], in the same way English
speakers distinguish *sun* from *sung*. In fact, even the Spanish speakers who do not use the
velar [ŋ] in word-final position recognize it as a signal of a word boundary between vowels
and know that [e-ná-g̣uas] cannot possibly mean *slip* or *petticoat*.

Note also that the rule stipulates that for word-final /n/ to be realized as a velar [ŋ],
it must precede a word beginning with a vowel or a pause—and, of course, a velar consonant due to regressive assimilation (P.A.). Thus *all* speakers say velar [ŋ] in the phrase
[uŋ-gá-to] **un gato** for this reason, but some, as we have indicated, also say [u-ŋí-xo] for
un hijo. They may also say [u-ní-xo] since there is no possibility of confusion as there
might be with **en aguas–enaguas** or **en hojas–enojas**.

Dialectal Variations of /m n ñ/

In the Caribbean (including the Puerto Rican and Cuban areas of the United States),
Central America, highland South America, and southern Spain, the word-final velar [ŋ] is
extremely common. As we have said, it is recognized as a word boundary signal even by
speakers of other dialects who do not use it—in Mexico, Colombia, the Southern Cone,
and Spain.

Contrasts with English

Although English has no palatal /ñ/, the sequence of /ny/, as in the words *onion* or
canyon, is close enough that it can be used in Spanish words with palatal /ñ/, even though
there is a discernible difference in Spanish between the last syllables of **Toño** [tó-ño] and
Antonio [aṇ-tó-ni̯o].

The main contrast between nasals in the two languages stems from the fact that in English a boundary feature called PLUS JUNCTURE, /+/, prevents regressive assimilation from taking place in many sequences of nasal + non-nasal. For example, just as in Spanish, we pronounce a velar [ŋ] before /k/ or /g/ in words like *bank* or *tango*, due, of course, to regressive assimilation to the following velar stop. But when a word boundary intervenes, we do not assimilate in English: *tan coat* [n-k] or *green grass* [n-g]. There is the temptation to do the same thing in Spanish and avoid the homorganic combination of nasal + non-nasal, which, however, happens in Spanish at word *boundaries*, too, unlike English. Thus an English speaker may say *[un-pé-so] instead of [um-pé-so] for **un peso**, *[en-fér-mo] instead of [eṃ-fér-mo] for **enfermo**, or *[en-gor-ɖár] instead of [eŋ-gor-ɖár] for **engordar.** Although such pronunciations are not really wrong, since phonemic contrasts between the nasals in Spanish disappear or are neutralized in this syllable-final position, they are not native-like Spanish pronunciations and can even sound strange in some cases.

Also, since /n/ and /ŋ/ are phonemic in English—as in *run-rung, sinner-singer*—you may be reluctant to imitate the use of word-final velar [ŋ] in Spanish when you hear it, and, worse, feel that it is somehow incorrect.

Spelling of /m n ñ/

/m/ is spelled with **m** everywhere in Spanish: **más, amo, inmediato.** However, the letter **m** sometimes represents /n/, as in **también, tampoco, álbum, réquiem**.

/ñ/ is spelled with **ñ** everywhere in Spanish: **ñandú, paño.**

/n/ is spelled with **n: no, mano, van, invitar, enfermo, ancho, tengo**, and, as we have indicated, even with **m** in some cases (**también, álbum**), reflecting regressive assimilation in the first case (**tan + bien**) and the fact that almost no native Spanish words end in /m/ in the second case: [ál-βun]. Remember also that the homorganic sequence [m-b] can be spelled four different ways in Spanish: **m b**, as in **álbum bonito** (**álbum** now *really* being pronounced with [m]) or **mb**, as in **hombre**; **m v**, as in **réquiem vistoso**; **n b**, as in **tan bonito**; and **n v**, as in **tan vasto** or **nv**, as in **invierno**.

Practice

A.

Your instructor will pronounce a series of words and phrases containing nasal consonants. Identify the nasal allophone according to its P.A., and then repeat the word or phrase. For example, if you hear **un peso**, *say "bilabial" since the point of articulation of this nasal is bilabial in the phrase* [um-pé-so], *and then repeat the phrase.*

1. en Filadelfia   3. mensual
2. antes   4. un vaso

5. en Chile	10. con huevos
6. enredar	11. infiel
7. enviar	12. ingerir
8. hinchar	13. piden tacos
9. inyección	14. un yerno

B.

Read or repeat the following sentences. Use velar [ŋ] at the end of a word preceding a pause or another word beginning with a vowel if your instructor tells you to. Remember the concepts "P.A.," "homorganic," and "regressive assimilation."

1. Hablan vasco.
2. Con hielo, por favor.
3. Se lo envié el año pasado.
4. Pongo aquí la parte ancha.
5. Quiero convertirlo en pesos.
6. Un chico enyesó el muro con la pala.
7. Es una persona de mucha confianza.
8. Buscan huevos de gallina en un huerto lleno de naranjos.
9. Intentan prender el fuego con fósforos húmedos. ¡Qué tonto!
10. Un jarro es mucho más grande que un vaso o que un cubo también.
11. Faltan un macho y una hembra para comenzar un grupo familiar.
12. Un señor con sus hijos pudieron terminar su trabajo en el jardín.
13. Un español, un portugués y un francés se fueron a trabajar a Brasil.
14. La canción famosa de *Casablanca* empieza: "Un beso no es nada más que un beso".
15. **Cónyuge** es un vocablo que significa **esposo**. Y de aquél tenemos la palabra **conyugal**.
16. Van a visitar Colombia, y pasar tiempo en Cali, en Manizales, en Cartagena, en Bogotá, en Medellín y en Bucaramanga, claro está.

C.

How many different ways, speaking allophonically, of course, can you think of to pronounce either the indefinite article **un** *or the preposition* **con**? *For example,* [um] *as in* **un peso** *or* [uŋ] *as in* **un carro**. *Put your phrases into Spanish sentences, such as* **Hay que pagar con** [kom] **pesetas.** *Do you know the P.A. of each different nasal?*

D.

Make a phonetic transcription of the following sentences. So far you have had the following consonants: /p t k b d g y w s ĉ f x m n ñ/. *Follow the same instructions as those given for previous transcription practices.*

1. En frente del convento de San Benito había un huerto lleno de naranjos.   [*careful speech*]
2. Un monje paseaba rezando sus oraciones en voz baja.   [*careful*]
3. Un chico estaba jugando con un gato que un padre le había enviado.   [*careful*]
4. ¿Esto es el comienzo de un cuento?   [*rapid; intonation*]
5. No, qué va. Son frases para ilustrar los alófonos de las consonantes nasales en español.   [*rapid; intonation*]
6. Enrique. Por favor, habla con él. Parece un hombre de confianza.   [*rapid; intonation*]
7. Los inviernos en Bolivia son fuertes, pero en Venezuela son calurosos.   [*careful*]
8. En Puerto Rico conviene llamar nenes a los niños porque los boricuas mismos los llaman así.   [*rapid; intonation*]

27

Lateral Consonants /l/ and /ĺ/

Allophones of /l/

The consonant /l/ has four principal allophones in Spanish: [l̪], a voiced dental lateral,[1] shown in the first diagram below; [l], a voiced alveolar lateral, shown in the second diagram; [l̀], a voiced alveolo-palatal lateral, shown in the third diagram; and [ĺ], a voiced palatal lateral, shown in the fourth diagram.[2]

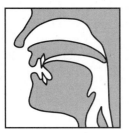
[l̪]

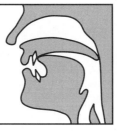
[l]

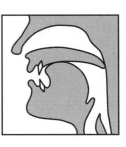
[l̀]

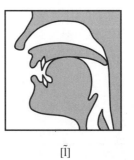
[ĩ]

[1] Actually the most significant part of laterals—the fact that the airstream passes by one or both *sides* of the tongue—cannot be shown in facial diagrams; thus all of the diagrams for the lateral sounds are identical to those for their non-lateral counterparts.

[2] In Castilian Spanish /l/ has another allophone: [l̺], a voiced interdental lateral, which, since it precedes only the interdental /θ/, as in **alzar**, is not heard in American Spanish and thus not practiced in this book. English has the same sound in *health*.

Description of /l/ Allophones

Just as with the nasals in the previous chapter, each of these lateral allophones is homorganic with a non-lateral, that is, they are articulated in exactly the same place in the vocal tract, usually due to regressive assimilation. The main difference between the lateral sounds and their non-lateral oral counterparts is the fact that for the former the airstream passes on one or both sides of the tongue (thus the term LATERAL), and for non-lateral oral sounds it passes over the tongue to escape out through the mouth.

For dental [ḷ] the tongue tip presses against the inside of the upper front teeth as it does for the stops [t] and [d]. As with all Spanish laterals, the vocal bands vibrate, and the air passes out on one or both sides of the tongue. Also the tongue for all Spanish laterals is relatively high and flat, especially as compared with its position for *l* sounds in English. The resulting sound is called impressionistically ''CLEAR'' or ''LIGHT,'' as opposed to the ''DARK'' sound of English [ɫ], which will be described below. These visual terms, of course, mean nothing until you connect them to the auditory impression, in which case they then seem to make sense. For Spanish alveolar [l] the tongue tip presses against the alveolar ridge, as it does for [n] or [r], and the air passes out on one or both sides of the tongue. For alveolo-palatal [l̩] the tongue tip is placed a bit farther back on the alveolar ridge where the palate begins, hence the term ALVEOLO-PALATAL. This is the same place of articulation of the affricate [ĉ] and the nasal [ǹ]. For palatal [l̃] the tongue tip rests against the lower front teeth. The dorsum humps up and makes extensive contact with the palate. This sound is very close to the sounds produced in the English word *million*.

Distribution of /l/

Most dialects of Spanish have only one lateral phoneme, /l/, which, like /n/, assimilates to the following consonant. To show this we can use the same device we did in the previous chapter on nasals—P.A.—to indicate that /l/ is homorganic with the following consonants. Thus the individual allophones do not have to be listed individually, although, again, we provide examples below the rule so you will be aware of what they are. In the following rule the *l* before P.A. is a small letter since we are talking about only one phoneme with no neutralization involved. In the nasal rule in the previous chapter we used a capital N before P.A. to show that there was a loss of contrast with *three* phonemes in this case: /m n ñ/. There is another important difference between nasals and laterals in Spanish. Remember that we had seven nasal allophones, ranging from bilabial [m] to velar [ŋ]. However, in the case of /l/ there are *no* bilabial, labio-dental, or velar laterals. This means that the only consonants that govern regressive assimilation with /l/ are /t d s n l r̄ ĉ y ñ/, that is, the dentals, alveolars, alveolo-palatals, and palatals. The bilabials, labio-dentals, and velars are excluded and go in the elsewhere part of the rule along with the word-initial, intervocalic, and absolute-final positions.

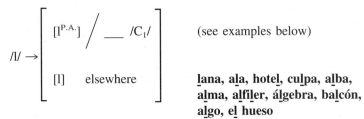

$$/l/ \rightarrow \begin{bmatrix} [l^{P.A.}] \Big/ \underline{\quad} /C_1/ \\ \\ [l] \quad \text{elsewhere} \end{bmatrix}$$

(see examples below)

**lana, ala, hotel, culpa, alba,
alma, alfiler, álgebra, balcón,
algo, el hueso**

/C₁/ represents the dental, alveolar, alveolo-palatal, and palatal consonants.

Examples of [l^{P.A.}]:

[l̪] (dental), as in **alto, el tipo, falda, el día**

[l] (alveolar), as in **salsa, el saco, balneario, el norte, alrededor, el ratón**

[l̠] (alveolo-palatal), as in **colcha, el chico**

[l̃] (palatal), as in **el ñoño, el yerno**

As you can see /l/ behaves quite like /n/ except that it has fewer allophones and, in the majority of dialects of Spanish, no phoneme with which to neutralize in syllable-final position as the nasal phonemes do.

Dialectal Variations of /l/

The last dialectal modification of /l/ occurs mainly in southern Spain but is also heard sporadically in the Caribbean countries and Chile: the replacement of /l/ with /r/ in syllable-final position. Thus an Andalusian who uses this pronunciation says the following sentence, **Lo encuentra al final de esta calle, señor**, as [lu̯eŋ-ku̯én-trar-fi-nár-ðéh-ta-ká-ye ‖ θe-ñó], with other interesting features such as *s*-modification, **ceceo**, and word-final *r*-deletion.

Contrasts with English

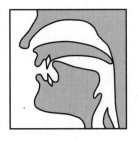

English [ɫ]

English [l] in syllable-initial position is not too different from Spanish alveolar "light" or "clear" *l*—although you can still hear the difference between Spanish **lana** and the English name *Lana*. But English [ɫ] in post-vocalic position, as in *bell, wheel, mile, build, halt, help,* is quite different. This [ɫ] is referred to as the "dark" *l* because of its velarized articulation and open vowel-like sound. In Spanish, regardless of its position in the word or the phonemic phrase, the alveolar [l] is pronounced with the tongue relatively flat and the sides against the inner surfaces of the upper molars (see the second facial diagram on page 248). But English "dark" [ł] is pronounced with no tongue contact at all with the upper articulators or very slight contact of the tongue tip. The middle of the tongue dorsum is lowered or concave and the back of the dorsum is raised toward the velum, giving it a *u*-like sound (see the facial diagram, in this section). This "dark" [ł] also exists in Catalan and Portuguese. It is particularly prominent in the upper Midlands, such as southern Pennsylvania and Ohio. Although its use in Spanish, in words like **mal, tal, hotel, sol, faltar, golpear**, does not change or affect meaning, it is extremely noticeable and foreign-sounding. One exercise for English speakers to practice pronouncing the light sound of Spanish alveolar [l] in syllable-final position, is to repeat the word *model*, for example, over and over, gradually softening the apical articulation of the tongue for the flap [d̂] sound, achieving at last the Spanish word **mal**.

Spelling of /l/

/l/ is spelled with **l** everywhere in Spanish: **l̲una, val̲e, al̲to, al̲ma, enl̲ace**.

Allophones of /l̃/

The phoneme /l̃/ (functional only in certain dialects in South America and Spain) has one principal allophone, [l̃], a voiced palatal lateral, shown in the fourth diagram at the beginning of the chapter.

Description of /l̃/ Allophone

Palatal /l̃/ is almost identical to the sound in the middle of the English word *million*. It is also similar to the sequence in Spanish of [li̲], as in the word **ali̲ar** *to ally*, but it is different enough so that this word contrasts with **hal̲lar** *to find* in all dialects of Spanish, including those, of course, that have palatal /l̃/ as a phoneme. This same palatal *l* exists in other languages, such as Italian **fig̲lio** and Portuguese **fil̲ho**.

Distribution and Dialectal Variations of /l̃/

/l̃/ → [l̃]   **l̲lama, el̲la, cal̲ló**

Most dialects of Spanish are **yeísta**, that is, there is no palatal /l̃/ phoneme; /y/ is used instead. This means that pairs like **hay̲a** and **hal̲la** or **se cay̲ó** and **se cal̲ló** are pronounced exactly alike, with [y] as the intervocalic consonant in all four of these words. However, in some dialects, these words are distinguished—with [y] in the first of each pair and palatal [l̃] in the second of each pair. This, then, makes this palatal *l* a phoneme /l̃/, heard in all words spelled with **ll**. The official name of this letter is **elle** in Spanish, but it is called **doble ele** by most everyone informally. These **lleísta** (as contrasted with **yeísta**) dialects are found in the highland regions of South America—central Colombia (particularly among older people), southern highland Ecuador, highland Peru, throughout Bolivia and Paraguay—and in rural areas, towns, and smaller cities in central and northern Spain. Madrid, however, is **yeísta**, and even in the **lleísta** areas, **yeísmo** is more and more widely used by younger speakers. Some linguists speculate that because of the same demographic and social factors that exist in most modern societies—more education, travel, watching television, listening to the radio, going to films—the palatal [l̃] will gradually disappear from Spanish as a phoneme. In fact, a common spelling error for uneducated and marginally educated speakers of Spanish is **ll** for **y**, as in *llo for **yo**, or vice versa, as in *****yegar** for **llegar**, indicating the lack of palatal /l̃/ as a phoneme.

As we indicated in Chapter 23, many Spanish speakers, particularly in Costa Rica, parts of Colombia, most of Argentina and Uruguay, and even parts of Spain, use the voiced palatal groove fricative [ž] (as in *measure*) instead of the palatal slit fricative [y]. This phenomenon is called **žeísmo** and extends to words spelled with **ll** as well as **y**. Female speakers in Argentina even devoice this sound and pronounce [š] in all these **y** and **ll** words.

Speakers in northern highland Ecuador are not **yeísta**—that is, they distinguish such pairs as **haya-halla, se cayó-se calló**—but in a still different fashion from **lleísta** speakers in Bolivia or rural central Spain, for example. They pronounce [ž] in words spelled with **ll** and [y] in words spelled with **y**, as in [bá-ža] **va__lla** *fence* versus [bá-ya] **va__ya** *go*. This actually, then, is neither completely **yeísta**, as in Mexico, nor completely **žeísta**, as in Argentina, nor even slightly **lleísta** as in Paraguay or rural central Spain, but a reverse of the first phenomenon, and a partial use of the second.

A further complication is the fact that many speakers from the **yeísta** areas learn **lleísmo** in school. They thus believe that it is really correct, so they occasionally use palatal [l̃] when they are on their best linguistic behavior, so to speak. However, if they are really **yeísta** speakers, the palatal [l̃] just disappears when they are conversing normally in an unmonitored fashion.

To sum up, here is the way speakers from four areas of Spanish America with their particular combinations of these different modes would pronounce the following two phrases, **Se cayó** "She/he fell down" and **Se ca__lló** "She/he was quiet." In this chart we use the + and − convention to show whether or not the dialect has the mode indicated. As you can see for Mexicans and Argentinians, for example, the words are homophones, but for Bolivians and northern Ecuadorians, for example, the words form a minimal pair.

Chart 24   Yeísmo, žeísmo, and lleísmo in American Spanish

	Se cayó.	Se calló.
+ yeísta − žeísta (Mexico, e.g.)	[se-ka-yó]	[se-ka-yó]
+ yeísta + žeísta (Argentina, e.g.)	[se-ka-žó]	[se-ka-žó]
+ lleísta − žeísta (Bolivia, e.g.)	[se-ka-yó]	[se-ka-ĩó]
− yeísta + žeísta (northern Ecuador, e.g.)	[se-ka-yó]	[se-ka-žó]

We could even modify the entry for Argentina by adding the pronunciation [se-ka-šó], which is characteristic of many women. However, men rarely use this pronunciation, and many women use [ž] as men do, thus the entry on the chart as it is.

And, finally, in these **lleísta** dialects the process of P.A. with /l/ is extended to the palatal /ĩ/ itself, as in **el llano** [eĩ-ĩá-no].

Although English has no palatal *l* phoneme, the sequence in words like *million* and *bullion* is virtually the same and can be easily substituted if you wish to use Spanish **lleísmo.**

Spelling of /ĩ/

/ĩ/ is spelled with **ll**, one of the three digraphs in Spanish (along with **ch** and **rr**), as in **llamar, valle**. As is the case with **ch**, Spanish dictionaries, lexical studies, and textbook vocabularies currently have a separate section for words beginning with **ll**, placing **llamar**, for example, after **luna** for this reason. However, the Spanish Royal Academy, following the UNESCO recommendation, recently announced that all their works published after 1998 would incorporate **ll** words in the **l** section of vocabularies, then placing **llamar** between **liviano** and **lobo**, for example. Again, it remains to be seen how soon and how widely this practice will be followed by other publishers.

Practice

A.

Your instructor will read one word or phrase in each numbered sequence, choosing at random. Identify the language by saying just **español** *if the word is Spanish, but if it is English, say* **inglés** *and give the corresponding Spanish word. Don't look at your books for obvious reasons. For example,*

gol   *goal*

(*Your instructor reads* **gol.**) *You say* **español.**

lana   *Lana*

(*Your instructor reads* Lana.) *You say* **inglés,** *and then say* **lana.**

1. del   *dell*
2. la   *lah* (as in *lah-de-dah*)
3. sol   *soul*
4. Lara   *"lotta"*
5. cal   *call*
6. lama   *llama*
7. tal   *tall*
8. hotel   *hotel*
9. les   *lace*
10. lid   *lead*
11. col   *coal*
12. tul   *tool*
13. lisa   *Lisa*
14. al   *all*
15. balsa   *balsa*
16. bol   *bowl*
17. mal   *mall*
18. fil   *feel*
19. loco   *loco*
20. sal   *Sol*

B.

Read or repeat the following phrases and sentences. Use [y] *for words spelled with* **ll** *unless your instructor requests a different pronunciation, such as* [ž] *or* [l̃] *or even* [ŷ].

1. Lo golpeó.
2. Se ponen esmalte.
3. Es muy sentimental.
4. El loro la cantó luego.
5. Volvió a lavarme el pelo.
6. El general es muy genial.
7. El gato contempló la lechuza.
8. Para ellos el alcohol es ilegal.
9. Ezequiel, esto es confidencial.
10. Luis la alaba a la luz de la luna.

11. Hay que lijarla con papel especial.
12. En el distrito federal el tráfico es fatal.
13. ¿Van a alojarse en un hotel o en un motel?
14. Se dice que está mal comer demasiada sal.
15. La llama, que se llamaba Lola, se lamía el lodo.
16. Este valle vale mucho; por eso, se llama ''Valle Feliz''.

C.

Answer the following questions, all of which request in their answers words and phrases that have occurred in Practices A and B. Then add something of your own about the item in your answer. For example,

[*instructor*] —¿Cómo se llama un lugar donde se alojan los viajeros en su viaje?

[*you*] —Ese tipo de lugar se llama ''motel''. Y la palabra ''motel'' es una combinación de las palabras ''motor'' y ''hotel''.

1. ¿Eres sentimental? ¿Cómo se ve?
2. ¿Puedes indicar el rango más alto del ejército?
3. ¿Qué pasa con un campo con poca hierba cuando llueve mucho?
4. ¿Qué pones en tu comida cuando no tiene mucho sabor?
5. ¿Cómo se llama la provincia, o el departamento, o el estado donde muchos países tienen su capital?
6. En los Andes del Perú o Bolivia, ¿cuál es el animal más común?
7. ¿Cuál es el ingrediente más notable del vino o de la cerveza?
8. ¿Cuál es el vegetal que también se llama repollo? En inglés tenemos casi la misma palabra para designar una ensalada especial.
9. ¿Cómo se llama el espacio entre dos montañas o alturas?
10. Hay una pintura especial, muy dura, que se usa también como cosmético. ¿Sabes lo que es? ¿Lo usas tú?

D.

Make a phonetic transcription of the following sentences. So far you have had the following consonants: /p t k b d g y w s ĉ f x m n ñ l/. Follow the same instructions as those given for previous transcription exercises. The answers are all given in the **+ yeísta – žeísta** mode. (If you don't understand this, check Chart 24 in this chapter's section on **Distribution and Dialectal Variations of Ñ/.**)

1. ¡Lo golpeó! ¡Llama a la policía! [*rapid speech; intonation*]
2. El coronel llamó al soldado, y le dijo que fuera al edificio federal. [*careful*]
3. Estaba en la parte central de la aldea de los rebeldes. [*careful*]

4. Quería ver si había llegado la carga de colchas.   [*careful; intonation*]
5. Cuando llegaron a la puerta del edificio, el guardia les gritó, —¡Alto!   [*careful; intonation*]
6. Alberto, la impresora necesita más papel.   [*rapid*]
7. ¿Sabes una cosa, Conchita? Esto de ''se calló'' y ''se cayó'' me tiene en la luna.   [*rapid; intonation]*
8. ¿Qué no comprendes? Es algo dialectal a fin de cuentas.   [*rapid*]

28

The Tap and Trill Consonants /r/ and /r̄/

Allophones of /r/ and /r̄/

The consonant /r/ has three principal allophones in Spanish: [r], a voiced alveolar tap, shown in the first diagram below; [r̄], a voiced alveolar trill, shown in the second diagram; and [r̥], a voiceless alveolar slit fricative, in which the tongue position is quite similar to that shown for [r] in the first diagram. The basic difference, to be described below, cannot be shown in a conventional facial diagram. The consonant /r̄/ has one principal allophone, [r̄], shown in the second diagram.

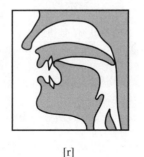

[r]   [r̄]

Description of /r/ and /r̄/ Allophones

For [r] the tongue tip quickly strikes the alveolar ridge once as the airstream passes through, creating a tap, or a very short stop sound (as in English wai*t*ing). For [r̄] the tongue tip, under great tension, strikes the alveolar ridge several times in rapid succession. This series of rapid taps or stops thus creates a trill. For [r̥] the tongue tip touches the alveolar ridge lightly, and the airstream passes through the slit formed by the two articulators. The vocal bands do not vibrate, making this sound very similar to the apico-alveolar [ṡ] or the palatal [š] (as in *she*). The tongue for [r̥], however, is somewhat flatter than for the former sound, and the tongue dorsum is lower than it is for the latter sound.

Distribution of /r/ and /r̄/

Although the tap /r/ and the trill /r̄/ are phonemic in Spanish, they actually contrast only in word-medial intervocalic position, as in **caro-carro**, **pero-perro**, **varios-barrios**. This is because the tap /r/, in what is known as DEFECTIVE DISTRIBUTION, never occurs at the beginning of a word in Spanish—the single *letter* **r** always represents the trill here, as in **rico**; tap /r/ never occurs after /l/, /n/, or /s/ since the letter **r** here often represents the beginning of a word that has been combined with a prefix ending in /l/ or /n/, as in **alrededor** or **enredar**; and either the trill [r̄] allophone or the tap [r] can occur in the syllable-final position, that is, within a word before a consonant. Thus in careful emphatic speech the word **puerta** can be pronounced either [puér̄-ta] or [puér-ta], the former pronunciation being more prevalent. In rapid speech either pronunciation occurs, with the latter being more prevalent.

/r/ in the absolute-final position (before a pause), in addition to the tap and trill possibilities mentioned above, can also be realized as the voiceless fricative [r̥]. Thus, for example, if the phrase **por favor** precedes a pause, it is either [por-fa-ƀór̄], [por-fa-ƀór], or [por-fa-ƀór̥], with the first pronunciation predominating in emphatic careful speech, just as it does within a word before a consonant.

The tap /r/ can occur elsewhere in the middle of words (other than after /l/ or /n/): **caro, tendré, abre, crema, tres**.

The trill /r̄/ occurs to the exclusion of /r/ at the beginning of words: **rico**. In addition, it is always heard within a word after /l/, /n/, and /s/ since the **r** here is very often really "word-initial" in the sense that it represents the beginning of a word that has been combined with a prefix ending in /l/ or /r/, as in **alrededor** [al-r̄e-đe-đór] or **enredar** [en-r̄e-đár]. There are only a handful of words where the trill /r̄/ follows /n/ or /s/ within a morpheme: **honra**, **Enrique**, and **Israel**, being virtually the only common examples. The trill, as we have stated, can also occur within a word between vowels, as in **carro**.

Thus, to sum up, /r/ and /r̄/ contrast in only one position in Spanish—intervocalically within a word: **caro-carro, varios-barrios, enterado-enterrado**.

The rule for /r/ (which does *not* show the defective distribution mentioned above):

$$/r/ \rightarrow \left[\begin{array}{ll} \begin{Bmatrix} [\bar{r}] \\ [r] \end{Bmatrix} \Big/ \underline{\hphantom{xx}} /C/ & \textbf{puerta} \\[2ex] \begin{Bmatrix} [\bar{r}] \\ [r] \\ [r̥] \end{Bmatrix} \Big/ \underline{\hphantom{xx}} \, \| & \textbf{por favor} \\[3ex] [r] \quad \text{elsewhere} & \textbf{tendré, abre, crema, caro} \end{array} \right.$$

The rule for /r̄/:

/r̄/ → [r̄]   **rico, carro, alrededor, enredar, Israel**

Dialectal Variations of /r/and /r̄/

The most common dialectal variations of /r/ and /r̄/ are the so-called fricative *r*'s. The voiceless variety [r̥] has already been described above, and the voiced version [ř], as you might expect, is exactly alike in all respects, except that the vocal bands vibrate for it. Both varieties are heard through Mexico, Central and South America. The voiced variety is most common in Costa Rica, Ecuador, Peru, Bolivia, Paraguay, and northern Argentina, and the voiceless in Guatemala, Chile, and Mexico. Also, as we indicated in the previous section, the voiceless [r̥] is commonly heard in all dialects of American Spanish in the absolute-final position, that is, before a pause. However, in the countries just mentioned this variety and its voiced counterpart replace /r/ in other positions, but particularly where the apico-alveolar trill /r̄/ occurs in standard speech as in **rico, carro**, **enriquecer**. Although the trill is considered correct and is the one taught in schools even in the areas where the fricative *r*'s are used, the latter sounds are used in everyday speech by all speakers in these areas. The sound is even heard in Spain, particularly in absolute-final position.

In the fricative *r* areas the voiceless [r̥] is particularly common as the second consonant of the cluster /tr/, causing the preceding /t/, through regressive assimilation, to have an alveolar rather than a dental articulation: **otro** [ó-t>r̥o]. Although this cluster sounds somewhat like the palatal [ĉ], it can easily be distinguished, as in **otro** versus **ocho**, for example.

In the Caribbean area—particularly Puerto Rico and the Dominican Republic (including the Puerto Rican speakers in the northeastern United States)—the standard voiced alveolar trill [r̄] alternates with a voiceless trill [r̥], as in **Puerto Rico** [pu̯ér-to-r̥í-ko] or **carro** [ká-r̥o]. The acoustic impression of this voiceless trill is that of a glottal aspiration or puff of air from the glottis before the voiced trill, and some linguists transcribe the sound in that fashion: [hr̄í-ko], [káh-r̄o]. However, since the vocal band vibrations are really for the following vowel rather than the previous trill, we prefer to write this sound with [r̥], indicating its voicelessness throughout its articulation.

In parts of Puerto Rico and the areas of the northeastern United States where Puerto Ricans live, another variety of the alveolar trilled /r̄/ is used, the voiced velar or uvular fricative [R] and its voiceless counterpart [X]. Neither of these *r*'s exist in English, although [R] is also heard in French (**rouge**) and German (**rauchen**). Thus many Puerto Ricans (either on the island or in the northeastern United States) pronounce the last word of their island of origin [Rí-ko] or [Xí-ko]. This latter sound is exactly the same one Castilian speakers use for /x/ (see Chapter 25). And since most Puerto Ricans say [hó-ta] for the word **jota** (the letter **j** or the Spanish dance), [Xó-ta] sounds to them like the word **rota**, *broken* but to a Spaniard like the letter or the dance. Context, of course, usually clarifies immediately.

Another dialectal modification of /r/ occurs in syllable-final position, that is, before a consonant or a pause, where the phoneme /l/ often replaces /r/. This is common in the Caribbean—even among educated speakers—but in particular in Puerto Rico and among Puerto Ricans in the northeastern United States. Thus with these speakers a sentence like **El doctor dijo que Roberto está muy enfermo** comes out [el̦-dok-tól̦-dí-ho-ke-Xo-β̥él̦-to-eh-tá-mu̯i-em̦-fél-mo].

The final dialectal variation of /r/ occurs also in syllable-final position, mainly before another consonant. Many Cubans and Cuban Americans change this syllable-final [r] to the same sound that follows it, in essence, producing a double consonant: **carne** is [kán-ne], **Carlos** is [kál-loh], **muerte** is [mu̯ét-te].

Throughout the Hispanic world the voiced alveolar tap [r] and the voiced alveolar trill [r̄] are taught in school and considered to be representative of the best pronunciation. However, the reality is that millions of Spanish Americans—including educated speakers—use these other varieties of /r/ and /r̄/ with great frequency.

Contrasts with English

English speakers occasionally have trouble with the tap /r/ at first until they realize that it is virtually the same sound as the English tap or flap [t̂] or [d̂], which exists in posttonic (after the stress) intervocalic position in probably hundreds of words: *butter, water, waiting, bidder, muddy, raider*. Some speakers contrast the /t/ and the /d/ in these words, but others make them exactly alike. At any rate, all are an acceptable equivalent for Spanish /r/. The first two syllables of the phrase *eight o'clock* are virtually identical to the Spanish word **era**. The first three syllables of the English maxim ''Better they than us'' are a near-enough equivalent—to start with at least—of the sounds in the Spanish word **verde**. This should demonstrate to you that the Spanish tap /r/ is a sound you have been using all your life in English.

In addition, the use of the English tap sounds in place of Spanish /d/, as in **todo, cada, modo** converts them into very different Spanish words: **toro, cara, moro**, respectively. As we pointed out in Chapter 22, the /d/ should be a fricative [ð], almost like the *th* of *father*, and the /r/ should be a tap or flap, almost like the *dd* of *fodder*.

Although you probably never realized it, English also has a voiceless fricative [r̥] after voiceless stops in words like *press, try*, or *cream*, quite close to the fricative *r* used in Guatemala, Ecuador, and other Spanish-American countries. However, you use this sound only as a part of the cluster voiceless stop + /r/, whereas the Spanish speakers who use it have virtually no restrictions on its place of occurrence.

The most common *r* in American English is the retroflex *r*, shown in the following facial diagram.

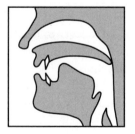

English [r̲]

As you can see, there is no tongue contact at all with the upper articulators, leading some phoneticians to analyze this English sound as a glide or semi-vowel. At any rate, it sounds very strange to the Spanish ear and is one of the most difficult sounds for them to master when learning English. The temptation is for them to make tongue contact somewhere with an upper articulator, but in English the tongue bunches up, and the tip is even sometimes slightly retroflexed (curved backward), and makes no contact of any kind with any articulators.

Although the Spanish tap /r/ is easy for English speakers to articulate for reasons explained above, the trilled /r̄/ remains a problem for many speakers of North American English, where this sound is absent. There are many tricks to help those of you having difficulty with it to pronounce it. Your current and past instructors have probably told you about them. The main recommendation we have here is to provide extreme tension in your tongue muscle, enough to keep the tip returning rapidly to the alveolar ridge as the exiting airstream forces it back. Although you should try to master it because it is the so-called prestige and correct /r̄/ in all dialects of Spanish, while you are waiting to achieve success, the fricative varieties, [ɹ̝] and [ř], are preferable to your standard retroflex [r]. Remember that the first of these two Spanish sounds is similar to the first sound of English *she* and the second to the middle consonant of *measure*.

Spelling of /r/ and /r̄/

Tap /r/ is spelled with **r** everywhere: **ahora, pero, quería, arte, normal, prisa, drama, crema**. As we stated above, sometimes the tap is trilled in syllable-final position: **parte, favor**, but it is still spelled with a single **r**.

Trilled /r̄/ is spelled with **rr** in the middle of a word between vowels: **ahorra, perro, querría**. This spelling is also used in compound words in which the first word ends in a vowel and the second word begins with the trill: **pelirrojo** (**pelo** + **rojo**) *red-headed*, **carirredondo** (**cara** + **redondo**) *round-faced*, **Monterrey** (**monte** + **rey**) *king's woods*. However, in words whose prefix ends in a consonant and root begins with a trilled /r/, a single **r** is used to represent the trilled phoneme: **subrayar** (**sub** + **rayar**) *to underline*, **subrogar** (**sub** + **rogar**) *to be a surrogate for*; **malrotar** (**mal** + **roto** + **ar**) *to squander*; **enrojecer** (**en** + **rojo** + **ec** + **er**) *to turn red*. There are only a handful of words where the trilled /r̄/ follows an /n/ or /s/ that is *not* the end of a prefix or the first word of a compound: **honra, Israel**, being two of the most common examples.

Practice

A.

Read the following groups of words, all containing intervocalic /t/, /d/, or /r/.

1. moto   modo   moro
2. cara   cata   cada

3. mido   miro
4. seta   sera   seda
5. lloro   yodo
6. dudo   duro
7. hablara   hablada
8. oda   hora
9. coto   codo   coro
10. para   pata

B.

Your instructor will read one word or phrase in each numbered sequence, choosing at random. Identify the intervocalic consonant phoneme by saying **ere** *if the word has an intervocalic /r/; then pronounce the corresponding Spanish word with the intervocalic /r̄/. But if the word has an intervocalic /r̄/, say* **erre**, *and pronounce the corresponding word with the intervocalic /r/. Thus if you hear* **pero**, *say* **ere** *and then* **perro**. *If you hear* **carro**, *say* **erre** *and then* **caro**.

1. ahora   ahorra
2. Viene el torero.   Viene el torrero.
3. varios   barrios
4. la vara   la barra
5. Formaron un coro.   Formaron un corro.
6. hiero   hierro
7. Es un cero.   Es un cerro.
8. foro   forro
9. amara   amarra
10. moro   morro
11. Está enterado.   Está enterrado.
12. deriva   derriba
13. para   parra
14. Su apellido es Lara.   Su apellido es Larra.
15. ¿aroma?   ¿A Roma?

C.

The following are English words, fragments, and phrases, many slangy or even meaningless. But, as a native speaker of English, you will know how to say them even if you don't know exactly what they mean. At any rate, they contain examples of intervocalic flap /t/ and /d/, all of which sound close enough to the Spanish tap /r/ so that you can substitute them in a corresponding Spanish utterance. The utterances will sound fine in Spanish—at least as far as /r/ is concerned! Give the meaning of your resulting Spanish utterance if asked.

1. *lot o'* . . .   6. *photo*
2. *eight o'* . . .   7. *toto*
3. *Moto*   8. *"moo dough"*
4. *pot o' tea*   9. *"Better they . . ."*
5. *meet a* . . .   10. *"Who gotta!"*

D.

Read or repeat the following phrases and sentences. By this time you know that there are various pronunciation possibilities for such consonants as /y/, /s/, and /x/. Your instructor has already indicated, or will now, how you should or can pronounce words containing these consonants. You also have some choices with regard to vowel combinations, but the speech and style with which you say the Spanish phrases and sentences should determine the vowel possibilities.

1. ¡Ahorra o nunca!
2. El pobre todavía no está enterado.
3. Perro que muerde no ladra. ¿Es así?
4. Ese carro es demasiado caro para mí.
5. Varios barrios tienen el mismo sistema.
6. César nunca dijo: "Vendré, veré y venceré".
7. Los famosos toros de lidia, Miura, son caros.
8. Gritaron: "¡A Roma!" La frase es tonta con **ere**.
9. No es un toro, es un becerro. ¿Sabes la diferencia?
10. Los arrieros derivan su nombre de la frase "¡Arre, arre!"
11. ¿Qué tiene el torero—una vara de hierro o una barra de hierro?
12. *Que será, será* es el título de una canción, pero no es español correcto.
13. Una fiesta de abril es el Domingo de Ramos. Otra es la Pascua Florida.
14. Una frase que describe los peligros que confrontan los toreros es "Más cuernos tiene el hambre".
15. La rima es "Erre con erre cigarro, erre con erre barril, rápido corren los carros cargados de azúcar del ferrocarril".
16. Se puede decir "Corro al coro" o "Voy en carro al coro", pero dudo que se diga por la multitud de **eres** y **erres**.

E.

Make a phonetic transcription of the following sentences. You now have had all the consonants of American Spanish: /p t k b d g y w s ĉ f x m n ñ l r r̄/, in addition, of course, to all the suprasegmentals and vowels, so nothing will be underlined. Follow the same instructions as those given for previous transcription practices.

1. Roberto y Enrique paseaban alrededor de la reja.   [*careful; intonation*]
2. Querían entregarle el recado al señor Rodríguez.   [*rapid*]

3. Israel, Siria e Irak no habían gozado de buenas relaciones.   [*careful*]

4. La cosa estaba enredada en el concepto de la honra, que, para estos caballeros, eran muy diferente del del honor.   [*careful; intonation*]

5. Cuando vimos al torrero, nos dimos cuenta del error que habíamos hecho. El tipo tenía una linterna, no una banderilla.   [*rapid; intonation*]

6. Un renglón subrayado en la hoja indica que debería aparecer en el libro en tipo de bastardilla.   [*careful*]

7. Le costó caro, ¿no? Es raro que no le haya irritado más.   [*rapid*]

8. ¿Cómo sabes que la palabra **subrogar** no tiene la misma combinación de consonantes que **sobra** o **ubre**?   [*rapid; intonation*]

29

Consonant Combinations in Spanish

Consonant Clusters and Sequences

Consonant combinations or sequences in Spanish are composed of two to four contiguous or adjoining consonants. As you may recall from Chapter 13, "Sound Groups in Spanish," a consonant sequence is simply a group of adjoining consonants, but if they are found in the same syllable, they form a cluster. The maximum number of consonants in a cluster in Spanish is two. Only twelve clusters can *begin* a phonemic phrase, a word, or even a syllable: /pr br tr dr kr gr fr pl bl kl gl fl/. These clusters are the stops + /r/, all the stops except /t/ and /d/ + /l/, and /f/ + both /r/ and /l/.

Two-consonant clusters can occur at the *end* of a syllable—the second one is always /s/—but only a few words end with consonant clusters. Some examples are **bíceps, fórceps, fénix** /ks/, **Pémex** /ks/, **clubs**. If the word is felt to be foreign, like **clubs**, many speakers even simplify the final cluster by eliminating the consonant before /s/, saying /klús/[1] or by adding an /e/, saying /klú-bes/.

In the middle of a Spanish word, a two-consonant sequence, if it is one of the twelve initial groups listed above, forms a cluster: **agradable** /a-gra-dá-ble/, **aplicar** /a-pli-kár/. Otherwise they are separated: **isla** /ís-la/, **pierde** /piér-de/.

Many Spanish words have three-consonant sequences in them, but, if the second and third consonants form one of the twelve possible initial groups, they cluster together to start the second syllable: **hombre** /óm-bre/, **asamblea** /a-sam-blé-a/. If the second and third consonants are not one of twelve possible initial groups, the first two cluster to end the first syllable: **constituir** /kons-ti-tuír/, **perspicaz** /pers-pi-kás/. The second consonant in these cases is usually /s/.

Within a word as many as four consonants can form a sequence in Spanish, but two consonants always cluster in the first syllable, the second virtually always being /s/, and

---

[1]Many of these examples are given in simplified *phonemic*, rather than *phonetic*, transcription since the specific allophones or variations are not significant in these matters of consonant combinations and consonant + vowel combinations. The analysis of such groups and their behavior forms a branch of phonology called PHONOTACTICS.

two—one of the twelve possible word-initial clusters listed above—begin the second syllable: **transcribir** /trans-kri-bír/, **explicar** /eks-pli-kár/. Even in these words many speakers simplify the sequence to three consonants by eliminating the first one in the sequence, saying /tras-kri-bír/ or /es-pli-kár/.

Across word boundaries (as long as there is no intervening pause, of course), four-consonant sequences are possible, but they are rare since so few Spanish words end in consonant clusters. However, three-consonant sequences are common: **el blanco** /el-blán-ko/, **hablan francés** /á-blan-fran-sés/.

Certain Spanish consonant sequences are troublesome to English speakers, usually because of one difficult consonant, whose difficulty is increased by the presence of a contiguous one. Consonant (/C/) + /r/ is often difficult because the second element, the tap /r/, occurs in English only in an intervocalic position (as an allophone of /t/ or /d/). You may be able to master these /Cr/ clusters more quickly if you at first insert a vocalic element, such as the schwa /ə/ (as in *appear*), between /C/ and /r/: **brisa** */bərísa/, **grande** */gəránde/. Such pronunciations, of course, are incorrect in Spanish, but when you find you can produce the tap /r/ with ease, you can then proceed to eliminate the /ə/ gradually and pronounce the cluster /Cr/.

Also difficult are word-medial clusters with the fricatives [ƀ đ ǥ] as the first element and [r] or [l] as the second, as in **abrir, podrá, agrio, hablar, siglo**. Since these fricatives alone can be troublesome for you, their combination with [r] and [l] requires even more concentrated practice for mastery.

Particularly difficult for English speakers is the sequence of /s/ + /r̄/, as in **los ricos** or **Israel**. Actually this same sequence is difficult in rapid speech for some Spanish speakers, who modify either or both consonants. So there is no reason why you should not do the same. The /s/ can be aspirated: [loh-r̄í-kos] or even eliminated: [lo-r̄í-kos]. The /r/ can even be made fricative: [ih-ṛa-él].

Another difficult consonant sequence for some English speakers is the sequence of /rC/, as in **perla, verde, mármol**. Again, sometimes inserting a schwa [ə] between the /r/ and the following consonant will help, as in *better they* for **verde** or *potter though* for **pardo**. The trilled [r̄], of course, is also acceptable in this position, and those for whom the trill is an easy sound to pronounce may find that it actually aids in the pronunciation of the above sequences, which also occur between words: **leer la noticia, hablar danés, ver más**.

Consonant Neutralization

Consonant sequences, in which the first consonant is syllable-final and the second syllable-initial, also require careful attention. Several things happen with the first consonant, the syllable-final one. In many cases, CONSONANT NEUTRALIZATION takes place, meaning that either of two consonants can be pronounced: either [t] or [đ] can end the first syllable of **Atlántico**, either [k] or [ǥ] can end the first syllable of **técnico**, either [r] or [r̄] can end the first syllable of **puerta**.

In the case of nasals, homorganic regressive assimilation to the following point of articulation (P.A.) takes place in the syllable-final position: [m] ends the first syllable of **invitar,** [m̪] ends the first syllable of **enfermo,** [n̪] ends the first syllable of **diente,** [n] ends the first syllable of **sensación,** [ñ] ends the first syllable of **mancha,** [ñ] ends the first syllable of **inyección,** and [ŋ] ends the first syllable of **tengo.** This same process happens across word boundaries, as in **un peso, con frío, tan tremendo, hablan sueco, un chino, ponen yeso,** and **estudian griego** (with the same sequence of nasals as listed in the previous sentence). Some English speakers are reluctant to use the homorganic nasals, probably because, although they too occur within words in English, they rarely occur across word boundaries, as in Spanish: [m] occurs in the word *impossible*, but not in the phrase *in Pittsburgh*; [ŋ] occurs in the word *income*, but not in the phrase *in Kansas*; and so forth. But complete nasal assimilation is the norm in Spanish—both within words and between words.

/s/ is a special case in this process since it has no voiced phonemic counterpart /z/, as English does. Yet you, as an English speaker, can utilize the phonetic realization of [s], as in **rascar,** and [z], as in **rasgar,** to help you identify the following phoneme, which has created the regressive assimilation in the first place. Thus, although the Spanish speaker knows that [los-pá-ños] and [loz-ɓá-ños] are **los paños** and **los baños,** respectively, because of the /p/ and /b/, you, as an English speaker, can also rely on the [s] and [z] for this same identification. The Spanish speaker, of course, normally doesn't even realize that there is a difference in the two *s*'s. But you do, and you can use this information to solve a common problem for English speakers, which is distinguishing the voiceless from the voiced stops: /p/ from /b/, /t/ from /d/, and /k/ from /g/. This is due to the lack of aspiration in Spanish and the timing of the subsequent voicing, which in Spanish is almost simultaneous for voiceless stops and slightly prior to the articulation for the voiced stops. (See Chapter 21 for a review of this phenomenon.)

Identical Consonant Sequences

All the sequences discussed so far contain *different* consonants, but two *identical* consonants also group together in Spanish. Identical-consonant sequences should not be confused with double *letters*, which, in the case of **ll** and **rr,** represent single sounds: /y/ and /r̄/, respectively, as in **ella** and **arre,** both of which have only one consonant sound.

Identical-consonant sequences, on the other hand, have two contiguous consonant *sounds* that are the same. They are rare within a word in Spanish, and many speakers simplify them to one in rapid speech. Thus **obvio** may be [óɓ-ɓio] or [ó-ɓio] , **innato** may be [in-ná-to] or [i-ná-to]. There are only a dozen or so Spanish words with /nn/—like **innecesario, innegable, innovador**—and either pronunciation is used. But virtually the only example in Spanish of a double consonant *within a morpheme* is the word **perenne** *perennial*, and since there is no other word with which it can be confused, most speakers are also indifferent here as to whether it has one /n/ or two. However, when these double consonants occur *across word boundaries*, such simplification may lead to a confusion of meaning: **el oro** /e-ló-ro/ is *the gold*, but **el loro** /el-ló-ro/ is *the parrot*; **Son hombres** /só-nóm-bres/ means "They are men", but **Son nombres** /són-nóm-bres/ means "They are names"; **Díganos** /dí-ga-nos/ is a singular **usted** command, but **Dígannos** /dí-gan-nos/ is a plural **ustedes** command. Thus in careful speech two equal consonants are likely to be distinguished from just one in such cases.

A few other identical-consonant sequences are theoretically possible but rare. /dd/ can occur between words, as in **La vi dejada** /la-bí-de-xá-da/ "I saw her unkempt", as opposed to **la vid dejada** /la-bíd-de-xá-da/ *the abandoned grape vine*, but there are few likely possibilities for confusion. A tap + trill, /r͡r̄/, is difficult, if not impossible, to hear and distinguish from just a strongly trilled /r̄/ since the tap and the following trill blend together and obscure the sound difference between **Ve ratones** /bé-r̄a-tó-nes/ "She/He sees mice" and **ver ratones** /bé-r̄a-tó-nes/ or even /bér-r̄a-tó-nes/ *to see mice*. Although a single /s/ between words is theoretically just as contrastive as a double /ss/ between words as the sounds in the above combinations, a prolonged double /s/ is equally difficult to distinguish from a short single /s/. Thus **Lo sabe** /lo-sá-be/ "He/She knows it," and **Los sabe** /los-sá-be/ "He/She knows them," or **las obras** /la-só-bras/ *the works* and **las sobras** /las-só-bras/ *the leftovers,* are usually identical in sound to each other in rapid conversation. Context again usually clarifies.

Enlace (Linking)

The most important consonant + vowel (CV) combination in Spanish is the one that occurs across word boundaries, forming linking or **enlace.** Because of Spanish syllabication, a single consonant between vowels always goes with the next vowel to form the next syllable whether within a word—**pelota** /pe-ló-ta/—or between words—**el otoño** /e-lo-tó-ño/—provided there is no pause, of course. No break of any kind occurs between the words: **las aves** *the birds* sounds exactly like **la sabes** *you know it*, both /la-sá-bes/.

One of the most important features of **enlace** is the fact that it obscures word boundaries in normal speech, word boundaries that many English-speaking students mistakenly try to indicate in their Spanish. Such misguided efforts interrupt the smooth flow of Spanish and create an unpleasant choppy sound. Instead of an utterance like **Los alumnos están en el aula** sounding like one long word in Spanish, /losalúmnosestáneneláula/, it comes out * /losʔalumnosʔestanʔenʔelʔaula/ (with ʔ representing a glottal stop, as in the English paralinguistic negative *uh-uh-uh-uhhhhh*). The proper, unbroken, smooth legato-like flow of Spanish, even at a relatively slow speed, is one of the reasons that it seems so fast to the English-speaking student.

There are a few cases in normal rapid conversational Spanish where word boundaries are indicated, but rarely with pauses and glottal stops as they are in English. For example, in the *s*-modification dialects, a word-final (or even morpheme-final) /s/ is often aspirated, as in **Los animales** [lo-ha-ni-má-leh] or **nosotros** [no-hó-troh]. Even here the word- or morpheme-final [h], because of **enlace**, begins the following syllable. The same is true of word-final velar [ŋ], in the dialects where this occurs. All Spanish speakers recognize the phrase [e-ŋá-g̶uas] as meaning **en aguas** *in waters* and not **enaguas** *petticoats* because they know (without knowing that they know) that velar [ŋ] between vowels can mean only one thing: the end of a word (or perhaps a morpheme). However, these are special cases. Out of context, in normal Spanish speech, there is no phonetic way to differentiate between **la s̱abes** and **las̱ aves**, or between **el̠ijo** and **el̠ hijo.**

Within the phonemic phrase the same phenomenon occurs even with words containing prefixes. Although the rules of Spanish spelling permit words with obvious prefixes or compounded words, such as **inoportuno, desagradable, s̱ubalimentación, aborigen**, or **bienestar,** to be hyphenated after the consonant in *writing* at the end of a line of text— **in-oportuno, des-agradable, sub-alimentación, ab-origen, bien-estar**, in *spoken* Spanish these boundaries are not observed. The only exception is the case we have already mentioned: velar [ŋ], where some speakers say [i-ŋo-por-tú-no] or [bi̠é-ŋes-tár], for example, showing the morpheme prefix-final or word-final /n/.

Consonant + Semi-Vowel + Vowel

Spanish combinations of consonant + semi-vowel + vowel—/CV̱V/—often represent a pronunciation difficulty for English speakers. In one corresponding English combination, /CyV/, the final vowel is almost always /u/, as in *few, beauty, cumulative*. Virtually all cases of this combination where the last vowel is not /u/ are foreign borrowings, and English speakers break these sequences into two syllables: *pati-o, fi-esta, Ki-ev, si-erra, Vi-etnam.* Then it is only natural for you to try to do the same in Spanish, saying *[pá-ti-o] for **patio**, *[fi-és-ta] for **fiesta**, *[a-di-ós] for **adiós** instead of the correct [pá-ti̠o], [fi̠és-ta], [a-ɸi̠ós], respectively.

English has a very limited distribution of words that begin with /CwV/: the consonant is usually /t d k s/, as in *twice, dwell, quit, swear*. However, in the Spanish pattern of /CV̱V/, in which V̱ is the semi-vowel [u̠] (corresponding to English /w/), the initial consonant can be virtually anything: **bueno, c̱uando, ḏueño, f̱uera, guante, J̱uan, ḻuego, ll̠ueve** (/y/), **m̱ueca, ṉuera, pues, ṟuana, s̱ueño, ṯuesto**. The situation here for English /w/ is virtually the same as that described above for the English glide /y/. In foreign borrowings into English and foreign words, English speakers break the /w/ and the following vowel into separate syllables: *pu-eblo, Bu-enos Aires, R-wanda*. Thus you may mistakenly do the same in Spanish, saying, *[pu-é-blo] for **pueblo** or *[fu-é-ra] for **fuera**, instead of the correct [pu̠é-ɸlo] and [fu̠é-ra], respectively.

A Spanish combination of CCV̱V is even more difficult because of the beginning /Cr/ or /Cl/, followed by the diphthong, as in **pliego, criada**, or **trueno.** The natural temptation for an English speaker is to say *[pli-é-go], *[kri-á-da], *[tru-é-no] instead of [pli̠é-g̶o], [kri̠á-ɸa], or [tru̠é-no].

The process of regressive assimilation occurs frequently in English, just as it does in Spanish. It is normal in English for the alveolar consonants /t d s z/ to turn into the closest palatal consonants /č ǰ š ž/ before the palatal glide /y/ plus another vowel. The /t/ of *rite* and *can't* becomes /č/ in *ritual* and *Can't you?*; the /d/ of *proceed* and *did* become /ǰ/ in *procedure* and *Did you?* ; the /s/ of *press* and *miss* becomes /š/ in *pressure* and *I'll miss you*; the /z/ of *close* and *please* becomes /ž/ in *closure* and *please you*. Occasionally this phenomenon even works its way into the spelling system. The name *Cajuns* gets its /ǰ/ from this assimilatory pronunciation of these people's name, *Acadians* /ǝkéyǰĭnz/, based on their original Canadian homeland of Acadia.

English has many words with these patterns that are almost exact cognates of Spanish words: *question*–**cuestión**, *cordial*–**cordial,** *delicious*–**delicioso**, *explosion*–**explosión**, *graduate*–**graduar**. The temptation is strong to follow the English pattern of regressive assimilation and say *[kụɛs-ĉón] instead of [kụes-tión], *[kor-ǰál] instead of [kor-điál], *[de-li-šió-so] instead of [de-li-sịó-so], *[ɛks-plo-žión] instead of [eks-plo-sịón], or *[gra-ǰu-wár] instead of [gra-đụár].

A further difficulty involving consonant + vowel combinations also involves English words that are cognate with Spanish words. The glide /y/ occurs in such English words as *regular, ridiculous, museum, future,* but the Spanish corresponding words, **regular, ridículo, museo, futuro,** have only [u] and no semi-vowel [ị] in any of them: [r̄e-ǥu-lár], [r̄i-đí-ku-lo], [mu-sé-o], [fu-tú-ro], respectively.

Spelling of Consonant Combinations

The spelling of consonant combinations is usually the same as that of the individual phonemes that make up the combinations. However, there are a few exceptions due to assimilation and neutralization.

For example, a word-final /n/ usually retains its normal spelling of **n**: **u̲n̲ beso, ta̲n̲ vasto.** But occasionally the phonetic reality produced by regressive assimilation (P.A.), namely [m], is reflected in the spelling system: **ta̲m̲bién** (really the result of **ta̲n̲ bien**), **ta̲m̲poco** (really the result of **ta̲n̲ poco**).

The trilled /r̄/, when it occurs within a word, is usually spelled **rr**, as in **ca̲rr̲o, aho̲rr̲a,** and with only one **r** at the beginning of a word: **r̲ico, r̲osa**. In words that contain prefixes ending in *consonants* before words beginning with **r**, the single **r** is also used to represent the trill: **al̲r̲ededor, en̲r̲edar, des̲r̲ielar, sub̲r̲ayar**. But if the prefix ends in a *vowel*, **rr** is used for the trill at the beginning of the root word: **a̲rr̲eglar, anti̲rr̲obo, peli̲rr̲ojo, auto̲rr̲adio, infra̲rr̲ojo.** There are only a few Spanish words where the trilled /r̄/ is spelled with a single **r** in the middle of a morpheme, that is, where there are no preceding prefixes or compounded words: **hon̲r̲a, Is̲r̲ael.**

The letter **x** also has special features. It often represents the consonant sequence /ks/, which can be a cluster, as in **ex̲poner** /eks-po-nér/ or **ex̲plicar** /eks-pli-kár/, or a bisyllabic sequence, as in **ex̲amen** /ek-sá-men/ or **ex̲acto** /ek-sák-to/. The /k/ in the last case, that is, when **x** represents a bisyllabic sequence, can be pronounced as a [k] or a [ǥ]: [ek-sá-men] or [eǥ-sá-men]. However, there is *never* progressive assimilation in these cases, meaning that /s/ is always realized as [s] and never as [z], as it is in the English words *exact, exam, exist*. One can say facetiously that "There are no *eggs* /égz/ in **examen**, only *egg salad* /êg+sǽlɨd/."[2]

Many speakers pronounce words in which the letter **x** precedes a consonant with just /s/: **exponer** /es-po-nér/ or **explicar** /es-pli-kár/. This tends to be characteristic of rapid speech, where the combination /ks/, explained in the previous paragraph, is used in careful slower speech.

Naturally in the *s*-modification dialects the letter **x**, when it represents /s/ at the end of the syllable, may also be pronounced with just a glottal aspiration: **explicar** [eh-pli-kár], **sexto** [séh-to].

There are also many common words where an intervocalic letter **x** represents only /s/: **taxi** /tá-si/, **exacto** /e-sák-to/, **auxilio** /au-sí-lio/.

To sum up, the letter **x** in Spanish may represent just [s], or [k-s], or even [ǵ-s], but *never* the voiced sibilant [z], as it so frequently does in English.

Practice

A.

Your instructor or a classmate will read the English word or phrase. You then say the corresponding Spanish cognate word or phrase. Occasionally, the Spanish word has a different meaning from the English one, even though the sounds are similar. For example, if you hear pure, *you then say* **puro**.

1. actually	13. residual	25. sexual
2. vision	14. appreciate	26. monument
3. bestial	15. ridiculous	27. express
4. delicious	16. salutations	28. ambitious
5. cordial	17. municipal	29. vehicular
6. simulate	18. exam	30. gracious
7. curious	19. naturally	31. puberty
8. situate	20. immune	32. illusion
9. discussion	21. question	33. music
10. casual	22. fury	34. perpetual
11. confusion	23. regular	35. malicious
12. exist	24. granular	36. punctual

[2]The symbol + in this case represents a pause-like feature in language, known as "plus-juncture," that marks a boundary of some sort. It has a variety of ramifications in English, but in this case, since it represents a word boundary, it prevents the normal progressive assimilation found in noun plurals and verb forms like *arms* /z/, *dogs* /z/, *digs* /z/, *harms* /z/.

B.

Read the following Spanish sentences. In this practice, it is important that you read rather than repeat since the spelling of the consonant combinations and consonant + vowel combinations is an important issue, too.

1. Es rojo, sí es rojísimo.
2. El hijo dijo: "Elijo éste".
3. Es extraño que exagere tanto.
4. Recuerde que Rosa Rodríguez no es rica.
5. Sí, para ellos **regar líquido** es **derramarlo.**
6. Tiene un examen en primeros auxilios con la Cruz Roja.
7. El subte es el modo favorito de transporte en Buenos Aires.
8. Los riojanos dicen que su vino puede resucitar a los muertos.
9. Se ha cortado la electricidad; por eso, no funcionará el refrigerador.
10. Cuando dicen **derramar,** es como si estuvieran diciendo **desramar.**
11. Don Quijote no tenía más remedio que emplear una ristra de cebollas.
12. Sí, allí a veces **verdad** suena **beldad,** y **es corta** suena **escolta.**
13. No, la expresión inglesa para **irritarse** o **enojarse** es **ver rojo,** no **ver ojo.**
14. No comprendo el anuncio de ese banco: "¡Ahorra o nunca!" ¿No es "Ahora o nunca"?
15. **Gracioso, delicioso** y **ambicioso** son lo que se llaman **palabras cognadas** o **afines.**
16. Las palabras **vidrio, cuadro** y **madre** tienen las mismas combinaciones consonánticas.
17. Nunca se pronuncia el sonido *zzzzzzz* en las palabras **examen, existencialista** ni **exactamente.**
18. También creo que es difícil pronunciar las palabras **criado, criollo, ruana** y **trueno** con sólo dos sílabas.
19. En algunos países lo llaman **el excusado,** en otros **el retrete,** en otros **el servicio** y en otros **el wáter.**
20. Una transcripción fonética representa la realidad, pero una transcripción fonológica no es más que una abstracción.

C.

Make a phonetic transcription of the following sentences. You now have had all the segmentals (vowels and consonants) and suprasementals (stress, pitch, junctures) of American Spanish. Follow the same instructions as those given for previous transcription exercises.

1. Es extraño que no existan esas cosas en este país.   [*careful speech; intonation*]
2. Pero después de examinar bien la situación, se dan cuenta de que es exactamente lo mismo en otros países también.   [*careful speech*]

3. Las acciones de los alumnos son inaplicables en este caso.   [*rapid speech*]
4. Le puso una inyección al chico a quien había mordido el perro rabioso.   [*rapid speech*]
5. ¡Allá en el rancho grande donde viven los chanchos, las gallinas, las ratas y los ñandúes!   [*rapid speech; intonation*]
6. ¿No es raro que estos exámenes no asusten a los estudiantes?   [*careful speech; intonation*]
7. Es absolutamente imprescindible que se subscriba usted a esas revistas guatemaltecas.   [*rapid speech*]
8. La decisión del árbitro fue innegable cuando se le oyó gritar: "¡Rudeza innecesaria!"   [*careful speech; intonation*]

30

Reviewing the Consonants of Spanish (CHAPTERS 20–29)

Consonants are sounded when the airstream is stopped or impeded in some way in the upper vocal tract or supraglottal cavities, that is, from the vocal bands up and out to the lips. There are three meaningful ways of classifying consonants in Spanish: place of articulation, manner of articulation, and voicing or the lack of it. Unlike the situation with English, Spanish dialects are determined much more by consonant variations than by vowel differences.

Five consonant features are very significant in the determination and analysis of Spanish dialects: /s/ modification, **yeísmo** (or the lack of it), /x/, /r̄/, and **seseo** versus **distinción**. This last named phenomenon really pertains only to the difference between American Spanish and Castilian or peninsular Spanish since all dialects of American Spanish are characterized by **seseo**.

Many speakers of Spanish, particularly in the coastal areas—the Caribbean countries (including, of course, Puerto Ricans and Cuban Americans now living in the continental United States), the Pacific coast of South America, and the River Plate region of South America—modify /s/ in the syllable-final position, either by aspirating it as [h] or by eliminating it entirely. This also happens in southern Spain and the Canary Islands.

Most dialects of Spanish, on both sides of the Atlantic, are **yeísta**, that is, the palatal /l̃/ phoneme is absent: **Se cayó** and **Se calló** are both pronounced exactly alike. Some speakers use other varieties of /y/, such as [ŷ] or [ž], but in words spelled both with **y** and **ll**. The distinction between /y/ and /l̃/ is usually referred to as **lleísmo** and characterizes the speech of inhabitants of the Andes highland areas of Colombia, Ecuador, Peru, and Bolivia and also of Paraguay. It is also found in central and northern Spain, although not among all speakers; it is not characteristic of the large cities. Madrid, for example, is basically **yeísta**. Younger speakers in general in Spain are **yeísta**, and thus **lleísmo** is slowly disappearing.

The **jota**, /x/, has three main varieties, which are also significant in determining Spanish dialects. Most speakers in the coastal areas of Spanish America—the Caribbean (including the U.S. mainland), Central America, most of Colombia—and many southern

Spaniards pronounce a glottal aspiration [h] in words like **jardín, mujer, joven, gitano, jugo.** Speakers of standard Castilian Spanish have a strong velar or uvular trill [X] in these words. All other Spanish speakers—in Mexico, the Andes highlands, the Southern Cone— have a velar fricative [x].

The trilled /r̄/ contrasts with the tap /r/ in all dialects of Spanish, as in **coro–corro.** The former sound has two principal manifestations in American Spanish: the standard, so-called correct and prestigious trilled [r̄], which is taught in schools and heard on radio and television. But many speakers in Central America and the Andean highlands have a fricative *r*, either voiced [řr] or unvoiced [r̥]. Many of these speakers, in formal situations, use the standard apical trill, but in informal situations they use the fricative varieties. Yet even speakers who use the standard trilled /r̄/ in word-initial and intervocalic positions occasionally use the unvoiced fricative [r̥] at the end of a phonemic phrase.

In Spain **distinción**—the contrast between /s/ and /θ/, as in **ves–vez**—is the so-called official norm, although many Spaniards, particularly in southern Spain and the Canary Islands, are **seseantes**, just as all Spanish Americans are. An interesting non-standard phenomenon is **ceceo**, characteristic of some regions of southern Spain, particularly the rural areas. This is the use of the interdental /θ/ in most words where standard Spanish uses /s/. However, **ceceo** speakers are not consistent in this usage and mix occasional /s/'s in with the /θ/. Some even have a sound which is halfway between the two, making it almost impossible for the listener to determine whether he is hearing /s/ or /θ/. **Seseo** is accepted all over Spain, although many Spaniards feel that North Americans who come to Spain should have learned and should use **distinción** rather than **seseo** since Spanish is not their native language as it is for **seseo**-speaking Andalusians.

The syllable-final position in Spanish—whether within a word, between words, or at the end of the phonemic phrase—is the most variable in the sense that many consonantal modifications occur there, most due to regressive assimilation. Also normally phonemic consonants neutralize or lose their contrast in this position. /k/ and /g/, for example, are contrastive, as in **callo-gallo**, but in the syllable-final position in certain instances either a voiced or an unvoiced sound can be used. The first syllable of **técnico** may be pronounced with either [k] or [g̃]. The same is true of /t/ and /d/, as in **Atlántico**, whose first syllable may end with either sound. Speech style is often the determining factor in these modifications. For example, in slow speech **Atlántico** may well have a [t], but in rapid speech assimilation causes voicing to [đ].

The phoneme /b/ often disappears completely in words beginning with **ob-** and **sub-** prefixes, as in **objeto** or **subjeto.** Also we can consider the intervocalic fricative varieties of the voiced stops /b d g/, that is, [β đ g̃], respectively, to be a type of assimilation since the open quality of the surrounding vowels causes the speech articulators to open up slightly, turning the intervening stops into fricatives. The consonants /y/ and /w/ are similar to /b d g/ in that each has different manifestations after pauses and nasals than in other environments. In the case of /y/, this variety is considered to be the affricate [ŷ]—as in **yo** or **inyección**, but in the case of /w/, for theoretical reasons, the analysis changes to /gu/—as in **huerta** or **un hueso.**

/s/, in addition to the modifications of aspiration or omission in the syllable-final position already mentioned, may be voiced, [z], due to regressive assimilation, before voiced consonants, as in **mismo**. This is particularly true of rapid speech; [s] in these cases—where there is lack of assimilation—is more characteristic of slow speech. Also some speakers in central Colombia and central Bolivia have an apico-alveolar, concave, retroflex [ś] with a prominent palatalized sound. This same type of /s/ is the norm in Castilian Spanish.

/ĉ/ has a fricative allophone, [š], which is heard in the Caribbean area and southern Spain. /f/ has a bilabial allophone, [ɸ], heard among many speakers in Central America and the Andean region of South America.

In the syllable-final position, /n/ shows almost complete regressive assimilation, with a range of varieties—all the way from bilabial to velar, each one matching the point of articulation of the following consonant. Thus, despite the fact that the word **invierno** is written with **n**, the following bilabial /b/ causes /n/ to be realized as [m]. /l/ is basically the same, except that there are only dental, alveolar, alveolo-palatal, and palatal varieties; there are no bilabial, labio-dental, or velar *l*'s in Spanish.

The number and occurrence of consonant clusters in Spanish is quite restricted in comparison with a language like English. Only twelve clusters, /pr br tr dr kr gr fr pl bl kl gl fl/, begin syllables or words, and only a handful of Spanish words end in consonant clusters, /ps/ and /ks/, being the most common. Thus Spanish sequences of three and four consonants in the middle of words or between words are always divided according to these restrictions. Some of these clusters are troublesome to English speakers, usually those with tap [r]. The equivalent sound in English, tap [t̂] or [d̂], never occurs as part of a cluster, as [r] does in Spanish.

Double consonants occur in Spanish—mainly between words, as in **el loro**, occasionally within words between morphemes, as in **innegable**, and in only one common word within a morpheme, **perenne**. Although some of these sequences are crucial to meaning, such as /nn/ (**Son hombres** versus **Son nombres**) or /ll/ (**el oro** versus **el loro**), some, such as /r̄r̄/ (**Ve ratones** versus **Ver ratones**) or /ss/ (**las obras** versus **las sobras**), are difficult to produce and perceive, and thus do not play an important phonemic role.

Enlace is the most important consonant + vowel combination in Spanish and one which English speakers need to observe scrupulously to avoid unwanted word separation and the resulting choppy rhythm. **Enlace** in compound words or words with prefixes ending in consonants is not observed in hyphenating a line of written text since it would violate word and morpheme boundaries. The compound word **bienestar** is hyphenated **bien-estar** when it comes at the end of a line on the page, but in speech, **enlace** holds and the word is always pronounced [bi̯é-nes-tár] or [bi̯é-ŋes-tár] . The same is true of a word like **inestable**, where the prefix is separated, when the word is hyphenated, **in-estable**, but not in speech, [i-nes-tá-ɸle].

Consonant + semi-vowel + vowel combinations in English usually produce either palatalization in the case of /y/ (/s/→/š/, as in *appreciate*) or hiatus in the case of /w/

(/w/→/u/, as in *pu-eblo*). Thus such Spanish words as **delicioso, situar**, and **fuera** are mispronounced because of these English patterns.

Many cognate words with this same English pattern are also troublesome because of the English speakers' temptation to insert a Spanish semi-vowel [i̯] (which corresponds to the English /y/) in such words as **futuro, ridículo, puridad**.

Practice

Write the answers to these questions and check them in Appendix C.

1. The three meaningful ways to classify consonants in Spanish are

   _____, _____,
   and _____.

2. *Voicing* and *function of the vocal bands* are basically the same thing in the analysis of consonant phonemes.   TRUE/FALSE

3. American Spanish does not have a /θ/ phoneme: the same sound as in English (a) *this;* (b) *think;* (c) *Thames.*

4. Pronouncing the /s/ of the Spanish word **asno** as a [z] instead of an [s] is an example of progressive assimilation.   TRUE/FALSE

5. Spanish /p/ often becomes phonetic ''zero.'' That is, it is not pronounced at all, in a word like (a) **aplicar;** (b) **septiembre;** (c) **apto.**

6. *Delayed voicing* with English voiceless stops /p t k/ creates a phenomenon known as _____.

7. Since /p/ and /b/ in Spanish are phonemic—contrastive and distinctive—just as they are in English, English speakers never have any trouble perceiving the difference between the two or pronouncing them properly.   TRUE/FALSE

8. Spanish [r] is virtually the same as the English sound _____.

9. One letter combination *never* used to spell the phoneme /k/ in Spanish words is (a) **ch;** (b) **qu;** (c) **k.**

10. Spanish words can begin with a stop [b] or a fricative [β̞], depending on their phonetic environment.   TRUE/FALSE

11. In Spanish sometimes a labio-dental [v] is heard due to (a) hypercorrection; (b) the influence of English and French; (c) the natural evolution of the language.

12. Spanish /d/ is pronounced as a stop after a pause and _____.

13. Spanish /g/ is spelled _____ before the vowels /e/ and /i/.

14. The [ž] sound of English (as in *measure*) or French (as in *Jacques*) is also heard in some dialects of Spanish.   TRUE/FALSE

15. The affricate sound [ŷ] is rarely heard as the initial sound in words spelled with (a) **ll-;** (b) **hie-;** (c) **y-.**

16. In its areas **žeísmo** is used by speakers of all social classes and educational levels. TRUE/FALSE

17. One of the only sound features characteristic of one sex in Spanish is (a) the devoicing of [ž] to [š]; (b) **lleísmo**; (c) **yeísmo**.
18. One of the features that distinguishes [w] from [u̯] is the fact that _____
_____.
19. The use of /gu/ in place of /w/ is considered incorrect by some speakers of Spanish.   TRUE/FALSE
20. The preponderance of Spanish place-names that begin with **Guad-** (a) shows that Spanish speakers have always had trouble with English words beginning with **w-**; (b) is due to recent rulings by the Spanish Royal Academy; (c) comes from the fact that Spanish speakers pronounced the Arabic word for *river bed* with a /g/-sound.
21. The deliberate misspelling of words in literary dialog to show the educational level of the speaker or perhaps his or her social dialect is called _____
_____.
22. The apico-alveolar [ś], heard in Spain and in Colombia, is also called the _____
_____ *s* because of the shape of the tongue.
23. The words **serrar** and **cerrar** form a minimal pair for most speakers in (a) central Colombia and parts of Bolivia; (b) central and northern Spain; (c) southern Spain and the Canary Islands.
24. One name given to the phonemic contrast of /s/ and /θ/ is _____.
25. This contrast characterizes the so-called official pronunciation of Spain. TRUE/FALSE
26. /s/ in all dialects of Spanish (a) voices occasionally due to regressive assimilation; (b) is normally omitted in syllable-final position; (c) often causes a following trilled /r̄/ to drop out.
27. **Ceceo** is considered correct by virtually all Spaniards.   TRUE/FALSE
28. The dialect of peninsular Spanish that most resembles Caribbean Spanish, at least as far as the sounds go, is the one spoken in (a) Madrid; (b) Bilbao; (c) the Canary Islands.
29. A common English term for **ceceo** is simply _____.
30. The sharp hissing dental [ş] of Mexican and Ecuadorian Spanish is unknown in North American English.   TRUE/FALSE
31. English speakers often mispronounce Spanish words with /s/ that are cognates of English words. An example of such a mispronounced cognate word would be (a) **caso**; (b) **física**; (c) **mozo**.
32. A Spanish *word* (not a proper name) spelled with the unusual combination **ze** or **zi** is _____.
33. /s/ is no longer spelled with **x** in the Hispanic world.   TRUE/FALSE
34. Spanish dictionaries and lexical lists have always put the word **chasquear** *after* the word **cura** because _____.
35. The pronunciation of the word **fuente** with a **jota** (/x/) instead of an /f/ is accepted as correct anywhere in the Spanish-speaking word.   TRUE/FALSE

36. The main difference between the Castilian [X] and [x] is (a) its point of articulation; (b) its voicelessness; (c) its manner of articulation.
37. The palatal sound [ç] is heard in a Spanish word like _____.
38. If a given dialect has [h] as its predominant **jota** sound, then (a) it is clearly an *s*-modification dialect; (b) it is probably spoken in a Southern Cone country; (c) the best analysis is to consider the phoneme itself as /h/, too.
39. The Spanish word for *Mexican* is spelled two different ways in the Hispanic world.   TRUE/FALSE
40. One nasal sound *not* heard in American Spanish is (a) [ṇ]; (b) [ŋ]; (c) [m̩].
41. When one sound is articulated in the same place in the vocal tract as another sound, we refer to the two sounds as _____.
42. The three nasal phonemes of any Spanish dialect contrast with each other only in the intervocalic position.   TRUE/FALSE
43. P.A. means (a) point of articulation; (b) position of the allophone; (c) palato-alveolar.
44. The pronunciation of **conmigo** with a [n-m] sequence rather than [m-m] or just [m] is due to the phonological process of _____.
45. The use of velar [ŋ] in Spanish never creates a phonemic contrast.   TRUE/FALSE
46. The pronunciation of nasals in English (a) normally shows assimilation across word boundaries; (b) never shows assimilation anywhere; (c) shows some assimilation, just as with Spanish nasals.
47. An example of a Spanish word whose spelling does not reflect the normal nasal pronunciation when the word is in the absolute-final position is _____ _____.
48. There are more lateral consonants in Spanish than nasal consonants.   TRUE/FALSE
49. Lateral consonants are so-named because (a) the airstream comes out on either or both sides of the tongue; (b) the tongue curves backward to articulate them; (c) the airstream comes out on either or both sides of the teeth.
50. The impressionistic term for Spanish [l], as opposed to the typical velarized word-final [ɫ] of English, is _____.
51. Some dialects of Spanish have a labio-dental *l*.   TRUE/FALSE
52. The use of the English velarized [ɫ] (a) contributes to a definite foreign-sounding accent in Spanish; (b) is not noticeable in Spanish in syllable-final position; (c) might make the listener think the speaker is from France or Portugal.
53. Even though the words **pollo** and **polio** are similar sounding in Spanish, they are always distinguished because _____.
54. Parts of South America are **lleísta.**   TRUE/FALSE
55. If the words **halla** and **haya** are pronounced exactly alike in Spanish, we can say that they are _____.

56. Most Spanish Americans pronounce pairs of words like **mayo** and **mallo** or **cayo** and **callo** exactly the same despite their different spelling.   TRUE/FALSE

57. Spanish dictionaries and lexical lists have normally placed the word (a) **allá** after **amo**; (b) **lujo** after **llover**; (c) **llama** after **luna**.

58. The little circle under a phonetic symbol like [ɼ̥] means _____
    _____.

59. Spanish tap /r/ can occur in any part of a word.   TRUE/FALSE

60. You can safely pronounce *either* a tap or a trill in the Spanish word (a) **revolución**; (b) **largo**; (c) **enterrado**.

61. The voiceless trill [ɼ̥] (a) is contrastive with the voiced trill [r̄] ; (b) is sometimes represented phonetically with an [h]; (c) is substandard in its areas of usage.

62. It is possible for the two completely different words _____
    and _____ to sound exactly alike when the first one is pronounced by a Spaniard and the second by a Puerto Rican.

63. If you hear /l/ for /r/ in syllable-final position in Spanish, you are almost certainly listening to a native speaker of an Oriental language like Vietnamese or Chinese. TRUE/FALSE

64. English has a sound almost exactly like the Spanish tap [r] in a word like (a) *today*; (b) *partly*; (c) *parent*.

65. An English word or phrase to help you pronounce the Spanish word **era** is
    _____.

66. All Spanish compound words or derived words containing a word beginning with **r-** , when used alone, spell the initial sound of this compounded or derived word with **-rr-**.   TRUE/FALSE

67. The following is *not* a syllable- or word-initial cluster in Spanish: (a) **sp-**; (b) **fr-**; (c) **gl-**.

68. One Spanish word ending with a consonant cluster is _____.

69. The second consonant of a word-medial, syllable-final consonant cluster in Spanish is almost always /s/.   TRUE/FALSE

70. Occasionally Spanish speakers themselves simplify a four-consonant sequence by (a) inserting a vocalic element like [ə] somewhere in the sequence; (b) eliminating the last consonant; (c) omitting the first consonant.

71. When two normally phonemic consonants lose their contrast in the syllable-final position, we refer to this as _____.

72. Even though [s] and [z] are not phonemic in Spanish, as they are in English, their presence can help you as an English speaker to determine the difference between two words in a minimal pair, such as **los codos–los godos**.   TRUE/FALSE

73. Two consecutive identical consonants in Spanish (a) most often indicate a boundary of some sort; (b) are common within morphemes; (c) are always reduced to just one.

74. Two consecutive identical consonants in Spanish that are very difficult to distinguish from just one are _____.

75. Two Spanish phrases containing the same individual sounds but with different meaning—like **un aparte** *an aside* (in the theater) versus **una parte** *a part*—are normally pronounced exactly alike in conversation.   TRUE/FALSE

76. One Spanish word that is divided differently in writing if hyphenated than in speech is ⎯⎯⎯⎯⎯⎯⎯⎯⎯⎯⎯⎯⎯⎯.

77. The Spanish monosyllabic combination of /CwV/ is often separated into two syllables by English speakers. This is somewhat puzzling because English has the same combination with no restrictions on either the C or the V of the combination.   TRUE/FALSE

78. The English consonants /t d s z/, when word-final, sometimes undergo a change in articulation, (a) due to progressive assimilation; (b) particularly when they are followed by a word beginning with /y/; (c) but this fact does not influence an English speaker's pronunciation of Spanish.

79. Can you name one Spanish word in which English speakers incorrectly insert the semi-vowel [i̯], despite the fact that there is no English cognate, as there is with **regular** or **futuro**, for example? ⎯⎯⎯⎯⎯⎯⎯⎯⎯⎯⎯⎯⎯⎯.

80. The facetious comment that ''there is *egg salad* in the Spanish word **examen**'' is meant to call your attention to the fact that there is no progressive assimilation from the /g/ to the /s/ in Spanish as there is in the English cognate word *exam*. TRUE/FALSE

31

The Orthography of Spanish

Although Spanish orthography is far more regular and informative than that of English and that of most languages Americans commonly study, it does have certain inconsistencies. These irregularities sometimes cause you not only to mispronounce unfamiliar words but even to misspell familiar ones.

"Silent" Letters

Spanish has several so-called "silent" letters[1]: **h, p**, and **u**. The letter **h**, except as part of the digraph **ch**, always represents silence: <u>honor</u> [o-nór]. When you began your study of Spanish, you may have allowed the presence of this to draw you into such incorrect pronunciations as *[há-ɸlo] for **hablo** or *[hám-bre] for **hambre**.

At one time a few specialized words like **psicología** or **psicólogo** were regularly spelled with **p**, which also was a superfluous letter, representing silence. The Spanish Royal Academy years ago recommended that these words be spelled without the initial **p** since virtually no one ever says them that way, /s/ being the initial sound. Today most dictionaries list these words both ways: **psicología** and **sicología**, with a note that the second spelling is preferred.

The letter **u** represents no sound in two cases: when it stands between either **q** or **g** and **e** or **i**, in order to represent the velar stops /k/ and /g/ before /e/ and /i/, as in **bus<u>q</u>ue** [bús-ke], **po<u>q</u>uito** [po-kí-to], **lle<u>g</u>ué** [ye-ǵé], and **lar<u>g</u>uísimo** [lar-ǵí-si-mo], respectively.

---

[1]The word "silent" is written with quotation marks because there really is no such thing as a "silent" letter. Letters neither make sounds nor do they remain silent. They are merely graphic representations of sounds and secondary in linguistic importance to them, as we observed back in Chapter 2, "Language and Linguistics." Everyone speaks a language, but not everyone writes his or her language for a variety of reasons. Conventional letters, although not nearly as good as phonetic symbols to represent speech sounds accurately, are nonetheless the primary way used in most cultures to achieve that goal. Occasionally letters are used in words where the sound no longer exists; thus we refer to them as "silent" letters. A better term might be "superfluous letters," but we will continue to use the conventional term in this book.

Digraphs and Double Letters

Spanish has three digraphs, which are two-letter combinations that stand for only one sound: **ch** for /ĉ/ as in **chico**, **ll** for /y/ (or /l̃/ in the **lleísta** dialects) as in **llevar**, and **rr** for /r̄/ within a word between vowels as in **corro**. The first two digraphs have no irregularities or problems—particularly now that the Spanish Royal Academy has recommended that dictionaries change their policy regarding them. The Academy in its own publications will begin listing the **ch** words in Spanish in their proper place in the **C** section (**charlar** after **cena** but before **cuna**) and likewise with **ll** words in the **L** section (**llevar** after **lana** but before **luna**) and not in separate **CH** and **LL** sections, respectively, as is done in probably most Spanish books you have seen.

However, there are a couple of irregularities with **rr** and the sound it represents. The trilled /r̄/ is always represented by a single **r-** letter at the beginning of a word, where the tap /r/ never occurs in Spanish. The exception to this are compound and derived words that contain as their second element a word with the trilled /r̄/ coming after a previous compounded word or prefix ending in a *vowel*. Thus you have **rojo** for *red*, but **pelirrojo** for *redhead*, **redondo** for *round,* but **carirredondo** for *round-faced.* A single **r** would incorrectly represent a tap /r/ in the dozens of Spanish words with this spelling pattern. But there is even an exception to this exception—namely the fact that the spelling of the trilled /r̄/ in the second word is spelled with only *one* **r** if the previous compounded word or prefix ends in a *consonant.* Thus you have **rayar** to *draw a line* and **subrayar** to *underline.* There are only a few Spanish words of this nature.

There are other double letters in Spanish, but they are *not* digraphs, as **ll** and **rr** are. A dozen or so Spanish words have **nn**, which, indeed, represent two /n/ sounds together (or perhaps one prolonged one) in careful speech: **innato, innegable, innecesario.**

There are also double vowel letters in Spanish. The main example is **ee**, which in careful speech with the proper stress can represents two /e/ sounds: **creer, lee.** These cases were taken up in detail in Chapter 18, ''Vowel Combinations in Spanish.'' One other vowel letter is also doubled: **oo**, as in **loor, cooperación.** Just as with **ee**, these two **o**'s sometimes represent two vowel sounds, depending on the stress and speech style. Double **aa** is found in just a few proper names, such as **Aaron** or **Saavedra.** Double **ii** and **uu** do not occur within words in Spanish.

In the case of all these double letters, the writing system, as usual, represents careful speech much more accurately than rapid speech.

Velar Consonants Before Front Vowels

We have already mentioned **u** as a silent letter in the combinations **qu** and **gu**, which represent /k/ and /g/, respectively, before the front vowels /e/ and /i/, as in **busque, poquito, llegué**, and **larguísimo.** The reason for this involves two other Spanish consonants, one being the velar **jota** /x/, and the other either /θ/ or /s/, depending on whether the speech mode is **distinción** or **seseo.**

Since the letter **g** alone before the vowels /e/ and /i/ represents the voiceless **jota** /x/, not the voiced /g/, as in **gente** or **gigante**, some other letter combination must be used to represent /g/ before the front vowels. All the Romance languages face this same problem: Italian uses **gh**, as in **ghetto** or **laghi**, French uses **gu**, as in **guerre** or **guillotine**, and Spanish, too, uses the "**u** solution," as in **llegué** and **larguísimo**.

As stated, in Spanish a **g** before **e** or **i** represents the voiceless **jota** /x/, as in **gente** and **gigante**. The fact that this combination of /xe/ or /xi/ is *also* spelled with **je** and **ji** is a matter of linguistic history. **Jefe** has exactly the same initial sound as **gente** despite the spelling. **Jinete** has exactly the same initial sound as **gigante**. You, as a student of Spanish, must just learn, like native Spanish speakers themselves, which words spell /xe/ and /xi/ with **g** and which with **j**.

The situation is simpler with /k/ before /e/ and /i/. **Qu** must be used in these combinations, such as **queso** /ké-so/ *cheese* or **quito** /kí-to/ *I remove*. The word **ceso** has either a /θ/ (in **distinción**) or an /s/ (in **seseo**) and means *I stop;* likewise with the word **cito** *I cite*. There are no other combinations as there are with **ge** or **je** and **gi** or **ji**, other than the small handful of foreign borrowings spelled with **k**, such as **kerosén** or **kilómetro**, for example.

Some books and instructors mislead you further by implying that if you spell **llegué** without the **u**—*llegé*— the Spanish-speaking reader will think you are trying to write the nonexistent word */ye-xé/. Or that if you spell **seguí** without the **u**—*segí*—the reader will think you are trying to write the nonexistent */se-xí/. The Spanish speaker, however, probably knows exactly what you mean even though you write these words incorrectly without the **u**, but he or she may think the same thing about you that you think about someone who spells *receive* in English as "*recieve*" or Spanish as "*Spainish.*" You are not fooled into thinking that there are two new words in English; nor does the Spanish speaker think there are two new words, *llegé* and *segí*, in Spanish either. Likewise, *buscé* is regarded by the Spanish speaker as just a spelling error for **busqué**. Communication goes on. Undoubtedly, there are cases where your failure to use a **u** for the combinations /ge/ and /gi/ will cause confusion, but they are few and far between. The opinion of the reader about the writer who makes such mistakes in spelling is another matter, which has little to do with linguistics.

A more likely problem is the fact that beginning students of Spanish may think that the letter **u** in these combinations represents a real /u/ sound and are thus drawn into such incorrect pronunciations as *[gué-r̄a] (instead of [gé-r̄a]) for **guerra** or *[kui-ós-ko] (instead of [kiós-ko]) for **quiosco**.

Since **u**, then, is "silent" and has the function of signalling /g/ as the consonant of the combination **gue** and **gui**, and **qu** shows that /k/ is the consonant meant in **que** and **qui**, what about combinations where there really is a /u/ sound? The spelling *verguenza represents the following nonexistent string of sounds in Spanish: /ber-gén-sa/ rather than the correct /ber-guén-sa/ *shame*, a word with a /u/ sound in it. Again native speakers of Spanish know what you mean, but the spelling is simply wrong. The **ü** now must carry a dieresis to show that it really represents the sound /u/ and is not "silent"—thus **vergüenza**.

The same solution is used for /gui/: **lingüista** is /lin-guís-ta/, the correct way to say *linguist*. *****Linguista** would be /lin-gís-ta/ and means nothing, although, once again, the native speaker probably knows exactly what you are trying to write—it is just a matter of good spelling.

The remaining combinations in this area are /kue/ and /kui/, once again with /u/ sounds. The letters **cue** spell the first one and **cui** the second one, as in **cuenta** and **cuidado. Ce** and **ci**, without the **u**, are used to spell /se/ and /si/ in **seseo** or /θe/ and /θi/ in **distinción**, as in **cena** and **cita**. Once again Spanish speakers probably recognize *****quenta** as **cuenta** or *****quidado** as **cuidado**, although there undoubtedly are cases in Spanish where the mistaken use of **qu** in these combinations could represent another word that could logically be used in place of the **cu** word.

Actually /kuV/ is the easiest of these troublesome combinations to spell: it is *always* **cuV**, as in <u>cu</u>ando /kuándo/, <u>cu</u>enta /kuénta/, <u>cu</u>idado /kuidádo/, <u>cu</u>ota /kuóta/. (The combination *****cuu** /kuu-/ does not exist in Spanish.)

Seseo **and** *Distinción*

The **seseo** of American Spanish and the non-**distinción** dialects in Spain create some minor orthographical problems, which may be a problem for native speakers as well as foreign learners of Spanish. One must learn the words in which /s/ is represented by the letters **s** or by **z** and **c** before **e** and **i**. This, of course, is not a problem for Castilian **distinción** speakers since **z** everywhere and **c** before **e** and **i** always represents /θ/, rather than /s/, as in ca<u>z</u>a *hunting* versus ca<u>s</u>a *house*, <u>c</u>epa *stump* versus <u>s</u>epa *know* (subjunctive of **saber**), <u>z</u>eta *Z* versus <u>s</u>eta *mushroo*m, po<u>z</u>o *well* versus po<u>s</u>o *I pose*, <u>c</u>ima *abyss* versus <u>s</u>ima *summit,* <u>z</u>umo *juice* versus <u>s</u>umo *great*, ve<u>z</u> *time* versus ve<u>s</u> *you see*. (The spelling combination of **ze** or **zi** is very rare in Spanish.) Virtually any speaker of Castilian Spanish will have no trouble spelling these words and any like it with the combinations of **z**, **ce**, **ci**, and **s**. Yet even educated **seseo** speakers make occasional mistakes with words of this nature, simply because they have no theta /θ/ sound to indicate which letters must be used. As we mentioned in Chapter 24, ''The Voiceless Consonants /s/ and /θ/,'' the common Spanish dish **gazpacho** is sometimes spelled **gaspacho** in southern Spain where there are many more speakers of **seseo** than of **distinción**.

Years ago many North American Spanish teachers advocated teaching their students Castilian **distinción**, often for this same reason: ease of spelling. This was not a convincing argument since all Spanish American children face this same problem in learning to write their own language. There may be other defensible reasons for North Americans to learn Castilian Spanish, but this is not one of them.

The most troublesome spelling combinations in Spanish are those resulting from the representation of velar consonants before front vowels, the representation of /s/ in American Spanish, and, to a lesser extent, the representation of /θ/ in Castilian Spanish. They are shown in Chart 25 with explanation and more examples following.

Chart 25   The Spelling of Spanish /k g x s θ/

Sounds heard	Letters used	Before . . .					Elsewhere
		/a/	/o/	/u/	/e/	/i/	
/k/	c	carne	cosa	cuna	—	—	lección, claro
	qu	—	—	—	queso	quitar	—
	k[+]	karate	kodak	kumis	kerosén	kilómetro	kodak
/kuV/	cu	cuando	cuota	—*	cuenta	cuidado	—
/g/	g	gato	gordo	gusto	—	—	grande, dogma
	gu	—	—	—	guerra	guitarra	—
/guV/	gu	guapo	antiguo	—*	—	—	—
	gü	—	—	—	vergüenza	lingüista	—
/x/ (or /h/)	j	jabón	joven	julio	jefe	jinete	reloj
	g	—	—	—	general	gitano	—
/s/	s	sala	sobre	sur	sentar	siglo	ves, mismo
	z[†]	zapato	zona	zurdo	zeta[‡]	zinc[‡]	vez, hallazgo
	c[†]	—	—	—	centro	cita	—
/θ/[#]	z	zapato	zona	zurdo	zeta[‡]	zinc[‡]	vez, hallazgo
	c	—	—	—	centro	cita	—

[+] The letter **k** occurs in Spanish in only a few foreign borrowings.

* This sequence of sounds does not exist in Spanish.

[†] Only in the **seseo** mode of American and non-Castilian Spanish since /θ/ does not exist here.

[‡] Only a few words and names in Spanish have **z** before **e** or **i**.

[#] Only in the **distinción** mode of Castilian Spanish where /θ/ is a phoneme.

You will notice in the preceding chart that there are many gaps, indicated by — . These gaps exist for several reasons. In some cases the sequence of sounds does not exist in Spanish, such as */guu/, for example. But in other cases, the letters that one might expect to be used are already taken. For example, **ce-** cannot be used for the sequence /ke/, as in **queso**, because these letters are used for the sequence /se/ in **seseo** or /θe/ in **distinción**, as in the word **centro**. Thus the letters **qu** are used; **k** is considered non-Spanish and is used in only a few foreign words. Likewise, the letters **ge-** cannot be used for the sequence /ge/, as in **guerra**, because they are already used for the sequence /xe/ as in

general. One might logically ask, why not use **je** for *all* cases of /xe/ in Spanish, but the use of **ge** or **je** for this sequence, seemingly arbitrary, is a matter of linguistic history. Some words, depending on their origin, have come down with **ge**, some with **je**—sometimes in a seemingly illogical fashion. The name **Jiménez** is based on **Gimeno** (although there is also a **Giménez**). But, returning to the representation of /ge/, the solution that Spanish uses is to insert a "silent" **u** after **g**, as in **guerra**.

Thus, most of these spelling combinations are logical and necessary. **Ja** and not **ga** must be used for /xa/, **jo** for /xo/, and so forth. But **je** versus **ge** is arbitrary; one must simply learn which set of letters is used for /xe/ in Spanish words. Likewise for **seseo** speakers, who must learn whether /s/ is spelled with **s**, as in **sello**, or with **c** as in **celo**, or whether it is spelled with **s**, as in **sala**, or with **z**, as in **zalamero**. This one, of course, is easy for a speaker of **distinción**, where these words begin with different sounds.

The spelling of **ze** and **zi** is very rare in Spanish, and the words with these combinations number only a few dozen, such as **Nueva Zelanda** *New Zealand* or **enzima** *enzyme* (**encima**, pronounced exactly the same way in all dialects of Spanish, means *on top.*) Furthermore, most Spanish words that are cognates of English words beginning with *ze-* begin with **ce-**: *zeal* **celo**, *zebra* **cebra**, *zero* **cero**.

Orthographical-Changing Verbs versus Real Irregular Verbs

By now you have probably recognized that these spelling patterns merit special consideration in grammar books, usually under the rubric of "orthographical-changing verbs." You have had to deal with **dirigir** and **dirijo**, with **buscar** and **busqué**, with **llegar** and **llegué**, with **comenzar** and **comencé**. Yet, strictly speaking, since there is a category known as "orthographical-changing verbs," there should also be one known as "orthographical-changing nouns" for **boca** and **boquilla** or **vez** and **veces**, and one known as "orthographical-changing adjectives" for **rico** and **riquísimo** or **capaz** and **capaces**, and one known as "orthographical-changing adverbs" for **cerca** and **cerquita** or **luego** and **lueguito**. This is because the spelling rules that created the class of verbs known as "orthographical-changing" in Spanish pertain to any part of speech in the entire language, not just verbs.

Most words in Spanish that, when inflected, cause one of the above consonants to be followed by a front vowel (/e/ and /i/) must undergo an orthographical change. People from **Santiago** are known as **santiagueños**; an affectionate term for **Diego** is **Dieguito**; an inhabitant of **Nicaragua** is a **nicaragüense**; baby talk for **agua** is **agüita**; an inhabitant of **Mendoza** is a **mendocino**; one person is **audaz** but two are **audaces**; **un poco** is *a little*, but **un poquito** is even less; and so forth throughout the entire language. As we have said, some of these changes seem unmotivated: why cannot an inhabitant of **Mendoza** be a *mendozino, why is it **comencé** and not *comenzé, why shouldn't the infinitive of **dirijo** be *dirijir or the infinitive of **cojo** be *cojer (or better yet, *kojer)? You, as a student, can learn the non-arbitrary combinations by applying logic: **Dieguito** does not have the sequence /xi/ as **gitano** and thus must be spelled with a **u**; **pocito**, with the sequence /si/, is a shallow pit or well in the ground, but **poquito**, with the sequence /ki/, is a word based on **poco.** But, although the spellings of **comencé** and **dirigir** seem arbitrary, they are just as necessary as the logical non-arbitrary spelling patterns.

These spelling patterns can be a source of great confusion to the student of Spanish (and occasionally to the teacher, too). Many do not realize at first that orthographical-changing verbs can be completely *regular* in their *sound* patterns. For example, neither the verb **buscar** nor the verb **dirigir** has any sound irregularity in any of its myriad forms. All forms of **buscar** in all tenses have /busk-/, and all forms in all tenses of **dirigir** have /dirix-/. Only the spelling varies: **buscar–busqué, dirigir–dirijo.** Thus a Spanish-speaking pre-schooler or an illiterate is totally unaware of any so-called irregularity or problem with either of these verbs, which, of course, are always given special attention in textbooks for foreigners.

A real *irregular* verb has *sound* changes—like **tener, tengo, tiene, tuve** or **saber, sé, supe, sepa.** Thus, **conocer** is *both* an irregular verb *and* an orthographical-changing one. The verb is irregular because of the /k/ inserted in the first-person singular of the present tense, /konósko/, which now must be spelled with a **c** since it precedes /o/: **conozco** (see Chart 25). The letter **z** is not a real irregularity at all since it represents the /s/ (or /θ/ of **distinción**) that is found in every single form of this verb in any of its tenses. The second **c** of **conocer** might be spelled with a **z**, *conozer, if Spanish spelling were completely logical. But in **conozco**—since Spanish spelling is based on **distinción** and /θ/ is now in the elsewhere position—/θ/ must be spelled with a **z**. Although seemingly paradoxical at first, the second **c** of **conozco** represents the real irregularity; the **z** is just a spelling change which represents the sound found in every single form of the verb.

To sum up, none of the above spelling alterations and patterns have anything to do with the various parts of speech as such but show up wherever the phonetic environment demands. The category of orthographical-changing verbs exists because, as you well know, Spanish verbs are at the core of Spanish grammar and require a great deal of time and effort for their mastery. But these spelling changes are the relatively easy aspect of Spanish verbs and pale in comparison with the real sound irregularities found in the Spanish verb system.

Other Spelling Irregularities

Several other spelling inconsistencies exist in Spanish. One is serious in all dialects of Spanish, the other only in the **yeísta** dialects, which, of course, are in the vast majority.

The letter **v** always represents the phoneme /b/, as does the letter **b**. All Spanish speakers occasionally confuse these two letters in spelling, but school children and semi-literate speakers frequently do. The common words for the letters **b** and **v** are **be** and **ve**, respectively. Since they both sound exactly alike, /be/ (the word **uve** for **v** exists but is not always used), teachers resort to a variety of terms to enable children to distinguish between the two letters in spelling. The letter **b** is called **b de burro** or **b alta** or **b grande**, and the letter **v** is referred to **v de vaca** or **ve corta** or **ve chica**. Some educated speakers occasionally attempt to pronounce **ve** with a labio-dental [v] to make this distinction, but normally the words for both letters come out the same.

Marginally educated Spanish speakers often spell common **b** words with **v** and vice versa. For example, **volver** can be found in any of the four possible spellings: ***volber, *bolver, *bolber**, and, of course, the right way. This spelling confusion has even found its way into proper names. The two family names **Velasco** and **Belasco** both exist and are pronounced exactly alike; however, the patronymic is always spelled with a **v: Velázquez.** One family name is **Baca**; another is **Vaca**—again both pronounced exactly alike. The first syllable of the name **Barga** is pronounced the same as that of **Vargas.** The family name **Rivera** was once commonly spelled **Ribera**. The pronunciation has not changed.

A similar problem is represented by the letters **ll** and **y**. Naturally, **lleísta** speakers rarely make mistakes with these letters since the digraph **ll** represents palatal /ʎ/ and the letter **y** the contrasting phoneme /y/. For them **valla** is not pronounced the same as **vaya**, yet for the vast majority of Spanish speakers, who are **yeísta**, they sound exactly alike. Thus one may find **yo** spelled as ***llo, llamar** as ***yamar**, and so forth.

There are a couple other minor spelling irregularities in Spanish, which seem completely arbitrary. The letter sequences **ue** and **ie** never begin words in Spanish. In the first case, the letter **h** is always placed first, as in **huelo, hueso, huevo.** In the second case, if the letter **i** really represents a vowel, **h** is placed first, as in **hielo, hierba, hiato.** But if the letter **i** would represent the consonant /y/, it is replaced by the letter **y**, as in **yerro** (from the stem-changing verb **errar**) or **yergue** (from the stem-changing verb **erguir**). The letter **i** after a vowel is never used to represent a word-final semi-vowel in Spanish: it is replaced by **y**, as in **ley, hay.**

It should be pointed out that spelling errors in Spanish of the type we have been discussing are characteristic mainly of school children and marginally educated speakers. Yet even the most highly educated Spanish speakers occasionally make misspellings of these types for the very same reason that highly educated English speakers misspell. Nevertheless, the average educated Spanish speaker makes far fewer spelling mistakes than an English-speaking counterpart for the simple reason that the writing system of Spanish is much more consistent and less idiosyncratic than that of English. For this reason, spelling bees are not an important educational activity in Hispanic countries. And rarely do educated Spanish speakers have to resort to their dictionaries for spelling purposes. In fact, you very soon may well find that your spelling in Spanish is more accurate than in your own native language, English. As we English speakers know only too well, if we are doing any serious writing, our dictionaries can never be very far away—more to aid us with spelling than to clarify lexical meaning.

Written Accents

The final aspect of Spanish spelling is the orthographic or written accent ´, which is used in certain words to indicate the position of the primary stress. The use of the accent mark has been standardized and is governed all over the Spanish-speaking world by rules originally formulated in past centuries and revised in the 1950s by the Spanish Royal Academy. These rules are observed by educated speakers mainly in *formal* writing, but are widely disregarded by everyone in informal writing. It is even not uncommon for native speakers of Spanish to ask foreigners who have mastered Spanish as a second language for help in the correct placement of these accents in a written text. This, of course, is because, although native speakers already know where the words of their own language are stressed, they do not know all the rules for written accent placement. But the written accent can be a very valuable tool for students of Spanish like yourselves to determine the correct pronunciation of unfamiliar words. For example, it shows you that the word **melodía** *melody* has four syllables with hiatus, rather than a diphthong, at the end, and the lack of an accent shows you that **parodia** *parody* has three syllables with a diphthong at the end. Although both words may have been new to you, a Spanish speaker knows what they mean already whether he finds ***melodia** incorrectly spelled without an accent or ***parodía** incorrectly spelled with one. Outside of serving this useful purpose, the written accent is another convention of the writing system, which, like spelling and punctuation, is followed by educated speakers in formal writing for social, rather than linguistic, reasons.

If you recall in Chapter 6, ''Stress in Spanish,'' we approached the problem of stress from the point of view of writing first. If you see written accents and certain word-final letters, they will guide you as to where to place the primary stresses in your pronunciation of the Spanish words you do not yet know. But in this chapter we will assume two things— first, just as native speakers of Spanish, you know how the words are pronounced, and, second, you also know how they are spelled. If you know these two things, the placement of written accents, outlined in the following rules, will be quite straightforward.

Rules for Written Accents in Spanish

Place a written accent over the stressed vowel in the following cases.

1. When a stressed /í/ or /ú/ comes in contact with another vowel *within* a word: **mío, país, gradúa, baúl**.

    This happens even if **h**, which has no phonetic value, intervenes: **prohíbe, búho.** There are two exceptions to this rule: one apparent and one real. In many words, as we now know, the letter **u** has no phonetic value; thus in **qui** and **gui** words a following /í/ does not really follow a /u/ sound and thus needs no written accent: **quito** /kí-to/, **seguir** /se-gír/. Also in words where a stressed /í/ follows a /u/ or a stressed /ú/ follows an /i/, there is no written accent: **ruido** /r̄uí-do/, **viuda** /biú-da/. Words like **aquí** and **seguí**, although apparently in this category, really have written accents because of rule 2, below.

2. In **aguda** (last-syllable-stressed) words ending in a vowel *letter* or the *letters* **n** or **s**: **pasó, andén, inglés.** Thus a written accent over the verb form **fió** shows you that it can be pronounced with two syllables in careful speech, but the lack of a

written accent over the verb form **dio** shows you that it can only be pronounced with one syllable.

3. In **llana** (next-to-last-syllable-stressed) words ending in any consonant *letter other than* **n** or **s**: c<u>é</u>sped, f<u>á</u>cil, <u>á</u>lbum, car<u>á</u>cter, l<u>á</u>piz. Notice that although the last word, **lápiz**, ends in an /s/ in American Spanish, it still falls under this rule because it is not spelled with **s** but with **z**. This is because, as we have said, Spanish spelling rules are based on **distinción**, where the word for *pencil* ends in a /θ/. Despite this, these rules are also followed scupulously in formal writing by all **seseo** speakers as well as those in Spain.

A word like **mío**, at first glance, may seem like an exception to this rule. It has two syllables, **mí-o**, but does *not* end in a consonant letter other than **n** or **s**. Then why an accent? Words like **pino** and **rico** have the same stress pattern and a similar syllabic structure, yet they do not have accents. This is because these words, **pino**, **rico**, and dozens more with the same syllabic structure are actually in the elsewhere situation. The hiatus of stressed /í/ and /ú/ has already been covered—as an exception—in rule 1, and now all **llana** words ending in a vowel letter, **n**, or **s** that do *not* have a stressed /í/ or /ú/ next to another vowel (like **pino**) are excluded, fit under none of the above rules, and thus have no accents.

4. In all **esdrújula** (third-to-last-syllable stressed) and **sobresdrújula** (fourth-to-last syllable stressed) words, *regardless of their spelling*: **rápido, énfasis, dígame, dígamelo, dándonoslas.** All **sobresdrújula** words in Spanish are verb forms with pronouns attached.

5. In all interrogative and exclamative words: **¿Dónde?, ¿Cómo?, ¡Qué lindo!, ¡Cuánto me alegro!**

A written accent is used in interrogative words even when they do not begin direct questions, but form indirect questions which are embedded in declarative statements: **No sé cuándo viene. No sabe qué hacer**.

6. In one of a pair of homonyms or homophones: **se** (reflexive pronoun) – **sé** (verb), **de** (preposition) – **dé** (verb), **tu** (possessive determiner) – **tú** (subject pronoun), **solo** (adjective) – **sólo** (adverb), **el** (definite article) – **él** (subject pronoun).[2]

There are relatively few words covered under rules 5 and 6, and perhaps these two rules could be telescoped into one. However, there are no exceptions to rule 5, but there are to rule 6. Usually the member of the homophonous pair that is a bound form unable to be uttered in isolation (see Chapter 6, ''Stress in Spanish'') has no accent—such as **se, de, tu**—whereas the free form that can be uttered in isolation—such as **sé, dé, tú**—carries a written accent. Monosyllabic verb forms like **dio, vi, vio, fui, fue** at one time carried written accents, but the Academy changed this practice in the revisions of the 1950s on

---

[2]Actually there is a seventh rule for just one word in Spanish, a rule that has nothing to do with sound or grammar. The word **o**, meaning *or*, has a written accent when it comes between *numerals*, as in **6 ó 7**, to make it clear to the reader that **o** is a letter and not the number **0**, which, without an accent, might make the text look like **607**. This is very much like the use of Ø in English texts to show that zero is meant and not a capital O.

the grounds that there are no other matching words in Spanish, unlike the case with **sé** and **dé**. But even so there are a few exceptions: **solo** *alone* is the free form, yet the bound form **sólo** *only* is the accented word. **Ve,** the imperative of **ir,** and **ve** *she/he sees* are homophones, and both are free forms. Yet neither has a written accent. **Para,** the preposition *for*, is unstressed in the stream of speech and thus has no accent. But neither does **para,** the third-person singular present tense form of **parar** *to stop*, which is stressed in the stream of speech.

In addition, the Spanish Royal Academy in its revisions of the 1950s said that demonstrative "pronouns" (really nominalized determiners), such as **este, estos, esa, aquel,** no longer needed written accents to distinguish them from their homophonous demonstrative "adjective" (really determiner) counterparts: **este libro, esa calle.** (This, of course, never included the neuters **esto, eso,** and **aquello,** which never had accents because they are unmatched by other words in Spanish.) However, many publications, pedagogical and otherwise, to this day put written accents over the free-standing so-called demonstrative "pronouns" and not over their bound counterparts: **Quiero éste,** but **Quiero este libro.** This is somewhat inconsistent since, although bound, the demonstrative "adjectives" also carry heavy stress in the stream of speech. The masculine singular word for *this* has a stressed initial syllable in the stream of speech, /éste/, whether it is a preposed demonstrative "adjective" (determiner)—**Quiero este libro**—or a free-standing demonstrative "pronoun" (nominalized determiner)—**Quiero éste.**

There are other inconsistencies in the Academy's pronouncements on written accents. They recommended, for example, that the word **huí** (and others like it—**construí, incluí.**) be written with an accent on the grounds that it is pronounced with hiatus in careful speech because of its morphemic structure. Thus **huí,** with hiatus and two syllables, contrasts with **fui,** with a diphthong and one syllable. But the Academy also recommended that words like **huir** itself, **huiste,** and **huisteis,** despite the same hiatus pronunciation with the stressed /í/ next to another vowel just like **huí,** be written *without* accents. Despite this, many dictionaries today write **huíste** and **huísteis** with accents to show the contrast between them and words like **fuiste** and **fuisteis,** which no one writes now nor ever did write with accent marks.

Adverbs ending in **-mente** that have accent marks really are covered by rules 2, 3, or 4, above, since they are considered by many to be two-word compounds with one heavy stress on the first element (adjective) and one on the **-mente.** A written accent is used if the adjective falls into one of the categories covered above. For example, **cortésmente** comes under rule 2 because of **cortés, fácilmente** under rule 3 because of **fácil,** and **rápidamente** under rule 4 because of **rápida.**

It should be obvious why the Spanish Royal Academy, when they concocted these rules, decided that the only two consonants included in rule 2 and thus excepted from rule 3 should be **n** and **s.** This was done simply to reduce the number of words in which written accents would be necessary. The letters **s** and **n** represent phonemes that so often inflect a noun or adjective from singular to plural or change the person ending of a verb with no effect whatsoever on the stress pattern: **casa–casas, alto–altos, habla–hablas–hablan.**

Otherwise if these two consonants were not excepted, all such inflected forms ending in **n** or **s** would require written accents: **casa—*cásas, habla—*háblan,** and thousands more like them in the language.

These rules are rigidly applied in formal writing, particularly in publications. This means that, since they are based on stress patterns, any word whose stress pattern *does change*—unlike those in the previous paragraph—loses or acquires a written accent, as the case may be. For example, **joven** /xóben/ is a **llana** word that ends in **n** and thus has no written accent. But the plural, **jóvenes** /xóbenes/, is now an **esdrújula** word and thus needs an accent. On the other hand, **razón** /r̄asón/ is an **aguda** word that ends in **n** and thus requires an accent. But now the plural, **razones** /r̄asónes/ is a **llana** word that does *not* end in one of the other consonants—**d, l, z**—and thus needs no accent. Or one can look at the same situation in reverse, so to speak. **Ingleses** /ingléses/ is a **llana** word that does not end in one of these other consonants, thus no accent. But the singular, **inglés** /inglés/, is an **aguda** word that ends in **s** and thus needs an accent. There are dozens, perhaps hundreds, of such words in Spanish whose stress category changes when inflected but nowhere near the number of words like **casa–casas** whose stress category does *not* change with inflection.

The written accent is frequently omitted from capital letters for typographical reasons: NACION or NACIÓN. This depends to a certain extent on the type font used, since with some fonts there is ample room over the capital letters for accent marks and in others there is not. It is also partly convention, since the reader almost always knows what the word in capitals is, with or without an accent mark. But the dieresis ¨ and the tilde ˜ over the **U** and the **N**, respectively, are another matter since they always indicate a phonemic difference that the reader might otherwise miss. There are very few minimal pairs with **u / ü**, such as GUITA *twine* versus GÜITA, a Mexican slang word for *money*, but many with **n / ñ**: SANA *healthy* versus SAÑA *anger,* CANA *gray hair* versus CAÑA *sugarcane, reed*.

A Final Look at Spanish Orthography

Spanish spelling, despite the irregularities, inconsistencies, and arbitrariness pointed out, is more nearly phonemic and thus a better system than our English one. There are good reasons for this. The majority of the sounds of Spanish have not changed appreciably in several hundred years. But even so, Spanish orthography has been periodically revised to represent the sounds as faithfully as possible and to make it easier for children and foreigners to learn. The pronunciation of English has changed substantially in the last 400 years—since Shakespeare's time—but the spelling has changed relatively little. In essence, then, English orthography is practically four centuries behind the times in comparison with the actual spoken language, but Spanish orthography, although not perfect, is relatively up-to-date.

The task of revising English orthography has been contemplated many times in the past, but extensive and meaningful revisions are now practically hopeless and out of the question—although there have been experiments with employing phonetic spelling temporarily during the teaching of reading in elementary schools. But eventually the transition to regular orthography must be made. Not only that, but spelling revision would create many other serious problems. It is hard to combat the strong public prejudice against tampering with deep-rooted traditions. Such experimental spellings as *nite* and *thru* have had only limited success. Changing English orthography would also necessitate a vast amount of reprinting. Either all children would have to be taught both the new and the traditional spelling systems, or all existing material would have to be reprinted, or certain things would have to be left eventually to become ancient documents, able to be read only by specialists—like medieval manuscripts today. Not everything could possibly be reprinted. Choices of what to reprint and what to leave in the eventually-to-be archaic spelling would have tremendous political, social, and ideological implications. Despite these pitfalls, however, major orthographical revisions have been carried out successfully in this century in several languages—such as Russian and Portuguese (in Brazil, at least). Yet the prospects for this in English, now a worldwide language, are dim, indeed.

Turning to Spanish, we see that there is much less need for major revision. Still there would be substantial difficulties. Literally hundreds of common everyday words would have to be spelled differently: **benir, yamar, ai, rrojo, cojer** (or **kojer**), and so on. And would *shoe* be spelled **zapato** in Spain but **sapato** in Spanish America, like *colour* in Britain and Canada, but *color* in the United States? Would **tampoco** be spelled **tanpoco** or would **tan poco** be spelled **tam poco**, and so on? It might be a good idea to put a written accent on every single word with primary stress in the stream of speech so no one would have to worry about the six rules for written accents. Also some decision would have to be made about spaces between words, usually phonetically unreal in spoken Spanish but visually necessary, or at least helpful, in written Spanish.

Spanish orthography, despite these inconsistencies and irregularities, is relatively sound compared with other important languages. In fact, it is really the main reason that Spanish enjoys its reputation as being such a comparatively easy language for foreigners to learn. True phonemic or phonetic spelling or transcription of languages like English or French has proven to be helpful in elementary textbooks for foreign students, but it seems quite pointless in elementary Spanish texts.

Correct spelling, fortunately or unfortunately, as one views it, is one of the standards that society in most developed countries uses to determine the level of education and culture of the individual who has produced the written text. Spelling Spanish correctly is relatively easy for the average American student of second-year Spanish and beyond. Speaking it correctly is clearly another matter.

Practice

A.

The following are sounds for some nonexistent but phonetically possible Spanish words. See if you can write them in conventional orthography. To be able to do this practice, you must make the following assumptions: (1) since Spanish spelling is based on Castilian Spanish, take this imaginary speaker to be a **lleísta** *speaker who uses* **distinción**—*that is, he/she uses both the palatal /ʎ/ and the interdental /θ/ phonemes; (2) none of these words has the letters* **h** *(except in the digraph* **ch***),* **k***, or* **w***; (3) none of these words is spelled with the rare combinations* **ze** *or* **zi***; (4) all instances of the phoneme /b/ are spelled with* **b***, never* **v***; (5) the sounds represent the way the words would be said in careful speech. Don't forget written accents. Then, when you are done, think of trying to do the same type of exercise in English!*

1. /weɾéke/	11. /muíxu/
2. /puθigaimá/	12. /guilení/
3. /sekeípetro/	13. /peɾiguáuguau/
4. /ʎuʎári/	14. /suaipaɾós/
5. /branisuába/	15. /θoifoθámal/
6. /xápemelos/	16. /ñoukulífaθ/
7. /muigilánturo/	17. /ɾulíakos/
8. /ĉoúbesa/	18. /xalabalú/
9. /tiúmed/	19. /suipiyeráθ/
10. /irguinstérne/	20. /doʎipárton/

B.

Write a written accent ´ on the words that require one, according to the six rules given in this chapter. The accented syllable is underlined. In the case of words that need a written accent, list the number of rule (see pp. 290–291) that governs the use of the accent. The dialect of Spanish is irrelevant here since written accents are used in the exact same way all over the Spanish-speaking world.

1. ima<u>gi</u>no	11. <u>na</u>car	21. <u>pre</u>ve
2. <u>vir</u>gen	12. far<u>ma</u>cia	22. <u>pien</u>
3. <u>jo</u>venes	13. a<u>na</u>lisis	23. <u>lus</u>tramelos
4. ri<u>qui</u>simo	14. tecnico<u>lor</u>	24. soli<u>citud</u>
5. Cozu<u>mel</u>	15. teori<u>camente</u>	25. ca<u>paz</u>
6. di<u>fi</u>cil	16. <u>ois</u>te	26. pau<u>pe</u>rrimo
7. di<u>fi</u>ciles	17. te<u>o</u>logo	27. <u>pi</u>o
8. <u>an</u>gel	18. <u>den</u>	28. pi<u>o</u>
9. <u>so</u>lo *(adj.)*	19. <u>fui</u>	29. <u>vio</u>
10. in<u>gle</u>ses	20. <u>ca</u>liz	30. constru<u>is</u>teis

C.

Continue to place accents on the words that need them, and cite the number of the rule that governs your decision. You may find some unfamiliar words, which you can look up in the end vocabulary. Many of these accents now depend on grammar as well as phonetics.

1. ¿Para donde vas?
2. Deme el primero.
3. Para el carro, quiero bajar.
4. Solo quiere jugar al domino.
5. Quiere jugar solo.
6. Levantandote temprano, podras llegar a tiempo.
7. Podremos llamar a la policia.
8. Aunque llueva, quiero quedarme aqui.
9. No se cuando llega.
10. El dia cuando llegue, no estare alli yo.
11. No sabre que hacer.
12. ¡Si que lo sabras!
13. Prefiero ese que tienes tu.
14. Y esta es para ti, Paquito.
15. Cuando llego el psicologo, me hizo una serie de preguntas tontisimas.
16. El acrobata llamo por telefono, se comunico con el farmaceutico y le pidio el antidoto para su compulsion irresistible de dar saltos mortales.
17. Los ingleses y los franceses discutiran la hegemonia de Rusia y Turquia.
18. La cancion tiene el titulo de ''Melodia de melancolia''.
19. No te dire como lo hizo pero lo completo en veintiuna horas.
20. El Credito Instantaneo: Usted tiene 12, 24, 36 o 48 meses para devolverlo.

32

A Final Look at Mastering the Sounds of Spanish

Learning the sound system of a new language is difficult for the average adult learner for one broad, all-encompassing and compelling reason: the native sound system is so ingrained in the learner that it constantly interferes with his or her efforts to acquire the foreign system. Thus the vast majority of pronunciation errors a language learner makes are predictable if one just examines the sound systems of the native language and the target language beforehand and focuses on the differences. This has been one of the main tasks of this book.

As we focus on these differences, we soon see that many, if not most, of the sounds of the target language are different in quality from those of the learner's native language. Not only that, but the few sounds that may be similar or even exactly the same are distributed differently and/or function differently. For example, English has an unaspirated [p] just as Spanish does but only within a word after /s/. However, in Spanish, all /p/ sounds are unaspirated, regardless of their phonetic environment. So you, as an English-speaking learner of Spanish, will undoubtedly sound the unaspirated [p] properly in the word **español**, where it follows /s/, but maybe not in a word like **paño**, where it is word-initial. The phonemic sets of the native and target language just don't match up neatly. Based on such contrastive analysis, the following six areas are where the average English speaker can expect to encounter problems in his or her efforts to master the sound system of Spanish.

I The Sounds of the Target Language Do Not Exist in the Native Language.

This is theoretically the most difficult for obvious reasons. Occasionally these new and strange sounds do not prove very difficult for some of you, but usually they do for the majority of you.

1. Probably the hardest Spanish sound for the typical English speaker is the trilled alveolar [r̄], which does not exist in any dialect of North American English

(although speakers of British and Scottish English occasionally use it for emphasis). One common mistake of English speakers is to substitute the friendlier tap [r], but this can create phonemic confusion: the adjective **caro** is not the noun **carro,** and the imperfect tense verb form **quería** is not the same as the conditional form **querría**.

2. Spanish light alveolar [l], with the tongue dorsum raised rather than lowered, is rare in English, although a similar *l*-sound can be heard at the beginning of a syllable. But at the end of syllables the normal English *l* is dark, that is, velarized [ɫ], and, although there is no phonemic confusion, this sound is quite prominent and unacceptable in Spanish in place of the light [l] in any phonetic environment.

3. The Spanish voiceless velar fricative [x] does not exist in North American English. Very often you substitute what you intuitively feel is the nearest sound. If you choose [h], of course, there is no problem since this is the sound used for **jota** by millions of Spanish speakers. But if you choose [k], phonemic confusion results: **vaca** is not **baja**, **curar** is not **jurar**, and so forth. Fortunately, the use of glottal [h] is an easy acceptable solution for those of you who simply cannot articulate a very good velar **jota**.

4. The Spanish voiced bilabial fricative [β] does not exist in English. Many of you choose a solution that is very noticeable although acceptable phonemically. In words spelled with **b** you may pronounce a stop [b], which can sound overly emphatic in a word like **abuela**, for example. In words spelled with a **v** you may pronounce the labio-dental [v], which is also occasionally heard in Spanish. The problem with this latter solution is that such a pronunciation may mislead you into thinking that Spanish speakers do this, too, and when you hear a word with the bilabial fricative [β], you may mistakenly think it must be spelled with **v**. Thus you may think that an unfamiliar phrase, like **la barca**, for example, must be spelled ***la varca**.

II The Sounds of the Native Language Do Not Exist in the Target Language.

This category represents almost as much a problem as the first one. In this case, you incorrectly intersperse your own native sounds in Spanish, creating a foreign accent once again, but for a slightly different reason.

1. The aspirated word-initial stops of English [pʰ tʰ kʰ] do not exist in Spanish, and their use in Spanish is conspicuous.

2. English retroflex [ɹ] does not exist in Spanish and its use is equally noticeable.

3. English dark velarized [ɫ] does not exist in Spanish, and its use is one of the most telling and unpleasant sounding features of an English accent.

4. The English open mid back vowel [ɔ] does not exist in Spanish, being a sound almost intermediate between the mid back [o] and the low central [a] of Spanish.

Thus its use, especially when stressed, obscures the difference between dozens of pairs of words, such as **hombre–hambre, lona–lana, cosa–casa**, and so forth.

5. English words are often separated or at least marked in the stream of speech by a pause-like feature called plus juncture /+/, a slight pause, or even a glottal stop. Since word boundaries within the phonemic phrase in Spanish are virtually meaningless—mainly because of **enlace**—any attempt to observe them in the above ways distorts the rhythm in an unnatural way. This is particularly done by English speakers in the case of contiguous identical vowels: **de español** is *[deʔes-pa-ñól] rather than [des-pa-ñól], **va a hablar** is *[váʔaʔa-blár] rather than [bá-ɸlár].

6. The most important English sound, however, which should never be used in Spanish is the mid central vowel, schwa [ə], as in *appear*, and its close counterpart, the high central vowel, barred *i* [ɨ], as in *sal̲a̲d*. These two vowels, of course, are characteristic of most unstressed syllables in English, but neither exists in Spanish. Not only do they create a foreign accent, but they blur many important grammatical contrasts: **daría** and **diría** sound alike when [ə] or [ɨ] is used in the first syllable of each, and likewise when either is used in the last syllable of **dieron** and **dieran**, for example. This may be the most noticeable and distracting feature of an English accent in Spanish.

7. The low front vowel [æ] of all dialects of English is commonly heard as the first sound of the diphthong [æw] throughout the eastern United States, Midlands, and South in such words as *town, mouse, round*. Since this vowel does not exist in Spanish, its use as the first part of the diphthong of words like **causa** and **aunque** is extremely noticeable.

8. English typically elongates all vowels and diphthongs before voiced consonants in a noticeable, although non-phonemic, manner. Compare the short and lengthened vowels in the following pairs in English: *sat–sad, face–faze, buck–bug, rip–rib, rich–ridge,* and so forth. Spanish vowels have the same length whether they precede voiceless or voiced consonants and whether they are stressed or unstressed. Lengthening the vowels of such words as **sí, sin, di, sal̲i̲r, ard̲i̲d** makes not only the individual vowels sound wrong, but adversely affects the rhythm of Spanish.

III The Phonemes of the Native Language Exist in the Target Language As Allophones.

What is meant by this category is that sounds in English that are contrastive and thus phonemic exist in Spanish but as allophones of one phoneme. This category is not nearly as serious a problem for you as learners of Spanish as it is for Spanish speakers learning English—simply because English has more phonemes than Spanish. You, as an English speaker, unnecessarily distinguish sound varieties in Spanish, which the Spanish speaker accepts as the same, perhaps without even realizing that they may be different. But this requires unnecessary effort on your part, and sometimes even causes you to think that certain Spanish sounds are wrong or characteristic of uneducated speech. But the Spanish speaker, to communicate properly in English, must learn to make another dozen or so contrasts that involve Spanish sounds that he/she has been considering basically the same.

1. The sounds [b] and [v] are phonemic in English (thus /b/ and /v/), as in *berry–very*, *verb–verve*, but Spanish [b] and bilabial [β̸], a near equivalent to labio-dental [v] are simply positional allophones of /b/, whose occurrence is predictable by a phonological rule stating the phonetic environments for both. The Spanish speaker has trouble distinguishing *berry* from *very*, *TV* from *TB*, and so forth, but the English speaker feels that there must be a difference between **tuvo** and **tubo** because of the spelling and may even feel that the stop [b] heard in a word like **enviar** is incorrect because it is spelled with a **v**.

2. The very same situation exists with English [d] and [ð], as in *ladder– lather* (thus /d/ and /ð/). But the corresponding sounds in Spanish, [d] and [đ], are once again positional allophones. The Spanish speaker confuses English words like *den* and *then*, but in your case there may be confusion of meaning. This is because a post-tonic (after the stress) /d/ in English is usually realized as a flap [d̂], as in *bidder* or *Canada,* and this sound is almost exactly the same as the Spanish tap [r]. Thus you may make **todo** sound like **toro**, **cada** sound like **cara**, and so forth. Notice that this is really a problem of *distribution*, since the proper sound exists in English as [ð]. But you may associate this sound only with the letters *th*, and thus do *not* expect to have to use it in words like **todo** and **cada**. The sounds in question exist in both languages; but they are distributed differently and function differently.

3. A very similar situation exists with English [y] and [ǰ], as in *yellow–jello* (thus /y/ and /ǰ/). The corresponding sounds in Spanish, [y] and [ŷ], are positional allophones and are also sometimes in free variation, depending on the emphasis desired. The Spanish speaker confuses English words like *yet* and *jet*, but you may feel that perhaps it is incorrect to use the affricate [ŷ] or even that its use can change the meaning of a word when used instead of [y]. You may feel that the word **yo** with this sound is somehow significantly different from the word **yo** with just [y]. Because of this basically distributional problem, the Spanish speaker misses the meaning, and you either waste effort overdistinguishing or acquire a mistaken notion about the Spanish language.

4. The same situation exists with English [s] and [z], as in *sue–zoo* (thus /s/ and /z/). The exact same sounds in Spanish are positional allophones and also occur according to the speech style. The Spanish speaker thus confuses English words like *fussy* and *fuzzy*, whereas you may feel that there is some significant difference between these sounds in Spanish. The word **mismo** said with a [z], instead of an [s], immediately attracts your attention whereas the Spanish speaker is hard pressed to hear the difference between the word with an [s] and with a [z]. In addition, you may correlate the sound [z] with the letter **z**, as in **zapato** or **caza**, which, of course, is completely wrong since the **z** in these words represents [s] in **seseo** and [θ] in **distinción**. However, there really is a [z] in the word **hallazgo**, but now because

of regressive assimilation, not spelling. This contrast, by the way, remains the most difficult and recalcitrant for a Spanish speaker. Even Hispanics who speak fluent and grammatically correct English—as a *second* language—usually pronounce such English words as *result, easy,* and *proposal* with [s] instead of [z].

5. However, the situation with the fricative sounds, [ž], as in *treasure*; [y], as in *layer;* [š], as in *pressure;* and the affricate [ĉ], as in *catcher*, is slightly different. The first sound exists in many dialects of Spanish in words like **ayer, llamar, pollo, raya**, but as an allophone of /y/. In English, however, this sound, [ž], contrasts with the second sound, [y], as in *pleasure* and *player.* Thus you may feel that Argentine **žeísmo**, with its [ž], is a strange-sounding dialect. Also you may feel that the use of the third sound, [š], instead of the fourth sound, [ĉ], in words like **chico** and **leche**, as heard in such Caribbean countries as Puerto Rico, Cuba, Venezuela, and Panama, is somehow strange or even incorrect because of the contrast in English of these two sounds, as in *sheep* and *cheap.* Thus all four of these sounds, [ž y š ĉ], exist in both languages, but the first two are allophones of the same phoneme all over the Spanish-speaking world, and last two are allophones of the same phoneme in many parts of the Caribbean. Spanish speakers find the new contrasts difficult, if not impossible at first, and English speakers feel that the use of these sounds in many cases is at least strange-sounding, if not incorrect.

IV Allophones in the Native Language Are Phonemes in the Target Language.

This is the smallest category but one of the most critical for English speakers learning Spanish.

1. English flap or tap [t̂] and [d̂], as in *latter–ladder* or *writer–rider,* are allophones of the stops /t/ and /d/, respectively, but both of these sounds (whose difference is difficult to detect in English) are practically the same as Spanish tap [r]. This sound in Spanish contrasts with /t/ and /d/, as in **moro–moto–modo**. Thus the use of the English flap or tap sound may cause you to confuse words like **foro** and **foto**, or **cara** and **cada**, and dozens more exactly like them.

V Some Phonemes and Allophones in Both Languages Have Different Distributions.

This category is very similar to category III and even partially overlaps it. It is quite serious in nature, perhaps even more so than category I—target language sounds that do not exist in the learner's language.

1. As we illustrated above, English [s] and [z] are phonemic—thus /s/ and /z/—but these two silibants are positional variants in Spanish, depending both on the style of speech and the quality of the following consonant. English speakers frequently

use [z] in syllable-initial position, where it never occurs in most dialects of Spanish and just occasionally in a few dialects. This is done particularly in words spelled with **z**, like **zorro** or **azul**.

2. Sometimes consonants, such as nasals plus stops or fricatives, combine in English without any regressive assimilation. This is virtually always true when such consonants are juxtaposed at word boundaries: *tan goat* has a normal alveolar [n] at the end of the first syllable, despite the following velar [g], but *tango* has a velar [ŋ] at the end of the first syllable because of regressive assimilation—just as in Spanish. The word *ingrown* sometimes has assimilation—like *tango*—and sometimes it does not—like *tan goat*. This is because now, instead of the nasal and following velar consonant occurring at word boundaries or within a morpheme, they occur within a word at morpheme boundaries, a type of intermediate category. Thus you, as a typical English speaker, may or may not use assimilation in these combinations, which, however, in Spanish *always* have regressive assimilation, regardless of the presence of word or morpheme boundaries. In Spanish **tengo**, **engrasar**, and **en Granada** all have a velar [ŋ] at the end of the first syllable, despite the fact that the first one occurs within a morpheme, the second one between morphemes within a word, and the third one between words.

3. English has almost no words with a single stressed vowel in syllable-final position. Stressed vowels are practically always followed by one of the three glides or semi-vowels: /y w h/, as in *see* /síy/, *go* /gów/, *poor* /pÚh/ (in the *r*-less dialects of New England, for example), or a consonant, thus closing the syllable, as in *sit* or *put*. Thus English speakers frequently add the corresponding semi-vowels [i̯ u̯] to stressed vowels in Spanish, as in **sí, yo, sé, tú**, saying *[síi̯], *[yóu̯], *[séi̯], and *[tʰuu̯], instead of the correct monophthongal [sí], [yó], [sé], and [tú], respectively. Spanish has two of the same diphthongal combinations as English—mainly /ei/— but they are *always* represented in writing and contrast with their monophthongal counterparts, as in **reino–reno** or **veinte–vente**, for example. The English diphthongs of [ii̯] and [uu̯] could also be included in category II, English sounds that do not exist in Spanish.

4. The English pattern of /CwV/, as in *swim*, is restricted in the sense that only certain consonants, such as /s g t /, for example, occur as C. The English solution for this combination in foreign borrowings with other consonants at the beginning is to insert the vowel /u/, turning it into /CuV/, as in *Rwanda, Bwana, pueblo*. Thus Spanish **fuera** becomes *[fu-é-ra], **pueblo** becomes *[pʰu-é-blo], instead of the correct [fu̯é-ra] and [pu̯é-β̸lo].

5. Spanish has hiatus (two syllable) and diphthong (one syllable) combinations for the same groups of vowels: **aun** (diphthong) versus **aún** (hiatus), **ley** (diphthong) versus **leí** (hiatus), **aula** (diphthong) versus **aúlla** (hiatus). But hiatus occurs only when the /í/ or /ú/ is stressed. Many English speakers, however, extend the hiatus pronunciation to Spanish diphthongs, mistakenly saying *[a-úŋ-ke] for **aunque**, or *[a-di-ós] for **adiós**, *[r̃e-í-na] for **reina**, *[de-ú-da] for **deuda**, and so forth.

This is done particularly when the diphthong is opening, that is, when the semi-vowel comes before, rather than after, the strong vowel.

6. Both English and Spanish use heavy stresses to distinguish meaning, but Spanish rarely puts a heavy stress on phrase-bound forms, such as definite articles, short prepositions, and object pronouns. English speakers often carry over their natural stress pattern, and, thinking of an English sentence such as "He didn't ask **you**, he asked **me**!", try to say ***No te lo pregunté, me lo pregunté**, not realizing that the Spanish solution for stressing such phrase-bound forms is a complete recasting of the sentence: **No te lo pregunté a ti, me lo pregunté a mí.**

VI   Miscellaneous Influences of the Native Language on the Target Language

Some sound problems are difficult to classify according to the above categories, but they are just as serious nonetheless.

1. The pronunciation of cognate words in Spanish is frequently influenced by their English counterparts. An unwanted [i] is inserted between the /C/ and the /u/ of such words as **ridículo, regular, peculiar**, because of *ridiculous, regular, peculiar* in English. Spanish dental and alveolar sounds are incorrectly palatalized before [i], as in **gracias, cordial, situar**, because this happens in English, as in *gracious, cordial, situate*. The vowel /a/ may be used in Spanish words with /o/, like **oficina, hospital, próspero** because of *office, hospital, prosperous*. And the stress is frequently misplaced in words like **deposito, comunica, acróbata, antídoto** because of English *deposit, communicate, acrobat, antidote*.

2. English pitch level /4/, used mainly for emphasis and contrast, is transferred to Spanish, where it is not really a discrete pitch level but the paralinguistic feature of overhigh, reflecting more about the speaker and the situation than the elements of the sentence being uttered. English pitch level /3/, normal at the end of statements, sounds too emphatic in Spanish because that is exactly its role in the Spanish intonational system, which has only three pitch phonemes /1 2 3/.

3. English has an uneven stress-timed rhythm with the interplay of long and short syllables, whereas Spanish has an even, legato, syllable-timed rhythm in which most of the syllables are of the same or nearly the same length. Not only does the English rhythm sound foreign in Spanish, but a concomitant feature is the use of the neutral vowel [ə], which can blur many crucial phonemic distinctions, thus changing lexical meaning (**calor** is not **color**) and grammatical categories, such as masculine versus feminine with adjectives (**generoso** is not **generosa**), preterit versus past subjunctive with verbs (**hablaron** is not **hablaran**), or present versus present subjunctive with verbs (**ayudan** is not **ayuden**).

4. Many North American students, for a variety of reasons, attempt to use **distinción** as it is used natively in Spain. Often at first, however, they (just as many Southern Spaniards) confuse /s/ and /θ/, typically substituting the former for the latter

incorrectly, as in the word **oficina**, saying [o-fi-sí-na]. Although this is not really wrong in the sense that most of the errors we have been discussing are wrong, it is regarded as an error coming from a North American in Spain. It is far better to opt for complete **seseo** and have a Spaniard wonder why you aren't using **distinción** than to try and fail to use **distinción** properly.

5. English has four stress phonemes / ´ ^ ` ˘ / , but Spanish has only two / ´ ˘ /, the weak one left unmarked in a phonetic or phonemic transcription. If you use all four degrees of stress while speaking Spanish, you are deforming the rhythm of Spanish, causing the words and phrases to have an uneven and choppy sound.

6. English can end a yes-or-no question with falling intonation and a terminal fall / ↓ /, particularly a long question. This can be done because English inverted word order immediately signals a yes-or-no question, and even though the voice more often rises, it can also drop in a question like, ''Were there many people at the party when you got there?'' / ↓ / However, this is impossible in Spanish since pitch alone usually is the principal way to signal such a question: **¿Había muchas personas en la fiesta cuando llegaste?** / ↑ / This same utterance, said with a terminal fall / ↓ / not only is a statement rather than a question, but it also probably makes your Hispanic friend wonder why you are telling him something he already knows.

7. Spanish typically uses a falling intonation and terminal fall / ↓ / with short elements that follow longer sentences: vocatives and tag phrases. English, however, prefers a terminal rise / ↑ / for such elements: ''Mary Ellen, please.'' / ↑ / (on the telephone) or ''Good morning, Frederick.'' / ↑ /. Thus, these rises, instead of terminal falls, are incorrectly carried over into equivalent sentences in Spanish: **María Elena, por favor; Buenos días, Federico.**

The above errors, of course, vary in the degree to which they interfere with communication and the role they play in the creation of an annoying or distracting foreign accent. This in itself interferes with communication in the social realm, often just as important as the linguistic realm. In your efforts to communicate, you are very interested in having your interlocutor attend to *what* you are saying, *not* to the *way* you are saying it. Naturally, not all of you make all or perhaps most of these errors as you are learning Spanish and starting to communicate with native speakers. Many of you just have a good ear and have been able to handle these problems quite easily—perhaps without expending a great deal of effort. But not all learners of a language are that fortunate. Some learners, in fact, feel that they will never be able to overcome these problems and give up too soon. The fundamental premise of this book is that there is always a chance if you know what the problems are beforehand, what the solutions are, and if you are willing to expend the time and effort to overcome these obstacles.

Fortunately, also, not all stumbling blocks are of equal difficulty and equal importance. For example, although Spanish fricative [β] does not exist in English, it is not a particularly difficult sound for you to articulate. Then, since stop [b] in its place is quite noticeable to Spanish speakers, you should make every effort to use the fricative sound in the proper places even though this has no effect on meaning at any time. On the other hand, although assimilating syllable-final nasals to the following consonant is the norm in Spanish, failure to do so rarely impedes communication and perhaps even goes unnoticed by the Spanish speaker. So an error of this nature is far lower on the scale of importance than the failure to use fricative [ƀ].

Following, then, is a different type of classification of these problem areas and the typical errors of English speakers learning Spanish. This classification is based on their degree of importance in acquiring a good Spanish accent.

Class A errors have the highest priority and, thus, demand the greatest effort and attention on your part—either because they involve sounds that are the most difficult for you to pronounce or because making them properly is essential to the acquisition of a good Spanish accent. These errors can seriously impede communication—either because a phonemic contrast is not observed or because they simply sound annoying or distracting to the native Spanish speaker. We will call them "critical."

Class B errors involve sounds that, while not natural at first for you as an English speaker to make, are not particularly difficult to articulate properly with a modicum of attention and practice. In addition, although failure to make these sounds properly is quite noticeable to the Spanish-speaking listener, it is not overly annoying or distracting. We will call them "serious but non-critical."

Class C errors involve sounds that are easy and natural for you to make once you realize that you should do so. In addition, failure to make them properly is probably ignored by the Spanish speaker, perhaps not even noticed. Some of these errors, although interesting for theoretical reasons, are trivial in the overall picture. One can call the mastery of these points "frosting on the cake," so to speak, since you can still sound relatively good in Spanish while occasionally making these slips. But if you can master all of these finer points, as well as those in Classes A and B, you will have acquired an authentic native-like accent—presumably the goal of all serious students of a foreign language. We will call them "important but not serious."

The list of errors in each class is not ordered since any of them may have a different degree of difficulty for any given speaker. The errors and the correct forms should be clear by now without a great deal of explanation and illustration. If you wish to review them, use the boldface indicators in brackets that follow each one to find them in the above contrastive classification.

Class A Errors—Critical

1. Substituting the neutral English vowels [ə ɨ] for unstressed Spanish vowels, thus blurring both lexical and grammatical contrasts, in addition to sounding conspicuously foreign: as in **sociedad–suciedad, anhelar–anular, pasaron–pasaran, hermana–hermano.** **[II]**
2. The use of English velarized or dark [ɫ] in place of the alveolar or light Spanish [l], especially in word-final position: as in **tal, hotel, mal.** **[I, II]**

3. Observing word boundaries in the stream of speech, with pauses or glottal stops. This is particularly true with contiguous identical vowels: as in **de español, va a hablar**. This, too, has a very damaging effect on the proper Spanish rhythm.   **[II]**

4. The use of the English aspirated stops [pʰ tʰ kʰ], especially in word-initial position, as in **paño, toma, cosa**. This is extremely conspicuous in Spanish.   **[II]**

5. The use of typical English galloping stress-timed rhythm rather than the smooth, legato, syllable-timed rhythm of Spanish. This is caused by the elongation of the stressed syllables, the shortening of the unstressed syllables, the replacement of many of these unstressed syllables with [ə] or [ɨ], and the use of the two intermediate degrees of stress—neither of which exists in Spanish.   **[VI]**

6. The use of the English flap [t̂ d̂] in place of Spanish intervocalic [t ð]. This usually causes a change in meaning, because the English sounds are really [r] in Spanish: as in **cata–cara, codo–coro**.   **[III, IV]**

7. The use of English retroflex [ɹ] in place of the Spanish tap /r/ and trilled /r̄/. Not only does it sound wrong, but it can blur meaning contrast: **caro–carro, enterado–enterrado**.   **[I, II]**

8. Adding semi-vowels or glides to all stressed vowels, as in **sí, sé, tú, yo**. Not only does this sound wrong in Spanish, but in the case of /e/ it blurs the contrast between **le–ley, pena–peina, vente–veinte**.   **[V]**

Class B Errors—Serious, but Non-Critical

1. Elongating all stressed vowels, particularly [a], as in **casa** *[ká:-sa]. Not only does this sound wrong, but it has a damaging effect on the even rhythm of Spanish.   **[II]**

2. The use of English vowels that do not exist in Spanish, such as [ɔ æ], blurring meaning distinctions—as in **hombre–hambre**—or creating strange-sounding diphthongs—as in **causa**, with [æu̯] in the first syllable rather than [au̯].   **[II]**

3. The misplacement of stress in cognate words: **imagino, deposito, acróbata, antídoto, demócrata**.   **[VI]**

4. Turning a diphthong into two syllables, particularly when the diphthong begins with the semi-vowel, as in **fuera, adiós**.   **[V]**

5. The use of Spanish tap /r/ in place of the trilled /r̄/, thus blurring contrasts like **caro–carro, enterado–enterrado**.   **[I]**

6. Stressing phrase-bound unstressed forms to show contrast or emphasis, as in ***La vi** instead of **La vi a ella** for "I saw **her**."   **[V]**

7. The use of occlusive [b d g] instead of the fricative [β ð ǥ], particularly in the intervocalic position. This makes these words sound unnecessarily emphatic in Spanish: as in **abuela, hablado, hago**.   **[I]**

8. Failure to use the appropriate terminal rise / ↑ / at the end of an ordinary yes-or-no question, especially a long one. Although English normally uses a rise here, too, the voice can drop since the opening inverted word order indicates question:

"Are there . . .?" versus "There are . . . ." Failure to end such questions in Spanish with rising intonation usually turns them into statements. **[VI]**

9. The use of all four English stresses, especially in long words, such as **responsabilidad** and **generalización**. This gives the words a strange galloping effect rather than the smooth even sound they should have. **[VI]**

10. The use of pitch level /4/, which is emphatic in English, but paralinguistic or extralinguistic in Spanish. Also the use of pitch level /3/, normal at the end of a statement in English, but emphatic in Spanish. This gives the learner's Spanish an excited, overly enthusiastic, and even affected cast. **[V, VI]**

Class C Errors—Important but not Serious

1. The confusion of /θ/ and /s/, usually because the learner is trying to make **distinción.** **[VI]**

2. The use of [s] instead of the voiced [z] before voiced consonants, in such pairs as **este–es de, rascar–rasgar.** This removes one way of distinguishing the following consonants, which often sound the same to English speakers. **[III, V]**

3. The use of a terminal rise / ↑ / after vocatives and tag phrases, as in **María Elena, por favor; Buenos días, Federico.** This often lends an overly interested or ingratiating tone to the learner's Spanish. **[VI]**

4. The failure to assimilate nasals to the following consonants, as in **un peso, un chico, un gato.** This often causes the learner to wonder about spelling, and to waste time and effort in trying to pronounce an [n] rather than [m]. **[V]**

To repeat our opening assertion in this book, there is a widespread misconception that Spanish is the easiest of all foreign languages for English speakers to learn. This is based on three principal factors. English has so many cognates with Spanish (**animal, televisión**). English now also has so many borrowings from Spanish (**sombrero, rodeo, fajitas**). But the main reason is the fact that Spanish spelling represents the spoken language so much more accurately and consistently than that of other languages commonly studied by North Americans, to say nothing of the English orthographical system, probably the worst of all.

Actually the Spanish *sound system* itself is as inherently difficult for North Americans as that of any other commonly studied European language and that of many non-European languages as well. But, nonetheless, with systematic and concerted effort—plus practice, practice, practice!—you can master it.

Review and Discussion

1. What is one main reason that makes learning the sound system of a new language difficult for the average learner?

2. If there are certain Spanish sounds that you feel you just cannot pronounce properly, at least for now, do you have to give up and do the best you can, or is there sometimes a viable solution?

3. Theoretically, who has a tougher time learning the sound system of the target language—you as a learner of Spanish or a Spanish speaker learning English? Why?

4. Which pronunciation mode of Spanish—**seseo** or **distinción**—do you think should be taught in North American schools and colleges? Support your opinion. Which one do you want to learn? Why?

5. Some native speakers of Spanish pronounce an intervocalic /s/ as [z] in some words, such as **pre̱sente, ha̱ce.** Why, then, won't your instructor let you get away with it in words like **re̱sidencia, propó̱sito, mo̱zo**?

6. How many English sounds can you name that for all practical purposes are exactly the same in Spanish? Does this mean you can just use them freely in Spanish and devote no more time or attention to them?

7. Do you think speakers of other languages make the same or similar pronunciation mistakes in Spanish that you do? Can you name a language where they do, and explain why? Can you name a language whose speakers might make *different* errors than you do and explain why?

8. What is the hardest Spanish sound or sound pattern to pronounce for you personally?

9. What is your most common pronunciation error in Spanish? Is it the same sound that you listed above in question 8? If not, why not?

10. Exactly what can you do to overcome the problems you mentioned in questions 8 and 9 above?

11. Do you consider acquiring an absolutely authentic Spanish accent of great importance for you personally? Why or why not?

12. Suppose you already have an authentic Spanish accent—either as a Spanish student who speaks another language natively or as a native speaker of Spanish. Is most of the material presented in this book then irrelevant for you? Why or why not?

Appendix A
Glossary of Linguistic Terms

*This glossary has three functions: (1) it provides the Spanish equivalent for the specialized, technical, and important terms found in capital letters in the text; (2) it gives a definition and/or explanation of these terms so it can serve as a quick reference section; (3) it can also be used as a study guide for test review. The first section is **English–Spanish** and includes the definitions and explanations; the second section, **Spanish–English**, omits obvious cognates. Important occurrences of the term are indicated by chapter numbers in brackets after the definition.*

English–Spanish

absolute initial **(posición) inicial absoluta**   The first sound of a breath group, that is, the first sound after a pause. [12, 13, 20]

acoustic phonetics **fonética acústica**   The study of speech sounds, their physical properties, their transmission, and their perception by the listener. [11, 12]

adjective **adjetivo**   A part of speech that modifies a noun and always carries a primary stress in the stream of speech in Spanish. [6]

adverb **adverbio**   A part of speech that modifies a verb and always carries a primary stress in the stream of speech in Spanish. [6]

affricate **(consonante) africada**   A consonant that starts as a stop and finishes as a fricative. [11]

allophone **alófono (variante fonética)**   An individual sound realization of a phoneme. [12]

alphabet **alfabeto**   The letters used in the writing system of a language. [2]

alphabetic writing **escritura alfabética**   A writing system that uses letters as symbols to represent the individual sounds of the language. [2]

alternate information question **pregunta alterna de información (pregunta pronominal alterna)**   A question that begins with an interrogative word, such as **qué, dónde, cómo,** which requests new information in its place. [7]

alternate statement **aseveración (afirmación) alterna**   An alternate statement, with another possible pitch level for the last stressed syllable: /2 2 1 ↓ / instead of /2 1 1 ↓ /. [7]

alternate yes-or-no question **pregunta alterna de sí o no (pregunta absoluta alterna)**
An alternate yes-or-no question with another possible pitch level for the last syllable:
/2 2 3 ↑/ instead of /2 2 2 ↑/. [7]

alveolar **alveolar**   The point of articulation produced with the tongue tip or blade against
the alveolar ridge, such as for [n]. [4, 11]

alveolar ridge **alvéolos**   The hard gum ridge immediately behind the upper front teeth.
[4]

alveolo-palatal **alveolopalatal**   The point of articulation produced with the blade of the
tongue against the point where the alveolar ridge meets the hard palate, such as for
[ĉ]. [11, 16, 25]

amplitude **amplitud**   The distance of the peaks of sound waves from point zero; the
sound wave property responsible for volume. [4]

Andalusian **andaluz**   From Andalusia, the region of Spain composed of the eight southern
provinces of Huelva, Sevilla, Cádiz, Málaga, Córdoba, Jaén, Granada, and Almería.
[3]

antepenult-stressed word **palabra esdrújula (palabra acentuada en la sílaba antepe-
núltima)**   A word stressed on the third-from-last syllable, such as **rápido**. [6]

article **artículo**   One subclass of the part of speech known as *determiner*, which modifies
a noun. [6]

articulatory description **descripción articulatoria**   A description of a language sound,
usually indicating its place and manner of articulation and whether it is voiced or
voiceless. [1, 11]

articulatory diagram **diagrama** (*m.*) **articulatorio**   Also called a *facial diagram,* a diagram of a side cutaway view of the vocal mechanism of a human being, typically
facing left. [11]

articulatory phonetics **fonética articulatoria**   The study of where and how speech sounds
are produced in the vocal tract. [2, 11]

aspiration **aspiración**   The puff of air expelled from the mouth during the articulation
of certain consonant sounds, like the initial [pʰ] in the English word *pill*, or the glottal
[h] for /s/ in the pronunciation of many Spanish speakers of the word e̲sto, for example.
[1, 12, 21]

assimilation **asimilación**   The process which causes one sound to take on some of the
characteristics of the one next to it. See also *mutual assimilation, progressive assimilation, regressive assimilation.* [20]

back vowel **vocal** (*f.*) **posterior**   A vowel, such as [u] or [o], pronounced with the tongue
retracted from a neutral position. [14]

Balearic Islands **Islas Baleares**   The Spanish islands of Ibiza, Mallorca, and Menorca,
located in the Mediterranean off the eastern coast of Spain. [3]

Basque **vasco**; **vascuence** (*m.* noun referring to the language)   The name of the ethnic
and linguistic group in north central Spain and their language. [3]

bilabial **bilabial**   The point of articulation produced with maximum closure by the two lips, such as for [b]. [11]

bilabiovelar **bilabiovelar**   The articulation, [w], produced with near closure by the two lips and also by the back of the tongue, which approaches the velum. [11]

blade of the tongue **predorso (corona) de la lengua**   The small area of the tongue between the tip and the dorsum. [4]

bound form **forma ligada**   A word that is never uttered alone but always accompanied by another part of speech, and, thus, normally does not take a primary stress in Spanish. [6]

break(ing) **hablar con voz quebrada (voz interrupta)**   A sound produced by the rapid opening and closing of the vocal bands with a series of relatively violent expulsions of the airstream and resulting sound waves, as in both laughing and crying. [9]

breath group **grupo fónico**   The stream of sounds occurring between two pauses. [13, 20]

bronchial tubes **bronquios**   The two tubes that connect the lungs to the trachea or ''windpipe'' in an inverted ''Y'' configuration. [4]

Canary Islands **Islas Canarias**   The Spanish islands of La Palma, Hierro, Gomera, Tenerife, Gran Canaria, Lanzarote, and Fuerteventura, located in the Atlantic Ocean off the coast of Morocco in northwestern Africa. [3]

capital **mayúscula**   Upper case letter. [13]

Castilian **castellano**   The Spanish language itself; also specifically the national standard dialect of Spain, spoken natively in central and northern Spain, as opposed to Andalusian (**andaluz**) or Mexican Spanish, for example. [1]

Catalan **catalán**   A Romance language spoken in northeastern and eastern Spain, including the Balearic Islands. [3]

ceceo *lisping*   The speech mode heard in Andalusian Spanish in which /s/ and /θ/ fail to contrast, the latter sound usually replacing the former. See ***distinction*** and **seseo**. [24, 31]

central vowel **vocal (*f.*) central**   A vowel articulated with the tongue in a neutral or central position with respect to the front and back of the mouth. [14]

chanting **hablar con sonsonete**   The vocal mode in which a succession of evenly timed syllables or words are produced at almost the same pitch and volume. [9]

chart **cuadro (gráfica, diagrama *m.*)**   A graphic display of information in tabular form, often divided into columns, rows, boxes, or the like. [11]

choice question **pregunta de selección múltiple**   A question in which two or more items or choices for the answer are given to one's interlocutor. [7]

''clear'' l **la *l* ''clara'' (alveolar)**   The [l] heard in Spanish, articulated with the tip of the tongue against the alveolar ridge and the tongue body relatively high with the sides touching the upper molars. The airstream passes around one or both sides of the tongue. [27]

click **chasquido (sonido ingresivo)**   A sound produced by sucking the air into the mouth as the tongue is released sharply from one of the upper articulators, rather than by expelling the air, as is normally done for most speech sounds. [9]

clipping **hablar con sílabas acortadas**   The vocal mode in which the sound is abruptly cut short at the end of each word, usually to express impatience, anger, or displeasure. [9]

closed syllable **sílaba trabada**   A syllable that ends in a consonant. [13, 20]

cluster **grupo consonántico**   Two or more consonants in the same syllable, either the beginning or the end of the syllable. Spanish clusters always have two consonants [13]

cognate **cognado (palabra cognada)**   A word in one language related to a word in another, usually of similar orthographic appearance although not necessarily similar in sound, and often meaning almost the same thing: **animal**–*animal*, **composición**–*composition*. [1, 19]

command **mandato**   A type of sentence in which the speaker tells his or her interlocutor to do something (or not to do it). [7]

complementary distribution **distribución complementaria**   The name given to the predictable occurrence of the allophones of one phoneme. [12]

complex vowel nucleus **núcleo vocálico complejo**   A syllable with two or three vowels, that is, a diphthong or triphthong, respectively. [14]

compound **vocablo compuesto**   A word composed of two words; the resulting meaning is sometimes not merely the sum of the meanings of each word or at least is not always immediately clear to the foreign listener, like Spanish **guardapolvo** *smock* (''dust-guard''), or English *whistle-blower.* [6]

condition **restricción**   The specific terms of a phonological rule, often indicated by superscribed or subscribed numbers or special symbols. [16]

confirmation yes-or-no question **pregunta de sí o no (pregunta absoluta) para confirmar**   A question requesting either an affirmative or a negative answer, but one in which the asker already expects a certain answer or one which indicates surprise or disagreement. [7]

conjunction **conjunción**   A part of speech used to join elements of a sentence. It may be *coordinating*, such as **y**, or it may be *subordinating,* such as **que**. [6]

conjunctive pronoun **pronombre clítico (pronombre conjunto)**   An object pronoun (direct, indirect, or reflexive), which is bound in the sense that it is never said alone but either before a verb as a separate word (**Lo vi**), or after a verb as part of one word (**Voy a verlo**). [6]

consonant **consonante** (*f.*)   A sound articulated when the airstream is blocked, impeded, or obstructed in some way as it leaves the vocal tract. [11]

consonant cluster **grupo consonántico**   Two or more consonants in the same syllable, either at the beginning or the end. Spanish clusters are always composed of two consonants. [13, 20]

consonant neutralization **neutralización consonántica**   The name for the loss of contrast between two phonemes. Consonant neutralization in Spanish always takes place in the syllable-final position, that is, either before another consonant or a pause. [29]

contrastive **contrastivo**   The characteristic of two sounds that are phonemic and, thus, determine meaning. [5]

coordinated elements **elementos coordinados**   Coordinated elements can be individual words (**papel y lápiz**), phrases (**con leche o sin leche**), or clauses (**Voy a la Oficina de la Decana, y voy a tratar de verla.**), all separated by coordinating conjunctions. [7]

cps **ciclos por segundo**   A sound wave's rise from point 0, its fall to 0 and below, and subsequent return to 0 is one complete cycle (see Diagram 2 in Chapter 4); the number of cycles of sound waves is their frequency, which, in turn, creates pitch. The more cycles per second, the higher the pitch; the fewer, the lower the pitch. [4]

crying **llanto (lamento, grito)**   A paralinguistic manifestation, often characterized by vocal breaking and extreme prolongation of syllables. [9]

culture **cultura**   The term "culture with a small *c*" is an anthropological concept, that is, the totality of the patterns of human behavior that often differ markedly from one ethnic and linguistic group to another. [2]

Culture **Cultura**   "Culture with a capital *C*" is an esthetic concept and refers to the artistic and literary endeavors of a small minority of any speech community—art, poetry, sculpture, music, philosophy. [2]

cycles per second **ciclos por segundo**   See *cps.* [4]

dark l **la *l* oscura (velarizada)**   The [ɫ] heard in syllable-final position in English, articulated with little or no contact between the tongue and the upper articulators. The middle of the tongue dorsum is lowered or concave, and the very rear of the dorsum is raised toward the velum. [27]

decibel **decibel** (*m.*)   A unit to measure the loudness of a sound. [5]

defective distribution **distribución defectuosa**   The distribution of a phoneme that does not occur in certain expected environments, like /r/ in Spanish, which never occurs at the beginning of a word. [28]

demonstrative **demostrativo**   One subclass of the part of speech known as *determiner*, which modifies a noun. [6]

dental **dental**   The point of articulation in which the tongue tip or blade makes contact with the back surface of the upper front teeth, such as for Spanish [t]. [11]

descriptive approach **enfoque** (*m.*) **descriptivo**   The approach to the study of language that describes the sounds and structures of the language as objectively and scientifically as possible with no attempt to determine the so-called correctness of any of the described elements. See *prescriptive approach.* [2]

determiner **determinante** (*m.*)   A part of speech that modifies a noun (rather than describes it as adjectives do). [6]

devoiced vowel **vocal ensordecida**   A vowel, which is normally voiced, articulated without any vocal band vibration, i.e., voicing. [14]

devoicing **ensordecimiento**   The articulation of a normally voiced sound without any voicing, i.e., vocal band vibration. Both vowels and consonants can be devoiced. See also *devoiced vowel*. [9]

diacritic **signo diacrítico**   A special mark used in writing systems to indicate sound modifications that cannot be represented just by letters, such as the ˜ used over Spanish **ñ** or the / through [ɸ] to indicate a fricative. [12, 16]

dialect **dialecto**   A variety of a language determined either by regional-geographic or socio-educational considerations or both. [1, 3]

diaphragm **diafragma** (*m.*)   The muscular wall separating the lungs and chest cavity from the digestive organs of the abdomen. Along with the lungs, it controls respiration. [4]

digraph **digrama** (*m.*)   Two letters that represent only one sound. For example, in Spanish **ch** represents /ĉ/, and in English *th* represents /θ/ or /ð/. [13]

diphthong **diptongo**   The combination of two vowels in a single syllable. [6, 13]

discrete **discreto**   The term used to describe clearly identifiable and separable units in any classification system. The individual segmental sounds of any language are discrete in the sense that they can be identified and analyzed separately from all other sounds. [5, 9]

disjunctive pronoun **pronombre disyuntivo**   In Spanish subject pronouns, such as **yo**, **ella**, and prepositional object pronouns, such as **mí, ti, ellos**, are disjunctive in the sense that they can be used without verbs and are also able to take primary stresses. [6]

dissimilation **disimilación**   The phonological process in which a sound is modified to become *unlike* an adjoining sound, the opposite of *assimilation*, as in Spanish **conmigo** with an alveolar [n] rather than the expected bilabial [m]. [26]

distinction **distinción**   The phonemic contrast in Castilian Spanish between /s/ and /θ/, as in **casa–caza**, sometimes mistakenly referred to as **ceceo**, in which both words are said with /θ/. See **ceceo** and **seseo**. [3, 24, 31]

dorsum of the tongue **dorso de la lengua**   The top of the tongue from the blade back to the root. [4]

drawling **hablar con enunciación lenta (arrastrar las palabras)**   The elongation of stressed syllables. *Drawling* is not normally a paralinguistic manifestation, but rather a normal feature of some dialects. [9]

egressive **egresivo**   This describes the outward flow of air, the normal way of producing all sounds in most languages. See *click*. [9]

eliminated **(vocal) eliminada (elisión de vocales)**   The dropping or omission of a vowel, either within words as in **cree** [kré], or at word boundaries as in **la abuela** [la-ɸué-la]. [18]

elsewhere **en los demás casos**   This describes the so-called normal, typical, expected, default position of occurrence of an allophone, after the exceptions have been dealt with. "Elsewhere" is a more economical way of describing what may be many environments remaining after the fewer exceptions have been stated. [12]

emphatic information question **pregunta enfática de información (pronominal)**   A question that begins with an interrogative word like **quién** or **dónde** and is said with falling intonation. However, the final stressed syllable of the emphasized word rises to pitch level /3/ rather than dropping to /1/. [7]

emphatic statement **aseveración (afirmación) enfática**   A statement in which the final stressed syllable of the emphasized word—usually the last one in the statement—rises to pitch level /3/ rather than dropping to /1/. [7]

enumeration **enumeración**   The listing of a series of several items: **Vamos a ver—una ensalada para comenzar, pan, carne para el plato principal, vino tinto para acompañarlo, flan de postre y café y aguardiente para rematar la comida.** [7]

epiglottis **epiglotis** (*f.*)   The thin, cartilaginous structure that covers the glottis during swallowing so that food or liquid will enter the esophagus rather than the larynx and breathing passage. [4]

esophagus **esófago**   The food tube connecting the throat to the stomach. [4]

exclamative **(palabra) exclamativa**   A word expressing emotion or emphasis, always said with a primary stress and written with an accent in Spanish: **¡Cuánto te quiero!**, **¡Qué lindo!** [6, 31]

external juncture **juntura externa (terminación)**   The behavior of the voice at pauses in the discourse, that is, a slight change in pitch, volume, and tempo as the vocal bands stop vibrating or phonating momentarily: rising ↑ , falling ↓ , and sustained →. [5, 7]

extra-linguistic **extralingüístico**   See *paralanguage*. [7]

extra high (pitch level) **super alto**   In Spanish pitch level /3/, used for emphasis and contrast, is extra high. In English pitch level /4/ is extra high. [7]

eye dialect **escritura dialectal**   A deliberate misspelling of a common word—usually in a literary piece—meant to indicate that the speaker is either uneducated, uncouth, or is speaking a non-standard dialect. [23]

facial diagram **diagrama** (*m.*) **facial**   See *articulatory diagram*. [1, 11]

falling juncture **terminación (juntura) descendente**   See *external juncture*. [5, 7]

falsetto **falsete** (*m.*)   A paralinguistic manifestation consisting of an artificial extremely high-pitched way of speaking, usually done by men to imitate women or children. [9]

farewell **despedida**   A phrase used to bid someone good-bye, normally said in Spanish with mid pitch level /2/ and a falling juncture. See *leave-taking*. [7]

flap **vibrante** (*f.*) **simple**   A consonant sound produced when the tip of the tongue, under tension, strikes the alveolar ridge once as the airstream passes through, like Spanish [r]. [11]

free form **forma libre**   A word that can be uttered alone, unaccompanied by another part of speech, such as nouns, adjectives, verbs, adverbs, and subject pronouns, all of which for this very reason are capable of taking primary stress. [6]

free variation **variación libre (no funcional)**   The name given to the occurrence of either allophone of one phoneme, such as Spanish [ŷ] and [y], either of which can be used in virtually any word in which /y/ occurs—with no change in meaning. [12]

fricative **(consonante) fricativa**   A sound produced when the airstream is forced through a narrow opening without being stopped but with resulting friction. [11]

front vowel **vocal (*f.*) anterior**   A vowel pronounced with the tongue pushed forward from a neutral position, such as [i] or [e]. [14]

function of the vocal bands **función de las cuerdas vocales**   If the vocal bands are tense enough to vibrate as the airstream passes through the glottis, the resulting phonation or sound wave production is called voicing. [11, 20]

function word **palabra gramatical**   A part of speech used to connect the major parts of speech—nouns, verbs, adjectives, and adverbs, such as the Spanish coordinators (**y, o**), articles (**el, las**), subordinators (**que, si**), and prepositions (**en, a, con, sobre**). [6]

functional **funcional**   The characteristic of a sound that contrasts phonemically with another, such as voicing in Spanish (/p/–/b/, /t/–/d/, /k/–/g/, and so on). See *phonemic*. [6, 12]

fused **(vocales) fundidas (diptongadas)**   The combination of two (or three) vowels in the same syllable, thereby creating a diphthong (or triphthong). One vowel of a diphthong (and the first and last of a triphthong) is always the semi-vowel [i̯] or [u̯]. [18]

Galician-Portuguese **gallego-portugués**   Galician is a regional language spoken in northwestern Spain and can be lumped with Portuguese to form a larger language group known as Galician-Portuguese. [3]

General American Spanish **español americano general**   General American Spanish is a group of dialects spoken natively mainly in Mexico, Central America, and the Andean region of South America, but the term also characterizes the speech of many educated speakers all over Spanish America and is heard as the principal form on radio and television. [1, 3]

glide **semivocal (*f.*) (semiconsonante *f.*)**   See *semi-vowel*. [11]

glottal **glotal**   The point of articulation of the consonant [h], for example, produced as the airstream passes through the glottis and rubs the vocal bands, producing friction, but in this case without accompanying vibrations. [11]

glottal stop **oclusiva glotal**   A sound produced by sharply closing or catching the vocal bands. It is not a segmental sound in either Spanish or English, but is used in both languages as a paralinguistic sound feature. [9]

glottis **glotis (*f.*)**   The triangular opening between the vocal bands through which the airstream passes in breathing or speaking. [4]

greeting **saludo**   A word or phrase to greet someone or open a conversation. [7]

groove fricative **(consonante) fricativa acanalada**   Also called a sibilant, a whistling or hissing sound produced as the airstream passes through a narrow, elongated groove or rill in the tongue tip or blade, which is pressed against the upper teeth, alveolar ridge, or palate: [s] and [z], for example. [11]

group initial   See *absolute-initial.* [12, 13, 20]

heavy stress **acento primario**   Stress is the relative loudness of a vowel, when compared to others in the same word or in the stream of speech, a feature functional in Spanish: **habló** versus **hablo**. [6]

hertz **hercio** (also **hertzio**)   The term, named after the German physicist, Heinrich Hertz, is now used for *cps* or *cycles per second. See cps.* [4]

hiatus **hiato**   The occurrence of two contiguous vowels in two linked syllables rather than fused into one: **mío** [mí-o], **leo** [lé-o], **caer** [ka-ér], for example. [13]

hieroglyphics **jeroglíficos**   Pictures or icons that represent objects, people, or concepts rather than individual sounds, such as the writing used by the ancient Egyptians and the classical Mayans. See *ideographs.* [2]

high back glide **semivocal (semiconsonante) alta (cerrada) posterior**   A semi-vowel or semi-consonant, like Spanish [u̯] or English [w], articulated like the vowel [u], except that it cannot be stressed or syllabic and thus necessarily forms one part of a diphthong. [14]

high back vowel **vocal alta (cerrada) posterior**   A vowel like Spanish [u], articulated with the tongue retracted from a neutral position and high in the mouth, that is, relatively close to the velum. [14]

high central vowel **vocal alta (cerrada) central**   A vowel like the English vowel [ɨ], the "barred *i,*" articulated with the tongue in a front-to-back neutral position and high in the mouth, that is, relatively close to the palate. [6, 14]

high front glide **semivocal (semiconsonante) alta (cerrada) anterior**   A semi-vowel or semi-consonant, like Spanish [i̯] or English [y], articulated like the vowel [i], except that it cannot be stressed or syllabic and thus necessarily forms one part of a diphthong. [14]

high front vowel **vocal alta (cerrada) anterior**   A vowel like Spanish [i], articulated with the tongue pushed forward from a neutral position and high in the mouth, that is, relatively close to the alveolar ridge. [14]

high pitch level **nivel tonal alto**   The highest significant level of voice pitch—in Spanish level /3/, in English level /4/. [7]

high vowel **vocal alta (cerrada)**   A vowel like [i] or [u], articulated with the tongue high in the mouth, i.e., relatively close to the palate in the first case or the velum in the second. [14]

homorganic **homorgánico**   The term used to describe two or more sounds articulated at the same point of articulation, such as bilabial [m] and [b]. [26]

hypercorrection **ultracorrección**   A misguided effort made by educated speakers to make their speech "correct" by replacing seemingly incorrect forms with those deemed to be correct, such as the pronunciation of labio-dental [v] in Spanish in a word like **viene**. [22]

Hz **hercio** (also **hertzio**)   See *hertz.* [4]

ideograph **ideograma** (*m.*)   A symbol used to represent semantic concepts, like words or morphemes, rather than individual sounds as letters do. Chinese writing is ideographic. See *hieroglyphics.* [2]

illiterate **analfabeto**   One who, for a variety of reasons, does not write his or her own language (provided it has a writing system to begin with, of course). [2]

implosive **(consonante) implosiva**   A sound produced by drawing the airstream into the mouth and vocal tract rather than expelling it as is normally done for most segmental sounds in language. See *clicks* for one type of implosive sound. [9]

indigenous **indígena**   Native to the area. In this book *indigenous* means native American or ''Amerindian'' as opposed to Spanish or European. [3]

information question **pregunta de información (pronominal)**   A question that begins with an interrogative word, such as **qué, dónde, cómo,** which requests new information in its place. The normal intonation pattern is /2 1 1 ↓ /. See *emphatic information question.* [7]

ingressive **(consonante) ingresiva**   See *click* and *implosive.* [9]

intensity **intensidad**   The volume of a sound, created by the amplitude of the sound waves, i.e., the distance of the peaks from point zero (see Diagram 3 in Chapter 4). Its linguistic result is stress. [5]

interdental **interdental**   The point of articulation produced by placing the tip or blade of the tongue between the upper and lower front teeth, such as for [θ]. [11]

interjection **interjección**   A sound, word, or phrase uttered to express an emotion, such as **¡Dios!,** *Shoot!,* **¡Ayyy!,** or *Owww!* [9]

interlocutor **interlocutor(-a)**   The person to whom one addresses his or her utterances or converses with. [5]

interrogative **interrogativo**   Questioning or asking. The term is also applied to certain adverbs, pronouns, and determiners that are used in information questions: **dónde, quién, cuántos,** etc. [6]

intonation **entonación**   The rises and falls of voice pitch to convey various types of meaning, such as interrogation, emphasis, contrast. [5, 7]

intonation language **idioma** (*m.*) **entonacional**   A language, like Spanish or English and all other European languages, where the rising and falling pitch of the voice is used to convey meaning such as interrogation, emphasis, contrast. [7]

intonational features **rasgos entonacionales**   The suprasegmental features that make up the intonation of the language: stress, pitch, juncture. [4]

intonational group **grupo entonacional (grupo fónico)**   Another term for *breath group* or *phonemic phrase*—the group of sounds occurring between two pauses. [13, 20]

item-and-arrangement **unidad y distribución**   The approach to language study that views the units of language as individual entities that occur in various patterns. For example, the phoneme /b/ in Spanish has two allophones, the stop [b] and the fricative [ƀ], each of which occurs in specific environments that one can describe, predict, and learn. [16]

item-and-process **unidad y proceso**   The approach to language study that views the units of language as related items, most of which occur as the result of an ordered process, chain, derivation, or series of rules, such as the consideration that the phoneme /b/ in Spanish in certain cases undergoes the process of "spirantization" or "fricativization," which produces fricative [β]. This same process produces other fricative sounds as well under the same or similar conditions. See *item-and-arrangement*. [16]

Judeo-Spanish **judeoespañol (ladino)**   The Spanish dialect spoken by the Jews who were expelled from Spain in 1492; also the language of their modern descendants, Sephardic Jews. [3]

juncture **terminación (juntura)**   See *external juncture*. [7]

kinesics **kinésica**   The study of body language, which includes such features as postures, gestures, and facial expressions. [10]

labio-dental **labiodental**   The point of articulation produced by placing the lower lip against the edges of the upper front teeth, such as for [f]. [11]

Ladino **ladino**   See *Judeo-Spanish*. [3]

language **lengua; idioma (m.); lenguaje (m.); habla**   A system of verbal communication, like Spanish or English (**lengua, idioma**); also a particular subclass of the broader system of communication, used for specific purposes and often by special groups, like adolescents, sports fans, etc. (**lenguaje**); also the human ability to use verbal communication (**habla**). [2]

larynx **laringe (f.)**   The "voice box" or muscular, cartilaginous structure below the throat in the breathing passage; it contains the vocal bands. [2, 4]

last-syllable stressed word **palabra aguda**   A word stressed on the last syllable, such as **co<u>mer</u>, ani<u>mal</u>, empera<u>triz</u>.** [6]

lateral **lateral**   A sound, like [l], articulated by expelling the airstream around one or both sides of the tongue rather than over the top. [11]

laughing **risa**   A paralinguistic sound manifestation made in a variety of ways, particularly the special manner in which the air is expelled through the glottis or even occasionally drawn back through it into the breathing passage. [9]

leave-taking **despedida**   A word or phrase used to close a conversation or say good-bye to someone. [7]

length (vowel length) **duración**   The time taken to articulate a vowel, like the distinctive long and short vowels of German. In English long vowels precede voiced consonants automatically, particularly when stressed. In Spanish there is very little difference in the length of vowels, regardless of the stress or phonetic environment. See *long vowels*. [11, 14, 18]

lengthened **prolongado**   A sound, usually a vowel, whose time of articulation is increased, such as the two identical consecutive vowels in rapid speech in Spanish if one is stressed: **cree** [kré:] rather than [kré-e], where they are linked in separate syllables. [11, 14, 18]

letter **letra**   A graphic symbol that represents a sound rather than a word, an object, a person, a concept, etc., as pictographs do. [13]

level juncture **terminación (juntura) suspensiva**   See *external juncture.* [5, 7]

light l **la *l* clara (alveolar)**   The Spanish *l*, [l], articulated with the tip of the tongue against the alveolar ridge and the tongue body relatively high and flat, as opposed to the *dark (velarized) l*, [ɫ], heard in English in syllable-final position, with the tongue dorsum lowered or concave and the back of the dorsum raised toward the velum. [27]

linguistic community **comunidad lingüística**   A group of people who all speak the same language. It can include various countries, like Mexico and Argentina for Spanish, or Canada and the U.S. for English. [2]

linked **(vocales) enlazadas**   The pronunciation of two or more vowels in separate syllables, but with a smooth unbroken transition rather than a break of any kind between them. [18]

linking **enlace** (*m.*)   Although the English term *linking* can refer also to vowels (see *linked*), the Spanish word **enlace**, as used in this book, refers almost exclusively to the situation in which the last consonant of a word preceding a word beginning with a vowel combines with this vowel to start the next syllable: **los alumnos** [lo-sa-lúm-nos]. [13, 20]

lip-rounding **redondeamiento de los labios (labios redondeados, labios abocinados)**   The automatic rounding of the lips as the tongue moves back for the vowels [u] and [o] in both Spanish and English, a redundant feature ignored in our analysis and requiring no particular practice on your part. [11]

lip-spreading **labios estirados (extendidos)**   The slight spreading of the lips as the tongue moves forward for the front vowels [i] and [e] in both Spanish and English. [11]

long subject **sujeto extenso**   A sentence subject can consist of many words, in which case the speaker often makes a juncture before moving on to the verb. [7]

long vowels **vocales largas**   In English long vowels occur almost automatically before voiced consonants, as in *maze, rib, skid,* and *flag.* In Spanish a long vowel is almost always the result of combining two identical vowels, one of which is stressed, into one long one, as in **creer** [kré:r]. See *lengthened.* [11, 14, 18]

low back vowel **vocal baja (abierta) posterior**   A vowel like English [ɔ], articulated with the tongue retracted from a neutral position and low in the mouth. Spanish does not have low back vowels. [14]

low central glide **semivocal baja (abierta) central**   A glide like English [h], articulated like the vowel [a], and heard in place of syllable-final /r/ in the so-called *r*-less dialects of the eastern and southern coastal U.S. and most other dialects of English all over the world. [14]

low central vowel **vocal baja (abierta) central**   A vowel like Spanish or English [a], articulated with the tongue in a front-to-back neutral position and low in the mouth. [14]

low front vowel **vocal baja (abierta) anterior**   A vowel like English [æ], articulated with the tongue pushed forward from a neutral position and low in the mouth. [14]

low pitch level **nivel tonal bajo**   In both Spanish and English the lowest tone of the voice, level /1/, is the sign of completion or finality in both statements and information questions. [7]

low vowel **vocal baja (abierta)**   A low vowel, such as the [a] of both Spanish and English, articulated with the tongue low in the mouth. [14]

lower (movable) articulators **articuladores inferiores**   The lower or movable articulators are the lower lip and the various areas of the tongue, all of which make contact or approach the upper or fixed articulators. *See upper (fixed) articulators.* [4]

lower front teeth **incisivos inferiores**   A lower or movable articulator, significant in Spanish and English only for the interdental [θ]. [4]

lower lip **labio inferior**   A lower or movable articulator, significant in Spanish and English for several sounds, such as [p] or [f]. [4]

manner of articulation **modo de articulación**   The manner in which the articulators contact or approach each other and modify the airstream in the production of consonants: stop, fricative, affricate, etc. [4, 11, 20]

maximum closure **contacto máximo (cerrazón máxima)**   The final position of the articulators as they contact or approach each other to modify the airstream in the production of consonants, that is, the point of articulation. [4, 11]

metrics **métrica (prosodia)**   The science of meter, or the arrangement and use of words in poetry, according to various factors, such as the position of the stresses and the number of syllables. [8]

mid back vowel **vocal media posterior**   A vowel like Spanish or English [o], articulated with the tongue retracted from a neutral position and about halfway up in the mouth. [14]

mid central vowel (unstressed) **vocal media central (inacentuada)**   A vowel like English [ə], as in *appear*, articulated with the tongue in a front-to-back neutral position and about halfway up in the mouth. This is the normal vowel in English unstressed syllables, thus the most common one and therefore the vowel of hesitation or uncertainty—"*Uh . . . er . . .*" [14]

mid central vowel (stressed) **vocal media central (acentuada)**   A vowel like English [ʌ], as in *cut*, articulated with the tongue in a front-to-back neutral position and about halfway up in the mouth. [6, 14]

mid front vowel **vocal media anterior**   A vowel like Spanish [e], as in **peso**, or English [ɛ], as in *pet*, articulated with the tongue pushed forward from a neutral position and about halfway up in the mouth. The tongue is slightly higher for Spanish [e] than for English [ɛ], thus the difference in phonetic symbols. [14]

mid pitch level **nivel tonal medio**   In intonation analyses the mid level of pitch is the so-called normal or default level /2/ used throughout most of the breath group until the end, where the pitch normally rises or falls. [7]

mid vowel **vocal media**   Mid vowels, such as [e] and [o], are produced with the tongue in an intermediate position between the lowest position, for [a], and its highest position, near the palate for [i] or the velum for [u]. [14]

minimal pair **pareja correlativa (pareja mínima)**   A pair of words whose pronunciation differs only by the presence of two sounds in the same position or "slot" of the two words, all others being exactly alike: **peso–beso**, *ether–either*. [12]

monophthong **monoptongo** A syllable whose nucleus is a single vowel. For example, the Spanish word **mil** has a monophthong, [i], but in the English word *meal* there are two sounds, a vowel [I] and a glide [y], thus a diphthong. [13]

Moors **moros** The North Africans who invaded Spain in 711 and conquered much of the Iberian peninsula in just a few years. They remained almost eight centuries in Spain until the last of the them were finally driven back to Africa in 1492. [3]

morpheme **morfema** (*m.*) A minimal unit of meaning—sometimes an entire word like **gato** or *cat*—but often just part of a word, like the **-dad** of **bondad** or the *im-* of *impossible*. [16, 18]

morphology **morfología** The study of the form of words and of their parts, that is, morphemes. [3]

morphophonemic changes **cambios morfofonológicos** The meaningful sound, that is, phonemic, changes that morphemes undergo for a variety of reasons, such as diphthongization (/e/–/ie/) in Spanish: **pensar–pienso**, or progressive assimilation (/s/–/z/) in English noun plurals: *cats–dogs*. [18]

mutual assimilation **asimilación mutua** Sometimes adjacent sounds exercise an influence on each other in both directions: progressively (first sound on the second) and regressively (second on the first), such as a word **enviar** where the nasal is realized as bilabial [m] due to regressive assimilation to the following bilabial /b/, and the /b/, in turn, is realized as a stop [b], due to progressive assimilation to the previous nasal. [22]

nasal **nasal** A sound in which the airstream, blocked somewhere in the oral cavity, passes out through the nasal cavity and nostrils: like [m]. [4, 11]

nasal cavity **cavidad (pasaje** *m.***) nasal** The air passage that extends from the nostrils back to the velum and uvula where it merges with the oral cavity and the pharynx. [4]

nasalizing (nasalization) **nasalización** Although consonants like [m] and [n] are nasal, the term *nasalizing* or *nasalization* usually refers to the pronunciation of vowels by expelling the airstream through the nasal cavity rather than the mouth. In some languages, like French and Portuguese, this is a significant feature in the vowel system. In Spanish and English, it happens automatically when vowels come in contact with nasal consonants. [9, 11]

negative **palabra de negación** In Spanish, negative words, such as **no, nada, nadie, ninguno** normally take primary stresses in the stream of speech. [6]

neutralization (with consonants) **neutralización consonántica** The phenomenon occurring when two consonant phonemes lose their contrast in certain cases, such as in Spanish syllable-final position. Although /t/ and /d/ are clearly phonemic (**tomar–domar** or **cata–cada**) either one can be used in a word like **ritmo**. The use of [s] or [z] in a word like **mismo**, however, is *not* a case of neutralization because these two sounds do not contrast anywhere in Spanish and are thus not phonemes like /t/ and /d/ are. [21, 26]

neutralize **neutralizar**   See *neutralization.* [21, 26]

nominalized form **forma sustantivada**   A nominalized form is any part of speech which functions as or replaces a noun, like **éste** (referring to **libro**, for example), as in **Éste me gusta más**. [6]

non-functional variation **variación no funcional**   See *free variation.* [12]

nostrils **fosas nasales (narices** *f.***)**   The openings to the nasal passage, through which the airstream exits in all nasal or nasalized sounds. [4]

noun **sustantivo (nombre** *m.***)**   One of the major parts of speech in language, used often as the subject—but also as an object—and always carrying a primary stress in the stream of speech in Spanish. [6]

numeral **número**   Numerals can be pronouns: **Uno, dos, tres...** or noun determiners: **Un vaso me basta, dos (vasos) me sobran**. Numerals always carry a primary stress in the stream of speech in Spanish. [6]

occlusive **(consonante) oclusiva**   The manner of articulation in which the airstream is stopped briefly and then abruptly released with a small explosion—[p], [d], [k], and so on. [11]

onomatopoeic **onomatopéyico** (*onomatopoeia* **onomatopeya**)   Paralinguistic sounds or ''words'' that are imitative and meant to replicate surrounding sounds: natural phenomena, man-made noises, animal cries, and the like. [9]

open syllable **sílaba libre**   A syllable that ends in a vowel, such as each of the four syllables in **a-ni-ma-do**. In Spanish this creates **enlace** between words: **lo-sa-mi-gos**. [13, 20]

open-ended choice question **pregunta abierta de selección múltiple**   A question that offers the interlocutor two choices with at least one more implied: **¿Quieres café ↑ o té? ↓** [7]

oral cavity **cavidad oral (cavidad bucal, pasaje oral)**   The oral passage, or mouth, starting at the pharynx and continuing past the tongue (over or beside it), to the teeth and lips. [4]

oral sound **sonido oral**   Sounds for which the airstream exits through the oral cavity or mouth rather than the nasal passage, the most common type in all languages. [4]

ordinary information question **pregunta común de información (pronominal)**   See *information question.* The word ''ordinary'' means that the intonation pattern is /2 1 1 ↓ /. See *alternate information question.* [7]

ordinary statement **aseveración común**   The intonation pattern for a sentence in which a statement or declaration is made is /2 1 1 ↓ /. See *alternate statement.* [7]

ordinary yes-or-no question **pregunta común de sí o no (pregunta absoluta)**   The intonation pattern for a yes-or-no question, in which the speaker requests confirmation or denial of the information already provided in the question, is /2 2 2 ↑ /. See *alternate yes-or-no question.* [7]

orthography **ortografía**   The rules of spelling, that is, the representation of speech sounds by graphic symbols. [1]

overfast **demasiado rápido**   A paralinguistic sound feature in which the speaker shortens all syllables, taking much less time to say them than normal. [9]

overhigh **demasiado alto**   A paralinguistic sound feature in which the speaker makes the pitch of his or her voice higher than the normally highest contrastive level in the intonational system, such as any pitch above level /3/ in Spanish or above /4/ in English. [9]

overloud **demasiado fuerte**   A paralinguistic sound feature in which the speaker makes the loudness of one syllable greater than necessary for normal primary stress. [9]

overlow **demasiado bajo**   A paralinguistic sound feature in which the speaker makes the pitch of his or her voice lower than the normally lowest contrastive level—/1/—in the intonational system. [9]

overslow **demasiado lento**   A paralinguistic sound feature in which the speaker draws out all the syllables of all the words, taking much more time to say them than normal. It is similar to drawling, except that overslow includes all syllables whereas drawling is usually done with just the stressed syllables. See *drawling*. [9]

oversoft **demasiado suave**   A paralinguistic sound feature in which the speaker makes the volume of most of the sounds far lower than normal for special effect. In whispering, however, all or most of the sounds are devoiced, whereas in oversoft the voiced sounds are still voiced. [9]

overtense **demasiado tenso**   A paralinguistic sound feature in which the speaker tightens the vocal bands to produce sounds that give the voice a tense, impatient, anxious, distraught effect. [9]

palatal **palatal**   The point of articulation produced with the dorsum of the tongue humped up against the hard palate, such as for [ŷ]. [11]

palate **paladar** (*m.*)   The hard roof of the mouth between the alveolar ridge and the velum or soft palate. [4]

paragraph **párrafo**   A group of sentences that deal with a particular idea. Paragraphs are indicated in writing either with spaces above and below, or with the first word moved or indented to the right of the left margin, or with both of these formatting devices. [13]

paralanguage **paralenguaje** (*m.*)   Vocal manifestations beyond the regular sound system of the language, articulated by speakers for special purposes, such as expressing emotion, imitating sounds made by animals or natural phenomena, and expressing certain semantic concepts, such as agreement, negation, approval. [9]

paralinguistic **paralingüístico**   See *paralanguage*. [7, 9]

penult-stressed word **palabra llana**   A word stressed on the next-to-last syllable, such as <u>ca</u>sa or <u>lá</u>piz. [6]

pharynx **faringe** (*f.*)   The throat cavity, below the velum and uvula, behind the tongue, in front of the throat wall, and above the epiglottis. [4]

phonation **fonación**   Sound produced by the vibration of the vocal bands. [4]

phone **fono (sonido)**   An individual sound without any specification of its function or patterning in the total system. [12]

phoneme **fonema** (*m.*)   A functional contrastive sound unit or family, usually consisting of two or more individual varieties, family members or allophones, and written between slash bars: /p b k/, etc. [11, 12]

phonemic **fonológico (fonémico)**   The contrastive or functional property of a phoneme or a group of phonemes, such as voicing in all languages. See *functional.* [5]

phonemic phrase **grupo fónico**   All the sounds between two pauses in the stream of speech, also referred to as a breath group. [20]

phonemic-phrase initial   See *absolute-initial.* [13]

phonemic writing **escritura fonémica**   Phonemic writing or spelling characterizes the orthographic systems of all European languages. The aim is to have each letter or graphic symbol represent one distinctive sound or phoneme in the language. Spanish spelling is much more phonemic than English spelling. [2]

phonemics **fonología (fonémica)**   The study of the functioning and patterning of sounds and sound groups in language. [2]

phonetic environment **contexto fonético**   Many phonemes have differing realizations or allophones in different phonetic environments, as in the preceding and/or following sounds, such as Spanish /b/, normally fricative, [β], between vowels but occlusive, [b], after nasals. [12]

phonetic similarity **similitud fonética**   If two of the three parameters—point of articulation, manner of articulation, and vocal band function—are the same, the sounds are considered to be phonetically similar. For example, /b/ and /d/ are phonetically similar because they are both stops and both voiced. But /d/ and /m/ are not phonetically similar because only one of the three parameters is shared: voicing. [12]

phonetic transcription **transcripción fonética**   The use of special symbols to represent sounds as consistently and accurately as possible, something that most conventional orthographical systems do not always do. [1]

phonetics **fonética**   The study of the production, transmission, and reception of speech sounds and their particular properties. [2]

phonology **fonología**   The study of the functioning and patterning of speech sounds. Not only are the properties of the sounds studied, as in phonetics, but also how the sounds determine meaning and pattern in the language, what processes they undergo, such as assimilation, devoicing, prevoicing, diphthongization, and so forth. [1, 2]

phonotactics **fonotáctica**   The study of how sounds combine and where they may or may not occur in the language, such as the following phonotactic considerations in Spanish: consonant clusters have only two phonemes, whether word- or syllable-initial or word- or syllable-final; /s/ is never the first member of word- or syllable-initial consonant cluster; tap /r/ never occurs at the beginning of a word. [29]

physiological phonetics **fonética fisiológica**   The study of the role that the body parts of the vocal tract play in the production of speech sounds, such as in phonation and articulation. [12]

pictograph **pictograma** (*m.*)   Pictures or icons used in the writing systems of some languages to represent objects, people, or concepts rather than individual sounds as letters do. Also called *hieroglyphics.* [2]

pitch **tono**   The musical tone of speech sounds determined by the frequency of the sound waves created by vibrations of the vocal bands. [4, 5]

pitch level **nivel tonal** (*m.*)   The relative height of the pitch of the voice. Spanish, for example, has three pitch levels: high /3/, mid /2/, and low /1/. [7]

place of articulation **punto de articulación**   The point at which the articulators approach or contact each other, that is, achieve maximum closure or their final position, whether close or far from each other, to produce the sound. [4, 11, 20]

plus juncture **juntura interna**   A boundary feature of English, /+/, which prevents certain phonological processes from taking place, or, conversely, causes them to take place. For example, English, does not assimilate nasals at word boundaries, *tan coat* or *green grass,* and often not even at morpheme boundaries, as in *income* or *ingrown,* due to the boundary feature of plus juncture, which is shown in a phonemic transcription of *income*, for example, after the alveolar /n/: /ín+kλm/. [26]

point of articulation **punto de articulación**   See *place of articulation*. [4, 11, 20]

Portuguese **portugués**   The official language of Portugal and one of the four languages of the Iberian peninsula, part of a larger group, Galician-Portuguese. [3]

possessive **posesivo**   A subclass of noun determiner. In Spanish the short pre-posed possessives—**mi, tu, sus**—do not normally carry primary stress in the stream of speech because they are bound, but long post-posed possessives—**mío, tuya, suyos**—always do because they are free. [6]

pre-antepenult-stressed word **palabra sobresdrújula**   A "word" stressed on the fourth-from-last syllable: **dígamelo, diciéndoselos**. All such "words" are really verb forms plus object pronouns. There are no regular individual **sobresdrújula** words in Spanish, that is, words that are not composed of verb + object pronoun. [6]

prescriptive approach **enfoque prescriptivo**   The prescriptive approach is concerned with correctness in language—the "true" meaning of words, grammatical rules, avoiding the so-called corruption and decay of the language. See *descriptive approach*. [2]

primary stress **acento primario**   The loudest syllable in a word, achieved by increasing the volume of the vowel in that syllable. Also referred to as *heavy stress* or, in the case of Spanish, just *stress* since there are no other degrees of stress as there are in English. [6]

progressive assimilation **asimilación progresiva**   The phonological process in which the preceding sound influences the second or following sound, causing it take on some of its characteristics, such as the bilabial nasal [m] in **hombre** causing the following /b/ to be realized as a stop, [b], since the two lips are already pressed together for [m]. [20, 22]

prosodic features **rasgos prosódicos**   These are also known as *intonational* or *suprasegmental* features of the language: stress, pitch, juncture. [4]

punctuation mark **signo de puntuación**   A special graphic symbol to mark a variety of phonemic, syntactic, and semantic features. Such marks vary from language to language even when the same alphabet is used: compare English quotation marks " " with « », frequently used in Spanish. [13]

qualifier **calificador (adverbio calificativo)**   A part of speech that intensifies or diminishes the force of an adjective, such as **muy, más, menos, poco**. Qualifiers are sometimes stressed in the stream of speech in Spanish. [6]

quavering **trémulo (con voz trémula)**   A paralinguistic sound feature in which the vocal bands are made to vibrate unevenly, lending an emotional or feeble effect to the speaker's voice. [9]

rasping **hablar con voz áspera**   A paralinguistic sound feature in which the air is forced through the glottis under great tension, causing the vocal bands to vibrate roughly and unevenly. [9]

r-less dialect (of English) **dialecto sin *r* (del inglés)**   A feature of many eastern and southern dialects of American English, standard British English, and, in fact, most dialects of English all over the world outside of North America. Speakers substitute a voiceless glide /h/ for a post-vocalic /r/, saying /páhk/ for *park*, /hǐh/ for *here*, /ðɛh/ for *there*. [3, 14]

reduced vowels **vocales reducidas (caducas)**   In some dialects of American Spanish, unstressed vowels—particularly those immediately before or after the main stress of the word—are shortened and can be represented by small superscribed letters in a phonetic transcription: **pos̲esiones** [po-s^e-si̲ó-nes], **ay̲udar** [a-y^u-d̶ár]. [14]

redundant **redundante**   A redundant sound feature is one that happens automatically below the level of awareness of the speaker, such as in Spanish, where vowels between nasal consonants are nasalized automatically or redundantly: **mano** [mã-no]. [11]

regressive assimilation **asimilación regresiva**   The phonological process in which the following sound influences the preceding sound, causing it take on some of its characteristics. For example, the bilabial stop [b] in **enviar** causes the preceding /n/ to be realized as a bilabial nasal, [m], since the two lips start pressing together for [b] somewhat in advance of this sound. [20, 22]

relative pronoun **pronombre relativo**   A pronoun in a relative or adjectival clause that refers back to a noun antecedent in the main clause: **Los alumnos que** (referring back to **alumnos** and thus governing a plural verb) **viv̲en en el recinto a veces comen en el centro**. Such pronouns do not normally carry a primary stress in the stream of speech in Spanish. [6]

replaced **(vocal) sustituida (trueque de vocales)**   This term refers to the replacement of unstressed /o/ by /u/, as in **to̲alla**, unstressed /e/ by /i/, as in **pe̲or**, and unstressed /i/ by /y/, as in **le̲yes**, under certain conditions—also referred to as vowel raising in the first two cases. [18]

resonance **resonancia**   The reverberation and resonating of the sound waves produced by glottal phonation in the three resonating chambers: the pharynx, the oral cavity, and the nasal cavity. These resonating frequencies are multiplied and combined as the size and shape of the first two chambers are changed by the lips and tongue, forming the sounds of human speech. [4]

resonance chambers **cámaras de resonancia**   See *resonance*. [4]

rhythm **ritmo**   A suprasegmental feature having to do with the time or relative length of stressed and unstressed syllables. Spanish has an even legato syllable-timed rhythm, since most syllables are of the same or almost the same length regardless of the stresses. English, on the other hand, has an uneven galloping stress-timed rhythm, since the primary stressed syllables are longer than those with lower degrees of stress. [5, 8]

rising juncture **terminación (juntura) ascendente**   See *external juncture*. [5, 7]

root of the tongue **raíz** (*f.*) **de la lengua**   The back of the tongue opposite the throat or pharynx wall. Neither Spanish nor English has sounds produced with the root of the tongue, known as pharyngeals. [4]

screaming **hablar con gritos (chillidos)**   A paralinguistic manifestation in which, under extreme emotion, the speaker tightens his or her vocal bands to such a degree that a series of extremely high-pitched and loud tones are emitted. [9]

secondary stress **acento secundario**   The second degree of stress in English, marked in transcription with a circumflex ˆ, typically used in the modifier in phrases consisting of modifier + noun, which has the primary stress: *a bîg hít, a stêel pláte*. [6]

segmental sound **sonido segmental**   An individual sound—consonant, vowel, or glide—in the stream of speech. [4]

semantic signal **señal semántica**   In paralanguage some sounds or words are used to convey semantic concepts rather than to express emotion or imitate nature, such as whistling, for example, in Spanish to indicate displeasure at an athletic event, or **Sssssssssssss** as a call for silence in any group. [9]

semi-consonant **semiconsonante** (*f.*)   See *semi-vowel*. [6, 11, 13]

semi-vowel **semivocal** (*f.*)   In Spanish, a semi-vowel or semi-consonant (also called *glide*) is either [i̯] or [u̯]. It is never stressed and necessarily forms one part of a diphthong, that is, a combination of two vowels in a single syllable. [6, 11, 13]

sentence **oración**   A traditional prescriptive definition is the useless and vague ''a complete thought.'' A descriptive definition is ''a syntactic unit consisting of a subject and a predicate (or verb phrase).'' [13]

sentence stress **acento de la oración**   In many sentences one word is more emphatic than the others, and its primary stress is thus louder than the primary stresses of the other words. In Spanish this is usually the first or last stressed syllable of the breath group and can be marked with a double accent in transcription: **¿Por qué dice esas <u>cosas</u>** [kő-sas]? [6]

separated **(vocales) separadas**   This refers to an artificial break between two vowels in the stream of speech—just a slight pause or a glottal stop [ʔ]. It is artificial in Spanish: **la abuela** is never pronounced naturally with separation [laʔa-βu̯é-la], but usually with elimination, [la-βu̯é-la]. [18]

sequence **secuencia**   Any string of adjoining consonants, with four being the maximum number within a word in Spanish. Sequences in Spanish can be divided into clusters, each with a maximum of two consonants. [13]

seseo The speech mode heard in many parts of Spain, particularly Andalusia, and through-out all of Spanish America, in which the phoneme /θ/ is absent, being replaced by /s/. See **ceceo** and *distinction.* [24, 31]

short vowels **vocales reducidas (caducas)** See *reduced vowels.* [14]

shouting **gritar** A paralinguistic manifestation in which the volume of most of the syllables is greater than expected, indicating special circumstances on the part of the speaker—either great emotion, the desire to attract someone's attention, the effort to be heard in a noisy environment. *Overloud* refers to the loudness of just certain syllables; *shouting* refers to all the syllables uttered by the speaker. [9]

sibilant **sibilante** (*f.*) See *groove fricative.* [11, 24]

simple preposition **preposición simple** A one-word preposition in Spanish, like **a, con, de, en**, as opposed to a compound preposition like **detrás de, en contra de**. [6]

slit fricative **fricativa hendida** A sound made by expelling the air through a wide (horizontal) and small flat opening formed by the two lips, by the lower lip and upper front teeth, by the tongue tip and the front teeth, by the tongue dorsum and palate, etc. [f] and [x] are slit fricatives, for example. [11]

soft palate **velo** See *velum.* [4]

Spanish **español (castellano)** The Romance language descended from Latin and now the national language of Spain and the Spanish American nations. It began as the peninsular dialect Castilian, which term is also used now to refer to Spanish. [3]

squeaking **chirriar (desentonar)** A paralinguistic manifestation in which most syllables are uttered at a higher pitch, but usually softer in volume than normal. Also many of the syllables are abruptly cut short in an unnatural manner. [9]

stop **(consonante) oclusiva** See *occlusive.* [11]

statement **aseveración (afirmación)** An utterance that provides information, as opposed to a question, which seeks information, or a command, which seeks action on the interlocutor's part. [7]

stress **acento de intensidad** The suprasegmental feature of loudness. In both Spanish and English, all polysyllabic words in isolation are spoken with one syllable louder than the others: **célebre–celebré**, *drafty–draftee.* [5, 6]

stress group **grupo de intensidad** In Spanish a group of unstressed syllables clustered around one primary stress: **Los hombres // que conocimos // en la fiesta // son futbolistas.** [6]

stress phrase **frase de intensidad** See *stress group.* [6]

stress shift **desplazamiento del acento** A few Spanish nouns shift the stress when pluralized, such as **régimen–regímenes, carácter–caracteres.** Many verbs ending in **-iar** and **-uar** also shift the stress: **enviar—envío, continuar–continúa**. [6]

stress-timed language **idioma** (*m.*) **de ritmo acentual** English is a stress-timed language. See *rhythm.* [8]

subordinated elements **elementos subordinados** Subordinated elements are dependent or subordinate clauses as opposed to independent or main clauses. [7]

substratum **sustrato** This term in linguistics refers to the people, and their language, of course, who were conquered by another group of people, whose language became dominant. However, sometimes the substratum language exercises an influence on the superstratum language of the conquerors. [3]

suprasegmental sound **sonido suprasegmental**   A suprasegmental sound is one that is overlaid onto the segmental sounds, usually the vowels. Suprasegmental sound features are stress, pitch, and vowel length, for example. [5]

syllable **sílaba**   The syllable is the smallest sound group in phonetics and can even consist of a single sound. Every Spanish syllable must have at least one vowel—V, as in **a**. *Open syllables* end in vowels; *closed syllables* end in consonants; two vowels in the same syllable form a diphthong: Spanish favors open syllables; thus CVCVCVCV is divided CV-CV-CV-CV **ca-pí-tu-lo**. This also happens between words within a breath group, creating linking or **enlace**: **Los alumnos están en el aula** /lo-sa-lúm-no-ses-tá-ne-ne-láu-la/. [13, 20]

syllabic writing **escritura silábica**   In some languages, like Japanese, the graphic symbols represent entire syllables rather than single sounds, units of meaning, words, or concepts. [2]

syllabication **silabeo**   The division of words and phrases into syllables. The rules for Spanish syllabication in speech are simple, consistent, and without exception. [13]

syllable-timed language **idioma** (*m.*) **de ritmo silábico**   Spanish is a syllable-timed language. See *rhythm.* [8]

syntax **sintaxis** (*f.*)   The patterns of arrangement of words, phrases, and clauses in a language. [3]

tag question **pregunta confirmativa**   A short question appended to a statement, seeking confirmation of what has been stated: **¿no?, ¿verdad?, ¿ves?, ¿sabes?** [7]

tap **vibrante** (*f.*) **simple**   See *flap.* [11]

terminal juncture **terminación**   See *external juncture.* [5, 7]

tertiary stress **acento terciario**   The third degree of stress in English, marked in transcription with a grave accent `, typically used on the second element of a compound with primary stress on the first element: *bláckbòard, Whíte Hòuse.* [6]

thanking **agradecer**   In Spanish the word **gracias** is normally said with the first syllable on pitch level /3/. If said with the first syllable on pitch level /2/ rather than /3/, it can imply, "No, thanks." [7]

tip of the tongue **punta (ápice** *m.*) **de la lengua**   The part of the tongue used in making most dental and many alveolar sounds. [4]

tone language **idioma** (*m.*) **tonal**   A language, like Thai, Chinese, or Vietnamese, in which pitch is manipulated to determine meaning on the lexical or word level. [7]

tongue **lengua**   The speech organ which is the principal lower or movable articulator. Its significant speech production parts are the tip, blade, dorsum, and root. [2, 4]

top of the tongue **dorso de la lengua**   The part of the tongue used in making some alveolar, most palatal, and all velar sounds. [4]

trachea **tráquea**   The so-called "windpipe" or breathing tube leading from the bronchial tubes up to the larynx and vocal bands. [4]

transliterate **transliterar**   The conversion of one set of symbols to another set to represent the same sequence of sounds. For example, English documents usually transliterate the Cyrillic characters of Russian into familar Roman letters. Thus Я вижу is transliterated as **Ya vizhu** *I see*. [12]

tremolo **trémulo (con voz trémula)**   See *quavering*. [9]

trill **vibrante** (*f.*) **múltiple**   The Spanish trilled [r̄], as in **carro**, is produced when the tip of the tongue, under great tension, strikes the alveolar ridge. The airstream forces the tongue tip back, but the muscular effort of the tongue keeps pushing the tongue tip forward against the alveolar ridge several times in rapid succession. [11]

triphthong **triptongo**   The combination of three vowels in a single syllable. In Spanish the first and third of these three vowels is always either the semi-vowel [i̯] or [u̯]. [13]

unbound form **forma libre (no ligada)**   See *free form*. [6]

unvoiced **sorda (ensordecida)**   A sound, such as [p] or [s], made without phonation, or vocal band vibrations, that is unvoiced or voiceless. This term can also refer to a normally voiced sound that is devoiced, such as the Argentinian palatal [ž], which is frequently devoiced to [š]. [4]

upper (fixed) articulators **articuladores superiores**   The upper parts of the mouth that do not move (or move slightly) in the production of speech sounds: upper lip, upper front teeth, alveolar ridge, palate, and velum. The lower or movable articulators make contact with or approach the upper articulators to produce segmental sounds. See *lower (movable) articulators*. [4]

upper front teeth **incisivos superiores**   One of the upper or fixed articulators, used in the articulation of labio-dental, interdental, and dental sounds. [4]

upper lip **labio superior**   Although the upper lip is considered an upper or fixed articulator, it moves very slightly in the production of bilabial consonants, such as [p] and [m], and to a fair degree for the back rounded vowels, such as [o] and [u]. [4]

uvula **úvula**   The flap of tissue hanging down from the velum. [4]

uvular **uvular**   The point of articulation produced as the tongue dorsum comes into contact with the uvula. (See *uvula*.) There are only two uvular sounds in Spanish: the strong voiceless trilled [X] (**jota**) of Castilian Spanish, sometimes uvular rather than velar, and the voiced trilled [R] of many Puerto Rican speakers, also sometimes uvular rather than velar. [11]

velar **velar**   The point of articulation produced as the tongue dorsum comes in contact with the soft palate or velum, such as for [k]. [11]

velum **velo**   The soft palate, the area behind the palate and in front of the uvula. [4, 11]

verb **verbo**   As a free form, along with nouns, adjectives, and adverbs, most verbs take primary stress in the stream of speech in Spanish. [6]

vocal bands **cuerdas vocales** The cartilaginous bands in the larynx, which can be tightened and made to vibrate as the airstream passes out from the trachea to create phonation or voicing. [4]

vocal tract **canal** (*m.*) **(pasaje** *m.***) vocal** The vocal tract, used in the production of speech sounds, includes the entire breathing passage, from the lungs to the nostrils, along with the oral cavity, tongue, lips, teeth, gums, and other parts of the upper digestive tract. [2]

vocative **vocativo** Your use of the title or name of the person to whom you are speaking: **señorita, Juan, amigo mío.** In Spanish the pitch usually drops on vocatives. [7]

voiced **sonoro** Sounds produced with vocal band vibration or phonation. [4]

voiceless **sordo (ensordecido)** Sounds produced without vocal band vibration, or phonation. See *devoiced.* [4]

voicing **sonorización** See *voiced.* [4, 11]

volume **intensidad** The loudness of sound produced by the amplitude of the sound waves. (See *amplitude.*) The volume of speech sounds is controlled by the muscular action of the vocal tract, including the diaphragm, lungs, trachea, and vocal bands. [4]

vowel **vocal** (*f.*) A sound articulated when the airstream is not blocked, impeded, or obstructed in any significant way as it leaves the vocal tract. The airstream, however, is always *modified* by the tongue, which controls the size and shape of the oral cavity and thus the color or quality of the vowels. [2, 11]

vowel length (duration) **duración vocálica** See *length* and *lengthened.* [11, 14, 18]

vowel raising **trueque** (*m.*) **de vocales** This refers to the replacement of the unstressed mid vowels /e/ and /o/ by the high vowels /i/ and /u/, respectively. See *replaced.* [18]

vowel reduction **reducción vocálica** See *reduced vowels.* [14]

vowel shortening **acortamiento vocálico** See *short vowels* and *vowel reduction.* [14]

weak stress **acento débil** The lowest degree of loudness of a vowel in a language like Spanish or English where stress is phonemic. In Spanish, where there are only two degrees of stress—strong (primary) and weak—weak stress is not marked in a transcription. [6]

whispered vowel **vocal ensordecida (cuchicheada, murmurada, susurrada)** See *devoiced vowel.* [14]

whispering **cuchicheo (murmullo, susurro)** A paralinguistic manifestation in which all vocal band vibrations are eliminated to make the speech sounds quieter and perhaps inaudible at more than a few feet from the speaker. [9]

word **palabra** A minimal free form or separable unit of speech. Some words, like nouns, verbs, adjectives, and adverbs, are completely free in the sense that they can be uttered in isolation. Others, like articles, prepositions, and conjunctions, are semi-bound in the sense that they can only be uttered next to free forms. [13]

yes-or-no question **pregunta de sí o no (pregunta absoluta)**   A question that provides all the necessary information to the interlocutor, asking either for confirmation or denial. [7]

Spanish–English

abocinados: labios —   rounded lips, lip rounding
acanalado   groove(d)
acento: — de intensidad   stress; **— de la oración**   sentence stress; **— débil**   weak stress; **— primario**   heavy, primary stress; **— secundario**   secondary stress; **— terciario**   tertiary stress
acortado   shortened
acortamiento vocálico   vowel shortening
afirmación   statement
agradecer   thanking
aguda   last-syllable stressed (word)
alvéolos   alveolar ridge
analfabeto   illiterate
anterior   front
ápice (*m.*) **de la lengua**   tip of the tongue
arrastrar las palabras   drawling
articuladores: — inferiores   lower (movable) articulators; **— superiores**   upper (fixed) articulators
aseveración   statement
áspera: hablar con voz —   rasping

Baleares: Islas —   Balearic Islands
bronquios   bronchial tubes
bucal   oral

caducas: vocales —   short, reduced vowels
calificador   qualifier
cámaras de resonancia   resonance chambers
cambios morfofonológicos   morphophonemic changes
canal vocal   vocal tract
Canarias: Islas —   Canary Islands
cavidad bucal   oral cavity
cerrada: vocal —   high vowel
cerrazón máxima   maximum closure
chasquido   click
chillar   screaming

chillido   scream
chirriar   squeaking
clítico: pronombre —   conjunctive pronoun
conjunto: pronombre —   conjunctive pronoun
con voz trémula   quavering, tremolo
consonante oclusiva   stop
contacto máximo   maximum closure
corona de la lengua   blade of the tongue
correlativa: pareja —   minimal pair
cuadro   chart
cuchichear   whispering
cuchicheos   whispers
cuerdas vocales   vocal bands

débil   weak
demás casos: en los —   elsewhere
demasiado: — lento   overslow; **— suave**   oversoft
desentonar   squeaking
despedida   farewell, leave-taking
desplazamiento del acento   stress shift
determinante (*m.*)   determiner
digrama (*m.*)   digraph
dorso de la lengua   dorsum of the tongue
duración   length

elisión de vocales   dropping, eliminating vowels
enfoque: — descriptivo   descriptive approach; **— prescriptivo**   prescriptive approach
enlace (*m.*)   linking
enlazado   linked
ensordecido   unvoiced, voiceless
ensordecimiento   devoicing
escritura dialectal   eye dialect
esdrújula   antepenult-syllable stressed (word)
estirados: labios —   spread lips

falsete (*m.*)   falsetto
faringe (*f.*)   pharynx
fónico: grupo —   breath group, intonational group, phonemic phrase
fono   phone
forma: — ligada   bound form; **— sustantival**   nominalized form
fosas nasales   nostrils
frase (*f.*) **de intensidad**   stress phrase

fricativa: — acanalada groove fricative, sibilant; **— hendida** slit fricative
fundido fused

gráfico chart
gritar screaming, shouting
grito scream, shout
grupo: — consonántico consonant cluster; **— de intensidad** stress group; **— fónico** breath group, intonational group, phonemic phrase

habla language
hablar con tono áspero rasping
hendida: fricativa — slit fricative
hercio hertz, Hz
hertzio hertz, Hz
hiato hiatus

idioma (*m.*)**: — de ritmo acentual** stress-timed language; **— de ritmo silábico** syllable-timed language
incisivo front tooth
intensidad volume
Islas Baleares Balearic Islands
Islas Canarias Canary Islands

jeroglífico hieroglyphics
judeoespañol Judeo-Spanish
juntura: — ascendente rising juncture; **— descendente** falling juncture; **— interna** plus juncture; **— suspensiva** sustained juncture

kinésica kinesics

labios: — abocinados lip-rounding; **— estirados** lip-spreading; **— extendidos** lip-spreading; **— redondeados** lip-rounding
ladino Judeo-Spanish
lamento crying
lento slow
ligado bound
llana penult-syllable stressed (word)
llanto crying

mandato command
mayúscula capital letter
minúscula small letter

murmullo   whisper
murmurar   whispering

narices (*f. pl.*)   nostrils
nariz (*f.*)   nose
nivel: — tonal alto   high pitch level; **— tonal bajo**   low pitch level; **— tonal medio**   mid pitch level
nombre   noun

oclusiva glotal   glottal stop
oración   sentence

palabra: — aguda   last-syllable stressed word; **— cognada**   cognate; **— esdrújula**   antepenult-syllable stressed word; **— gramatical**   function word; **— llana**   penult-syllable stressed word; **— sobresdrújula**   pre-antepenult-syllable stressed word
paladar (*m.*)   palate
pareja correlativa   minimal pair
párrafo   paragraph
predorso de la lengua   blade of the tongue
pregunta: — absoluta   yes-or-no question; **— confirmativa**   tag question; **— de selección múltiple**   choice question; **— pronominal**   information question
pronombre: — clítico   conjunctive pronoun; **— conjunto**   conjunctive pronoun; **— disyuntivo**   disjunctive pronoun; **— relativo**   relative pronoun
prosodia   metrics
punta de la lengua   tip of the tongue

quebrada: hablar con voz —   breaking

raíz (*f.*) **de la lengua**   root of the tongue
rasgos entonacionales   intonational features
redondeados: labios —   lip-rounding
risa   laughing
ritmo acentual   stress timing

saludo   greeting
semiconsonante   glide, semi-consonant, semi-vowel
semivocal   glide, semi-consonant, semi-vowel
señal semántica   semantic signal
signo diacrítico   diacritic
sílaba: — libre   open syllable; **— trabada**   closed syllable
silabeo   syllabication
similitud fonética   phonetic similarity

sobresdrújula pre-antepenult-syllable stressed (word)
sonido sound, phone; — **ingresivo** click
sonorización voicing
sonoro voiced
sordo voiceless, unvoiced
superior upper
suspensivo sustained
sustantivado nominalized
sustantivo noun
sustrato substratum
susurrar whispering
susurro whisper

terminación external, terminal juncture
tonal (*adj.*) pitch
tono (*n.*) pitch
trabada: sílaba — closed syllable
tráquea trachea
trueque (*m.*) **de vocales** vowel replacement

ultracorrección hypercorrection
unidad: — y distribución item-and-arrangement; — **y proceso** item-and-process

variación no funcional free variation
variante fonética allophone
vasco Basque
vascuence (*m.*) Basque
velo soft palate, velum
vibrante (*f.*): — **múltiple** trill; — **simple** flap, tap
vocablo compuesto compound
vocal: — abierta low vowel; — **alta** high vowel; — **anterior** front vowel; — **baja** low vowel; — **caduca** short, reduced vowel; — **cerrada** high vowel; — **ensor-decida** devoiced, whispered vowel; — **media** mid vowel; — **posterior** back vowel; — **prolongada** long vowel; — **reducida** short, reduced vowel; — **sorda** devoiced, whispered vowel; —**es diptongadas** fused vowels; —**es fundidas** fused vowels; **cuerdas —es** vocal bands; **elisión de —es** dropping, eliminated vowels; **trueque de —es** vowel replacement, vowel raising
voz: hablar con — áspera rasping; **hablar con — interrupta** breaking; **hablar con — quebrada** breaking; **hablar con — trémula** quavering, tremolo

Appendix B
Sound Charts

Consonant Phonemes of General American Spanish

Points of Articulation

MANNERS OF ARTICULATION	bilabial	labio-dental	dental	alveolar	palatal	velar	bilabio-velar	glottal
STOPS	p b		t d			k g		
FRICATIVES		f		s	y	x	w	(h)
AFFRICATES					ĉ			
NASALS	m			n	ñ			
LATERALS				l	(l̃)			
TAP				r				
TRILL				r̄				

Most dialects of American Spanish have only 18 consonant phonemes: they have *either* /x/ *or* /h/, thus the parentheses around the latter phoneme on the chart on page 338; only the **lleísta** dialects have palatal /l̃/, thus the parentheses around this phoneme.

Vowel Phonemes of General American Spanish

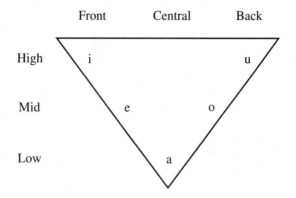

Tongue Position

Suprasegmental Phonemes of General American Spanish

Stress   primary /´/   weak / / (unmarked)

Pitch   /3/ high   /2/ _mid_   /1/ low

Terminal Junctures   rise / ↑ / fall / ↓ / sustained /→/

Consonant Allophones of General American Spanish

Points of Articulation

MANNERS OF ARTICULATION	bilabial	labio-dental	dental	alveolar	alveolo-palatal	palatal	velar	bilabio-velar	glottal
STOPS	p b		t d				k g		
SLIT FRICATIVES	p̶ b̶	f v	d̶	ř̥ ř		ç y	x g̶	w	h
GROOVE FRICATIVES			s̩ z̩	s ś z ż	sˡ	š ž			
AFFRICATES					ĉ	ŷ			
NASALS	m	m̩	n̩	n	ǹ	ñ	ŋ		
LATERALS			l̩	l	ì	ĩ			
TAP				r					
TRILL			r̥̄ r̄				X	R	

(handwritten note under STOPS: oclusiva)
(handwritten note under SLIT FRICATIVES: fricativa)

The standard sibilants or groove fricatives of General American Spanish, alveolar [s] and [z], are made with the tongue blade curved down, giving the tongue a convex shape. The so-called retroflex *s* or **s espesa**, [ś], and its voiced counterpart, [ż], are also alveolar—thus they are in the same box above—but they are made with the tongue tip at right angles with or even retroflexed as it touches the alveolar ridge, giving the tongue a concave shape.

Vowel Allophones of General American Spanish

Tongue Position

	Front	Central	Back

High	y
	i̯
	  i
			w
			u̯
			  u

Mid	e		o
Low		a	

Consonant Phonemes of American English

Points of Articulation

MANNERS OF ARTICULATION	bilabial	labio-dental	inter-dental	alveolar	palatal	velar	bilabio-velar	glottal
STOPS	p b			t d		k g		
FRICATIVES		f v	θ ð	s z	š ž			(h)
AFFRICATES					č ǰ			
NASALS	m			n		ŋ		
LATERALS				l				
GLIDES				r	y		w	h

All the glides in English also function as consonants at the beginning of the syllable. In addition, /h/ in this position has fricative properties—thus the parentheses on the chart.

Vowel Phonemes of American English

Tongue Position

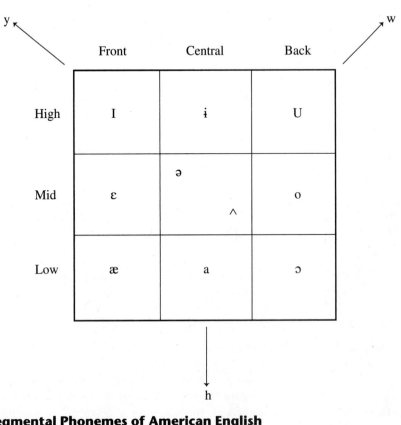

	Front	Central	Back
High	I	ɨ	U
Mid	ε	ə / ʌ	o
Low	æ	a	ɔ

Suprasegmental Phonemes of American English

Stress   primary /ˊ/   secondary /ˆ/   tertiary /ˋ/   weak /ˇ/

Pitch   /4/ extra high   /3/ high   /2/ _mid_   /1/ low

Plus Juncture   /+/

Terminal Junctures   rise /↑/   fall /↓/   sustained /→/

Appendix C
Answer Key

This Answer Key contains suggested answers for all Review and Discussion sections, as well as all Practices. For some of the Review and Discussion open-ended questions, only a few brief suggestions are made to give you an idea of some of the ways in which you can respond. More specific instructions will be given for phonetic transcription practices when they come up.

2 Language and Linguistics

1. Several important things characterize human language as opposed to the communication systems of animals. Two are the human brain—intelligence—and the uniquely-shaped vocal tract of humans, which permits them to make the most basic of speech sounds—vowels. You should be able to think of other unique characteristics of human speech, such as the combination of a relatively small number of sounds into a infinite number of meaningful words, phrases, and sentences.

2. A baby at first is physically able to make practically every possible human sound. But it quickly begins to discard those that are absent from the language of the surrounding individuals in favor of the ones it hears over and over. It begins to see how these sounds can be used in a practical way. As it learns these particular sounds, it begins to abandon those it never hears. Ultimately these abandoned sounds, most of which exist in other languages, become stranger and more and more difficult to the child as it grows older. In fact, some of these ''foreign'' sounds become almost impossible to learn by the average adult language learner. The question, then, is one of environment—nurture—and not heredity—nature.

3. Language is one of the most important manifestions of culture with a small *c*, i.e., the patterns of human behavior, since every single human being performs them. It is also true that it is possible to learn a foreign language well without learning its culture, but the reverse is absolutely impossible.

4. If you have read Spanish or Spanish-American literature, looked at examples of Spanish painting, or listened to Spanish-American music in your Spanish language classes in high school or college, you have been exposed to Hispanic Culture (with a capital *C*).

5. Language is really the ''noises you make with your face'' (sounds) and not the ''scratches you make with your fist'' (letters) because of the simple fact that all human

beings do the former, but millions of people, for all sorts of reasons, do not do the latter. The writing system is not the language, but merely represents it—often inconsistently and imperfectly. Nevertheless, writing is undeniably a valuable tool in the teaching and learning of language and in its transmission from one generation of native speakers to the next. Although it is possible to learn to speak a foreign language well without learning to write it, it is easier and more efficient if writing is brought into the picture at some stage. Also most people feel that to be truly educated, you must become adept at writing the language in question as well as speaking it.

6.   Letters represent sounds; pictographs (also hieroglyphics and ideographs) represent things, people, and concepts. Letters are a much more precise and efficient way of representing language although many important peoples with great cultures—such as the ancient Egyptians and the modern Chinese—have relied principally on pictographic rather than alphabetic writing.

7.   Prescriptive: ''In English never end a sentence with a preposition.'' ''Just pronounce it the way it's written.'' ''Pretty soon, if American English keeps on degenerating, we will be unable to communicate with speakers of British English.'' '' 'It's me' is wrong; it should be 'It is I'.'' ''It is incorrect to say **Le escribí una carta a mis padres.''** ''It is incorrect to say **¿Cuál libro vas a comprar?** It should be either **¿Qué libro... ?** or **¿Cuál de los libros... ?''** ''The best (most beautiful, most correct) Spanish is spoken in. . . .''

Descriptive: ''Most speakers of American English use the word *will* or just the contraction *'ll* for the future tense. If they do use *shall*, they do not use it instead of *will* to indicate determination in . . . (most Americans cannot even state the rest of the prescriptive rule about *will* and *shall* because such a rule has never been true of conversational English).'' ''Millions of Americans use *ain't* regularly in their speech to replace various contractions like *isn't, aren't, hasn't*, and as a contraction for the nonexistent **am't*.'' (Refer to note 1 in Chapter 6.) ''Many Americans pluralize the word *you* with such forms as *you all, y'all, youse,* and *you'uns.* Some also have possessive forms for them, such *y'all's books* or *you'uns' books.'' ''Millions of Americans use double negatives.'' ''Millions of Spanish speakers say **Le escribí una carta a mis padres, ¿Cuál libro vas a comprar?, ¿Cuándo fuistes a México?, ¿Qué tenés (vos)?''** ''Many Spaniards refer to their governmental aid checks as their **suicidio** rather than their **subsidio** (in all seriousness, of course).'' ''Many Mexicans say **pos** instead of **pues**.'' ''Many educated Spanish speakers forget whether certain words are spelled with **v** or **b**, and with **s** or **z**.''

3 Language and Dialects

1.   Everyone has an accent in the sense that he or she necessarily speaks a dialect of the language. Of course, if one speaks the default or standard dialect, this is not noticeable to most other speakers of the language, because they do, too. On television, for example, Mississippians and Bostonians sound to the millions of Americans who are not from those places like they have an accent. Probably, though, an Iowan does not sound

like he or she has an accent to the millions of Americans who are not from Iowa. This, of course, is because, unlike Mississippians and Bostonians, Iowans speak General American. But General American, too, is a dialect in itself and any of its speakers sound "funny" in Manchester, England, or New Delhi, India.

2.   Usually different dialects of the same language have mutual comprehensibility, the same writing system, and basically the same grammar. This is particularly true of English and Spanish although not so much so for some other languages, like German and Italian (there is not always mutual comprehensibility between dialects of these languages) or Serbian and Croatian (each of these two dialects uses a totally different alphabet but practically the same words and grammatical structures).

3.   One dialect of a given language usually emerges as the dominant and thus standard or default dialect. This dialect then becomes identified as the language, and, for a variety of reasons, the other dialects are often left to decline in the number of speakers and importance. The best example for us is Spanish, which began as Castilian, one of many dialects on the Iberian peninsula descended from Latin. But for historical reasons, Castilian speakers came to be the dominant political, military (with the toughest fighters), and cultural force on the peninsula. Thus Castilian, as the most important dialect, became the language of Spain. Except for Portuguese, Catalan, and Basque, which are now languages, too, other Romance (late Latin) dialects, like Aragonese, Galician, Asturian, Leonese, have declined in importance, and some are even on the brink of extinction.

4.   Dialects can be geographical or regional, but also social, based on such factors as socio-economic class, age, sex, profession, and contact with other languages. Our approach to the study of Spanish has concerned itself almost exclusively with the former approach to dialectology.

5.   You must answer this one yourself, of course.

6.   The four languages of the Iberian peninsula are Spanish, Portuguese, Catalan, and Basque.

7.   Many Sephardic Jews, descended from the Jews who were expelled from Spain, along with the Moslems (Moors), in 1492, settled in eastern Mediterranean countries, and centuries later, Israel. Today these particular Israelis still speak Spanish (Judeo-Spanish or **ladino**) and publish materials in Spanish—sometimes with Latin characters as all other Spanish speakers do and sometimes in Hebrew characters.

8.   There are two principal theories to explain this fact. One is that the majority of the Spaniards who emigrated to the Americas were from southern Spain or at least had lived there for a considerable period of time before emigrating and thus basically transplanted their variety of Spanish to America. Another is that American Spanish, under the influence of later settlers from Spain, underwent certain similar sound changes at about the same time in history. Thus, American and southern peninsular Spanish evolved in the same direction but somewhat independently or indirectly. And, of course, the children of the more recent Spanish immigrants to Spanish America grew up speaking more like their peers than their parents.

9.   There are several important indigenous languages, with millions of speakers, in Spanish America today: Nahuatl in Mexico, Mayan in Meso-America, Quechua in the Andean regions of South America, Aymará in the same area, and Guaraní in Paraguay.

10.   You could try to delineate these divisions on the basis of the substratum or indigenous language mentioned in the previous question. Or you could base your division on lowland versus highland areas of Spanish America. Or you could make your division on the basis of the coastal versus the inland areas. These last two divisions are similar, but not the same since there are inland areas of Spanish America that are not really mountainous or even highland, such as the grasslands and low-lying agricultural areas of interior Venezuela, Paraguay, Uruguay, and Argentina.

11.   This is yours to answer.

4 Producing Speech Sounds: Phonation

1.   The *nasal cavity* is vital to speech since the airstream for all nasal sounds, such as [m], [n], and the nasalized vowels of languages like French, Portuguese, and Polish, passes through it rather than through the oral cavity. The *diaphragm*, along with the lungs, is used in respiration, which, of course, provides the airstream for all speech sounds. The *glottis* is the opening between the vocal bands through which the airstream passes for all speech sounds. When the bands are tightened during phonation or voicing, the glottis changes size and shape.

The *molars* play no role in the production of speech sounds (although the front teeth are important). Likewise with the *sinuses,* which, although they have some effect on the quality of one's voice, do not distinguish individual speech sounds in any way. The *epiglottis* covers and protects the air passage during the ingestion of food and liquid, but has no function in speech.

2.   Closing off the glottis, or the opening between the vocal bands, in essence creates a long column of air between that point through the entire breathing passage all the way to the lungs and diaphragm. This holds the diaphragm steady and enables one to tense the abdominal muscles, an action necessary for a variety of human exertive activities.

3.   Adult males normally have deeper voices than adult females for two principal reasons: they have thicker vocal bands, which vibrate at a slower rate and thus produce a deeper tone, and their resonance chambers, such as the pharynx and nasal cavity, are larger, thus producing lower frequencies as well.

4.   Phonation or voicing is created by tightening and relaxing the vocal bands as the airstream passes through the glottis, or opening between them. They vibrate and produce sound.

5.   All languages rely on phonation or voicing for the absolutely necessary ingredient of all human speech: vowels. Also languages use phonation or voicing to distinguish between consonants articulated in the same place and in the same way, such as [p] and [b], [s] and [z].

6.   The three resonating chambers are the throat or pharynx, the nasal cavity, and the mouth or buccal (oral) cavity.

7.   When you have a head cold and your nasal passages are blocked or at least narrowed, you cannot articulate nasal sounds properly—just the opposite of the popular notion. [m] sounds like [b], [n] like [d], and so forth. The average lay person knows that the nasal passage is obviously involved but does not really know how.

8.   To make a sound louder, you must increase the amplitude of the sound waves resulting from the vibration of the vocal bands produced during phonation. This is done by expelling the air from the lungs and up through the trachea and larynx with greater muscular force. The peaks of resulting sound waves are farther from point zero, that is, have greater amplitude. This is exactly what an electrical amplifier does to the sound waves in a stereo or public address system, although here the energy source is electrical, of course.

9.   To make a sound higher, you must increase the frequency of the sound waves, by tightening the vocal bands, thus producing more sound waves or cycles per second (also known as Hertz or Hz). This can be done artificially with voice recordings by increasing the speed of the tape or disk.

10.   Vowels are produced without significant obstruction or blockage in the vocal tract. Consonants result when the airstream is blocked or impeded in some significant way.

6 Stress in Spanish

*(Many of the practices from this point on are oral and are thus recorded on cassette, where the answers are provided. However, in practices like **A** and **G** in this chapter, where you are to respond in some way other than by just repeating or answering, answers are provided here in this Answer Key, too. The answers to written practices, of course, are not recorded and are provided only here.)*

A. [*also* recorded]

1. **llana**   2. **esdrújula**   3. **sobresdrújula**   4. **aguda**   5. **aguda**   6. **llana**
7. **llana**   8. **sobresdrújula**   9. **esdrújula**   10. **llana**   11. **aguda**   12. **llana**
13. **llana**   14. **aguda**   15. **llana**   16. **llana**   17. **sobresdrújula**   18. **aguda**
19. **llana**   20. **llana**   21. **sobresdrújula**   22. **llana**   23. **aguda**   24. **llana**

B.–F.   Oral Practices

G.

1. Es un amigo suyo.   2. A mí me gusta la lucha libre. (Me gusta la lucha libre a mí.)   3. No lo ha visto nadie.   4. O es un loco o es un genio la persona que siempre se habla a sí misma.   5. ¿La conoces a ella? (¿A ella la conoces?)   6. No es vídeo tuyo (El vídeo no es tuyo); no lo puedes tomar.   7. ¿También le gusta la lucha libre

a él/a ella? (¿A ella/a él también le gusta la lucha libre?)   8. Creo que la Mafia se llama entre los "miembros" "Cosa nuestra".   9. Tampoco lo comprendo a él.   10. ¿Por qué siempre critica lo que escribo yo?

H.

1. Se comunica con los ingleses por medio del teléfono.   2. Sí, es (or es) lo que llaman ustedes un carácter, pero tenemos muchos caracteres como él por aquí.   3. Imagínese que ya se va la señora Martínez.   4. El chico cuyo padre era el candidato demócrata el año pasado es (or es) alumno mío.   5. —¿Tienes suficiente papel? —Sí, esta caja me basta.   6. Figúrese, me contó la anécdota en la que no pudieron encontrar el antídoto a tiempo.   7. —Solicito ayuda de unos alumnos que sean muy, muy (*likelihood of primary stress is indicated by repetition of word* **muy**) diligentes, con mucha responsabilidad. —¿Los has encontrado? —Todavía no y francamente no me lo explico.   8. —Celebre usted la llegada de un hombre tan (or tan) célebre. —Ya lo celebré.

7 Intonation in Spanish

A.–R.   Oral Practices

S.

1. ¿Cuándo tienen que comenzar?

2. Quiere sacar este vídeo por dos días.

3. ¿Cómo te va, hombre?

4. ¿Sabe usted el número de su apartamento?

or ¿Sabe usted el número de su apartamento?

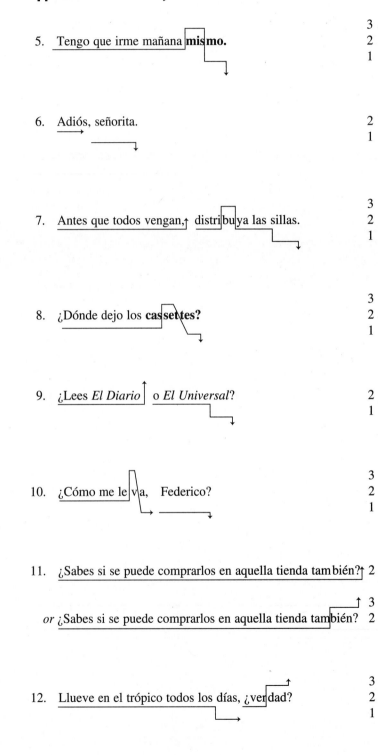

5. Tengo que irme mañana **mismo.**

3
2
1

6. Adiós, señorita.

2
1

7. Antes que todos vengan, distribuya las sillas.

3
2
1

8. ¿Dónde dejo los **cassettes?**

3
2
1

9. ¿Lees *El Diario* o *El Universal*?

2
1

10. ¿Cómo me le va, Federico?

3
2
1

11. ¿Sabes si se puede comprarlos en aquella tienda también? 2

or ¿Sabes si se puede comprarlos en aquella tienda también?

3
2

12. Llueve en el trópico todos los días, ¿verdad?

3
2
1

8 The Rhythm of Spanish

A.–C. Oral Practices

9 Spanish Sounds Beyond the System

    1.   *Paralanguage* refers to sounds beyond the regular system of segmental (vowels and consonants) and suprasegmental sound features (stress, pitch, juncture). They are considered beyond the regular system because they are so numerous, so varied, so individualized that they defy systematic analysis and organization into discrete classes, units, degrees, and levels, as we do with vowels, consonants, stress, and pitch.

    2.   By causing your vocal bands to *break*, you can create such paralinguistic vocalizations as crying, laughing, quavering, and tremolo.

    3.   In English we can make *ingressive* or *implosive sounds*, such as a bilabial click—used to represent a kiss or to call a dog, an alveolar click with the tongue tip and blade—used to express disapproval (*Tsk-Tsk!*), a lateral click with the sides of the tongue—used to urge on a horse, to express satisfaction or approval, and so on. You can probably think of more, but remember, to answer this question properly you must cite sounds made by pulling the air back *into* your mouth rather than by expelling it.

    4.   *Interjections* are paralinguistic sounds that accompany our actions and express our emotions. Sometimes they are actual words (found in the dictionary), such as Spanish **¡Caramba!, ¡Vaya...!** or English *Shoot!, No way!*, but more often they are made-up words, such as Spanish **¡Ayyyy!, ¡Upa!** or English *Whew!, Boooo!* You can probably think of many more in your own language. Careful—some of them are a bit dubious for polite company!

    5.   *Onomatopoeic sounds* are paralinguistic sounds meant to imitate or represent sounds around us: man-made noises, natural phenomena, animal cries. In Spanish a gunshot is **¡Pum!**, an insect makes the noise indicted by the verb **zumbar**; in English an object falls into the water with a *Splash!*, and a thunderbolt goes *Crash!* Once again you can think of many more. Notice that the Spanish equivalents do not seem to sound as right to us as the English sounds, and vice versa for the Spanish speakers.

    6.   *Semantic signals* substitute for words to express ideas or semantic notions. In Spanish **¡Misimismisi!** in a falsetto voice is used to call a cat; **Este...** indicates hesitation, uncertainty, or pausing while searching for the next words. In English vocal band breaking (laughing) indicates humorous approval or almost the opposite, scorn and derision; a prolonged *Shhhhhhh!* is a call for silence. You can probably come up with many more.

    7.   There is no good explanation for the fact that so many of these *paralinguistic vocalizations* in both Spanish and English use sounds and sound patterns absent in the normal phonetic inventory of each language. One possible explanation is that speakers want to call attention to these ''words,'' and one way to do it is to use unfamiliar or strange

sounds and sound combinations. Another is that these vocalizations are the vestiges of sounds made thousands and thousands of years ago by humans before they possessed language. At any rate, these vocalizations are universal in the sense that all human beings use them. Yet they are also language specific since they vary from language to language even in the case of onomatopoeic sounds, which purport to represent sounds that would seem to be the same to all humans. Two of the best sources for these paralinguistic manifestations are comic strips, where they must be represented graphically in the balloons above the characters' heads, and some educational children's television programs.

8.   You must answer this one on your own.

9.   Again, this one is for you.

10.   Even though noises in the real world probably sound exactly alike to human beings everywhere, our choice of sounds or words to represent them is undoubtedly influenced greatly by our own language and is often purely conventional. In English at an early age in children's literature, comic strips, television, and advertising we get used to seeing the representation of a rooster's crow as *Cockaaadoodledoooo!* But Spanish-speaking children see **¡Quiquiriquíííí!** in their environment. Thus our own word is the first one that occurs to us to represent the sound, although, if we think better of it, we may feel it is really not very accurate and perhaps not even as good as the foreign word for the same sound. It would be interesting to see how bilinguals handle these matters—especially if they are exposed to the influences mentioned above in both langauges on a fairly equal basis from an early age. Maybe there is someone in your class who can answer this.

10 Reviewing the Melody of Spanish (CHAPTERS 5–9)

1. false   2. (a)   3. false   4. phonemic (functional, contrastive)   5. false   6. a particular species of bird   7. false   8. free form   9. (c)   10. **porque** is unstressed because it is a subordinating conjunction, but the **qué** of **por qué** is stressed because it is an interrogative   11. (a)   12. **aguda, llana, esdrújula** (also **sobresdrújula**)   13. (c)   14. true   15. They are cognates, that is, related words, with different stress patterns from their English counterparts.   16. (a)   17. true   18. (a)   19. true   20. vocative   21. false   22. (c)   23. interrogative, interrogative   24. (b)   25. true   26. (b)   27. syllable-timed   28. (c)   29. true   30. false   31. **¡Achís!**   32. (c)   33. true

11 Producing Speech Sounds: Articulation

1.   The upper or fixed articulators are the upper lip, the upper front teeth, the alveolar ridge, the hard palate, the velum, and the uvula. The lower or movable articulators are the lower lip and the tongue (tip, blade, dorsum, root). The terms "fixed" and "movable" must not be taken in an absolutely literal way, but rather relatively, since the upper

lip moves slightly in the articulation of some sounds and the uvula moves as the airstream flows between it and the tongue dorsum.

2.   Place (point) of articulation, manner of articulation, and function of the vocal bands (voicing or the lack of it).

3.   Glottal, uvular, velar, palatal, palato-alveolar, alveolar, dental, interdental, labio-dental, bilabial.

4.   English has /p/ *pat*, /b/ *bat*, /t/ *time*, /d/ *dime*, /k/ *curl*, /g/ *girl*. Spanish has the same six: **peso, beso, tía, día, callo, gallo**.

5.   The manner of articulation known as affricate is in a sense a double articulation since it starts as a stop and ends as a fricative, like the English palatal [č] of *church*, or the Spanish palatal [ŷ] of ¡**yo**! German has a bilabial, labio-dental affricate [pf], as in **Pferd** *horse,* and an alveolar affricate [ts], as **Zeit** *time.*

6.   All dialects of English have exactly the same alveolar tap, as in *water,* that Spanish does, as in **caro**, except that in English, due to linguistic convention, it is represented by the phonetic symbol [t̂] and in Spanish by [r]. Thus the English phrase *eight o'* or *ate a* and the Spanish word **era** are virtually identical, at least as far as the consonants go. American English does not have trills anymore, although at one time Americans in very formal and dramatic speech—particularly on the stage—could use the same alveolar trill heard occasionally in British English today: "Thrrrree times, milords!" Scottish English has this trill also.

7.   Since the airstream in the oral tract is blocked, obstructed, or impeded in some significant way for the production of consonants, we find place and manner of articulation (these obstructions) a very convenient way of describing and/or classifying consonants. But the airstream flows out relatively unimpeded in the production of vowels, which are determined more by the size and shape of the oral cavity. This in turn is controlled by the position of the tongue, so for Spanish and English we classify vowels in a two-dimensional configuration based on the front-to-back and high-low position of the tongue. For other languages, like French and German, other parameters, such as lip-rounding and nasalization, are necessary, too.

8.   The vowel triangle is the graphic representation of the positions of the tongue in the production of vowels as seen from a side view. It is perfect for a three-vowel system /i a u/, like Classical Quechua, or a five-vowel system, like Spanish, where there are no central vowels. But in English there are central vowels produced with the tongue not at the perimeter of the vowel triangle, as it is for Spanish. Thus, a quadrangular configuration seems more appropriate to represent English vowels than a triangle.

9.   There is no point in marking vowel nasalization or lip-rounding in a phonetic transcription in Spanish since both features happen obligatorily and automatically below the level of awareness of Spanish speakers. Vowels between nasal consonants and sometimes before them—as in **mano** or **enfermo**—are automatically nasalized. Both back vowels in Spanish, [u] and [o], have automatic lip-rounding, and both front vowels, [i] and [e], have no lip-rounding, but rather slight lip-spreading. But both features have to be

indicated in some way in a phonetic transcription for a language like French, since neither is automatic and both are phonemic and contrastive.

10.   Things do not come out perfectly or neatly in any analysis or description of sounds in language. There are at least two disadvantages to the traditional place-and-manner of articulation system that we use in this book. First, the parameters used for consonants must be changed for vowels, as we have indicated above. Place and manner of articulation are replaced by tongue position since it determines the size and shape of the oral cavity. Second, some important consonantal distinctions must be indicated with additional descriptors that cannot be shown on a traditional place-and-manner of articulation chart. For example, there are various types of *s*'s in Spanish; two distinct types are both voiceless alveolar groove fricatives and thus fit in the same compartment of our consonant chart. Other systems of phonetic analysis in which these objections are answered—such as generative phonology—are extremely detailed, complicated, and have limited value to the foreign-language student. The last objection is perhaps the most serious. The interlocutor interprets speech sounds on the basis of *perception*, not articulation, since he or she obviously cannot actually see what is going on inside the speaker's mouth. Yet our system is based almost exclusively on *articulation*, not acoustics or auditory reception. However, the pedagogical advantages of the system used in this book far outweigh the theoretical advantages of other systems of phonetic analysis. Using this system, we feel you can learn to articulate all these sounds like a native speaker of Spanish and thus acquire an authentic Spanish accent. It is doubtful that this could happen if you approached the matter with other systems of phonetic analysis.

12 Contrasting the Sounds of Spanish

1.   Although a baby can make an infinite variety of sounds, only a relatively small number of them is used in the language spoken by its caregivers. Thus the baby gradually learns only the sounds it hears and which elicit desired responses, discards the many it does not hear, and narrows the range down to the two or three dozen of its own language.

2.   Unfortunately, practically every linguistics book uses a slightly different set of symbols, although there is a significant number used in almost all books. This situation exists for a variety of reasons—some substantive and some rather trivial. Certain symbols seem better suited to one language than to another, certain ones have become traditional among linguists that work in a given language, certain ones are a holdover from the typewriter days, certain ones don't look right in a given type font, and certain ones are used because linguists disagree on the exact properties of the sounds they represent. One quick example: some very prestigious Spanish phonetics books used [ɲ] as the symbol for palatal *n*, as in **año**, whereas others, like this book, use [ñ]. If you had to produce this symbol on a keyboard, which one would you use and why?

3.   **Boldface** type is used in this book to represent conventional Spanish orthography in an English text, like the word **año** in the preceding answer 2. It is also used for conventional orthography in examples from other languages—like **lait** for French or **Staat**

for German. *Italics* is used for English words and glosses in an English text: "**Año** means *year* in English." It is also used for letters, like palatal *n*, and also to emphasize English words in a text: "**Ceceo** does *not* characterize the speech of most Spaniards from central and northern Spain." Square brackets enclose *phonetic* transcription, like the word **bobo**, which is transcribed [bó-ƀo]. Slash bars enclose *phonemic* transcription, like /bóbo/ for the word in the previous sentence. By the way, notice other differences between these last two transcriptions.

4.   No, we will not try to transcribe every Spanish sound that is known to exist, although it might seem to you at times that we do. First of all, there is no complete agreement among linguists as to how many of these sounds there are and exactly what they are. And, even if there were complete agreement, it would be an unnecessary waste of time because many of these sounds are pronounced automatically and below the level of awareness of both the native speaker of Spanish and you as a foreign learner of Spanish. If you pronounce the words **quiso** and **caso** very slowly in Spanish, even lingering over the first syllables, you will notice that even though both of them are transcribed with the same initial consonant symbol [k], there is quite a difference in the placement of the tongue against the roof of the mouth for each. (This, of course, has *nothing* to do with the spelling differences, **qu** and **c**.) Try it again and notice exactly where your tongue touches. The same is true of English: try *keep* and *cop*. In some languages these two different *k*'s are phonemically distinct, but not in Spanish and English. In fact, they are even difficult to perceive unless your attention is drawn to them. Even then some of you may not get the difference. So why try to distinguish them in transcription? Try a variety of words with *s* in English. Are all the *s* sounds exactly alike from a precise phonetic point of view?

5.   If you tried to make lists of common English words with these different varieties of /p/, you would not be helping the foreigner very much, although it might cause you to realize that each variety of /p/ kept appearing in a certain position in all these words you were collecting. And this, of course, is the key to solving the problem. You would realize that aspirated [pʰ] occurred at the beginning of all your *p*-initial words, like *pit, pat, pill*, or in the middle of the words between vowels, the second one of which was stressed, like *appear, oppose, impel*. You would realize that all the unaspirated [p] sounds occurred after *s*, like *spit, spat, spill, aspire, dispel*. And you would realize that all the unreleased [p-] sounds occurred at the end of the words, like *lip, cup, top, sleep*. Thus it would be much more helpful to try to convey this information as simply as possible to your friend so that he or she would understand the principle involved and be able to *predict* the correct variety of /p/ in advance on his or her own and get new words, like *pour, spore, depose, rap, right* without consulting long lists of words.

6.   A phoneme is a family or group of sounds that function meaningfully in the language. The phoneme has properties that, when taken together, make it different from every other phoneme in the language since none of them have the exact same combination of properties. For example, /p/ and /b/ in both Spanish and English are bilabial stops, but they are distinct because one is voiced and the other is not. /p/ and /t/ are both voiceless stops, but they are distinct because one is bilabial and the other is dental (in Spanish) or

alveolar (in English). /b/ and /m/ are both voiced bilabials, but they are distinct because one is a stop and the other is a nasal. Each of the phonemes mentioned above and many others in both languages have at least a couple of members in its family, that is, allophones, that occur in predictable environments but whose properties do not contrast with each other. For example, all varieties of /d/ in Spanish or /p/ in English function the same way, although these varieties (allophones) have discernible differences. Yet their similarities are more important than their differences. The crucial contrastive feature of /d/ in Spanish is that it is voiced and dental, not that it is a stop or a fricative, because it is both of these, in certain environments. The crucial contrastive feature of /p/ in English is that it is a voiceless bilabial stop, not that it is aspirated, unaspirated, or unreleased, because it is all of these, in certain environments. The Spanish word **cada** may sound funny with a stop [d], instead of a fricative [ɖ], but it is still **cada**. The English word *pill* may sound funny with an unaspirated [p], instead of an aspirated [pʰ], but it is still *pill*. But **cada** with a *voiceless* intervocalic consonant is no longer **cada**, but **cata**, a very different word. And *pill* with a *voiced* initial consonant is not longer *pill*, but *bill*, a very different word. The right allophones make your language sound normal, natural, native-like; but the right phonemes allow it to be understood and thus permit communication to take place—whether in a native-like manner or not.

7.   An asterisk * in this book means that the form is impossible, ungrammatical, or nonexistent in the language—like ****quiería** or ***huerreque** in Spanish or **am't* (the contraction of *am* and *not*) in English. In historical linguistics, however, it is used to represent a word that linguists are pretty sure actually existed but for which no written record or documentation has ever been found, like ***capitia**, thought to have been the word for *head* at a previous time in Spanish. We perhaps could use the * in this way before the names of supposed historical personages like *King Arthur, *Robin Hood, or *Count Dracula. You probably can think of more.

8.   The quickest way to prove the existence of a phoneme in language is to find a minimal pair. For example, in Spanish **p<u>a</u>so – p<u>e</u>so** or **mes<u>a</u>s – mes<u>e</u>s** and dozens of such pairs of words show the existence of two vowel phonemes: /a/ and /e/. The same for English with *l<u>o</u>t – l<u>e</u>t* or *sw<u>a</u>pped – sw<u>e</u>pt* to prove the existence of /a/ and /ɛ/.

9.   Sometimes it is hard, if not impossible, to find a minimal pair to prove the existence of a phoneme. Usually a native speaker's intuition is reliable here, and, if the native speaker feels there is a phonemic difference between two sounds, he or she is probably right. Sometimes a near minimal pair is sufficient. A near minimal pair is two words that differ in more than one place, such as *illusion* and *dilution,* to prove the existence of /ž/ and /š/ as phonemes in English, even though the second word begins with a /d/. This is enough for native speakers to be able to decide that the two sibilants in question are phonemes. The best technique, however, in lieu of real minimal pairs, is the one outlined in the answer to 10, below.

10.   If the linguist finds all the phonetically similar phones of the supposed phoneme and begins to tally their distribution, significant patterns begin to emerge. For example, in the case of Spanish /d/, the linguist will find that the stop allophone [d] and the fricative

allophone [ɖ] never seem to occur in the same environment. This leads him or her to doubt that they are phonemes, since there is no possibility of contrast, and leads him or her to suspect that they are allophones of the same phoneme. A quick check of two words, such as [lá-do] and [lá-ɖo], shows that, since these two words are felt to be the same by the native speaker, the two phones in question are allophones of the same phoneme and not distinct phonemes.

11.   The reason for giving the exceptional or unusual cases first in a phonological rule is simply one of economy. The exceptions are always fewer in number and much easier to state. Thus, if they are excluded, then the majority of cases, for example, the elsewhere environments, do not have to be stated individually. It is simpler and quicker to state the few exceptions than the numerous typical cases.

12.   Complementary distribution means that one allophone of a phoneme does not occur in certain environments where the other or others do. In Spanish, [d] and [ɖ] are mutually exclusive in their distribution, leading the linguist to suspect that they are allophones rather than phonemes, which usually contrast somewhere in the language in the form of a minimal pair. Occasionally, however, allophones of the same phoneme do appear in the same environment without changing the meaning. This is free or non-functional variation. In English, for example, although the various allophones of /p/ are in complementary distribution most of the time, occasionally the aspirated allophone [pʰ] is used in word-final position, as in the very emphatic pronunciation of the word *up*. Most of the time, however, the unreleased allophone [p⁻] occurs. Since there is no change in meaning, and the environment is exactly the same, and the native speaker is often unable to hear the difference or explain it if he or she does hear it, we refer to this as pure free variation. The problem arises when foreign learners of English, especially those who are speakers of a language where these two sounds are important, wonder why one is used sometimes and the other at other times.

13.   A phonological rule or formula is really a statement of the way native speakers handle the phoneme in question. Native speakers use the language, and the linguist attempts to describe this usage and summarize it in the form of a rule or statement, one that will be particularly useful to the foreign learner of the language so he or she will be able to use the phoneme exactly as native speakers do. Thus, for native speakers of Spanish, the phonological rules you see are summaries or statements of their linguistic behavior. But for you, as a foreign learner of Spanish, the rule is a prescription or guideline for your pronunciation so that you will sound native-like. The native speaker provides the input to the rule; you, as a student, view the output as a model for your own pronunciation.

14.   The nul symbol [Ø] represents silence only in the sense that the phoneme in question is not sounded or pronounced where indicated. In the /d/ rule for Spanish, this symbol means that in certain cases no /d/ is pronounced, such as at the end of a word or in the **-ado** ending. Thus silence simply means non-occurrence or omission. In English an example of this would be the zeroing out of the /k/ phoneme in the middle of the word *Arctic* or the colloquial pronunciation of the word *picture*, which sounds like *pitcher* when the /k/ is omitted.

13 Sound Groups in Spanish

A.

1. a-bo-ri-gen 2. cons-truc-ción 3. buey 4. le-che-ro 5. tran-qui-li-zar
6. hay 7. de-sas-tro-so 8. pai-sa-no 9. a-ún 10. cau-di-llo 11. in-no-va-
ción 12. ma-lo-grar 13. cons-tan-te 14. a-ho-gar 15. pa-ís 16. que-brar
17. gra-duáis 18. ins-trui-do 19. sub-ver-sión 20. i-nhu-ma-no 21. ha-bi-
tuar-se 22. ca-os 23. trans-plan-te 24. deu-da 25. ex-tra-or-di-na-rio 26. pa-
se-ar 27. aun-que 28. ho-mo-ge-nei-dad 29. sub-ra-yar 30. a-hí 31. ho-
yue-lo 32. dí-a 33. ins-ti-tu-ción 34. ahu-ma-do 35. co-rrió 36. ob-viar
37. po-e-sí-a 38. a-ma-rrar 39. o-í-do 40. ba-úl

B.

1. e-la-ni-mal 2. e-lhi-jo 3. la-hi-ja 4. lahi-ji-ta 5. la-shi-jas 6. ha-bla-nes-
pa-ñol 7. sua-ve 8. mia-mi-go 9. mi-sa-mi-gos 10. pa-ra-es-tehi-ji-to
11. se-ve-í-a-mui- (*or* mu-i-) bien *or just* mui-bien 12. e-nE-cua-dor 13. so-
nhom-bres 14. son-nom-bres 15. la-so-bras 16. las-so-bras 17. la-o-dio
18. ha-bleus-ted 19. la-hon-ra 20. po-re-la-mo-ra-mi-pa-tria 21. la-is-la-se
-ha-lla-e-nel-Me-di-te-rrá-ne-o.   22.   Las-lla-mas-van-por-las-ca-lles-de-
Cuz-co. 23. La-chi-ca-del-ga-da-co-rrió-tra-sel-pe-rro. 24. Tie-nes-que-sub-ra-
yar-to-dos-lo-se-le-men-to-sin-te-re-san-tes. 25. El-chi-cha-ro-se-cul-ti-va-mu-cho-
en-Puer-to-Ri-co. 26. A-mi-hi-ja-no-le-gus-tan-pa-ra-na-da-las-co-rri-das-de-to-ros.
27. El-bú-ho-es-ta-ba-de-ma-lhu-mor ‖ y-no-qui-so-can-tar. 28. Se-pro-hí-be-fi-
jar-car-te-le-se-nes-tos-mu-ros-de-la-ciu-dad. 29. E-lár-bi-tro-gri-tó-en-vo-zal-ta, ‖
"¡Ru-de-zain-ne-ce-sa-ria!" 30. To-dos-los-miem-bros-de-nues-tra-cla-se-se-re-ú-
ne-ne-nes-ta-au-la-en-la-plan-ta-ba-ja.

C.

1. In Practice A items 2, 6, 8, 10, 11, 18, 19, 21, 24, 25, 27, 28, 31, 33, 34, 35, 36
have *diphthongs*. In Practice B items 4, 7, 8, 10, 11 (2), 12, 17, 18, 20, 23, 24, 25,
28, 29 (2), 30 (3) have *diphthongs*. Notice that items 11, 29, and 30 each have more
than one. In Practice A items 3 and 17 have *triphthongs*. Practice B has no *triphthongs*.
2. In Practice A items, 9, 14, 15, 22, 25, 26, 30, 32, 37 (2), 39, 40 have vowels in
hiatus. Notice that item 37 has two cases. In Practice B items 3, 10, 11 (2), 17, 19,
21 (4), 25, 26, 27 (2), 28, 29, 30 (3) have vowels in hiatus. Notice that items 11, 21,
27, and 30 each have more than one case. 3. In Practice B items 3, 21, 26 the words
hija, isla, and **hija,** respectively, all have stressed /í/ because they are all nouns and
are thus stressed in the stream of speech. They have no written accents due to the
rules of Spanish spelling. 4. In Practice B items 1, 2, 5, 6, 9, 12, 13, 15, 20 (3), 21,
23, 24 (2), 27, 28 (2), 29 (2), 30 (2) have **enlace.** Notice that items 20, 24, 28, 29,
and 30 each have more than one.

15 The Low Vowel /a/ and the Mid Vowels /e/ and /o/

A.–E. Oral Practices

F.

As the instructions at the end of Chapter 15 indicated, these transcription answers contain all the correct symbols, even though we have not taken all of them up yet. The symbols we have had thus far—[a e o]—are underlined; thus in succeeding chapters there will be more and more sounds underlined. As always there will be a few cases where there is more than one possible answer. Check with your instructor if you are convinced that one of your symbols, although not given in this Answer Key, is correct.

1. [pa-pá-ƀá-a-la-ƀá-na-pa-ra-ƀlár-le-ar-nál̩-do-a-rá-na]
2. [ál-ƀa-ro-es-tá-a-lé-ǵre ‖ i-ki-sás-ƀá-a-kom-pa-ñá-ra-pa-pá-kuan̯-do-ƀá-ya]
3. [bus-ka-rán-r̄e-kuér-ɖos-pa-ra-tó-ɖa-la-fa-mí-lia]
4. [el̩-dok-tór-ke-ƀús-ko-nó-es-tá-en-su-kon-sul̩-tó-rio ‖ ez-ɖe-sír-suo-fi-sí-na ‖ si-no-e-ne-los-pi-tál]
5. [prón̩-to-lo-to-mó]
6. [el-koŋ-gré-so-ɖe-on̩-dú-ras-kom-ple-tó-tó-ɖo-lo-po-sí-ƀle]
7. [e-nel̩-tró-pi-ko-lou-mi-yá-ron ‖ ki-tán̩-do-le-ló-ro-yel-fós-fo-ro-ke-r̄o-ƀó]
8. [bí-ƀeus-té-ɖem-pa-na-má]
9. [bés-lo-ke-á-sen]
10. [eŋ-ké-kúr-so-pién-sa-sa-sé-ré-se-tra-ƀá-xo]
11. [pién-so-a-sér-lo-e-nés-ta-klá-se]
12. [e-lóm-brei-sus-pa-rién̩-tes-ƀi-ƀe-ne-ne-ló-tro-pué-ƀlo]
13. [bís-te-la-es-tá-tua-ɖe-ɖoŋ-ki-xó-ten-la-ká-ye-me-ɖi-na-sé-li]
14. [kré-o-ke-se-yá-ma-sí-e-les-tá-ɖo-ɖe-ko-lo-rá-ɖo-po-rel-ko-lór-ɖe-la-tié-r̄a]
15. [r̄e-kuér-ɖe-nus-té-ɖes-ke-las-pér-las-nó-pa-ré-sem-ba-lió-sas ‖ pe-ro-el-r̄éi-las-kié-re-pa-ra-pa-ǵár-las-ɖéu-ɖa-se-neu-ró-pa]

16 The High Vowel /i/

A.–E. Oral Practices

F.

This time the allophones of the vowels /a e o i/ will be underlined.

1. [iǵ-ná-sio-e-sum-pai-sá-no-mí-o]
2. [bi-ƀí-a-mo-se-nel-míz-mo-pa-ís ‖ bo-lí-ƀia ‖ á-se-ɖie-si-séi-so-ɖie-si-sié-te-á-ños]
3. [i-é-so-es-kó-mo-sein̩-te-re-só-en-lo-sa-sún̩-toz-ɖe-mia-mí-ǵo-sói-lo]

4. [i-lo̯im-por-tán-tes-ke-βi̯é-ne-a-la-si̯u-đá-đa-yu-đár-len-la-far-má-si̯a]

5. [es-tói̯-se-ǵú-ro-đe-la-pro-nun-si̯a-si̯ón-de-pa-lá-βras-ko-mo-a-lér-xi̯a ‖ e-ner-xí-a ‖ e-mo-r̄á-xi̯a ‖ i-me-lo-đí-a ‖ kṷan̯-do-βé-o-las-tíl̯-des ‖ ez-đe-sír-lo-sa-sén̯-to-ses-krí-tos]

17 The High Vowel /u/

A.–E.   Oral Practices

F.

This time nothing will be underlined since we have had all the vowels and none of the consonants.

1. [au̯ŋ-ke-nó-sé-a-la-káṷ-sa-đe-la-đéṷ-đa ‖ lo̯u-mí-ya-mú-ĉo]
2. [la-pe-lí-ku-la-ú-ne-se-nel-sí-neṷ-ró-pa]
3. [bá-mo-sa-to-má-re-láṷ-to ‖ ú-ǵo]
4. [bṷé-no ‖ pú-se-lá-ǵu̯a-kí ‖ i-a-ó-ra-wé-le-a-ú-mo]
5. [kṷi-đá-đo ‖ a-kí-ú-βo̯u-nak-si-đén̯-te-đe-ǵu̯á-ǵu̯a-sá-seṷ-noz-đí-as]
6. [kṷán̯-tos-ki̯é-res ‖ si̯é-te-u-ó-ĉo]
7. [pṷe-seṷ-sé-βi̯o ‖ nó-es-ni-βṷé-no-ni-fu̯ér-te-ni-su̯á-βe-ni̯ú-til]

18 Vowel Combinations in Spanish

A.–G.   Oral Practices

H.

Although we have had all the vowels, this time only vowel combinations *will be underlined. Remember that the assumption is that these sentences are being read or spoken in* careful *speech.*

1. [la-á-ma-kon̯-tó-đa-su-ál-ma]
2. [nó-kré-o-ke-los-po-é-ta-se-pa-sé-em-po-rés-ta-βe-ní-đa]
3. [me-si̯én̯-to-a-o-ǵá-đo]
4. [mei̯-ma-xí-no-ke-te-í-βa-sa-lau̯-ni̯ón]
5. [ke-rí-a-đi̯e-si-séi̯-so-đi̯e-si-si̯é-te ‖ pe-ro-nó-ái̯-a-kí-más-ke-kín-se]
6. [pi̯én-so-ke-és-đe-ku̯a-đór]
7. [su-á-βe-és-su̯á-βe]
8. [i-é-so-nó-es-ŷé-so]
9. [si-én̯-tras ‖ lo-si̯én̯-te-sen-se-ǵí-đa]
10. [sá-βe-él-ke-la-kó-sa-nó-pṷé-đe-mé-nos-kem-pe-o-rár]

I.

Only vowel combinations *are underlined. This time the speech is* rapid. *In the few cases where there is more than one possibility, the most likely vowel is indicated in the regular line of phonetic transcription and the alternate immediately above in its complete syllable.*

1. [lá-ma-koṇ-tó-đa-su̯ál-ma]
      -kréu̯-   -pu̯é-
2. [nó-kré-o-ke-los-po-é-ta-se-pa-sém-po-rés-ta-ƀe-ní-đa]
3. [me-si̯én-tu̯au̯-ǵá-đo]
4. [mi̯-ma-xí-no-ke-tí-ƀa-sa-lu̯-ni̯ón]
                                             -ái̯-
5. [ke-rí-a-đi̯e-si-séi̯-so-đi̯e-si-si̯é-te ‖ pe-ro-nó-á-ya-kí-más-ke-kín-se]
6. [pi̯én-so-kéz-đe-ku̯a-đór]
7. [su̯á-ƀe-su̯á-ƀe]
8. [yé-so-nó-ez-ŷé-so]
9. [si̯éṇ-tras ‖ lo-si̯éṇ-te-sen-se-ǵí-đa]
                                          -pi̯o-
10. [sá-ƀél-ke-la-kó-sa-nó-pu̯é-đe-mé-nos-kem-pe-o-rár]

19 Reviewing the Vowels of Spanish (CHAPTERS 14–18)

A. Oral Practice

B.

1. true   2. [I ɛ æ ɨ ə ʌ U ɔ]   3. true   4. (a)   5. devoiced   6. false   7. (c)
8. true   9. (c)   10. It is represented in writing, either with the letters **ei**, as in **reina**, **veinte**, or **ey**, as in **ley** or **rey**.   11. true   12. semi-vowel (glide)   13. (c)
14. condition   15. false   16. (a)   17. false   18. (a)   19. **y** (as in **hay**), **i** (as in **isla**), and **hi** (as in **hijo**).   20. (a)   21. between vowels when the second one starts a word, as in **siete u ocho**, or when it ends a word after a vowel and precedes a word beginning with a vowel, as in **Bernabeu es un estadio.**   22. (c)   23. [æ]   24. true
25. (b)   26. true   27. (b)   28. style of speech, stress, word and morpheme boundaries, the nature of the vowels themselves   29. true   30. before the same vowel when stressed (as in **mi hijo** or **su humo**) or when it occurs before /a e o/ at morpheme or word boundaries in careful speech (as in **fió**, **mi amigo** or **graduar**, **su oficina**.)
31. false   32. (a)   33. careful (slow)   34. true (as in **me imagino** or **lo único**)
35. (b)   36. **la oficina** [la-o- . . .], [lo- . . .], or [lau̯- . . .]; **la esposa** [la-es- . . .], [les- . . .], or [lai̯s- . . .]

21 The Voiceless Consonants /p t k/

A.–E.   Oral Practices

F.

As we indicated in the instructions, now only the consonants will be underlined, chapter by chapter. Of course, even though the vowels are no longer underlined, you are expected to know all these allophones.

1. [pá-ɸlo   kié-ro-to-má-ru-na-tá-sa-ɖe-té]   2
                                                                1

2. [to-más   a-tí-te-ǵús-ta-má-sel-xú-ǥo-ɖe-na-rán̠-xa↑   2

   o-la-kó-ka-kó-la]   2
                                                                1

3. [el-se-més-tre-ɖe-la-es-kué-la-e-le-men̠-tál-ko-mién-sa-prin-sí-pios-ɖe-se-tiém-bre]

4. [kí-so-kom-prá-run-lí-tro-ɖe-ke-ro-sén ‖ pe-ro-na-tu-rál-mén̠-tel-kiós-ko-nó-te-ní-a-és-tas-kó-sas]

                                                                3
5. [po-ɖrí-a-to-má-rum-po-kí-to-ɖe-ké-so]↑   2

6. [bus-ké-un̠-ték-ni-ko-pa-ra-ke-me-a-yu-ɖá-ra-kon-la-kom-fek-sión̠-ɖe-lát-las]

22 The Voiced Consonants /b d g/

A.–G.   Oral Practices

H.

Alternate possibilities will be indicated immediately above the regular line of transcription, but only *alternatives for the sounds we have had thus far. Check with your instructor if you do not understand any of these alternatives.*

                     -tu̯a-   3
1. [bié-ne-ɸe-ní-to-a-ɸér-tel-sá-ɸa-ɖo]↑   2

2. [nó ‖ ké-ɸá ‖ bá-ɸi-si-tá-ra-pá-ɸlo ‖ ke-ɸí-ɸem-be-ne-su̯é-la]

                    -ku̯a-
3. [bík-tor-fu̯é-al-ƀaŋ-ko-a-kam-bi̯á-run̄-ĉé-ke-pa-ra-kom-prá-rel-ƀo-lé-to]
4. [e-d̶u̯ár-d̶o-me-d̶í-xo-ke-r̄ei̯-nál̦-do-le-d̶e-ƀí-a-mú-ĉo-d̶i-né-ro]

                         -di̯aṇ-
5. [ku̯aṇ-do-me-ƀi̯ó ↑ me-pre-ǥuṇ-to-d̶óṇ-de-aṇ-dá-ƀa-   2

        -du̯e-
    r̄e-nál̦-do-e-nés-toz-d̶í-as]   2
                          └───┘   1

                          -ru̯é-re-
6. [le-r̄es-poṇ-dí-ke-nó-sa-ƀí-a-ná-d̶a ‖ pe-ro-é-ra-e-ƀi-d̶éṇ-te-ke-nó-me-kre-í-a]
7. [ke-rí-a-fu-ǥár-se-d̶e-lal̦-d̶é-a ‖ pe-ro-nó-es-tá-ƀa-se-ǥú-ra-ke-pu-d̶i̯é-ra-kom-ple-
    tár-la-ma-ni̯ó-ƀra-ko-nék-si-to]

                                                                          3
8. [le-ǥri-tá-ron   gu̯ár-d̶i̯a   béŋ-ga   béŋ-ga]   2
   ─────────────→   └─┐   └─┐   └─┐   1
                          └→   └→   └→

                          -tel-
9. [kom-prél-ƀes-tí-d̶o-por-ke-me-ǥús-tai̯l-ko-lór-né-ǥro ‖ i-por-

    ki̯a-   -ru-
    ke-a-d̶e-má-sé-rau̯-na-ǥráŋ-gáŋ-ga]

         -d̶á-o-   -o-
10. [é-mos-tar-d̶á-d̶o-d̶e-ma-si̯a-d̶o-ti̯ém-po ‖ d̶á-te-prí-sa ‖ a-ká-ƀa-yá]

23 The Voiced Consonants /y/ and /w/

A.–C. Oral Practices

E.

    yá-┐   -ŷe-   3
1. [ŷá-ma-me-d̶es-pu̯és-d̶e-ye-ǥár]   2
              └─┐   1
                └→

    yé-
2. [ŷé-na-la-ko-ná-ǥu̯a ‖ i-próṇ-to-se-kom-ber-ti-rá-eñ-yé-lo]

                    -ŷá-   -ŷá-   -ŷe-   3
3. [las-ŷá-mas-ŷá-nó-a-b̶í-ta-nés-ta-pár-te-d̶el-b̶á-ye   sá-b̶es]↑   2
   _____→   1

4. [los-w̲a-k̲é-ros ‖ k̲on-sus-w̲a-rá-ĉes ‖ k̲u-b̶rį́é-ron-las-w̲é-ỵas-d̶e-los-w̲é-sos]

                        -ŷa-   -yér-   3
5. [di-xís-te-k̲e-la-g̲ra-mí-ỵa-se-ú-sa-p̲a-ra-sér-ŷér-b̶a-má-te]↑   2

                    -ŷa-
6. [nó ‖ la-g̲ra-mí-ỵa-es-yér-b̶á ‖ pe-ro-k̲ré-o-k̲e-los-g̲áu̯-ĉos-k̲om̩-

                                        -ŷa-
   fun̩-d̶í-an-la-p̲a-lá-b̶ra ‖ i-em-pe-sá-ro-na-ỵa-már-la-yér-b̶a-es-pe-sị̲al-

   yér-
   ŷér-b̶a]

                    -ŷá-   -ŷa-   -ya-   -ŷa
7. [si-la-yá-b̶e-yá-nó-es-tá-e-nel̄-ŷa-b̶é-ro↑   dón-de-se-á-ya]   2
   _____   1
   -ŷá-

                    -ŷá-
8. [em-mé-xi-k̲o-ỵá-ma-na-lo-sa-me-ri-k̲á-nos-w̲é-ro-so-g̲ué-ros ‖ a-p̲e-sár-d̶e-k̲e-nó-
   tó-d̶os-só-mos-r̄ú-b̶įos]

24 The Voiceless Consonants /s/ and /θ/

A.–C. Oral Practices

D.
                    -b̶ós-
1. [o-í-mo-s̲u-na-b̶óz-mis-te-rịó-sen-la-r̄e-si-d̶én-sị̲a]   2
   _____   1

                                                        -ŷa
2. [ob̶-s̲er-b̶é-k̲e-al̩-tí-po-nó-le-g̲us-tá-b̶a-el-ĉo-rí-s̲o-en-s̲u-p̲a-é-ỵa]

3. [ál-g̲o-me-r̄o-só-el-b̶rá-s̲o]   2
   _____   1

4. [el-pre-si-d̶én̩-te-míz-mo-sa-lịó-d̶e-s̲ụo-fi-sí-na-sin-sa-pá-tos]

5. [ái̯-u-na-ǵráṇ-ḍi-fe-rén-si̯a-eṇ-tre-xú-ǵo-i-sú-mo]   3
                                                                   2

6. [un-r̄e-frám-pa-ra-la-per-só-na-ke-nó-es-ka-pás-ḍes-pe-rár ‖ és ‖ nó-se-ǵa-nó-sa-
   mó-ra-e-nú-na-ó-ra]

7. [se-fu̯é-ro-na-líz-la-pa-ra-ǵo-sár-ḍe-mú-ĉaz-ḍi-ɓer-si̯ó-nes ‖ pe-ro-se-trans-for-
   má-ro-ne-náz-nos]

                   -sas ‖ i-   -ŷe-

8. [us-me-á-ɓa-las-r̄ó-sa-si-pen-sa-ɓa-en-los-ḍi-as-ku̯aṇ-ḍo-ye-ǵá-ron-lo-sas-té-ka-
   sa-é-sas-r̄e-xi̯ó-nes]

9. [só-r̄o-nó-a-sí-a-la-se-ñáḷ-ḍe-la-krú-si-no-ḍe-la-lé-tra-sé-ta]   2
                                                                     1

                                                          3

10. [só-r̄o   ké-és   u-na-ni-mál nó ɓó-ɓo é-rum-per-   2
                                                                           1

                                                          3

so-ná-xe-ko-no-sí-ḍo-ḍe-la-te-le-ɓi-si̯ón]   2
                                                                       1

25 The Voiceless Consonants /ĉ f x (h)/

A.–C. Oral Practices

D.

                                                 -xé-

1. [i-si̯é-roŋ-kons-tru-í-ru-na-r̄é-xa-pa-ra-pro-te-çé-rel-xar-ḍín]

             -bri̯o-   -ŷá-

2. [su-nóm-bre-o-fi-si̯á-les-fran-sís-ko   pe-ro-lo-yá-mam-páǹ-ĉo]   2
                                                                       1

                                                          3

3. [sal̀-ĉí-ĉa nó ki̯é-ro-ĉo-rí-so és-to-tál-méṇ-te-ḍi-fe-réṇ-te]   2
                                                                       1

4. [sí ‖ es-kom-fú-so ‖ la-ko-sí-na-es-la-es-tú-fa ‖ ke-seŋ-kuéṇ-tra-en-la-ko-sí-na]

5. [blas-fé-mi̯a-e-sel-sus-taṇ-tí-βo ↑ pe-ro-βlas-fe-má-re-sel-βér-βo]   2
                                                                            1

6. [las-pa-lá-βras-fu̯é-ra ‖ fu̯ér-te ‖ i-fu̯é-ǥo ‖ nó-se-pro-nún-si̯aŋ-koŋ-xó-ta-si-no-ko-né-fe]

        -xi-
7. [em-mé-çi-ko-ké-pre-fi̯é-reṇ-de-sír   ĉí-ko ↑ o-pe-ké-ño]   2
                                                                  1

8. [é-se-ĉíz-mes-ĉa-βa-ká-nu̯i-ĉo-káṇ-te ‖ pe-ro-sói̯-lo ‖ ku̯éṇ-ta-me-más ‖ por-fa-βór]

26 The Nasal Consonants /m n ñ/

A.–C.   Oral Practices

D.

1. [em-fréṇ-te-ɖel-kom-béṇ-to-ɖe-sam-be-ní-to-a-βí-a-uŋ-wér-to-

    ŷé-
    yé-no-ɖe-na-ráŋ-xos]

    un-   -xe-
2. [um-móŋ-çe-pa-se-á-βa-r̄e-sáṇ-do-su-so-ra-si̯ó-ne-sem-bos-βá-xa]

        -ŋuŋ-
3. [uṅ-ĉí-ko-es-tá-βa-xu-ǥáṇ-do-ko-nuŋ-gá-to-ke-um-pá-ɖre-le-a-βí-a-em-bi̯á-ɖo]

    -tu̯e-   -ɖi̯uŋ-   3
4. [és-to-e-sel-ko-mi̯éṇ-so-ɖeuŋ-ku̯éṇ-to]   2
                                                1

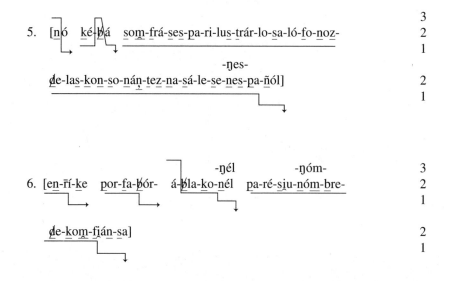

5. [nó   ké-b̸á   som-frá-ses-pa-ri-lus-trár-lo-sa-ló-fo-noz-   3
                                                                 2
                                                                 1
   -ŋes-
   d̸e-las-kon-so-nán-tez-na-sá-le-se-nes-pa-ñól]   2
                                                    1

                                 -ŋél   -ŋóm-   3
6. [en-r̄í-ke   por-fa-b̸ór-   á-b̸la-ko-nél   pa-ré-s̨iu-nóm-bre-   2
                                                                   1

   d̸e-kom̨-f̨ián-s̨a]   2
                       1

7. [lo-s̨im-b̨iér-no-sem-bo-lí-b̸ia-som̨-fu̯ér-tes ‖ pe-ro-em-be-ne-su̯é-la-s̨oŋ-ka-lu-ró-
   s̨os̨]

                           -ŷa-
8. [em̨-pu̯ér-to-r̄í-ko-kom̨-b̨ié-ne-ya-már-né-ne-sa-loz-ní-ños-por-ke-loz-   2

   -yá-ma-ŋa-
   b̸o-rí-ku̯az-míz-moz-loz-ŷá-ma-na-sí]   2
                                            1

27 The Lateral Consonants /l/ and /l̃/

A.–C.   Oral Practices

D.

                 -pi̯ó-   yá-   3
1. [lo-g̸ol̨-pe-ó̸   ŷá-m̨a-la-po-li̯-s̨í-a]   2
                                                            1

         -ya-
2. [el̨-ko-ro-nḗl-ŷa-m̨ó-al-s̨ol̨-dá-d̸o ‖ i-le-d̸í-xo-ke-fu̯é-ra-le-d̸i-fí-s̨i̯o-fe-d̸e-rál]
3. [es̨-tá-b̸a-en-la-pár-te-sen̨-trál̨-de-lal̨-de-a-d̸e-los-r̄e-b̸él̨-des̨]

-ŷe-
4. [ke-rí-a-b̶ér-si-a-b̶í-a-ye-g̶á-d̶o-la-kar-g̶a-d̶e-kól̀-ĉas]   2
1

-ŷe-   -ŋa-
5. [kual̯-do-ye-g̶á-ro-na-la-pu̯ér-ta-d̶e-le-d̶i-fí-si̯o ↑ el-g̶u̯ár-d̶i̯a-   2

3
les-g̶ri-tó   ál̯-to]   2
1

6. [al̯-b̶ér-to ‖ lim-pre-só-ra-ne-se-sí-ta-más-pa-pél]

-ŷói̯-   -ŷó-   3
7. [sá-b̶e-su-na-kó-sa ↑ koǹ-ĉí-ta és-to-d̶e-se-ka-yói̯-se-ka-yó-   2
1

3
me-ti̯é-nen-la-lú-na]   2
1

8. [ké-nó-kom-prén̯-des ‖ é-sál-g̶o-d̶i̯a-lek-tá-la-fín̯-de-ku̯én̯-tas]

28 The Tap and Trill Consonants /r/ and /r̄/

A.–D. Oral Practices

E.

-b̶ér-   -ŋal-
1. [r̄o-b̶ér-to-i-en-r̄í-ke-pa-se-á-b̶a-nal-r̄e-d̶e-d̶ór-d̶e-la-r̄é-xa]   2
1

-ŋen̯-   -káu̯-al-
2. [ke-rí-a-nen̯-tre-g̶ár-lel-r̄e-ká-d̶u̯al-se-ñó-r̄o-d̶rí-g̶es]

iz-   ei̯-   -naz-
3. [is-r̄a-él ‖ sí-ri̯a ‖ e-i-rák-nó-a-b̶í-aŋ-go-sá-d̶o-d̶e-b̶u̯é-nas-r̄e-la-si̯ó-nes]

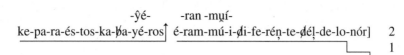

-ŋel-
4. [la-kó-sa-es-tá-ƀa-en-r̄e-đá-đa-e-nel-kon-sép-to-đe-la-ón-r̄a ↑   2

         -ŷé-   -ran -mu̧í-
  ke-pa-ra-és-tos-ka-ƀa-yé-ros⌝ é-ram-mú-i-đi-fe-rén̠-te-đél̠-de-lo-nór]   2
                                                1

5. [ku̧an̠-do-ƀí-mo-sal̠-to-r̄é-ro ↑ noz-đí-mos-ku̧én̠-ta-đe-le-r̄ór-   2

  ke-a-ƀí-a-mo-sé-ĉo el̠-tí-po-te-ní-u-na-lin̠-tér-na nóu̧-na-ban̠-   2
                                                 1
       -ŷa
  de-rí-ya]   2
                1

         -ŷá-   -xai̯n-
6. [un-r̄eŋ-glón-suƀ-r̄a-yá-đo-en-la-ó-xa-in̠-dí-ka-ke-đe-ƀe-rí-a-pa-re-

          -ŷa
  sé-ren̠-tí-po-đe-ƀas-tar-đí-ya]

         é-   -li̯á-ŷai̯-   -o-
7. [le-kos-tó-ká-ro ‖ nó ‖ éh-r̄á-ro-ke-nó-le-á-yai̯-r̄i-tá-đo-más]

8. [kó-mo-sá-ƀes-ke-la-pa-lá-ƀra-su-r̄o-ǥár-nó-ti̯é-ne-la-míz-ma-   2

  kom-bi-na-si̯ón̠-de-kon-so-nán̠-tes-ke-só-ƀra ↑ o-ú-ƀre]   2
                                             1

29 Consonant Combinations in Spanish

A.–B. Oral Practices

C.

<pre>
     -ses-   -ek-   -ŋé-   -ŋés-
1. [é-seks-trá-ño-ke-nó-eg̱-sís-ta-né-sas-kó-sa-se-nés-te-pa-ís]   2
                                        └──────┐   1
                                               ↓
</pre>

<pre>
        -ḏek-   -si̯óŋ
2. [pe-ro-ḏes-pu̯és-ḏeg̱-sa-mi-nár-b̯i̯én-la-si-tu̯a-si̯ón ‖ se-ḏáŋ-ku̯éṇ-

        -sek-   -ŋó-   -bi̯éŋ
ta-ḏe-ke-seg̱-sák-ta-méṇ-te-lo-mís-mo-e-nó- tros-pa-í-ses-tam-bi̯én]
</pre>

<pre>
                       -ŋi-   -ŋés-
3. [la-sak-si̯ó-nez-ḏe-lo-sa-lúm-no-só-ni-na-pli-ká-ꝑle-se-nés-te-ká-so]
</pre>

<pre>
                  -ŋal̀
4. [le-pú-su-niñ-ŷek-si̯ó-nal̀-ĉí-ku̯a-ki̯en-le-a-ꝑí-a-mor-ḏí-ḏu̯el-pé-r̄o-r̄a-ꝑi̯ó-so]
</pre>

<pre>
   ┌-ŷái̯┐   -ŷí-   3
5. [a┤yái̯├nel-r̄áǹ-ĉo-g̱ráṇ-de-ḏoṇ-de-ꝑí-ꝑen-los-ĉáǹ-ĉos-laz-g̱a-yí-   2
                                                      ─────

        -la-
   naz-lah-r̄á-ta-si-loz-ñaṇ-dú-es]   2
                         └─────┐   1
                                ↓
</pre>

<pre>
   -ez-   -sek-   -ŋa-
6. [nó-es-r̄á-ro-ke-és-to-seg̱-sá-me-nes-nó-a-sús-te-na-lo-ses-tu-   2
   ───────   ─────

                                                          3
   ┌──────────────────┐↑   2
   ḏi̯áṇ┤tes]↑─────────┘↑
</pre>

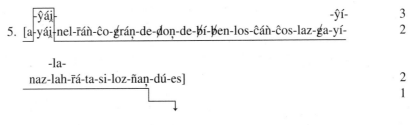

<pre>
   é-   -ḏa-é-sa-
7. [e-saꝑ-so-lú-ta-méṇ-tim-pre-siṇ-dí-ꝑle-ke-sus-kri-ꝑís-te-a-é-sah-
</pre>

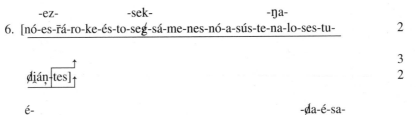

<pre>
        -wa-
   r̄e-ꝑís-taz-g̱u̯a-te-mal̩-té-kas]
</pre>

-lár-
8. [la-ḍe-si-si̯ón̯-de-lár-ɓi-tro-fu̯é-in-ne-ǵá-ɓle-ku̯an̯-do-se-le-   2

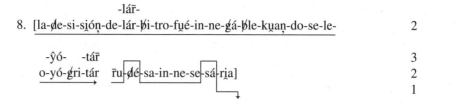

-ŷó- -táɾ   3
o-yó-ǵri-tár   ɾu-ḍé-sa-in-ne-se-sá-ri̯a]   2
                                                                                        1

30 Reviewing the Consonants of Spanish (CHAPTERS 20–29)

1. place (point) of articulation, manner of articulation, voicing (or lack of it)   2. true
3. (b)   4. false   5. (b)   6. aspiration   7. false   8. [t̂] (or [d̂])   9. (a)   10. true
11. (a)   12. after /l/ and /n/   13. **gu**   14. true   15. (b)   16. true   17. (a)
18. [w] is a consonant; the tongue body comes so close to the velar region that there
is often slight friction or mild turbulence   19. true   20. (c)   21. ''eye'' dialect
22. retroflex (or concave)   23. (b)   24. **distinción**   25. true   26. (a)   27. false
28. (c)   29. lisping   30. false   31. (b)   32. **zeta, zinc, zigzaguear**   33. false
34. They have a special section for words beginning with **ch-**, coming between the
c- and the **d-** sections.   35. false   36. (c)   37. **gente** or **gitano**   38. (c)
39. true—**mejicano** in Spain, **mexicano** everywhere else   40. (a)   41. homorganic
42. true   43. (a)   44. dissimilation   45. false   46. (c)   47. **álbum, réquiem**
48. false   49. (a)   50. clear (light) *l*   51. false   52. (a)   53. **pollo** has an
intervocalic palatal [ĺ], and **polio** has an alveolar [l], followed by the semi-vowel [i̯]
54. true   55. homophonous   56. true   57. (c)   58. that the sound is voiceless
59. false   60. (b)   61. (b)   62. **jota, rota** or **bajo, barro**   63. false   64. (a)
65. *ate a* or *eight o'*   66. false   67. (a)   68. **bíceps, fórceps, fénix**   69. true
70. (c)   71. neutralization   72. true   73. (a)   74. /r/ and /r̄/ or /s/ and /s/
75. true   76. **bienestar, desagradable, inoportuno** 77. false   78. (b)   79. **película** or **montículo**   80. true

31 The Orthography of Spanish

A.

1. ***huerreque** (Remember what the asterisk is for?)   2. ***pucigaimá**   3. ***sequeípetro**   4. ***llullari**   5. ***branisuaba**   6. ***jápemelos**   7. ***muiguilánturo**
8. ***choúbesa**   9. ***tiúmed**   10. ***irguinsterne**   11. ***muiju**   12. ***güilení**
13. ***perriguauguau**   14. ***suaiparrós**   15. ***zoifozámal**   16. ***ñouculífaz**
17. ***rulíacos**   18. ***jalabalú**   19. ***suipiyeraz**   20. ***dolliparton**

B.

1. —   2. —   3. **jóvenes** (rule 4)   4. **riquísimo** (rule 4)   5. —   6. **difícil** (rule
3)   7. **difíciles** (rule 4)   8. **ángel** (rule 3)   9. —   10. —   11. **nácar** (rule 3)

12. —   13. **análisis** (rule 4)   14. —   15. **teóricamente** (rule 4)   16. **oíste** (rule 1)   17. **teólogo** (rule 4)   18. —   19. —   20. **cáliz** (rule 3)   21. **prevé** (rule 2) 22. **píen** (rule 1)   23. **lústramelos** (rule 4)   24. —   25. —   26. **paupérrimo** (rule 4)   27. **pió** (rule 2)   28. **pío** (rule 1)   29. —   30. **construísteis** (rule 1)

C.

1. **dónde** (rule 5)   2. **Déme** (rule 6)   3. —   4. **Sólo** (rule 6), **dominó** (rule 2) 5. —   6. **Levantándote** (rule 4), **podrás** (rule 2)   7. **policía** (rule 1)   8. **aquí** (rule 2)   9. **sé** (rule 6), **cuándo** (rule 5)   10. **día** (rule 1), **estaré** (rule 2), **allí** (rule 2)   11. **sabré** (rule 2), **qué** (rule 5)   12. **Sí** (rule 6), **sabrás** (rule 2)   13. **ése** (rule 6, although many publications follow the Academy's ruling and leave off the accent in these demonstrative ''pronouns''), **tú** (rule 6)   14. **ésta** (rule 6, but also **esta**; see answer 13, above.)   15. **llegó** (rule 2), **psicólogo** (rule 4), **tontísimas** (rule 4) 16. **acróbata** (rule 4), **llamó** (rule 2), **teléfono** (rule 4), **comunicó** (rule 2), **farmacéutico** (rule 4), **pidió** (rule 2), **antídoto** (rule 4), **compulsión** (rule 2)   17. **discutirán** (rule 2), **hegemonía** (rule 1), **Turquía** (rule 1)   18. **canción** (rule 2), **título** (rule 4), **melodía** (rule 1), **melancolía** (rule 1)   19. **diré** (rule 2), **cómo** (rule 5), **completó** (rule 2)   20. **Crédito** (rule 4), **Instantáneo** (rule 4), **ó** (the ''7th rule,'' just for the word for *or*, **o**, when used with numerals)

32 A Final Look at Mastering the Sounds of Spanish

1.   The native language sound system is so ingrained in the learner that it constantly interferes with his or her efforts to acquire the foreign system.

2.   In a few cases there are acceptable Spanish sounds that are easier for you as an English speaker which can be substituted for the difficult sounds. For example, the glottal [h], which exists in English, can properly be substituted for the velar [x], which does not. Or the fricative *r*, [ř], similar to the [ž] sound, as in *measure*, can be substituted for the trilled [r̄], which does not exist in American English. Although the fricative [ř] is not used in all dialects of Spanish, it is preferable everywhere to the typical English retroflex [r̠], which does not exist at all in Spanish.

3.   Theoretically, Spanish speakers have a harder time learning the sound system of English than you do of Spanish, for the simple reason that English has more phonemes and, thus, more contrasts than Spanish. This is theoretical, of course, and is often not the case in practice.

4.   There is no right or wrong answer to this question. The facts, however, are that there are far more **seseo** speakers of Spanish in the world than **distinción** speakers. **Seseo** is acceptable in Spain even to speakers who do not use it, and it is theoreticaly easier for foreigners because it requires one fewer phonemic contrast for them to make. However, **seseo** creates some spelling problems that do not exist with **distinción**: the **seseo** speaker

may be unsure of whether unfamiliar /s/ words are spelled with **s**, **z**, or **c**; a **distinción** speaker *always* knows.

5.   The pronunciation of intervocalic /s/ as [z] is heard only in certain words and in certain dialects of Spanish. But in *no* case in Spanish does it have anything to do with the spelling. Also, in many cases, it sounds strange—even wrong. Thus, as an English speaker, you should be careful to avoid the pronunciation of intervocalic [z], particularly in cognate words, like **residencia**, **propósito**, **visual**, or words spelled with **z**, like **cazar**, **mozo**, **empezar**, where you are most tempted to use it.

6.   The following sounds exist in both English and Spanish: [p b k g f θ ð ç h s z š ž č ŷ m n ŋ a o]. But be sure you realize that such sounds as English aspirated [pʰ] or Spanish fricative [b̸] are *not* included in this group for reasons you should know by now. Also you cannot use the English sounds in the above group freely in Spanish without being sure of their phonetic environment, which determines the use of almost all sounds in both languages. For example, just because the English stop [b] also exists in Spanish does not mean that you can use it in a word like **abuela**.

7.   Speakers of other languages, depending on the sound structure of these languages, make many of the same mistakes you do in Spanish and many different ones, too. French speakers have the same problem you do with Spanish /b/ ([b] or [b̸]) because /b/ and /v/ are phonemic in French just as they are in English: **boire** *to drink*–**voir** *to see*. Since Spanish and English are both intonation, rather than tone languages, you do not make mistakes trying to discern or use the imaginary tones or pitch levels of individual Spanish words. But speakers of tone languages like Thai, Chinese, or Vietnamese have difficulty on this score with both Spanish and English. Your instructor may be able to provide more examples of this nature.

8.   This is for you to answer. But try also to determine the reason for the difficulty that the Spanish sound or sound pattern presents to you.

9.   Again, this is for you to answer. If your answer for this question is not the same as your answer for question 8, it may have something to do with the frequency of the sound in Spanish or its distribution. Try to determine this.

10.   This is for you and your instructor to answer.

11.   This is for you to answer.

12.   The answer to this one is also individual and may very well depend on your own future career plans—or your own feelings about education in general.

Appendix D
Practice Dialogs

The following dialogs are intended to provide you with pronunciation practice and also phonetic transcription practice, if your instructor wishes. They are recorded, and suggestions for how to practice with them are given on the tape. Your instructor may suggest other ways to work with these dialogs in or out of class, such as reading with a classmate or transcribing portions of the dialog either from the textbook or from the tape recordings.

Dialog 1   Tareas postergadas

MICAELA: ¿Ya averiguó los pasajes a España? Dicen que allá en los Estados Unidos son más baratos.

CARMENZA: Todavía no he tenido tiempo, pero esta semana, el lunes, voy a la agencia de viajes.

MICAELA: ¿Y le consiguió el libro a su hermano?

CARMENZA: Mami, he estado muy ocupada; lo que pasa es que ustedes ni se imaginan qué es esto de la vida como estudiante universitaria.

MICAELA: Yo sí entiendo, pero es que su hermano le pidió el favor hace muchos días y usted no lo ha hecho.

CARMENZA: Sí, ya lo sé. Pero... él no lo necesita ahora. ¿Verdad que no? Él puede esperar un poco más, ¿no?

MICAELA: Bueno, sí. Pero... y... la cámara de fotografía de Mauricio, ¿ya la averiguó?

CARMENZA: ¡Tampoco!

MICAELA: Yo no sé qué es lo que pasa, pero ninguna de las cosas que le han pedido las ha hecho.

CARMENZA: Lo siento, mamá, pero le prometo que este mismo lunes comenzaré a hacerlo.

Dialog 2   Los 32 centavos

OVIDIO: ¿Puedes creer lo que me pasó?

DIANA: No tengo ni idea, cuéntame.

OVIDIO: Pues que recibí la cuenta de mi tarjeta de crédito y como estaba más bien desocupado, decidí revisar las cuentas de ellos. Resulta que había una diferencia de 32 centavos a favor de ellos.

DIANA: ¿Y? ¡Treinta y dos centavos no es nada!

OVIDIO: ¿No? Pues figúrate que yo no pienso lo mismo. Además la cuestión no son los 32 centavos. ¿Tú sabes cuánto gana un banco con 32 centavos extra con todos los clientes que piensan lo mismo que tú?

DIANA: Bueno, la verdad es que no.

OVIDIO: Pues en eso me puse a pensar y llamé a la oficina. La telefonista tenía la misma actitud que tú tienes; es más, me dijo que costaría más arreglar el error que dejarlo como estaba. En otras palabras, me dijo que yo tenía que pagar 32 centavos por su error.

DIANA: Pero... ¿y qué pasó al fin y al cabo?

OVIDIO: Tanto alegué y alegué con la señorita esa que al fin y al cabo me arreglaron mi problema.

DIANA: Tú siempre andas metiéndote en problemas. ¿No crees?

OVIDIO: No, por el contrario, tú te la pasas evitándolos, cerrando los ojos como si no estuvieran allí.

DIANA: Ahora, por favor, no empieces conmigo que yo no tengo el más mínimo deseo de discutir contigo.

OVIDIO: Claro, si ya lo sé, siempre andas evitándome.

Dialog 3   Indocumentados

PAULA: Fabri, ¿puedes creer lo que presentaron en la televisión acerca de ese par de indocumentados?

FABRICIO: ¿Qué pasó? Ya ni veo noticias.

PAULA: Pues que dos... yo ni sé qué eran, policías, agentes... lo que sea... cogieron a dos inmigrantes ilegales a bolillazos.

FABRICIO: Y... ¿cómo lo supo la gente?

PAULA: Pues, figúrate, que tuvieron la mala suerte de que en esos momentos pasaba un helicóptero de un canal de televisión y ¡filmaron todo, todo lo que pasó!

FABRICIO: Pero... y ¿qué les van a hacer a los tipos esos?

PAULA: No estoy segura. Lo que sé es que los suspendieron pero dizque con sueldo. ¿Tú puedes creer eso? Es que como están las cosas, ya nada me extraña.

FABRICIO: ¿Cómo así que los suspendieron con sueldo? Después que golpearon a ese par de esta manera y ¿les pagan? ¡Qué barbaridad!

PAULA: Sí, pero no creo que eso sea lo peor de todo; me imagino que muy pronto los reintegran.

FABRICIO: ¡Ojalá que no! Acuérdate que Toño también anda por ahí indocumentado y si lo agarran, que no le vayan a tocar esos ''agenticos'' del ''desorden''!

PAULA: Mira, Fabri, si yo hubiera sabido que las cosas eran como eran, nunca en mi vida hubiera salido de mi tierra como indocumentada.

FABRICIO: ¡Qué! ¿Qué estás diciendo? Si es que todos los días aprende uno algo nuevo. ¡Nunca me habías dicho que viniste de ilegal!

PAULA: Fabri, esa es una larga historia. Yo estaba más joven, ignorante de los peligros de un viaje de esta clase y con ganas de aventurear.

FABRICIO: ¿Cuántos años tenías?

PAULA: Como veintidós.

FABRICIO: La verdad es que siempre me pareciste un poco arriesgada pero nunca pensé que pudieras haber hecho algo así.

Dialog 4   Los niños y el fútbol

JUAN: ¿Ya conoció el niño de Clara?

ALEJANDRO: No, todavía no, pero me han dicho que es bonito y que se parece al papá.

JUAN: Yo no sé si será bonito; lo único que se me ocurre pensar es que ojalá no sea tan necio ni tan insoportable como el otro que tienen.

ALEJANDRO: No, hermano, lo que pasa es que a usted no le gustan los niños; no importa cómo sean, a usted no le gustan ni poquito. Pero espérese y verá que cuando tenga los suyos no va a haber quien se lo aguante de papá malcriando los culimbos.

JUAN: ¡Qué va, hermano! Yo pa' eso de papá no sirvo y menos hoy en día como están las cosas de caras: los pañales, la leche, los remedios. Ya no se puede ni tener familia.

ALEJANDRO: ¿Y si Sofía sale embarazada? ¿Qué va a hacer entonces?

JUAN: No sé, pero lo mejor es que por ahora no pensemos en problemitas. Mejor hablamos de otra cosa. ¿Verdad que estuvo en la goleada que le metió Colombia a Argentina?

ALEJANDRO: ¡Qué va! Ganas no me faltaron, estuve sí pero solamente sentado frente al televisor, tomando traguito y haciendo fuerza. A lo último cantaba de la dicha. No lo podía creer, la primera vez que Colombia lo golea. ¿Y usted, dónde estaba?

JUAN: Ese día tuve tan mala suerte que se fue la luz en mi casa; luego me llamaron por teléfono de urgencia que tenía que ir a la casa de mi vecino.

ALEJANDRO: ¿Qué pasó?

JUAN: ¡Si por lo menos hubiera pasado algo! Pero la verdad es que todo fue falsa alarma; para cuando me di cuenta que no había ni incendio ni nada y que todo estaba bien, ya el partido se había acabado y yo me quedé con las ganas de verlo. Y usted, ¿qué hizo después del partido?

ALEJANDRO: Me fui para *El Rincón Clásico* y allí estuvimos todos celebrando hasta las cuatro de la mañana que nos echaron porque iban a cerrar. Fue una noche de maravilla.

Appendix E
Bibliography

The following references are divided into two groups: those dealing principally with Spanish phonetics and phonology, and those dealing with English phonetics and phonology and related general linguistics topics. This bibliography is selective and omits works on specific dialects of Spanish.

Spanish

Alarcos Llorach, Emilio. (1965) *Fonología española,* 4a ed. Madrid: Gredos.

Allison, Kathy Oppelt. (1993) "A Computer-Assisted Comparative Acoustic and Perceptual Analysis of Spanish and English Intonation and Its Application for Foreign Language Instruction." Ph.D. diss., Pennsylvania State University.

Ávila, Raúl. (1974) "Problemas de fonología dialectal." *Nueva Revista de Filología Española.* 23: 369–81.

Azevedo, Milton M. (1992) *Introducción a la lingüística española.* Englewood Cliffs, NJ: Prentice-Hall.

Barrutia, Richard, and Armin Schwegler. (1994) *Fonética y fonología españolas: teoría y práctica.* New York: John Wiley & Sons.

Bjarkmann, Peter C., and Robert M. Hammond, eds. (1989) *American Spanish Pronunciation: Theoretical and Applied Perspectives.* Washington, DC: Georgetown U. Press.

Bowen, J. Donald. (1956) "A Comparison of the Intonation Patterns of English and Spanish." *Hispania* 39: 30–35.

Boyd-Bowman, Peter. (1956) "The Regional Origins of the Earliest Spanish Colonists of America." *PMLA* 71: 1152–72.

———. (1963) "La emigración peninsular a América: 1520–1539." *Historia Mexicana* 13: 165–92.

———. (1968) "Regional Origins of the Spanish Colonists of America: 1540–1559." *Buffalo Studies* 4: 3–26.

———. (1972) "La emigración española a América: 1560–1579" in *Studia hispánica in honorem R. Lapesa,* 2 vols. Madrid: Gredos. II: 123–47.

Canfield, D. Lincoln. (1962) *La pronunciación del español en América.* Bogotá: Instituto Caro y Cuervo.

———. (1967) "Trends in American Castilian." *Hispania* 50: 912–18.

———. (1981) *Spanish Pronunciation in the Americas.* Chicago: U. of Chicago Press.

Cotton, Eleanor G., and John M. Sharp. (1988) *Spanish in the Americas.* Washington, DC: Georgetown U. Press.

Craddock, Jerry R. (1981) "New World Spanish" in Charles A. Ferguson et al, eds. *Language in the USA.* Cambridge: Cambridge U. Press, pp. 196–211.

Cressey, William W. (1978) *Spanish Phonology and Morphology: A Generative View.* Washington, DC: Georgetown U. Press.

Dalbor, John B. (1980) "Observations on Present-Day **seseo** and **ceceo** in Southern Spain." *Hispania* 63: 5–19.

———. (1980–81) "Tres mitos de la fonética española." *Yelmo* 46–47: 12–14.

Del Rosario, Rubén. (1979) *El español de América,* 2a ed. Río Piedras, PR: Edil.

Departamento de Geografía Lingüística, C.S.I.C. (1973) *Cuestionario para el estudio coordinado de la norma lingüística culta: I—Fonética y fonología.* Madrid: Consejo Superior de Investigaciones Científicas.

González-Bueno, Manuela. (1993) "Variaciones en el tratamiento de las sibilantes. Inconsistencia en el seseo sevillano: Un enfoque sociolingüístico." *Hispania* 76: 392–98.

Harris, James W. (1969) *Spanish Phonology.* Cambridge, MA: M.I.T. Press.

———. (1970) "Distinctive Feature Theory and Nasal Assimilation in Spanish." *Linguistics* 58: 30–37.

Henríquez Ureña, Pedro. (1921) "Observaciones sobre el español en América." *Revista de Filología Española* 8: 357–90.

Izzo, Herbert J. "Andalusia and America: The Regional Origins of New-World Spanish" in Ernst Pulgram, ed. *Studies in Romance Linguistics.* Ann Arbor: Dept. of Romance Languages, U. of Michigan, 1984, pp. 109–31.

Klein, Philip W. (1992) *Enfoque lingüístico al idioma español.* New York: Peter Lang.

Kvavik, Karen. (1976) "Research and Pedagogical Materials on Spanish Intonation: A Re-examination." *Hispania* 59: 406–17.

Lado, Robert. (1957) *Linguistics Across Cultures: Applied Linguistics for Language Teachers.* Ann Arbor: U. of Michigan Press.

Lantolf, James P. (1976) "On Teaching Intonation." *Modern Language Journal* 60: 267–74.

Lapesa, Rafael. (1964) "El andaluz y el español de América" in *Presente y futuro de la lengua española,* 2 vols. Madrid: Ediciones Cultura Hispánica. II: 173–82.

Lipski, John M. (1989) "Beyond the Isogloss: Trends in Hispanic Dialectology." *Hispania* 72: 801–09.

———. (1989) "Latin American Dialectology: Some Recent Contributions." *Hispanic Linguistics* 3, i–ii (Fall): 270–300.

Lope Blanch, Juan M. (1968) *El español de América.* Madrid: Ediciones Alcalá.

———, ed. (1977) *Estudios sobre el español hablado en las principales ciudades de América.* México, DF: Universidad Nacional Autónoma de México.

———. (1987) "Fisionomía del español en América: Unidad y diversidad" in Humberto López-Morales and María Vaquero, eds. *Actas del Ier Congreso Internacional sobre el español de América.* San Juan, PR: Academia Puertorriqueña de la Lengua Española.

Macpherson, Ian R. (1975) *Spanish Phonology: Descriptive and Historical.* Manchester: Manchester U. Press. New York: Barnes and Noble.

Malmberg, Bertil. (1965) *Estudios de fonética hispánica,* tr. Edgardo R. Palavecino. Madrid: Consejo Superior de Investigaciones Científicas.

———. (1970) *La América hispanohablante: Unidad y diferenciación del castellano.* Madrid: Editorial Istmo.

Navarro, Tomás. (1957) *Manual de pronunciación española,* 5a ed. New York: Hafner.

Nuessel, Frank H. (1982) "Eye Dialect in Spanish: Some Pedagogical Implications." *Hispania* 65: 346–51.

Quilis, Antonio. (1970) *Fonética española en imágenes.* Madrid: La Muralla.

———. (1973) *Album de fonética acústica.* Madrid: Consejo Superior de Investigaciones Científicas.

———. (1981) *Fonética acústica de la lengua española.* Madrid: Gredos.

———, and Joseph A. Fernández. (1966) *Curso de fonética y fonología españolas para estudiantes angloamericanos,* 2a ed. Madrid: Consejo Superior de Investigaciones Científicas.

Real Academia Española. (1958) "Nuevas normas de prosodia y ortografía (nuevo texto definitivo)." *Boletín de la Real Academia Española* 38: 343–47.

Resnick, Melvyn C. (1969) "Dialect Zones and Automatic Dialect Identification in Latin American Spanish." *Hispania* 52: 553–68.

———. (1975) *Phonological Variants and Dialect Identification in Latin American Spanish.* Paris: Mouton.

Rona, José P. (1964) "El problema de la división del español americano en zonas dialectales" in *Presente y futuro de la lengua española,* 2 vols. Madrid: Oficina Internacional de Información y Observación del Español. I: 216–26.

Stockwell, Robert P., and J. Donald Bowen. (1965) *The Sounds of English and Spanish.* Chicago: U. of Chicago Press.

———, ———, and Ismael Silva-Fuenzalida. (1956) "Spanish Juncture and Intonation." *Language* 32: 641–65.

Torreblanca, Máximo. (1988) "La pronunciación española y los métodos de investigación." *Hispania* 71: 669–74.

Whitley, M. Stanley. (1986) *Spanish/English Contrasts.* Washington, DC: Georgetown U. Press.

Wieczorek, Joseph A. (1991) "Spanish Dialects and the Foreign Language Textbook: A Sound Perspective." *Hispania.* 74: 175–81.

Zamora-Munné, Juan C., and Jorge Guitart. (1988) *Dialectología hispanoamericana,* 2a ed. Salamanca: Almar.

English and General

Albright, Robert W. (1958) *The International Phonetic Alphabet: Its Backgrounds and Development.* Bloomington: Indiana University Research Center in Anthropology, Folklore and Linguistics, no. 7.

Bronstein, Arthur J. (1960) *The Pronunciation of American English: An Introduction to Phonetics.* New York: Appleton-Century-Crofts.

Buchanan, Cynthia D. (1963) *A Programed Introduction to Linguistics: Phonetics and Phonemics.* Boston: D.C. Heath.

Falk, Julia S. (1978) *Linguistics and Language: A Survey of Basic Concepts and Implications,* 2nd ed. New York: John Wiley & Sons.

Gelb, Ignace J. (1952) *A Study of Writing: The Foundations of Grammatology.* London: Routledge and Kegan Paul.

Gleason, H.A., Jr. (1961) *An Introduction to Descriptive Linguistics,* revised ed. New York: Holt, Rinehart and Winston.

Hockett, Charles F. (1958) *A Course in Modern Linguistics.* New York: Macmillan.

International Phonetic Association. (1957) *The Principles of the International Phonetic Association.* London: IPA.

Ladefoged, Peter. (1971) *Preliminaries to Linguistic Phonetics.* Chicago: U. of Chicago Press.

———. (1982) *A Course in Phonetics,* 2nd ed. New York: Harcourt Brace Jovanovich.

Malmberg, Bertil. (1963) *Phonetics.* New York: Dover.

Pike, Kenneth L. (1943) *Phonetics.* Ann Arbor: U. of Michigan Press.

———. (1945) *The Intonation of American English.* Ann Arbor: U. of Michigan Press.

Pulgram, Ernst. (1965) "Consonant Cluster, Consonant Sequence, and the Syllable." *Phonetica* 13: 76–81.

Shearer, William M. (1963) *Illustrated Speech Anatomy.* Springfield, IL: Charles C. Thomas.

Sloat, Clarence, Sharon H. Taylor, and James E. Hoard. (1978) *Introduction to Phonology.* Englewood Cliffs, NJ: Prentice-Hall.

Smalley, William A. (1964) *Manual of Articulatory Phonetics,* revised ed. Tarrytown, NY: Practical Anthropology.

Trager, George L. (1958) "Paralanguage: A First Approximation." *Studies in Linguistics* 13: 1–12.

———. (1961) "The Typology of Paralanguage." *Anthropological Linguistics.* 3:17–21.

Vocabulary

*The following types of words have been omitted: (1) easily recognizable Spanish cognates; (2) obviously derived words, such as diminutives, superlatives, and -**mente** adverbs if the adjective is listed; (3) high frequency structure words, such as articles, prepositions, pronouns; (4) past participles of listed infinitives unless they have a different meaning as nouns or adjectives; (5) individual verb forms with a few low frequency exceptions, such as* **yergue** *(from* **erguir***); (6) words that a third-year student would reasonably be expected to know unless the word is required as an answer in one of the practices.*

The gender of masculine nouns ending in -**o,** -**l,** -**r,** *and* -**ista** *is not listed. The gender of feminine nouns ending in* -**a,** -**ción,** -**d,** -**ie,** *and* -**z** *is not listed. Most proper nouns that the student might not know are given. Radical changes and verb irregularities are listed in parentheses after the infinitive: for example,* **gemir (i, i)***, the first* **i** *being for the present tense, the second* **i** *for the third-person preterit forms. Other irregular verbs are simply indicated as such and can be checked elsewhere if necessary: for example,* **argüir** *(irr.),* **erguir** *(irr.). Spelling irregularities are not listed if they can be deduced: for example,* **ahogar** *must have a* **u** *after the* **g** *anywhere before* **e***,* **alzar** *must have c instead of* **z** *anywhere before* **e***, etc.*

Most phrases are cross-listed for each important word, with — representing the alphabetized word: for example, **baja: planta —** *ground floor for* **planta baja** *ground floor.*

Words from other foreign languages are listed only when their meaning is not given in the text in which they occur.

The letters **ch** *and* **ll** *are not treated separately but are listed in their proper order in the* **c***'s and* **l***'s, respectively.*

abrelatas (*m. sing.*) can opener
abrir paso to open the way, step aside
abyecto abject, utterly hopeless
acosar to harass, pursue relentlessly
acoso harassment, pursuit
acróbata (*m., f.*) acrobat
acudir to come, go to help
adivinar to guess
adular to flatter
afín related, similar

agarrar to grab, seize
agonizante dying
agrio sour
aguantar(se) to bear, stand, endure
aguardiente (*m.*) brandy
ahogar to suffocate, smother, drown
ahorrar to save, accumulate
ají (*m.*) red pepper, chili pepper
ajo garlic
alabar to praise

alba   dawn

alcalde   mayor, justice of the peace, magistrate

alcatraz (*m.*)   pelican

aldea   village

alegar   to argue, bring forth proof to win an argument

alfabetización   literacy

alfiler   pin

alojarse   to stay, be housed, take lodging

alquiler   rent

alzar   to raise, lift

amarrar   to tie, fasten, moor

amígdala   tonsil

amo   master, head, owner

ancla   anchor

andén (*m.*)   platform in a station, sidewalk (*Colombia*)

anglosajón   Anglo-Saxon

anhelar   to desire, long for

Aníbal   Hannibal (247–183 B.C.), *Carthaginian general who fought the Romans*

ánimo   spirit, courage

anorak (*m.*)   hooded jacket

antaño   long ago, yesteryear

antídoto   antidote

antirrobo   antitheft

aparte (*m.*)   aside (*theater*)

apuntar   to note, jot down

apunte (*m.*)   note

árbitro   umpire, referee

ardid (*m.*)   ruse, trick

argüir (**y**) (*irr.*)   to argue

arriero   teamster, muleteer

asno   donkey, ass

astro   heavenly body

asustar   to frighten, startle, scare

ataúd (*m.*)   coffin

atún (*m.*)   tuna

augusto   august, magnificent

aula   classroom

auxilio   aid, help

ave (*f.*)   bird, fowl

aventurear (*also* **aventurar**)   to risk it, take a chance

avergonzar (**üe**)   to shame, embarrass

averiguar (**ü**)   to find out; to inquire, investigate, check on

avestruz (*m.*)   ostrich

avivar   to quicken; to encourage

azahar   orange blossom

azar   chance, fate, happenstance, random occurrence

bacalao   cod

Baco   Bacchus (*god of wine*)

baja: planta —   ground floor

bala   bullet

balneario   spa, health resort

balsa   raft; pool, pond

banderilla   *barbed dart used in bullfighting*

barra   bar, rod

bastón (*m.*)   cane

baúl   trunk

becerro   yearling calf

Bensalem   *suburban town near Philadelphia*

Bernabeu   *soccer stadium in Madrid*

betún (*m.*)   shoe polish

bienestar   well-being; welfare

billetera   wallet, billfold

bis   twice; Encore!

blasfemar   to swear, curse

blasfemia   oath, curse; blasphemy

bloc (*m.*)   note pad

bobo   fool

boina (**boína** *in Colombia*)   beret

bol   punch bowl

boleto   ticket

bolillazo   blow caused by a billy club (*Colombia*)

bombilla   drinking straw; light bulb

boquilla   mouthpiece (*music*); cigarette holder

boricua (*m., f.*)   Puerto Rican

botar   to throw away, discard

botín (*m.*)   booty

brillo   shine

brío   vigor, spirit, verve

brújula   compass

bucle (*m.*)   curl, ringlet (*hair*)

búho   owl

bustia (*Catalan*)   mailbox (*for mailing letters*)

butano   butane

buzón (*m.*)   mailbox (*for mailing letters*)

caja   box; cash register

cal (*f.*)   lime (*chemical*)

calar   to penetrate, soak through

calcetín (*m.*) sock

cáliz (*m.*) chalice; calyx (*outer covering of flower petals*)

callar to silence, quiet

callo callus

camión (*m.*) truck; bus (*Mexico*)

camiseta undershirt, T-shirt

camposanto cemetery

cana gray hair (*one strand*)

cancha court (*sports*); soccer field

cancho boulder

canguro kangaroo

cántaro pitcher, jug; **cántaros: llover a —** to pour, rain heavily

capilla chapel

carcajada guffaw, loud laugh

carestía scarcity, shortage

careta mask

carga load

carne (*f.*) **de vaca** beef

carnicero butcher

carrera race; career; major (*college*)

cartel poster, placard

cartílago cartilage

casa cuna day-care center; nursery; foundling home

casa de correos post-office

casualmente by chance, ''it just so happens ...''

caucho rubber

cebra zebra

ceja eyebrow

cejudo with bushy eyebrows

celo zeal, fervor; (*pl.*) jealousy

cepa stump; vine

cerdo pig, hog

cerilla match (*to ignite*)

cerro hill

cesar to stop, cease

césped (*m.*) lawn

chabacano vulgar, coarse, cheap

chaleco vest

chamaco little boy, kid

chancho hog

chao bye, so long

Chapultepec *large park in Mexico City, with castle-fortress*

charlar to chat, talk informally

charlatán (*m.*) chatterbox, ''bigmouth''; con man, ''quack''

chasquear to click (*one's tongue*)

chaval lad, boy, kid

chícharo pea

chicle (*m.*) chewing gum

chiflado crazy, foolish

chisme (*m.*) gossip

chocante shocking

chorizo pork sausage

chueco crooked; lame

Cid (*m.*) *Moorish name given to Rodrigo Díaz de Vivar, Spanish national hero (eleventh century)*

circo circus

cloaca sewer, drain

cobrar to charge; to collect, get, draw (*pay*)

cochino (*n.*) hog, pig; (*adj.*) filthy, dirty, messy

cocina kitchen; stove

codo elbow

cofre (*m.*) storage chest, case

cohete (*m.*) rocket

col (*f.*) cabbage

colcha bedspread, quilt

colorado red; colored

combustible (*m.*) fuel

conseguir (i, i) to get, obtain

copa glass, goblet; cup, trophy

cordura sanity

cornada thrust with the horns, goring

correos: casa de — post-office

cortado: café — coffee with cream (milk)

corte (*f.*) court (*law*)

cota quota, share; number, figure

coto enclosed pasture; game preserve

Cozumel *island off the Caribbean coast of Mexico's Yucatan peninsula*

coya queen (*Incas*)

crédito credit

criollo native American, (*as opposed to Spanish or European*)

cu (*f.*) letter *q*

cuadra city block; stable

cubo bucket, pail

cubrecama (*m. or f.*) quilt, bedspread

cuchara: meter su — to butt in, put one's ''two cents' worth'' in

cuenta account; bill

cuerno: Más —s tiene el hambre ''Hunger has more horns'' (*Spanish saying to explain why young boys from poor families*

*take up such a dangerous but potentially
lucrative activity as bullfighting)*
cuero leather
culimbo brat (*Colombia*)
cuna: casa — day-care center; nursery;
   foundling home
cuñado brother-in-law
cursi cheap, affected, showy, "cutesy", trite,
   flashy, in bad taste
Cuzco *city in highlands of Peru*

danés Danish; Dane
decana dean
déjà vu (*French*) "already seen"
dejado unkempt, untidy, slovenly;
   abandoned
derribar to knock down; to overthrow
descalzo barefoot
descantar to clear of stones
desfile (*m.*) parade
desperdicio waste
desprender to unfasten, loosen, detach,
   separate
desrielar to derail
Diario *Mexico City daily newspaper*
dibujar to draw, sketch
dicha happiness; good luck
dirigir to direct, lead
discante (*m.*) *stringed instrument*
diseño design
dizque they say
domar to tame
dominar to dominate, control
Domingo de Ramos Palm Sunday
dominó (*m.*) dominoes
dramaturgo dramatist
dulzura sweetness

ea *exclamation used to attract attention*
ele (*f.*) letter *l*
embarazada pregnant
empeñado determined, insistent, bent
encima over, on top; besides, in addition
enderezar to straighten
engrasar to grease
enhorabuena congratulation(s)
enjaular to cage, coop up, lock up, put in
   jail
enredar to entangle, snarl, complicate
enterar to inform

enterrar (**ie**) to bury
entrada ticket
entumecido numb, asleep (*limbs*)
enyesar to plaster; to put in a plaster cast
ere (*f.*) letter *r*
erguir (*irr.*) to raise, lift, put up straight
erre (*also* **doble ere**) (*f.*) letter *rr*
esbelto slim, slender, lithe, graceful
esbozo sketch, outline
esmalte (*m.*) enamel, nail polish
espeso thick (*liquid*)
espina thorn
estacionamiento parking
estacionar to park
estanco *government-run store, such as for
   stamps, tobacco, alcoholic beverages*
estufa stove
excusado bathroom, restroom, toilet

faca long knife, dagger
facha face (*slang*); look, appearance (*often
   unfavorable*)
faja band, sash; girdle; strip
fajitas (*pl.*) *Mexican meat dish*
farmacéutico pharmaceutical
farol streetlight; lantern
fastidiar to bother, annoy, "bug"
felicitar to congratulate
fénix (*m.*) phoenix (*mythical bird that, after
   destroying itself by fire, arose from its own
   ashes to live again*)
fiar (**í**) to trust
fil derecho leapfrog
filosofar to philosophize
flan (*m.*) flan (*custard dessert*)
flojo weak, feeble, limp; weak, not skilled
fluorita fluorite (*mineral*)
foro forum
forro lining
fósforo match (*to ignite*)
frac (*m.*) dress coat, tails
fracasar to fail
friolera trifle, bauble
fuerza: hacer — to root (for), cheer (on)
fugarse to flee

gafas (*pl.*) eyeglasses
gala ostentation; finery
gallina hen
gallo rooster

gama gamut, range, scale; doe
gana desire, whim, urge
gandul lazy person, loafer
ganga bargain
ganso goose
gayo jay, bluejay
gema gem
gemir (i, i) to moan
ginebra gin; **Ginebra** Geneva
girar to spin, whirl
godo Goth
goleada high score, "whipping" (*soccer*)
golondrina swallow (*bird*)
golpear to hit, strike
goma rubber; eraser
gordura obesity
gorra cap
gorrión (*m.*) sparrow
gozar to enjoy
gozne (*m.*) hinge
grabar to record; to engrave
gramilla grass; lawn; football field
Grau, Jacinto *Spanish dramatist (1877–1958)*
grito shout, cry, scream
grúa crane, derrick
guaca (*see* **huaca**)
guagua bus (*Caribbean countries and northeastern U.S.*)
guante (*m.*) glove
guapo good-looking, handsome (pretty); "tough-guy," bully
guaquero (*see* **huaquero**)
guarache (*m.*) (*see* **huarache**)
guardabrisa (*m. or f.*) windshield
guardaespaldas (*m. sing.*) bodyguard
Guayaquil *coastal city of Ecuador*
güero (*see* **huero**)
güipil (*see* **huipil**)
gusano worm

hacer fuerza to root (for), cheer (on)
hacha axe
hacienda ranch; treasury
¡Hala! Hey!, Wow!, Gee! (*indicating surprise or consternation*)
hallazgo find, discovery
hambre: Más cuernos tiene el — (*see* **cuerno**)
hampa underworld

hazmerreír (*m.*) laughing-stock, butt of jokes
hegemonía hegemony, leadership, prominent influence
helar (ie) to freeze
hembra female
hiato hiatus, break, gap
hiena hyena
hierba grass
hígado liver
hilo thread
hinchar to swell
hondureño Honduran, Honduranian
hoyuelo dimple
huaca (*also* **guaca**) tomb, funeral mound; buried treasure, valuables
huaquero (*also* **guaquero**) *individual who finds and steals treasure and other valuables at graves, tombs, and archaeological sites*
huarache (*m.*) (*also* **guarache**) Mexican sandal
hueco hollow
huella track, trace; print
huero (*also* **güero**) blond, fair; North American (*Mexico, Central America*)
huerta vegetable garden
huerto orchard
hueso bone
huida flight
huipil (*also* **güipil**) *brightly-colored, embroidered smock, dress (Mexico, Central America)*
huir (y) to flee
humillar to humiliate
humito thin wisp of smoke
humo smoke
husmear to scent, smell, sniff

imperio empire
impermeable (*m.*) raincoat
impresora printer (*machine*)
incendio fire
indicio indication, sign, hint
indocumentado illegal immigrant
ingerir (ie, i) to ingest
innato innate
innegable undeniable
innovador innovative
inquilino tenant

insoportable   unbearable
instantáneo   instant, instantaneous
invalidez   disability
inverosímil   unlikely, improbable, not realistic
irlandesa   Irish (*female*)

jactarse   to brag, boast
jalar (*also* **halar**)   to pull, haul, tow
jama   small iguana (*Honduras*)
jaqueca   severe headache, migraine
jareta   *sewn fold in garment to hold belt or drawstring*
jaula   cage
jinete (*m.*)   horseback rider, jockey
jornada   working day
joya   jewel
juez (*m.*)   judge
jugo   juice
Jujuy   *city in western Argentina*
juntar   to join
jurar   to swear, take an oath

kiosco (*also* **quiosco**)   kiosk, stand, stall
kumis (*m.*)   fermented mare's milk

laca   lacquer
lacre (*m.*)   sealing wax
ladino   Judeo-Spanish, Sephardic
ladrar   to bark
lait (*French*)   milk
laja   flagstone
lamer   to lick
lana   wool
lanza   spear, lance
lanzador   pitcher (*baseball*)
Lara   *a family name*
lástima   pity, shame
lastimar   to hurt, harm, injure
lechar   to milk; to nurse
lechero (*n.*)   milkman; (*adj.*) milk, dairy
lechuza   owl
legar   to bequeath
lento   slow
lerdo   slow(-witted); clumsy
libre: lucha —   wrestling
lícitamente   legally
lid   contest, fight
lidia   bullfighting
ligar   to tie, bind

lijar   to sand, smooth
Lillo   *a family name*
liso   smooth, even; plain, unadorned, without letters, designs, or pictures (*garments*)
lisonjear   to flatter
llano (*adj.*)   flat, smooth, even; (*n.*) plain, flatland
llavero   key case, key ring
llover (ue) a cántaros   to pour, rain heavily
lobo   wolf
lóbrego   sad, dark, gloomy
lodo   mud
Loja   *city in Ecuador*
lona   canvas
loor   praise (*poetic*)
loro   parrot
lozano   lush, luxuriant
lucha libre   wrestling
luchar   to fight, battle, struggle
luna: tener en la —   to have (one) confused, dumbfounded, stumped
lustrar   to shine

madurar   to age, mature; to think up, "cook up," "hatch"
maguey (*m.*)   *fiber from cactus plant*
magullar   to bruise
maíz (*m.*)   corn
malcriar (í)   to spoil, pamper
mallo   mallet
malograr   to damage, spoil
maniobra   maneuver
masaje (*m.*)   massage
masajista (*m., f.*)   masseur(-euse), trainer (*sports*)
mate (*also* **yerba —**) (*m.*)   *type of tea drunk in Argentina, Uruguay, and Paraguay; also the pot from which the tea is drunk*
media   stocking
Medinaceli   *street in Madrid*
medir (i, i)   to measure
melancolía   melancholy
melodía   melody
mensual   monthly
mesera   waitress
meter su cuchara   to butt in, put one's "two cents' worth" in
minutero   minute hand (*timepiece*)
Miura   *a family name*
moco   mucus

módico moderate, reasonable
moho mold, mildew
monja nun
monje (*m.*) monk
mono (*n.*) monkey; (*adj.*) cute
morder (ue) to bite
moro Moor
morro snout
mortal mortal; **salto —** somersault
motilar to cut someone's hair very short
muaré moiré (*watered silk*)
mudarse to move, change residence
mueca grimace, ''face''
muro wall (*outside*)
mus (*m.*) a card game

nácar mother-of-pearl
nafta naphtha; gasoline (*Argentina*)
nariz nose; nostril
necio difficult, hyperactive (*children*)
nene (*m.*) baby, small child
nido nest
noticias (*pl.*) news
nuera daughter-in-law
numen (*m.*) poetic inspiration, talent

ñandú (*m.*) *South American ostrich*
ñoño timid, shy; insipid; spineless; feeble

obra work (*individual work*)
obviar to obviate, prevent, eliminate, remove
oda ode
odio hatred
oficio job, profession, occupation
ola wave
oler (hue) to smell (*both to perceive an odor and to give off an odor*)
oloroso fragrant, scented
ombú (*m.*) *Argentinian tree*
oso bear (*animal*)

paca bale
padrino godfather; best man (*wedding*); protector, sponsor, patron
paisano countryman
paja straw
pájaro bird
pala shovel
pana corduroy
panal beehive

pañal diaper
paño cloth
papa potato
parada stop (*transportation area*)
paraguas (*m. sing.*) umbrella
parar to stop
pararrayos (*m. sing.*) lightning rod
pardo dull brown; dark gray
parecerse (*irr.*) **a** to look like
parra grapevine
partidario supporter, backer, partisan, follower
partido game, athletic contest
Pascua Florida Easter
pasillo hall, corridor
paso: abrir — to open the way, step aside
pata paw; leg (*animal, furniture*)
paupérrimo very poor, impoverished
pe (*f.*) letter *p*
peca freckle
pegar to hit, beat; to glue, paste
peinado hairdo
peinadora hairdresser
peinar to comb
pelar to peel
pelirrojo redhead
pellón (*m.*) sheepskin, saddle blanket
Pémex *informal name of* **Petróleos Mexicanos** (*Mexican national oil company*)
peña cliff, rock
penado convict
peón (*m.*) unskilled laborer, farmhand
perito expert, qualified person
Pérsico Persian
perspicaz perspicacious, shrewd, discerning
pesar (*v.*) to weigh; to grieve; (*n.*) sorrow, grief
pez (*m.*) fish (*animal*)
piar (í) to chirp, peep
piel (*f.*) skin; fur
pillar to pillage; to grasp, catch
piña pineapple
pío pious, holy
piojo louse
pisar to step, tread
piso floor, story (*building*); apartment, condominium (*Spain*)
pista track, racetrack, course; court (*sports*)
planta baja ground floor

pliego sheet (*paper*)
plomero plumber
plumero feather duster
poetisa poet (*female*)
polo pole; polo
porito (*dim. of* **poro**) pore
posar to sit, pose
postre (*m.*) dessert
premio prize
prender to seize, grasp; to turn on (*light*); to light (*fire*)
presto quick, swift, prompt
prevé (*3rd-person sing. present of* **prever**) he/see foresees
propósito purpose, aim, intention, objective
psicólogo psychologist
pulga flea
purito (*dim. of* **puro**) pure

quebrar (ie) to break
qué dirán (*m.*) public opinion (*literally, ''What will they say?''*)
¡qué va! What do you mean?, No way!
queja complaint
quejarse to complain
quemar to burn (*transitive*)

rabioso furious; rabid
Ramos: Domingo de — Palm Sunday
rango rank
rascar to scratch
rasgar to tear, rip
raya line, streak; **rayas: a —** striped
recado message
reclutar to recruit
refrán (*m.*) proverb, saying
régimen (*pl.* **regímenes**); (*m.*) diet; regime
rehén (*m., f.*) hostage
rehusar (ú) to refuse
reintegrar to reinstate
reja iron grating
remar to row
rematar to finish off, bring to a conclusion, put on the finishing touch
remedio medicine; cure
renglón (*m.*) line (*of writing*)
repollo cabbage
réquiem (*m.*) requiem
reseco parched, too dry

retrete (*m.*) toilet, restroom
reuma (*m.*) rheumatism, arthritis
reumático rheumatic, arthritic
revisar to review, check, audit
rezar to pray
rimar to rhyme, write verse
rincón (*m.*) corner (*inside*)
rosado pink
rozar to rub, brush against
ruana square, heavy poncho or cape
rudeza roughness
rueca spinning wheel
Rusia Russia

sábana sheet
sabor taste, flavor
sacacorchos (*m. sing.*) corkscrew
sacapuntas (*m. sing.*) pencil sharpener
saco bag
salchicha sausage
salto jump; **— mortal** somersault
salvavidas (*m. sing.*) life preserver
San Pedro de Macorís *city in the Dominican Republic noted for its high number of major league baseball players*
Santo Domingo *capital of Dominican Republic*
sarampión (*m.*) measles
sellar to stamp
sello stamp
señal (*f.*) signal
septimazo *slang term used in the Colombian capital Bogotá for an evening stroll down Seventh Avenue (**la Séptima Avenida**)*
sera large basket
serio serious
serrar (ie) to saw
servicio service; restroom
seseo *the name for the pronunciation mode of all Spanish American and some peninsular dialects of Spanish, in which the Castilian phoneme /θ/ is replaced by /s/*
seso brain
seta *type of mushroom*
silbar to whistle, hiss
simular to simulate, pretend
siseo hiss(ing)
sobras (*pl.*) leftovers
sobre (*m.*) envelope; (*prep.*) over, on

solicitar to request, seek
soltero bachelor
sombría (*fem. adj.*) shaded, dark; sad, gloomy
sombrilla parasol
sonoro sonorous, loud, resonant; voiced (*phonetics*)
soplico slight puff
subalimentación undernourishment
sublevar to incite, cause to rebel
sucursal (*f.*) branch, subsidiary
sudadera sweatshirt
sueco Swedish, Swede
sueldo salary, wages
suevo Swabian (*from a district of southern Germany*)
suizo Swiss
sur south
sutileza subtlety

taba anklebone; *gaucho game*
tanza fishing line
tapa lid, cover, top; snack (*served with drinks in bars*)
tapar to cover, hide; to stop up
teja roof tile
tener (*irr.*) **en la luna** to have (one) confused, dumbfounded, stumped
tenia tapeworm
tenis (*m.*) tennis
tilla *part of a ship's deck*
tinto (*adj.*) dyed, stained; (*n.*) red wine; black coffee (*Colombia*)
Tlacotalpan *town on eastern coast of Mexico*
tlapalería hardware store (*Mexico*)
Tlaxcala *city in southern Mexico*
toallero towel bar
tojo furze (*leguminous plant*)
tomado drunk, tipsy
torrero lighthouse keeper, tower guard
tostar (*ue*) to toast
traguito (*dim. of* **trago**) drink; drinking (*alcoholic beverages*)
trama plot (*literature*)
tregua truce
trepar to climb
trigo wheat
trillo threshing machine; path, track

tripulación crew
trocito (*dim. of* **trozo**) bit, piece, chunk, fragment
troncar to cut off, mutilate
trueno thunder
truncar to truncate, cut off, shorten
tul tulle (*thin, fine cloth*)
turno turn; shift (*work schedule*)
Turquía Turkey

unir to unite (*transitive*); —**se** to unite (*intransitive*)
Universal *Mexico City daily newspaper*
usanza usage, custom

vaca: carne (*f.*) **de —** beef
vacilar to hesitate
valla fence, barricade; hurdle
vascuence (*m.*) Basque (*language*)
veraneo summer vacation trip
verdura greenness; (*pl.*) greens, green vegetables
vero skunk; marten
vidrio glass (*material*)
vista view
vistoso showy, colorful, attractive
viuda widow
volar (*ue*) to fly
vos you (*2nd-person singular familiar pronoun used with its own verb forms in many Spanish American countries, such as Costa Rica and Argentina*)
vuelta turn; trip; lap (*sports*)

wáter toilet, bathroom, water closet

xenofobia xenophobia, fear and hatred of things foreign
xilófono xylophone

yacer (*irr.*) to lie, recline
yámbico iambic (*type of verse*)
yegua mare
yema egg yolk; fingertip
yerba grass, weed; **— mate** *type of tea drunk in Argentina, Uruguay, and Paraguay*
yerbabuena mint

yergue (*3rd-person sing. present of* **erguir**) he/she raises, lifts, puts up straight

yerno   son-in-law

yeso   plaster, gypsum

yod (*f.*)   yod (*tenth letter of the Hebrew alphabet, now used as the name for the semi-vowel* [i̯])

yodo   iodine

zalamero   flattering, wheedling

Zamora   *city and province in northwestern Spain*

zorro   fox

zumo   juice

zurdo   left-handed; clumsy

Index

All numbers refer to chapters. Chapter numbers for widely used terms, such as vocal bands, *are given only for the first and/or principal treatment, followed by* **etc.** *A dash —* *indicates repetition of the key word. Material in the Practices is not included here.*